REGIONAL SCIENCE
PERSPECTIVES FOR THE FUTURE

Also by Manas Chatterji

ANALYTICAL TECHNIQUES IN CONFLICT MANAGEMENT

ARMS SPENDING, DEVELOPMENT AND SECURITY (*co-editor*)

DISARMAMENT, ECONOMIC CONVERSION AND MANAGEMENT OF PEACE (*editor with Robert E. Kuenne*)

DYNAMICS AND CONFLICT IN REGIONAL STRUCTURAL CHANGE (*editor with Robert E. Kuenne*)

ECONOMIC ISSUES OF DISARMAMENT (*editor with Jurgen Brauer*)

ECONOMICS OF INTERNATIONAL SECURITY (*co-editor*)

ENERGY AND ENVIRONMENT FOR THE DEVELOPING COUNTRIES (*editor*)

ENERGY, REGIONAL SCIENCE AND PUBLIC POLICY (*editor with P. L. van Rampuy*)

ENVIRONMENT AND HEALTH IN DEVELOPING COUNTRIES (*co-editor*)

ENVIRONMENT, REGIONAL SCIENCE AND INTERREGIONAL MODELING (*editor with P. L. van Rampuy*)

HAZARDOUS MATERIALS DISPOSAL: Siting and Management (*editor*)

HEALTH CARE COST CONTAINMENT STUDY: An Econometric Survey

HEALTH CARE MANAGEMENT AND POLICY: An Analytical Approach

MANAGEMENT EDUCATION IN COUNTRIES IN TRANSITION (*co-editor*)

MANAGEMENT AND REGIONAL SCIENCE FOR THE DEVELOPING COUNTRIES

NEW FRONTIERS IN REGIONAL SCIENCE (*editor with Robert E. Kuenne*)

REGIONAL SCIENCE IN DEVELOPING COUNTRIES (*co-editor with Yang Kaizhong*)

SPACE LOCATION AND REGIONAL DEVELOPMENT (*editor*)

SPATIAL, ENVIRONMENTAL AND RESOURCE POLICY IN THE DEVELOPING COUNTRIES (*editor with Peter Nijkamp, T. R. Lakshann and C. R. Pathak*)

TECHNOLOGY TRANSFER IN THE DEVELOPING COUNTRIES (*editor*)

Regional Science: Perspectives for the Future

Edited by

Manas Chatterji
Professor of Management
Binghamton University
State University of New York
and Honorary Distinguished Professor of Management
Indian Institute of Management, Calcutta

Foreword by Walter Isard

First published in Great Britain 1997 by
MACMILLAN PRESS LTD
Houndmills, Basingstoke, Hampshire RG21 6XS and London
Companies and representatives throughout the world

A catalogue record for this book is available from the British Library.

ISBN 0-333-62908-6

First published in the United States of America 1997 by
ST. MARTIN'S PRESS, INC.,
Scholarly and Reference Division,
175 Fifth Avenue, New York, N.Y. 10010

ISBN 0-312-15930-7

Library of Congress Cataloging-in-Publication Data
Regional Science : perspectives for the future / edited by Manas Chatterji.
p. cm.
Includes bibliographical references and index.
ISBN 0-312-15930-7
1. Science—Developing countries. 2. Science and state--Developing countries. I. Chatterji, Manas, 1937- .
Q127.2.R43 1996
338.9—dc20 96-7067
CIP

This book is printed on paper suitable for recycling and made from fully managed and sustained forest sources.

10 9 8 7 6 5 4 3 2 1
06 05 04 03 02 01 00 99 98 97

Printed in Great Britain by
The Ipswich Book Company Ltd
Ipswich, Suffolk

To regional scientists, past, present and future

Contents

List of Tables and Figures x

Foreword by Walter Isard xiv

Notes on the Contributors xvi

1 Introduction 1
Manas Chatterji

2 Urban Systems and Regional Development 7
Masahisa Fujita and Paul Krugman

3 Linked System of Enterprise, Regional and National Input–Output Accounts for Policy Analysis 26
Karen R. Polenske

4 Dynamic Price Patterns in Spatial Oligopolistic Markets: The Impact of Lagged Quantity Adjustments 43
Richard Schuler

5 Spatial Aspects of Knowledge Networks: The Case of Scientific Collaboration at a Distance 70
Martin Beckmann

6 Measuring the Regional Quality of Life 80
Jean H. P. Paelinck

7 Innovative Environments: Concept and Application 88
Marc-Urbain Proulx

8 Intergenerational Transfers in a Framework of Fused Regional Accounts 108
Stan Czamanski

9 Uncertainty as a Management Evaluation Tool for Infrastructure Projects 127
Kingsley E. Haynes, Fred Y. Phillips and Rajendra K. Srivastava

10 Simulating Regional Systems: A System Dynamics Approach 144
Colin Lee

11 Applied Spatial Informatics as a Framework for Natural Disaster Mitigation 166
George G. van der Meulen

12 Climate Change and the Social Sciences: Global and Regional Issues 181
Peter Nijkamp and Celeste Wilderom

13 Regional Planning Implications of Climate Changes 197
Antoine S. Bailly

14 Economic Geography with Division of Labour and Amenity Difference 207
Wei-Bin Zhang

15 Comparative Analysis of Intercity Agglomeration
Tatsuhiko Kawashima, Iwan Azis and Michael Tane 219

16 The North American Free Trade Agreement: Implications for US Regions 232
Niles Hansen

17 Regional Science and New Regional Policy in Russia 248
Alexander Granberg

18 Socioeconomic Transformations in Central and Eastern Europe from the Perspective of Regional Science 263
Ryszard Domański

19 Integration Processes and Foreign Investment in Central Europe: A Regional Perspective 272
Tadeusz Marszał

20 The Trends of the 1990s: Humanity and Business Facing a World of Multiple Choices 289
Alain Sallez

21 Dynamic Take-off: Accelerating Effects of a Continental Expressway 296
Hirotada Kohno, Yoshiro Higano and Yuji Matsumura

22 Identifying the Direct and Indirect Economic Effects of Electric Power Development Projects 314
Toshiyuki Hayashi and Sid Saltzman

23 A Multi-Regional Model for China Based on Price and Quantity Equilibrium 326
Asao Ando and Takanori Shibata

24 Incorporating a Disaggregate Model for Trip Generation, Trip Distribution and Mode Choice 345
Ryosuke Ando, Shogo Kawakami and Naojiro Aoshima

25 Planning for National Development: An Agenda Guided by the Socioeconomic System's Social Philosophy 361
Stanley C. W. Salvary

26 MegaProject Impact Assessment 384
Roger R. Stough and Kingsley E. Haynes

27 Regional Science and Nation State Development 399
Takashi Takayama and John Williams

Index 411

List of Tables and Figures

Tables

3.1	US managerial accounting	28
3.2	US financial accounting	30
3.3	Chinese enterprise input-output accounting	34
4.1	Payoff summary for binary choice, intertemporal pricing game	62
4.2	Payoff summary for binary choice, intertemporal pricing game	63
4.3	Payoff summary for binary choice, intertemporal pricing game	64
4.4	Payoff summary for binary choice, intertemporal pricing game	65
6.1	Mixed multicriteria matrix	84
6.2	Substitution rates	85
9.1	Attrition pattern for 116 new projects	136
15.1	Two-dimensional matrix for analysis of spacial redistribution of city population	220
15.2	Spacial-cycle framework for a system of cities	220
15.3	Spacial-cycle implications of ROXY Index values for inter-city analysis	222
15.4	Values of ROXY Index and its marginal values	224
16.1	Leading states in exports to Mexico and in employment generated by trade with Mexico, 1992	234
21.1	Partition into zones	303
21.2	Industrial classification	303
21.3	Planning horizon	303
21.4	Maximum permissible limit of loan balance borrowed from overseas	305
21.5	Construction pattern of the proposed Asian Expressway Network	305
21.6	Case setting	306
21.7	Values of objective functions	310
23.1	Correlation coefficients between Beijing tables estimated for 1985 and compiled for 1987	335
24.1	Evaluating results for the temporal transferability of the destination choice model	353

24.2 Evaluating results for the temporal transferability of the mode choice model 355
24.3 Evaluating results for the temporal transferability of the trip generation model 355
24.4 Statistics on the number of tours for non-workers based on tour patterns in one day 357
26.1 Type of megaproject by motivating factor 386

Figures

2.1 Circular causality in spatial agglomeration of firms and workers 10
2.2 Examples of possible equilibrium spatial configurations ($m = 1$) 15
2.3 A monocentric spatial configuration 16
2.4 Potential curves for the monocentric configuration under various N 16
2.5 Two types of symmetric duocentric configuration 18
2.6 Potential curves for Duo-A configurations 18
2.7 Three types of tricentric configuration 19
2.8 An example of a hierarchical system of cities 19
2.9 City size ratio for Tri-A equilibria 22
3.1 Procedure for annual comprehensive enterprise planning, People's Republic of China 37
3.2 An integrated system of input-output accounts 39
4.1 Logistic market share adjustment mechanism for products requiring first-hand confirmation 49
4.2 Concave market share adjustment mechanisms for low-cost confirmation of product attributes 51
4.3 Spatial market allocations under mill pricing 53
7.1 Circumstances favourable to the new theory 89
7.2 The octagon of innovative environment 94
7.3 The actors of the innovative environment 98
8.1 Master matrix 110
8.2 Sectoral flows matrix 123
8.3 Income and consumption matrix 124
8.4 Governments' programmes and investments matrix 125
9.1 Infrastructure project evolution 128
9.2 Commitments *vs* expenditure 131
9.3 Impact of Go-On-Skip-No Go decision on committed costs 135

9.4	ROI probability estimate	138
10.1	Feedback loops in a simple system	148
10.2	The structure of the Susquehanna River Basin Model	153
10.3	The structure of the Regional Utility Simulation Model	156
10.4	Influence diagram for ECCO	161
11.1	General program structure	169
11.2	Animation and elaboration of a cyclone disaster by applied spatial informatics	170
11.3	Elaboration of global seawater level rising by applied spatial informatics	171
11.4	Data elaborated by applied spatial informatics	173
11.5	Animation and elaboration of a volcanic eruption disaster by applied spatial informatics	175
11.6	Comprehensive land use and spatial planning design images	177
11.7	Simulated emergency announcements and evacuation of inhabitants of a flooding polder	178
12.1	A payoff matrix	186
13.1	Human reactions to national hazards	201
13.2	The relationship between climate change and human choices	202
13.3	Major stages of the planning process	204
14.1	The one-city and one-farm system	208
15.1	Definition of the ROXY Index for inter-city analysis	221
15.2	Diagrammatic interpretation of spacial-cycle path by means of ROXY Index value for inter-city analysis: wavelike cyclic form	223
15.3	Calculation of ROXY Index based on annual growth ratio	225
15.4	ROXY Index in wavelike cyclic form	226
15.5	ROXY Index in circular cyclic form	227
19.1	Number and ownership structure of business entities in Poland, 1992	279
19.2	Number and structure of private companies in Poland, 1991–2	280
19.3	Capital structure of companies with foreign capital in Poland, 1992	281
19.4	Spatial distribution of employment in companies with foreign capital in Poland, 1992	282
19.5	Number and value of foreign investment by branches, 1993	283

19.6 Number and value of foreign investment by country, 1993 284
19.7 Locational preferences of German investors in Central and Eastern Europe, 1992 287
21.1 Optimum transport investment allocation to the Asian Expressway Network by period (Case 1) 307
21.2 GNP derived from the model 311
23.1 Composition of a national input–output table and its regional distribution 329
23.2 The procedure to estimate regional tables and inter-regional trade 334
23.3 Aggregated railroad network and the virtual project examined 336
23.4 Inter-regional trade flows estimated for the case of without and with project 338
23.5 Principal components of regional price indices 341
23.6 Principal components of economic indicators 342
24.1 Typical tour patterns 346
24.2 The nested logit model with $L = 1$ 349
24.3 Depiction of the nested logit model for non-workers' travel demand modelling 357
25.1 Technological frontier and substitution possibilities 366
27.1 Three elements of environment and their interaction 401
27.2 Nation state and rest of the world interaction differential game scheme 403

Foreword

The occasion of the first Beijing International Conference on Regional Science for Developing Countries, which motivated the publication of this book and contains a number of the papers presented, marks another major step in the development of the interdisciplinary field of regional science. It not only signifies the spread of this field to another vast area of our planet and its many peoples and cultures, but also points up new needs and directions for regional science – new needs to contain looming inadequacies, and new paths for continuing and sustainable development.

One development in the field of regional science is crystal clear – namely the burgeoning of its breadth. Consider the many different topics covered in this book. Start with the headings of first five chapters:

1. Urban Systems and Regional Development.
2. Linked System of Enterprise, Regional and National Input–Output Accounts for Policy Analysis:
3. Dynamic Price Patterns in Spatial Oligopolistic Markets: The Impact of Lagged Quantity Adjustments.
4. Spatial Aspects of Knowledge Networks: The Case of Scientific Collaboration at a Distance.
5. Measuring the Regional Quality of Life.

Continue through the rest of the book, or pick up the 1994 programme of the North American Regional Science Association, or the recent programmes of the European and the Pacific Region Associations. This rapid movement in all directions, involving healthy and lively networking with numerous other social and physical science organizations and professions, is indeed extremely fruitful. At the same time it creates an urgent need for an up-to-date identification of the core of regional science – one that can be interpreted flexibly and revised and supplemented appropriately with respect to the particular requirements and attributes of a given university's graduate programme and research projects. My 1960 book, *Methods of Regional Analysis*, is no longer adequate; it is obsolete. For example, it contains nothing about regional econometrics, social accounting (SAM), and computable general equilibrium (CGE) models. Moreover, its treatment of input–output, linear programming, industrial complex and gravity models is outdated. Still more, its channels of synthesis, aimed at connecting and integrating models and methods, need to be restated, revised and perhaps completely discarded and replaced by new integrative frameworks, particularly in light of the revolutionary advances in computer technology since 1960.

The need for the development of a new book on models and methods was keenly appreciated at the North American Regional Science meetings held at Niagara Falls, Canada, November 1994 – a need especially urgent in order to provide a common ground and stock of knowledge to which advances in the diverse research directions we are now pursuing could be connected. Such a book would facilitate more effective communication and recognition of the many contributions being realized. We must recognize that we are no longer the small group we were in the past, when effective communication could be achieved on a face-to-face basis at conferences.

At the North American 1994 conference, first steps were taken to initiate the development of a book for graduate study, and also a new undergraduate textbook to replace my *Introduction to Regional Science*, also out-of-date. Additionally, steps were taken to develop an organization to facilitate the exchange of ideas and experiences among universities which offer graduate programmes in regional science and closely related areas. It was judged that had such an organization existed, it would have assisted greatly in efforts to maintain the Department of Regional Science at the University of Pennsylvania, and that in the future it can be effective in enhancing and amassing support for regional science and closely related educational and research programmes, both existing and new, at other universities.

Once again, I wish to indicate my pleasure at the publication of the diverse contributions in this book. I look forward to continuing fruitful progress in Regional Science and closely related fields in all parts of the world, whether from Departments of Regional Science (the existence of which can easily be justified) or strictly non-departmental interdisciplinary programmes, each type of organization having distinct advantages, and each also justifiable.

Cornell University WALTER ISARD

Notes on the Contributors

Asao Ando is Associate Professor of Information Sciences at Tohoku University, Japan.

Ryosuke Ando works for Katahira to Engineers Inc. Tokyo, Japan.

Iwan Azis is Professor of Economics, University of Indonesia, and Visiting Professor of City and Regional Planning, Cornell University, USA.

Naojiro Aoshima is Professor of Civil Engineering at Gunma University, Japan.

Antoine S. Bailly is Professor of Geography at the University of Geneva, Switzerland.

Martin Beckmann is Emeritus Professor of Economics at Brown University, USA and the Technical University of Munich, Germany.

Manas Chatterji is Professor of Management at Binghamton University (SUNY) in Binghamton, USA, Honorary Distinguished Professor of Management, Indian Institute of Management, Calcutta, India, and Guest Professor, Peking University, Beijing, China.

Stan Czamanski is Professor of Economics at Florida International University, USA.

Ryszard Domański is Professor of Spatial and Environmental Economics at the Academy of Economics Poznań, Poland.

Masahisa Fujita was formerly Professor of Regional Science at the University of Pennsylvania, USA.

Alexander Granberg is Chairman of Council for Location of Productive Forces and Economic Cooperation in Moscow, Russia.

Niles Hansen is Professor of Economics at the University of Texas at Austin, USA.

Toshiyuki Hayashi is associated with the Japan International Cooperation Agency, Tokyo, Japan.

Kingsley E. Haynes is University Professor of Public Policy at George Mason University in Fairfax, VA. USA.

Yoshiro Higano is Professor at the Institute of Agriculture and Forest Engineering at the University of Tsukuba, Japan.

Walter Isard is Emeritus Professor of Economics, Cornell University, USA.

Shogo Kawakami is Professor of Civil Engineering at Nagoya University, Japan.

Tatsuhiko Kawashima is Professor of Economics at Gakushuin University, Japan.

Hirotada Kohno is Professor Emeritus of Economics at the University of Tsukuba, Japan.

Paul Krugman is Professor of Economics at the Massachusetts Institute of Technology, USA.

Colin Lee is Senior Lecturer in the School of the Built Environment at Coventry University, UK.

Tadeusz Marszal is Professor of Spatial Economy and Geography at the University of Łódź, Poland.

Yuji Matsumura is lecturer at the University of Tsukuba, Japan.

Peter Nijkamp is Professor of Economics at Free University, The Netherlands.

Jean H. P. Paelinck is Professor Emeritus of Theoretical Spatial Economics at Erasmus University, Rotterdam, The Netherlands.

Fred Y. Phillips is Professor of Management in Science and Technology at the Oregon Graduate Institute of Science and Technology, Portland, USA.

Karen R. Polenske is Professor of Regional Political Economy and Planning at the Massachusetts Institute of Technology, USA.

Marc-Urbain Proulx is Professor of Economics at the University of Quebec, Canada.

Alain Sallez is Chair Professor of Urban Economics in ESSEC, Ecole Supérieure des Sciences Economiques et Commerciales, France.

Sid Saltzman is Professor of City and Regional Planning, Cornell University, USA.

Stanley C. W. Salvary is Professor of Accounting at Canisius College, USA.

Richard Schuler is Professor of Economics at Cornell University, USA.

Takanori Shibata is an Associate with Fukuyama Consultants, Inc., Japan.

Rajendra K. Srivastava is Professor of Marketing and the Jack R. Crosby Regent's Chair in Business Administration at the University of Texas at Austin, USA.

Roger R. Stough is Professor of Public Policy at George Mason University, Fairfax, Virginia, USA.

Takashi Takayama is Professor of Economics in the Faculty of International Studies, Tokiwa University.

Michael Tane is a member of the research staff at the University of Indonesia and the University of Illinois-Urbana, USA.

George G. van der Meulen is Chairman of Compuplan Foundation, Institute for Applied geo-Spatial and Environmental Informatics, in Mill, The Netherlands.

Celeste Wilderom is a Full Professor in Organization and Management at Tilburg University, Department of Business Administration, Tilburg, The Netherlands.

John Williams is Assistant Lecturer in Economics at the University of Western Australia.

Wei-Bin Zhang is Associate Professor at the Institute for Future Studies in Stockholm, Sweden.

1 Introduction

Manas Chatterji

It has been almost fifty years since regional science was born. That was an auspicious time. In economics and the other social sciences, a revolution was taking place. The emphasis was more along theoretical and mathematical lines and the advent of computers helped progress this development. The end of the Second World War and decolonization of the developing countries led to a new emphasis on geographical space. It followed the modern day transportation revolution. The role of time was already being captured through economic model building; regional science drew attention to space as one of the primary factors affecting human economic activity. Accordingly, some say that the appropriate name of the new discipline should have been Spatial Science. However, although this name would have captured the micro aspects of human interaction, the aggregate macro aspect would have been lost.

Regional science starts with the geographical distribution of population and its demographic aspects, namely fertility, mortality, life expectancy, and migration. Physical characteristics like rainfall, soil, vegetation, and consequently agricultural practices vary greatly over space and are clearly linked with human factors. However, regional scientists did not investigate those factors and most of the contributions came from economics and not from physical geography. Of course, a considerable amount of work has been done in the area of the environment, and it has been effectively tied with human factors. Although air pollution models have been used extensively, water pollution literature in regional science has been largely neglected. Further, the regional conflicts arising out of the sharing of water resources, a fertile area for research, have not been investigated.

The starting point in regional science is the definition and demarcation of a region. Since Isard's *Methods of Regional Analysis* (1960) there has been a great deal of discussion about what constitutes a region. However, because of the availability of data an administrative definition is usually taken. The phenomenal growth of geographical information systems (GIS) has greatly advanced the field of measurement and the availability of data.

Although Isard provided the theoretical structure of regional analysis including political, social, economic and environmental variables, most research has been done with economic variables. Very little work is available using the political/social variables in regional science. Following closely the work of national income accounts, parallel developments have taken place with regional and interregional income and social accounts. The development of regional accounts is crucial for the application of more sophisticated tools like econometric models and input–output analysis. This contribution is distinctive enough to stand as a separate field, comparable to national income and product accounts. This however, cannot be said about regional cycle analysis.

Regional scientists turned their attention to forecasting models, starting with economic base theory. Although Czamanski (1973) made some unique contributions in this area, the base theory has not been changed substantially. However, in input–output analysis, significant innovations, both theoretical and empirical, have taken place. In comparative cost analysis new ideas are needed. A great potential exists for industrial complex analysis but this method has not been used effectively by regional scientists since Isard's (1959) groundbreaking study. There has been enough work on programming models in a regional framework and gravity models, in conjunction with transportation science, have made great strides. The most promising original work has been in spatial statistics, pioneered by Jean Paelinck (1979). An excellent beginning was made in the theoretical development of a time–space framework by Isard and Liossatos (1979), but that research has not been followed up. Therefore, although regional science has had a fantastic record of development over its first fifty years, its renewal and the development of new avenues are called for in the twenty-first century.

The most obvious need is for regional science to focus on developing countries, where the opportunity is greatest. For this purpose, the regional scientists in these countries should take the responsibility themselves for developing analytical tools. The existing tools originating in the developed countries are not applicable. A companion volume *Regional Science for Developing Countries* edited by K. Yang and me includes some such contributions. Many countries like the former Soviet Union, Poland, etc., are in a state of transition from a strict centralized system to a decentralized one. It is expected that, for some time, a cooperative public–private system will be in use in these countries. Since regional science tools have been devised in a free enterprise economic system, it is necessary to modify these tools for use in those areas where regional transformation is taking place. In Europe and the

Pacific Rim, the forces of integration are operating. NAFTA, ASEAN, and many other regional groupings are coming up, and the development of these spatial organizations will have different regional impacts. Privatization and investments by multinational corporations will create a special type of spatial configuration. Considerable scope exists in extending regional science methodology to analyze local public finance. The same opportunity exists in the area of hazardous waste management, where the location of a facility is not based on minimizing the transportation cost but by maximizing the distance from the community. Other areas where significant work can be done are (1) agricultural regional planning, (2) health care planning, and (3) conflict management, etc.

This book contains a number of selected contributions from some well-known regional scientists. For the past two decades, economic development and international trade have been dominated by interchanges between cities. Fujita and Krugman try to model the formation and growth of cities in terms of macroeconomics. They intend to develop a more realistic model taking into consideration political restriction, national geographic features, history, and customs. Polenske presents an input–output system where the policy question at the local, regional, national, and international levels are linked and where the analysis can readily, instantaneously, and simultaneously respond to a particular policy decision.

In the tradition of Hotelling and Beckmann, Schuler illustrates the optimal dynamic pricing strategies. He also considers the effect of customer response on demanded quantities. In terms of public policy, his analysis emphasizes the speed of customer response in estimating the intensity of competition in an oligopolistic market. Martin Beckmann presents a very innovative approach to estimating collaborations between scientists who are spatially separated. For this analysis, he uses the Cobb-Douglas production function. In his article on measuring the regional quality of life, Paelinck uses a multi-criteria matrix and shows how to consider a non-measurable variable in modeling. The definition of environment, the concept of a 'successful' innovative environment, organizational culture, and environment are the focus of Proulx's thesis.

Czamanski, who started his career doing research on social accounts, now extends his thinking to environmental factors in social accounts and the impact of human capital on social accounts. For this purpose he designs a set of accounts matrix from which input–output and investment multipliers can be computed.

The choice of an investment project depends on the rate of return on investment (ROI) or cost-benefit (C/B) analyses. However, both require the assumption of some amount of uncertainty in demand and supply. Haynes, Philips, and Srivastava use this uncertainty factor in the selection of a capital project in addition to ROI and C/B ratio. This paper presents the risk behaviour of an organization and provides operational guidelines for how managers should estimate project costs. Colin Lee presents a Forrester-type simulation model of urban and regional growth using the demographic sector, housing sector, etc. He thinks that his computer modeling, simulation, and policy analysis, coupled with the use of quantitative models, can do a better job than just these models alone. The practical usefulness of computer technology in natural disaster planning is shown by Van der Veulen.

A new topic in regional science, namely the regional dimension of climate changes, is presented by Nijkamp on a theoretical level and by Bailly from a practical point of view. Zhang attempts to provide a microeconomic geographical model involving the demand and supply of various commodities, price structure, and spatial diffusion of labour with its preferences. He also considers the labour force and locational factors. Kawashima, Azis, and Tane examine the spatial distribution process of population in the thirty largest cities in Japan and present a spatial-cycle hypothesis.

There has been a considerable amount of research on the North American Free Trade Association (NAFTA). Niles Hansen translates its impact on different US regions as the national growth rate is very much determined by regional growth rates. According to him, although NAFTA will be mutually beneficial, its effect on the US will be small. In the short run, the effect may be negative, but in the long run it will be positive but small. A potential area of research for regional scientists is the change in regional structure due to the collapse of communism in Russia. How to manage this change in countries in transition has been discussed in another publication (Chatterji, Domanski, 1996). An eminent Russian regional scientist, Alexander Granberg presents an excellent account of the threats and opportunities in regional development policies in Russia. Contrary to other predictions, he thinks that state integrity will be preserved, and that it is unlikely that the existing administration of territorial units will be integrated into state entities. Domanski follows up the analysis of transition in Poland. According to him there will be regions with moderately advanced urban–industrial agglomerations offering considerable external economies at only a moderate rate. There will be (1) a high level of monopolization, (2) underdevelopment, (3) social conflict, (4) unequal access to regional and national potentials, and (5) varying efficiency of local governments. With respect to the question of the role of industries in regional development, Sallez thinks that the environment will possibly be the most important factor in economic competition between firms. A regional perspective on the investment behaviour of international firms in Poland is provided by Marszal. Despite the strategic location of Poland, the availability of cheap skilled labour, and the speed of transportation, it will still take some time to attract significant foreign investment. This is due to a poor communication infrastructure, an insufficient banking system, lack of information, and high inflation.

Kohno and Higano embark on a dynamic multiregional, multi-industrial, multi-transport mode optimal programming model involving an Asian Express Network (AEN). It is an ambitious project indeed. If anything, it will energize other researchers to seek alternative approaches.

Hayashi and Saltzman contend that the indirect economic effect of electric power generators is so large that the conventional method of cost benefit analysis may not be good enough. Consequently, they propose a semi input–output model and demonstrate how it can be used. In a similar vein, Ando and Shibata propose a multi-regional model to evaluate the impact of transport projects on the regional economy. The model is applied to China and its 29 provinces for the year 1985. The results are fairly reasonable in the sense that the transfer input will promote both domestic and external trade.

The paper by Ando, Kawakami, and Aoshima investigates the effect of trip distribution on the desegregated model combining trip generation, trip distribution, and mode choice. The logit model was defined at three levels: (1) parameter level – transferring the model system without any change, (2) variable level – transferring the model system with the re-estimation of all coefficients, and (3) structure level – transferring the model system with new coefficients for the old coefficients. Salvary presents a paper on regional political economy emphasizing that the national leaders pay particular attention to local voices and participation. Stough and Haynes examine the spatial and temporal issues of mega projects and intergenerational problems. It is also necessary to address the conflict management aspect, which also needs significant intellectual inputs. This topic also requires consideration of the alternatives of equilibrium and optimization versus the disequilibrium and chaos approach. The concluding paper by Takayama and Williams presents a comprehensive, structural game theory model for a transition economy which emphasizes the need for coordination of national and regional development plans, and above all a unified political leadership.

The articles in this book share the common theme that the changing political scene and socioeconomic structures of nations require new ways of thinking. The established methods of regional science developed in the last 50 years have lost relevance. I hope the twenty-first century will bring forth these new insights.

References

Chatterji, M. and R. Domanski (eds) (1996) 'Urban and Regional Management in Countries in Transition' *Studie Regionlalla*, vol. 5, Committee for Space Economy and Regional Planning, Polish Academy of Science, Warsaw, Poland.

Czamanski, S. (1973). *Regional and Interregional Social Accounting* (Lexington Books, DC Heath, Cambridge, Mass.).

Isard, W. and T. Vietorisz (1959) *Industrial Complex Analysis and Regional Development* (MIT Press).

Isard, W. and P. Liossatos (1979) *Spatial Diagnosis and Optimal Space–Time Development* (North Holland Co., New York).

Paelinck, J. (1979) *Spatial Econometrics* (Farnborough, England: Sexton House).

2 Urban Systems and Regional Development

Masahisa Fujita and Paul Krugman

INTRODUCTION

Since the 1950s, one of the most notable phenomena in world economic geography has been the rapid urbanization being experienced by most countries. Today, in most developed countries and many developing countries, more than 70 per cent of the population resides in cities. Although in the past, urbanization was almost synonymous with industrialization, the recent progress of so-called 'deindustrialization' has brought about a renewed trend of further urbanization in many countries. As a consequence, the economic activities of most countries are dominated by cities at present. Furthermore, cities are becoming more important, not only for each national economy but also for the world economy and trade. For example, the trade among many countries has been dominated increasingly by the exchange of the goods produced in their cities.

Recently, the urbanization trend has been especially strong in East Asia, which as a whole has been experiencing the most rapid economic growth in the world since the 1970s. As a consequence, in most East Asian countries in the 1990s, a disproportionate share of population and manufacturing industries is concentrated in their primal cities. This in turn has brought about a marked disparity between the core region and peripheral regions in each country. Although many governments in East Asia have striven to decentralize industry to curb the growth of their primal cities, their efforts have not been very successful.[1]

Given the increasing urbanization trend and the increasing prominence of cities in national and world economies, an obvious question of importance for economists is how to model the formation and growth of cities in terms of microeconomics. This question is important not only for positive theory but also for policy purposes. Indeed, in order to develop effective policies which curb the growth of present primal cities, and to promote the growth of peripheral cities, it is essential to understand the mechanism behind the formation and growth of cities.

In order to investigate this question, one must first note that the growth of cities in a modern economy hinges less on the locational advantages attributable to first nature (such as climate, or mineral deposits), which are becoming increasingly less important, than on the self-reinforcing advantages of second nature or agglomeration economies. Second, note that cities differ from each other not only in size but also in function. In an economy, typically, cities together constitute some form of *hierarchical system.*

What we need, then, is an economic theory that can explain the formation and change of a hierarchical city system in an economy. Unfortunately, however, it seems that no microeconomic model yet exists that can generate a hierarchical system of cities in the general equilibrium context of a national (or international) economy. Although countless articles have been published on 'central place theory' since the pioneering work by Christaller (1933), no formal microeconomic model of central place theory seems yet to have been developed.[2]

In developing a microeconomic model of urban systems, a key question is how to explain the formation of cities as a result of interactions among individuals. In other words, how to model the endogenous forces of urban agglomeration in terms of microeconomics? In this chapter, we propose a microeconomic model of endogenous urban agglomeration, based on the Chamberlinian monopolistic competition behaviour of firms (which provide a continuum of differentiated products).[3] Furthermore, we examine the potential capability of the model in yielding a variety of urban systems, and investigate its usefulness for designing effective regional development strategies.

The plan of the chapter is as follows. In section 2, we present an informal description of the model. First, a formal model is presented, then we examine possible equilibrium spatial configurations of the economy. In the next section, by examining the structural stability of equilibria, we investigate linkages between our model and big push or growth pole models of economic development advocated by early development theories. Finally, possible future research directions are discussed.

PRODUCT VARIETY AND URBAN AGGLOMERATION

In this section, first we discuss informally why monopolistic competition based on product variety in *consumption goods* would result in the formation of a system of cities, then we demonstrate that a similar argument can be made based on product variety in *intermediate goods.*

Suppose we have a given population of homogeneous workers. Each worker consumes a homogeneous agricultural good (*A*-good) together with several groups of manufactured goods (*M*-goods), where each group of *M*-goods consists of a large variety of differentiated goods. Because of scale economies in product-specialization, each variety of each group of *M*-goods is supposed to be produced by a single firm (by using labour as its sole input) which chooses its f.o.b. price monopolistically (in the sense of Chamberlin). The homogeneous *A*-good is produced by constant-returns-to-scale technology using labour and land. All workers are assumed to be free to choose their location. In this context, the mechanism for the formation of a hierarchical system of cities is as follows.

First, let us assume that there is only one group of *M*-goods (together with the *A*-good). In this context, if a large variety of *M*-goods is produced in a city, this variety of goods can be purchased at lower prices there when compared to more distant places. Thus, given a nominal wage rate, because of tastes for variety, the real income of workers (= consumers) becomes higher. This, in turn, will induce more workers (= consumers) to migrate there. This increase in the number of consumers (= workers) will create a greater demand for *M*-goods there, which in turn can support a greater number of specialized firms. (Note that because of scale economies at the individual-firm level, a large number of firms can be supported only when the total demand for *M*-goods is sufficiently large.) This implies the availability of an even greater variety of *M*-goods in the city. Figure 2.1 depicts this circular causality in spatial agglomeration of firms and workers through a *forward linkage* (where the availability of a greater variety of *M*-goods increases the real income of workers there) and *backward linkage* (where a greater number of consumers can support a greater number of specialized firms). In other words, through these forward and backward linkages, scale economies at the individual firm level are transformed into increasing returns at city level.

It is, of course, not always necessary for all firms to agglomerate at one location. If the *M*-goods in question are close substitutes for each other (or transport costs of *M*-goods are high), then some firms may find that by moving away from the central agglomeration and primarily serving farmers in a fringe agricultural area, they can earn a greater profit. In this case, then the equilibrium spatial system will contain multiple cities.

Next, let us assume there are two groups of *M*-goods, where each group consists of a large number of similar but differentiated goods.

Figure 2.1 Circular causality in spatial agglomeration of firms and workers

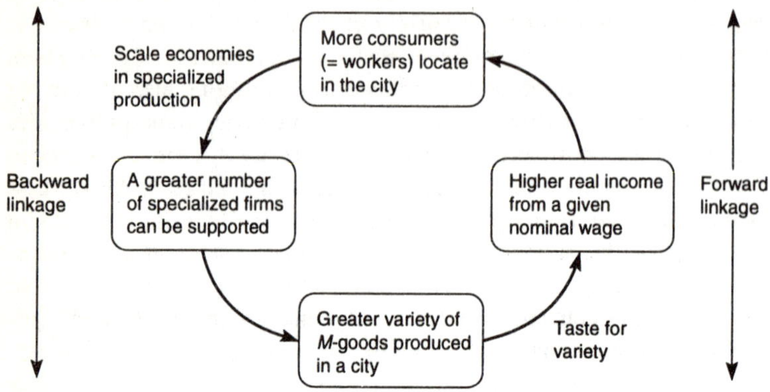

Suppose further that goods in the first group are highly differentiated (and hence their price-elasticity is low), while those in the second group are close substitutes for each other (thus price-elasticity is high). Then, provided that transport costs for both groups of *M*-goods are not much different, it is quite possible that the first group of *M*-goods is provided mainly at the central dominant city, while the second group is provided not only in the dominant city but also in smaller cities. If so, we have a hierarchical system of cities. In this way, by introducing many groups of *M*-goods, a more complex hierarchical system of cities would be generated.

Note that since we assume that no pair of differentiated goods is perfectly substitutable, the output of any firm will be consumed by every consumer in the economy (provided that the utility function is of a CES type). Therefore, *there will be trade between every pair of cities*. Thus the system of cities from our model resembles more that of Pred than that of Cristaller (1933) (recall that Christaller's system is purely tree-shaped).

Next, in our discussion above, the basic force of spatial agglomeration was generated through product variety in consumption goods. A similar model of spatial agglomeration can be developed by introducing product variety in intermediate goods. For example, suppose that a homogeneous *M*-good is produced (by *M*-firms) using labour and variety of differentiated (producer) services. Because of scale economies in product specialization, each service is assumed to be supplied monopolistically by a single *S*-firm. In this context, we can reread Figure

2.1 as follows: if a large variety of services is prodced in a city, then this variety of services can be purchased at lower prices there (assuming the f.o.b. pricing by *S*-firms). Thus, because of complementarity among servies, the productivity of *M*-firms becomes higher in the city. This, in turn, will induce more *M*-firms to agglomerate there. Then, this increase in the number of *M*-firms will create a greater number of specialized *S*-firms. In turn, this implies a greater variety of services in the city. Thus, as before, this process creates a circular causality in the spatial agglomeration of *M*-firms and *S*-firms (as well as their workers). Such an agglomeration force caused by product variety in producer services can partly explain a concentration of specific industry in a city (for example, the consumer electronics industry in Tijuana, Mexico; the computer industry in Silicon Valley in the USA; the headquarters of multinational firms in Tokyo).

A FORMAL MODEL OF A SPATIAL ECONOMY

In this section, we present a formal model of a spatial economy that represents the basic ideas above in concrete terms. For the formation and growth of cities in the real world, the product variety in both consumption goods and intermediate goods is important. However, for simplicity, in the rest of the chapter we focus on the product variety in consumption goods.[4] Our model here is based on Fujita and Krugman (1993), which in turn is an extension of Krugman (1993b).[5]

Consider a long, narrow country, in which area is represented by one-dimensional, unbounded location space, $X = \mathbb{R}$. The quality of land is homogeneous and the density of land is equal to 1 everywhere. The country has a continuum of homogeneous workers with a given size, N. Each worker is endowed with a unit of labour, and is free to choose any location and job (that is, manufacturing work or agricultural work) in the country. The consumers of the country consist of the workers and landlords. All landlords are attached to their land (like weeds), and consume the entire revenue from land (that is, land rent) at their location.

Each consumer consumes a homogeneous agricultural (*A*-goods) together with m groups of manufactured goods (*M*-goods), where each group i of *M*-goods ($i = 1.2 \ldots, m$) consists of a continuum of differentiated goods of size n_i. (Here m is given, and each n_i is determined endogenously.) All consumers have the same utility function, given by:

$$U = z_0^{\alpha_0}\prod_{i=1}^{m}\left[\int_0^{n_i} z_i(\omega)^{\rho_i}\, d\omega\right]^{\alpha_i/\rho_i}, \tag{2.1}$$

where z_0 represents the amount of the consumption of *A*-good, $z_i(\omega)$ is the consumption (density) of each product $\omega \in [0, n_i]$ in group i; and α_0, α_i and ρ_i are positive constants such that $\alpha_0 + \Sigma_{i=1}^{m}\alpha_i = 1$ and $0 < \rho_i < 1$. Note that a *smaller* ρ_i means that consumers have a stronger preference for variety in products of group i. Suppose that a consumer has an income, Y, and faces a set of prices, p_0 (for the *A*-good) and $p_i(\omega)$ (for each product ω in group $i = 1, 2, \ldots, m$). Then, by choosing the consumption bundle that maximizes (2.1), subject to the budget constraint,

$$p_0 z_0 + \sum_{i=1}^{m}\int_0^{n_i} p_i(\omega) z_i(\omega)\, d\omega = Y, \tag{2.2}$$

the demand functions of the consumer can be obtained as:

$$z_0 = (\alpha_0 Y)/p_0, \tag{2.3a}$$

$$z_i(\omega) = (\alpha_1 Y/p_i(\omega))(p_i(\omega)^{-\gamma_i}\Big/\int_0^{n_i} p_i(\omega)^{p-\gamma_i}\, d\omega), \tag{2.3b}$$

for each $\omega \in [0, n_i\}$ and $i = 1, 2, \ldots, m$, where $\gamma_i = \rho_i/(1 - \rho_i)$. Note from (2.3b) that the demand for any product in group i has the same price elasticity, E_i, given by $E_i = 1/(1 - \rho_i) = 1 + \gamma_i$. Thus, E_i increases as ρ_i (or γ_i) increases. Substitution of (2.3) into (2.1) yields the following indirect utility function:

$$U = Y\left(\prod_{i=0}^{m}\alpha_i^{\alpha_i}\right) p_0(y)^{-\alpha_0}\prod_{i=1}^{m}\left(\int_0^{n_i} p_i(\omega)^{-\gamma_i}\, d\omega\right)^{\alpha_i/\gamma_i} \tag{2.4}$$

Next, the *A*-good is assumed to be produced under constant returns, where each unit of *A*-good consumes a unit of land and a_0 units of labour. (In this chapter, land is used for *A*-good production only.) Each *M*-good is produced with labour only. All products of the same group i have the same production technology under increasing returns such that the total labour input, L_i, for production of q_i of any product in group i is given by $L_i = f_i + a_i q_i$, where f_i is the fixed labour requirement and a_i the marginal labour input. We assume, for simplicity, that the transport cost of each good takes Samuelson's iceberg form: if a unit of a product in group i ($i = 0, 1, \ldots, m$) is shipped over a distance d, only $e^{-t_i d}$ units actually arrive.[6] In other words, in order to receive a unit of the product at distance d, $e^{t_i d}$ units of the product must be dispatched.

Because of scale economies in specialized production of M-goods, each variety of each group i is assumed to be produced by a single, specialized firm. If a firm locates at $x \in X$ and produces a product in group i, it chooses an f.o.b. price $p_i(x)$, so as to maximize its profit at the Chamberlinian equilibrium. By the assumption of iceberg transport technology, then the effective (delivered) price, $p_i(y \mid x)$, for consumers at location $y \in X$ of any product in group i produced at location x is given by:

$$p_i(y \mid x) = p_i(x)e^{t_i|y-x|}. \tag{2.5}$$

Given the delivered price function above, it can readily be verified that the price elasticity of the total demand for any product in group i is independent of the spatial distribution of the demand, and equals the price elasticity, E_i, of each consumer's demand. Thus, given the equilibrium wage rate, $W(x)$, at x, by the equality of the marginal revenue and marginal cost, $p_i(x)(1 - E_i^{-1}) = a_0W(x)$, the optimal f.o.b. price for the firm (at location x) can be obtained as:

$$p_i(x) = a_iW(x)/\rho_i, \qquad i = 1, 2, \ldots, m. \tag{2.6}$$

Then, if q_i is the output of the firm, its profit at location x equals:

$$\begin{aligned}\pi_i(x) &= p_i(x)q_i - W(x)(f_i + a_iq_i)\\ &= W(x)\{a_i(\rho_i^{-1} - 1)\, q_i - f_i\}\\ &= a_i\gamma_i^{-1}W(x)(q_i - \gamma_i f_i/a_i).\end{aligned} \tag{2.7}$$

Therefore, given any equilibrium configuration of the economy, if a firm in M_i-industry operate at x, then by the zero-profit condition, its (equilibrium) output must be equal to:

$$q_i^* = \gamma_i f_i/a_i, \tag{2.8}$$

which is a constant independent of location.

Consequently, the unknowns of the model left are: (i) the price, $p_0(y)$, of the A-good at each y; (ii) the wage rate, $W(y)$, at each y; (iii) the land rent, $R(y)$, at each y; (iv) the equilibrium utility level, u, of workers; (v) the spatial distribution of workers; (vi) the spatial distribution of the production of M-goods in each group i; and (vii) the transport/trade pattern of each good.

A spatial configuration is in equilibrium if all workers achieve the same highest utility, the maximum profit of all active firms equals zero, and the equality of the demand and supply of each good is attained. In particular, we must make sure that no existing M-firm could increase its profit by moving away from its present location. To express this *location equilibrium condition* precisely, suppose an M_i-firm locates at x, and let $D_i(x)$ represent the total demand for the product of that firm from the entire economy. Then, setting $q_i = D_i(x)$ in (2.7) and using (2.9), the profit of the firm is given by $\pi_i(x) = a_i\gamma_i^{-1}W(x)(D_i(x) - q_i^*)$, which implies that $\pi_i(x) \gtreqless 0$, as $D_i(x) \gtreqless q_i^*$. For convenience, let us define:

$$\Omega_i(x) \equiv D_i(x)/q_i^*. \tag{2.9}$$

Then it follows that $\pi_i(x) \gtreqless 0$ as $\Omega_i(x) \gtreqless 1$. Therefore, if $n_i(x)$ represents the equilibrium number of M_i-firms at each location x, the location equilibrium requires that:

$$\Omega_i(x) \leq 1 \quad \text{for all } x, \tag{2.10}$$

and

$$\Omega_i(x) = 1 \quad \text{if } n_i(x) > 0, \tag{2.11}$$

which together assure that no firm can earn positive profit at any location, and existing firms earn just zero profit. Following Krugman (1993), we call $\Omega_i(x)$ the (market) *potential function* of M_i-industry, which represents the relative profitability of each location for M_i-firms.

EQUILIBRIUM SPATIAL CONFIGURATION

First, suppose we have only one group of M-goods (that is, $m = 1$ and hence $i = 1$ always). For this simple case, Figure 2.2 depicts examples of possible equilibrium spatial configurations.[7] Suppose that the transport cost for the A-good is much higher than that of M-goods. Then, as depicted in Figure 2.2(a), no transportation of the A-good will occur, and the production of M-goods will take place everywhere in the agricultural domain. (In Figure 2.2(a), the height represents the density distribution of M-good firms, and the horizontal line represents the endogenously-determined domain of the land used for agriculture.) In the opposite situation, we shall have Figure 2.2(b), where all manu-

Figure 2.2 Examples of possible equilibrium spatial configurations ($m = 1$)

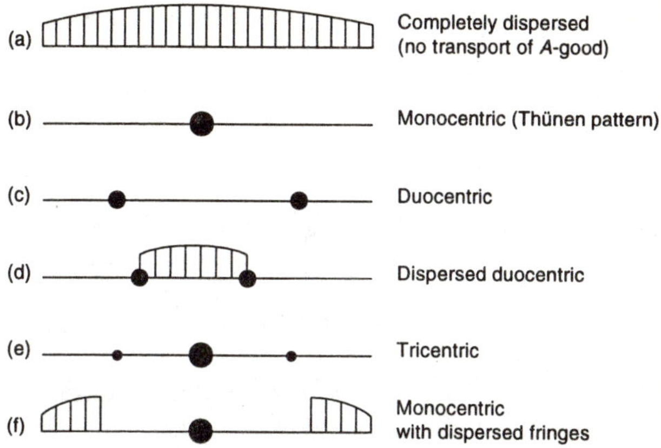

facturing takes place at one location (the metropolis). This is the case as in the *Isolated State* (von Thünen, 1826). Between (a) and (b) above, a variety of equilibrium spatial configurations is conceivable. For example, Figure 2.2(c) represents the case where manufacturing takes place in two cities. Note that since every manufacturing firm is specialized in one product and each consumer consumes every kind of M-good produced, we have trade of M-goods between the two cities (as well as between the cities and the agricultural area). It can be shown that when two major cities locate very closely, then the possible equilibrium configuration is not (c) but (d) in Figure 2.2, where an *industrial belt* (that is, a mixed area of manufacturing and agriculture) will emerge between the two cities. Figure 2.2(e) and 2.2(f) present other possible examples. It is shown in Fujita and Krugman (1993) that multiple equilibria are quite possible.

Under exactly what conditions will each configuration above be in equilibrium? First, let us consider the case of the monocentric configuration depicted in Figure 2.3 (which corresponds to Figure 2.2(b)), where the agricultural area extends from $-l$ to l, and the production of all M_1-goods takes place in the city located at $y = 0$. We can show this case as follows. If $\alpha_0 t_0 > (1 + \rho_1)\alpha_1 t_1$ (for example, A-good transport cost t_0 is very large), then the monocentric configuration can never be in equilibrium; while if $\alpha_0 t_0 \leq (1 + \rho_1)\alpha_1 t_1$ and $\alpha_1 \geq \rho_1$ (that is, M_1-goods are highly differentiated), then the monocentric configuration is always equilibrium. Therefore the most interesting case is when $\alpha_0 t_0 \leq (1 + \rho_1)\alpha_1 t_1$ and $\alpha_1 < \rho_1$. In this case, we can show that the

Figure 2.3 A monocentric spatial configuration

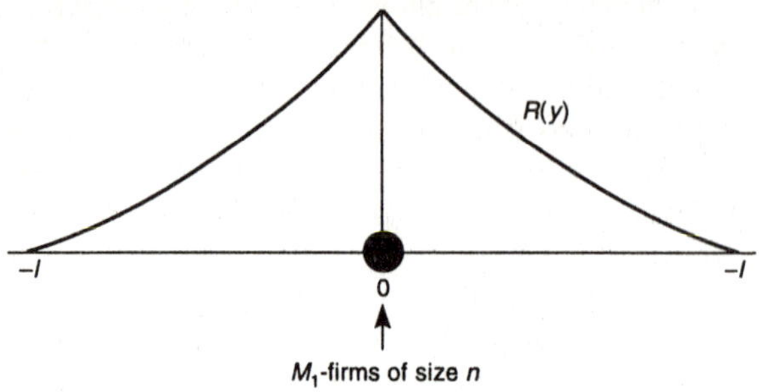

Figure 2.4 Potential curves for the monocentric configuration under various N

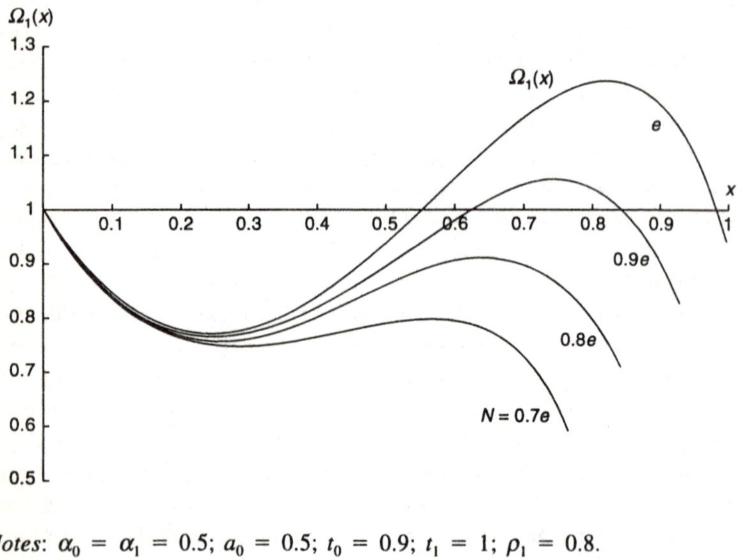

Notes: $\alpha_0 = \alpha_1 = 0.5$; $a_0 = 0.5$; $t_0 = 0.9$; $t_1 = 1$; $\rho_1 = 0.8$.

monocentric configuration will be in equilibrium only when the population N of the economy is sufficiently small. Figure 2.4 demonstrates the final conclusion graphically, which depicts the potential curve (at the right of $x = 0$ at which the city locates) under each value of N. When $N = 0.7e$, for example, $\Omega_1(x) < 1$ for all $x \neq 0$. Hence, no existing firms in the city would deviate, and the monocentric configuration is in equilibrium. On the other hand, if $N = 0.9e$, for example, then

$\Omega_1(x) > 1$ in the periphery. So, some firms would deviate from the city, and hence the monocentric configuration cannot be in equilibrium.

When the monocentric configuration is not in equilibrium, which configuration could be in equilibrium? Obvious candidates are the duocentric configurations shown in Figure 2.5. In these (symmetric) duocentric configurations, the production of M_1-goods takes place in two cities of equal size located at $x = -b$ and $x = b$ respectively. In the Duo-A configuration, the agricultural hinterlands of two cities are connected; while in the Duo-B configuration they are separated. First, let us consider the Duo-A configuration. Given that $N = e$ (and other parameters specified at the bottom of Figure 2.6), Figure 2.6 depicts the potential curves (associated with the Duo-A configuration) under various values of b (recall that when $N = e$, the monocentric configuration is no longer in equilibrium). We can see from Figure 2.6 that when b is between 0.3 and 0.5 (that is, the two cities are not too close yet not too far), the Duo-A configuration can indeed be in equilibrium. We can also show that under the same set of parameters, the Duo-B configuration is in equilibrium for any given value of b greater than 0.65. Recall that each M_1-firm is producing a different kind of M-good in Group 1. Therefore, in either case of duocentric equilibrium configuration in Figure 2.5, two cities trade different kinds of M_1-goods to each other (and also export them to agricultural hinterlands).

Next, Figure 2.7 presents three possible types of (symmetric) tricentric spatial configurations. In a *Tri-A configuration* (the top), the excess A-good will always be transported inwardly. For this to happen, the two side-cities must be relatively small in comparison with the central city. Hence, they can be interpreted as *satellite cities* of the central metropolis. In contrast, in a *Tri-B configuration* (the middle), each city has its own agricultural hinterland. Thus, the economy consists of a system of three *regions*, each having its own core city. Finally, a *Tri-C configuration* (the bottom) consists of three *semi-isolated states*. Note, however, that since the M_1-goods produced in any one city will be exported to two other states, the three states are in fact not isolated economically.[8]

In all the examples so far, cities are different in size only: they are functionally the same. But now suppose that we have two groups of M-goods (that is, $m = 2$). Then, it is possible to have a hierarchical system of cities. For example, the transport costs for the two groups are similar, but the products in Group 1 are highly differentiated (that is, ρ_1 is small) while those in Group 2 are close substitutes for each other (that is, ρ_2 is large). Then, as depicted in Figure 2.8, it is

Figure 2.5 Two types of symmetric duocentric configuration

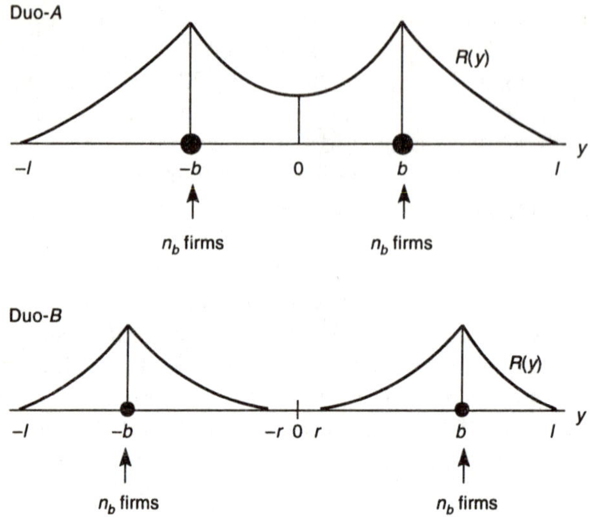

Figure 2.6 Potential curves for Duo-A configurations for b = 0.2 to 0.6

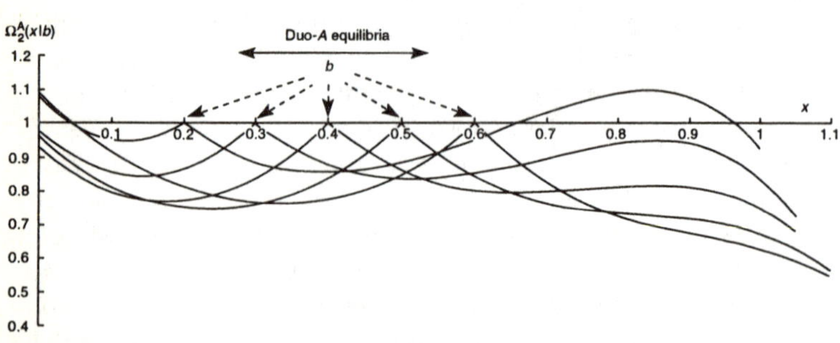

Note: $\alpha_0 = \alpha_1 = 0.5$; $a_0 = 0.5$; $t_0 = 0.9$; $t_1 = 1$; $\rho_1 = 0.8$; $N = e$.

possible that the *M*-goods of Group 1 will be produced mainly at the central dominant city, while those of Group 2 will be produced in several small cities as well as in the dominant city.[9]

Figure 2.7 Three types of tricentric configuration

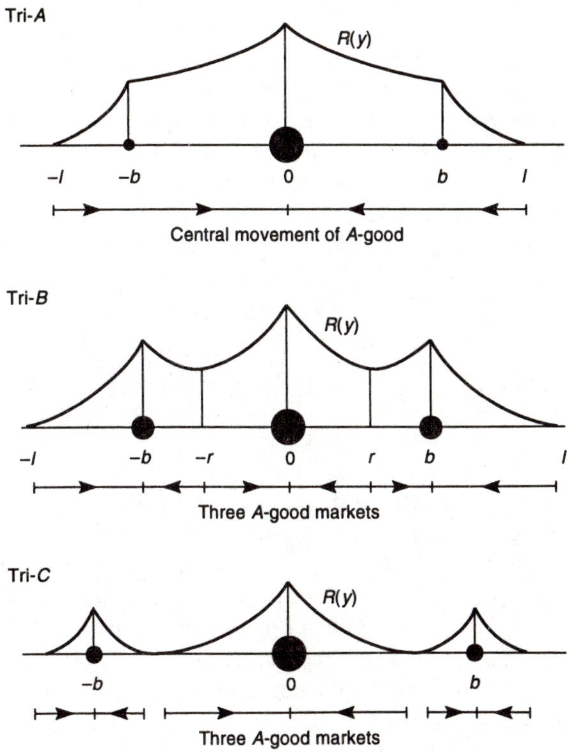

Figure 2.8 An example of a hierarchical system of cities

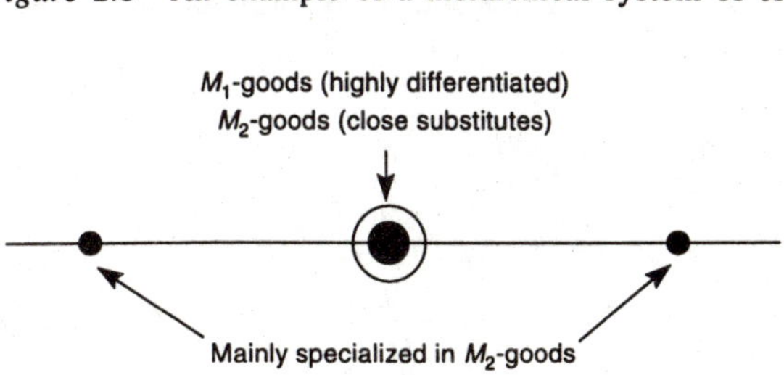

STRUCTURAL INSTABILITY OF MULTIPLE EQUILIBRIA AND REGIONAL DEVELOPMENT STRATEGIES

Given that our model of space economy yields a high degree of multiple equilibria, in this section we examine the stability of (static) equilibria obtained above. The stability analysis is important, for two reasons. First, since unstable equilibria would rarely be observed in the real world, the stability analysis helps to narrow down the range of observable equilibria. Second, and more importantly, the dynamic relationship among (static) equilibria provides useful information on regional development strategies, as illustrated below.

Following Krugman (1993b), we consider the following dynamic adjustment process of our spatial economy. Take any time $t \in \mathbb{R}$, and suppose that the production of M_1-goods takes place in J cities, $j = 1, 2, \ldots, J$, where each city j locates at x_j. Let $N_j(t)$ be the population of each city j (that is, the size of workers in city j) at time t. Then, given the fixed total size of workers in the economy by N, the size of agricultural workers (A-workers) at time t is given by $N_A(t) = N - \Sigma_j N_j(t)$. Here, we assume that at each given moment of time t, the population of each city is fixed, and hence $N_A(t)$ is also fixed. We assume, however, that at time t all A-workers are free to choose their location, but they remain to be A-workers. Given this population distribution, $N_j(t)$, $j = 1, 2, \ldots, J$ and A, we solve the model for $U_j(t)$ (together with all other unknowns), where $U_j(t)$ is the equilibrium utility level of workers in city j, or that of A-workers if $j = A$. Then, for each pair of $j, k = 1, 2, \ldots, J$ and A, the rate of migration from k to j is assumed to be given by $\sigma N_j(t)\{U_j(t) - U_k(t)\}N_k(t)$. That is, workers move away from a low-utility city (or A-job) toward a high-utility city (or A-job). Hence, for each $j = 1, 2, \ldots, J$ and A, the net change of population at time t is given by:

$$\dot{N}_j(t) = \Sigma_k \sigma N_j(t)\{U_j(t) - U_k(t)\}N_k(t), \tag{2.12}$$

or, since $\Sigma_k N_k(t) = N$, by setting $\bar{U}(t) \equiv \Sigma_k N_k(t)\, U_k(t)/N$ we have that:

$$\dot{N}_j(t) = \sigma N_j(t)\{U_j(t) - \bar{U}(t)\}N. \tag{2.13}$$

Using this dynamic model, we can examine the stability of each (static) equilibrium.

Let us fix parameters, for example, as follows:

$$\alpha_0 = \alpha_1 = 0.5;\ a_0 = 0.5;\ a_1 = 1;\ t_0 = 0.9;\ t_1 = 1;$$
$$\rho_1 = 0.8;\ f_1 = 1;\ N = 0.75e. \qquad (2.14)$$

Then, it turns out that under this identical set of parameters, the following configurations are simultaneously in equilibrium:[10]

(i) the monocentric configuration;
(ii) the Tri-*A* configuration for *each* value of $b \in (0,0.8)$;
(iii) the Duo-*A* configuration for *each* value of $b \in (0.35, 0.4)$; and
(iv) the Duo-*B* configuration for *each* value of $b \geq 5.2$,

where the parameter b in (ii) represents the distance of each satellite city from the central metropolis; while in (iii) and (iv), b represents a half of the distance between the two cities (refer to Figures 2.4 and 2.6).

Among the four types of equilibrium configuration above, it turns out that *all Tri-A equilibria are (locally) unstable, while the rest of equilibrium configurations (that is, Mono, Duo-A and Duo-B for each b) is (locally) stable.* The stability of Mono, Duo-*A* and Duo-*B* equilibria is based on the fact that the total population of the economy $N = 0.75e$ is more than three times of $\hat{N}(\simeq 0.6)$ under which the monocentric equilibrium achieves the highest equilibrium utility. On the other hand, instability of Tri-*A* equilibria is not surprising if we recall that the satellite city of any Tri-*A* equilibrium is very small in comparison with the central metropolis (and hence the system is basically unstable).

The instability of Tri-*A* equilibria provides a linkages between our model and big push or growth pole models of economic development advocated by early development theorists such as Rosenstein-Rodan (1943), Perroux (1950), Myrdal (1957) and Hirshman (1958). That is, suppose that at present the spatial configuration of the economy is monocentric, and that the planners of the economy intend to develop cities in the hinterland of the unique metropolis. The question is, what are the minimum sizes of these new cities that will lead to self-sustained growth? Let us consider the case of two new cities to be created at symmetric locations. Then, in the context of present example, Figure 2.9 provides the answer, where $N_b(b)/N_0(b)$ represents the ratio of the population in each satellite city (*s*-city), $N_b(b)$, and the population in the central city, $N_0(b)$, under each value of b.

That is, let us fix any $b \leq 0.8$ in Figure 2.9, then the value of $N_b(b)/N_0(b)$ provides the minimum size of each *s*-city (in comparison with

Figure 2.9 City size ratio, N_b/N_0, for Tri-*A* equilibria

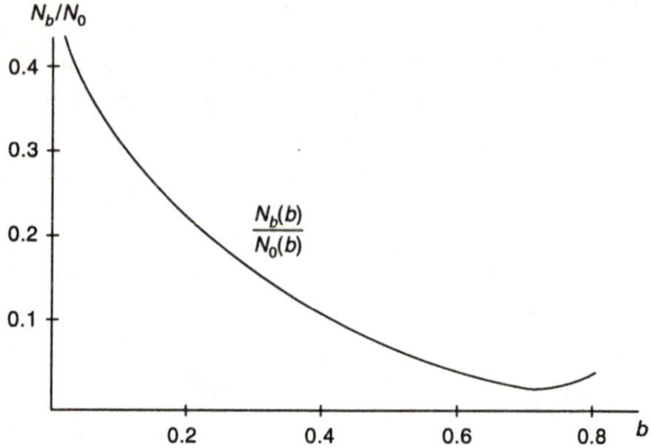

Note: $\alpha_0 = \alpha_1 = 0.5$; $a_0 = 0.5$; $a_1 = 1$; $t_0 = 0.9$; $t_1 = 1$; $\rho_1 = 0.8$; $f_1 = 1$; $N = 0.75e$.

the size of the central city) that is necessary to initiate a self-sustained growth of each new *s*-city.[11] In particular, the necessary size of each *s*-city is minimum when each is created at distance $b \simeq 0.7$ in Figure 2.9. In this sense, $b = 0.7$ represents the best candidate for the location of growth-pole. More generally, unstable equilibrium configurations of our model provide the information on the threshold sizes of new cities to be set in self-sustained growth.

CONCLUSION

In this chapter, we have presented a microeconomic model of urban systems, and examined its possible usefulness in designing effective regional development strategies. Our analysis of the model in this chapter, however, is preliminary, and a great deal of work remains to be done in the future. First, we must examine thoroughly the case of multiple groups of manufactured goods. Second, an interesting direction in which to extend the model is to consider multi-locational firms. That is, suppose that each firm consists of multiple units (for example, HQs, R&D units, and manufacturing plants) which can be located separately. Then, since different units will follow different agglomeration forces (for example, availability of business services and convenience of face-to-face communication for HQs, availability of engineers for R&D units, and accessibility to consumers for manufacturing plants), we shall be able to develop a richer class of spatial models.[12] Eventually, by introducing into such basic models various realistic features (such as political restrictions, natural geographic features, and historical and cultural elements), we shall be able to develop a realistic regional model that would be useful in studying the future economic geography of a nation or group of nations, and in designing effective regional development strategies.

Notes

The author is grateful for the financial support by Grant in Aid for Research 08403001 of the Ministry of Education, Science, and Culture in Japan in conducting this research.

1. A notable exception has been China, where strong economic measures on housing and food allocation in cities have been very effective in curbing the growth of the country's biggest cities. However, if China continues to promote its market economic policy, there is a strong possibility that the primal cities will start growing rapidly in the near future.
2. Although there have been many attempts to develop formal models of central place/urban system theory, these are either partial or without reference to space. For example, in Henderson (1987), no space is explicitly considered.
3. For a systematic discussion of a variety of possible models of endogenous spatial agglomeration, see Fujita (1990).
4. For spatial agglomeration models based on product variety in intermediate goods, see, for example, Fujita (1990).
5. Krugman (1993b) developed a microeconomic model of a spatial economy, which can explain the formation of a metropolis at some specific location in a given continuous geographical space. Our model here generalizes Krugman's model by introducing multiple types of manufactured goods and by considering more than one metropolis (or city).
6. Without changing the essential results of the chapter, we can replace $e^{-t_i d}$ by any decreasing function, $f_i(d)$, of d such that $f_i(0) = 1$.
7. See Fujita and Krugman (1993) for a description of the conditions under which each configuration in Figure 2.2 emerges as an equilibrium. However, given the present state of the research, some configurations have not yet been shown to be an equilibrium, and more work is called for. Note also that although only symmetric configurations are depicted in Figure 2.2, all equilibrium configurations need not be symmetric.
8. For detailed discussions of these tricentric configurations and other types of equilibrium spatial configurations (for $m = 1$), see Fujita and Krugman (1993).
9. For detailed analyses of hierarchical urban systems (with $m > 2$), see Fujita, Krugman and Mori (1993).

10. For details of the discussion below, see section 7 of Fujita and Krugman (1993). Although we have confirmed the four types of equilibrium configurations indicated below, they are not necessarily exhaustive of all possible equilibrium configurations. The identification of all possible equilibrium configurations, however, is left for the future.
11. Since our stability analysis is local, it informs only that if a newly created Tri-*A* configuration is such that $N_b(b)/N_0(b)$ is above the curve in Figure 2.9, then these *s*-cities will achieve self-sustained growth. In order to know what new (stable) equilibrium configuration this original Tri-*A* configuration will eventually lead to, we must conduct a global dynamical analysis of the economy, which is left for the future. For an example of global dynamical analyses of urban systems (in the context of our present model), see Mori (1993a, 1993b).
12. For spatial economic models with multiunit firms, see, for example, Ota and Fujita (1993).

References

Christaller, W. (1933) *Die Zentralen Orte in Suddeutschland*, trans. by C. W. Baskin (1966) as *Central Places in Southern Germany* (Englewood Cliffs, NJ: Prentice-Hall).

Fujita, M. (1990) 'Spatial Interactions and Agglomeration in Urban Economics', in M. Chatterji and R. E. Kunne (eds), *New Frontiers in Regional Sciences* (London: Macmillan).

Fujita, M. and P. Krugman (1993) 'A Monopolistic Competition Model of Urban Systems and Trade', mimeo, Department of Regional Science, University of Pennsylvania, Philadelphia.

Fujita, M., P. Krugman and T. Mori (1993) *Urban Hierarchy and Regional Development*, Department of Regional Science, University of Pennsylvania.

Henderson, J. V. (1987) 'Systems of Cities and Inter-city Trade', in P. Hansen *et al.* (eds) *Systems of Cities and Facility Location* (Chur, Switzerland: Harwood Academic Publishers) pp. 71–119.

Hirshman, A. (1958) *The Strategy of Economic Development* (New Haven, Conn.: Yale University Press).

Krugman, P. (1991) *Geography and Trade* (Cambridge, Mass.: MIT Press).

Krugman, P. (1993a) 'First Nature, Second Nature, and Metropolitan Location', *Journal of Regional Science*, vol. 34, pp. 129–44.

Krugman, P. (1993b) 'A Dynamic Spatial Model', mimeo, Department of Economics, Massachusetts Institute of Technology.

Mori, T., (1993a) 'Structural Stability Analysis of Urban Systems', *Working Papers in Regional Science*, No. 161, Department of Regional Science, University of Pennsylvania, Philadelphia.

Mori, T. (1993b) 'Structural Stability Analysis of Urban Systems and Trade Patterns, mimeo, Department of Regional Science, University of Pennsylvania, Philadelphia.

Myrdal, G. (1957) *Economic Theory and Underdeveloped Regions* (London: Duckworth).

Ota, M. and M. Fujita (1993) 'Communication Technologies and Spatial Organization of Multi-unit Firms in Metropolitan Areas', *Regional Science and Urban Economics*, forthcoming.

Perroux, F. (1950) 'Economic Space: Theory and Applications', *Quarterly Journal of Economics*, vol. 64, pp. 89–104.

Rosenstein-Rodan, P. (1943) 'Problems of Industrialization of Eastern and South-eastern Europe', *Economic Journal*, June–September.

Von Thünen, J. H. (1826) *Der Isolierte Staat in Beziehung auf landwirtschaft und Nationalekonomie*, Hamburg.

3 Linked System of Enterprise, Regional and National Input–Output Accounts for Policy Analysis

Karen R. Polenske

Most input–output analysts make macroeconomic studies at regional, national, or even global levels. Recently, some analysts have begun to work in an exciting new area of research where they construct input–output accounts at the microeconomic – individual firm – level. In a previous paper, Polenske (1989) discussed briefly how corporation input–output accounts can be linked to regional and national input–output accounts. Because of the increased interdependence in economic activity, not only must macro planners be aware of policy changes by firms, but firm managers must also be aware of relevant policy changes happening in the regional, national and international spheres. A linked input–output system of accounts provides an excellent means of portraying these relationships. The purpose of this chapter, therefore, is to extend this important concept in two ways.

First, we compare three major accounting systems used by corporations and show how an input–output accounting system is a necessary complement to the more familiar managerial and financial accounting systems currently used extensively by US firms. Second, we provide more details on the structure of a system of enterprise, regional and national accounts, and the ways such an accounting system can be used for policy analyses in China.

MANAGERIAL, FINANCIAL, AND ENTERPRISE INPUT–OUTPUT ACCOUNTS

Major changes are taking place in the field of corporation accounting in the USA and other countries. In order to compare managerial, financial and enterprise input–output accounts, we shall look at each in terms of the types of account available, data used, purposes served, and users of the accounts.

Three of the most vocal advocates of changes in the accounting system are Robin Cooper, Robert S. Kaplan and H. Thomas Johnson. They have written widely on the subject (for example, Cooper (1987); Cooper and Kaplan (1991); Kaplan (1984, 1985, 1986); Kaplan and Atkinson (1989); Johnson (1988, 1992), Johnson and Kaplan are also co-authors of a prize-winning book, *Relevance Lost: The Rise and Fall of Management Accounting* (1987), in which they provide an especially useful description of the history of the present management accounting system and why it does not meet the needs of modern managers. In Table 3.1, we summarize US managerial accounting, using the Johnson–Kaplan division of three stages in the development of these accounts: (1) those developed for single-activity organizations, which were dominant from the early nineteenth century up to 1910; (2) those developed for multiactivity organizations, dominant from 1900 to 1920; and (3) those developed for multi-divisional organizations since the 1920s. These type of accounts are used by US firms to plan and control the internal operation of corporations efficiently, providing comprehensive monetary and non-monetary information on the current performance and future directions of a firm.

Managerial accounts, however, have at least five shortcomings (Dudick, (1987); Foster and Horngren (1988); Lammert and Ehrsam (1987); Polenske (1989, pp. 379–80)). First, they do not provide adequate measurements for the evaluation of division performance within firms. Second, they do not provide complete accounting information for management decisions. Third, they are not designed to support the operation and strategy of the firm. Fourth, although they are relatively effective means of determining efficient uses of direct labour and materials, corporations now need means to assess the short-term and long-term performance of the company in the broader regional, national and global arena. Fifth, they focus managers' attention on costs rather than on quality and flexibility.

In Table 3.2, three major types of financial accounting statements are presented: (I) balance sheet, (II) income, and (III) cash-flow (also

Table 3.1 US managerial accounting

Type of statement	*Data used*	*Purposes served*	*Users of statement*
Developed for Single-activity Organizations (early nineteenth century to 1910)			
I Conversion cost system			
Double-entry cost accounts for direct-labour, material and general overhead costs	Direct labour, direct and indirect material, overhead	Monitor and evaluate the output of internally directed processes, monitor employee performance, provide incentives for workers to achieve productivity goals	Owners and top-level management
Operating ratio (railroad)	Operating expenses, revenues	Compare variations of subunits to total performance	Owners and top-level management
Gross margin (distribution)	Sales receipts, cost of goods sold, department operating expenses	Monitor department performance and compare departments to the company's overall performance	Owners and top-level management
Stockturn (distribution)	Inventory turnover	Same as gross margin	Owners and top-level management
II Scientific management			
Standard rates for material and labour input	Direct labour, direct and indirect material, overhead	Gauge efficiency of tasks or processes, cost control, inventory valuation	Owners and top-level management
III Strategic product costing			
All costs, including direct overhead costs to products	Direct labour, direct and indirect material, overhead	Evaluate overall profitability of the organization	Owners and top-level management

Developed for Multi-activity Organizations (1900–20)			
IV Single-activity accounts			
All single activity accounts	See single-activity organization	Efficient and effective performance in specialized activities	Department managers
Modified single-activity	See single-activity organization	Overall goal: harmonize actions in departments with overall goals of the firm	Central management
V Return on investment (ROI)			
Asset accounting	Sales, payroll, manufacturing costs, plant & equipment costs	Compare performance of each department with performance of entire firm, efficient allocation of capital among activities	Central management
VI Budgets			
Cash, income and capital, cash-flow forecasts, sales forecasts	Projected sales, product prices, input costs, other income, construction costs	Co-ordinate and balance internal resource flows from raw materials to final customers	Central management
Developed for Multidivisional Organizations (1920s)			
VII Overall management accounting system from multi-activity firm			
	See multi-activity organization	Perform the role of markets for capital and managers, especially to evaluate and motivate managers	Central management
VIII Return on investment			
	See multi-activity organization	Delegate to division managers the entire responsibility for using capital efficiently	Division managers

Source: Compiled by K. R. Polenske, L. Bleiberg and A. Malhotra from H. T. Johnson and R. S. Kaplan (1987) *Relevance Lost: The Rise and Fall of Management Accounting* (Boston, Mass.: Harvard Business School).

Table 3.2 US Financial accounting

Type of statement	*Data used*	*Purposes served*	*Users of statement*
I Balance sheet Gives snapshot of investing and financing activities of firm as of a specific date	Double-entry accounts which maintain the following equality among accounts: assets = liabilities plus owners' equity Types of account: (i) Asset accounts (ii) Liability accounts (iii) Equity accounts	Shows the economic resources (assets) of firm and claims (liabilities or equity) on these resources Enables assessment of management's discharge of its 'stewardship' responsibility towards owners	Investors, creditors and government regulatory agencies
II Income statement Gives results of operating activities of firm for specific period of time	Double-entry revenue and expense accounts Net income = revenues minus expenses (i) Revenue accounts: sales revenue, interest revenue, rent revenue, etc. (ii) Expense accounts: cost of goods sold, salaries expenses, interest expenses, depreciation expenses, etc.	Indicates firm's operating performance during the period Enables assessment of management's discharge of its 'stewardship' responsibility towards owners	Investors, creditors and government regulatory agencies

III Cash-flow statement			
Gives cash flows arising from operating, investing and financing activities of firm for specific time period	(i) Balance sheet accounts: cash, accounts receivable, accounts payable, etc. (ii) Income statement accounts: sales revenue, cost of goods sold, depreciation expenses, etc.	Indicates liquidity/viability of firm Shows 'sources' and 'uses' of firm's cash Enables assessment of management's discharge of its 'stewardship' responsibility towards owners	Investors, creditors and government regulatory agencies

Source: Compiled by K. R. Polenske, L. Bleiberg and A. Malhotra from S. Davidson *et al.* (1988) *Financial Accounting: An Introduction to Concepts, Methods, and Uses* (Chicago, Ill.: Dryden Press).

called flow-of-funds). Whereas managerial accounts are designed primarily for use by owners and managers of the corporation, financial accounts are designed for a vastly different set of users, namely, investors, creditors and regulatory agencies. They provide aggregate data on the financial performance of a corporation that are used by investors in the corporation to help make investment decisions, and by the government to determine the base for corporation tax. Thus the data used and the purposes served by the financial accounts also vary from those of managerial accounts (Davidson *et al.*, 1988). In addition to some of the deficiencies as mentioned above for managerial accounts, financial accounts do not provide a reliable measurement of corporate performance because, for their own purposes, managers may often be able to misrepresent the short-term profits of the corporation (Polenske, 1989, p. 379).

Thus managerial and financial accounts do not provide corporation managers and the public at large with a comprehensive set of accounting information, and they cannot be used directly to implement basic planning procedures such as sensitivity analysis, linear programming and interdivision linkages. A third type of accounting system that helps to fill in some of the gaps of managerial and financial accounts is available, namely, corporation (enterprise) input–output accounts. These accounts have been used in China since the early 1960s and have been, or are being, used in several other countries, such as Belgium, Italy (La Noce and Latorre, 1988), Portugal (Pimpao, 1979) and the former Yugoslavia (Filipic, 1985, 1986). Here, we focus on the uses in China.

In Table 3.3, the type of statement, data used, purposes served, and users for (Chinese) enterprise input–output accounts are summarized. As in the case of the managerial accounts, the users are primarily managers; however, the input–output accounts appear to be used extensively in China by managers at all production levels. According to the managers we interviewed, they derive many benefits from the use of an enterprise input–output account, a few of which are detailed below.

First, it merges many aspects of statistical, managerial and financial accounts into one system and can be generalized to include physical and value accounts.

Second, it provides a systematic method for collecting statistical data on products, production units and plants to build a foundation for an automated information management system. Immediate uses include: (i) tracking distribution of outputs; (ii) tracking purchase of inputs; and (iii) showing how to balance production within individual production units and for the entire enterprise. The established database can then be used for the economic responsibility system to be adopted by the enterprise.

Third, managers use it to produce a systematic set of targets and production quotas for production units and the enterprise as a whole. They also incorporate the account into an enterprise input–output model (especially a dynamic model), which is very useful for long-term forecasting. Techniques they use to produce targets and quotas are: (a) direct input coefficients; (b) total input coefficients (direct plus indirect); (c) linear programming model; and (d) sensitivity analysis.

Fourth, managers also expand the account for use in an optimization input–output model to make efficient use of scarce resources possible, so as to maximize enterprise profits. Inputs to the model given by enterprise programme managers include: (a) set of goals; and (b) measures to verify attainment of goals.

Fifth, the account provides a link to input–output accounts (and models) for an industrial sector, geographic region, entire nation, or even other countries. An enterprise–regional–national–global set of accounts can increase the understanding of economic constraints and opportunities both at the micro and macro levels.

On three of the author's visits to China (1988, 1990 and 1992), managers were met who were using enterprise input–output accounts in six different enterprises (Anshan Iron and Steel Corporation; Hualin Rubber Corporation; North China Pharmaceutical Corporation; Baoding Woollen Mills; Tsinghua Rubber Corporation; and Yunnan Tin Corporation). The exact number of enterprises using these accounts in China is not known, but in Hebei Province alone over 600 enterprises may have prepared 1992 enterprise input–output accounts. Li Bingquan and others from the Institute of Systems Science at the Chinese Academy of Science have held several training sessions in recent years, attended by many different corporations, and they are asked regularly by different enterprises to help in establishing such accounting systems. From the accounts we have reviewed, the structure of the accounts are similar in many respects from one enterprise to another, but each is designed to fit the specific needs of the enterprise.

Throughout the world, managers' experience in the use of input–output accounts is far more restricted than their experience in using managerial and financial accounts. A few examples of the limited information available in English include: Filipic (1986) for the Split shipbuilding industry in the former Yugoslavia; La Noce and Latorre (1988), for the Instituto La Riconstruzione Industriale (IRI) in Italy;

Table 3.3 Chinese enterprise input–output accounting

Type of statement	*Data used*	*Purposes served*	*Users of statement*
Used from 1964 onwards			
I Physical input–output table			
Gives the input and output flows for the entire enterprise in physical units	Technological (physical) characteristics of all products. Specifically, input coefficients (direct and indirect) for products of individual production units. (The physical table is classified using processes and products) Demand characteristics of all products. Specifically, demand for outputs of each production unit by other production units and external users	Shows technological variations among production units. Enables comparisons among units producing the same product Helps management make production plans, organize supplies of raw materials and determine amounts of internal transportation required	Central and production-unit managers
Used from 1980 onwards			
II Value input–output table			
Gives the input and output flows for the entire enterprise in value units	Data are similar to those used in physical table, only they are in value (price times quantity) terms. (The value table is also classified using processes and products)	Allows internal cost-accccunting and cost comparisons among production units Makes profit calculations available:	Central and production-unit managers

		(a) profit from internal transactions, (b) profit from external sales Includes calculated items, such as depreciation, interest and taxes Facilitates long-term planning and forecasting when used to develop comprehensive balances and economic efficiency projections	
III Optimization input–output table			
Gives the optimal combinations of inputs and outputs for the entire enterprise. It is usually static but also can be dynamic.	Technological characteristics and final production data are combined into a system of equations Production constraints, such as labour and materials, and financial and other constraints, are imposed upon the input–output system	Solution of optimization model permits: (i) revenue maximization by selection of product combination that yields largest profits; (ii) cost minimization, by selection of input combination that achieves lowest costs	Central and production-unit managers
IV Physical-value input–output table			
	Data from both the physical and value tables are combined (physical quantities, values and detailed prices)	Unifies managerial, financial and input–output accounting: has advantages of physical and value tables	Central and production-unit managers

Source: Compiled by K. R. Polenske, L. Bleiberg and A. Malhotra from K. R. Polenske and Chen Xikang (eds) (1991) *Chinese Economic Planning and Input-Output Applications* (Hong Kong: Oxford University Press) chs 16–19.

Li Bingquan (1991), a general discussion of the applications in Chinese enterprises; Tong Renchang (1991), a specific application of enterprise input–output tables in China; and Zhang Renjia *et al.* (1991), a specific application of the input–output accounts for planning at the Anshan Iron and Steel Corporation (AISC) in China. Filipic presented his sophisticated system of accounts at the eighth international input–output meetings, and it is also available in a book (written in Serbo-Croatian), so that we shall not discuss it further here. The Italian work is also available in published form. In addition, a publication in French has recently been received (Pimpao, 1979) on the construction and application of an input–output account for a petrochemical complex in Portugal, and there is also a publication available (only in Portuguese) of its use for Air Portugal (TAP) (Pimpao, 1990). Thus we found that the use of enterprise input–output accounts has so far been relatively restricted outside China.

CHINESE ENTERPRISE INPUT–OUTPUT ACCOUNTS

At AISC, managers have been using the input–output accounts for many management decisions since 1964. By 1989, the AISC staff had constructed their eighth input–output account, the most recent to date being for 1987, having already constructed accounts for 1964, 1977, 1978, 1980, 1981, 1983 and 1985. The 1987 accounts contain a comprehensive set of data on the distribution of output and purchase of inputs for more than 1000 types of product and for each of 40 plants (Zhang Renjia *et al.*, 1991). The first accounts were constructed using physical units only, but the most recent are an integrated set of physical, value, plant and product accounts. In Figure 3.1, we show how the AISC enterprise relates its enterprise planning to the state plans. Details on the many uses to which the AISC input–output accounts have been put are available in the publication already cited, and in two publications by Polenske (1989, 1991). AISC is just one of many enterprises in China currently constructing input–output accounts for management decisions. As far as it can be discerned, enterprises in all the provinces are constructing and using such accounts, although the exact number, nor how diverse the uses really are, cannot be determined. Workshops are held, and enterprises send representatives to them to be trained in input–output accounting.

Figure 3.1 Procedure for annual comprehensive enterprise planning, People's Republic of China

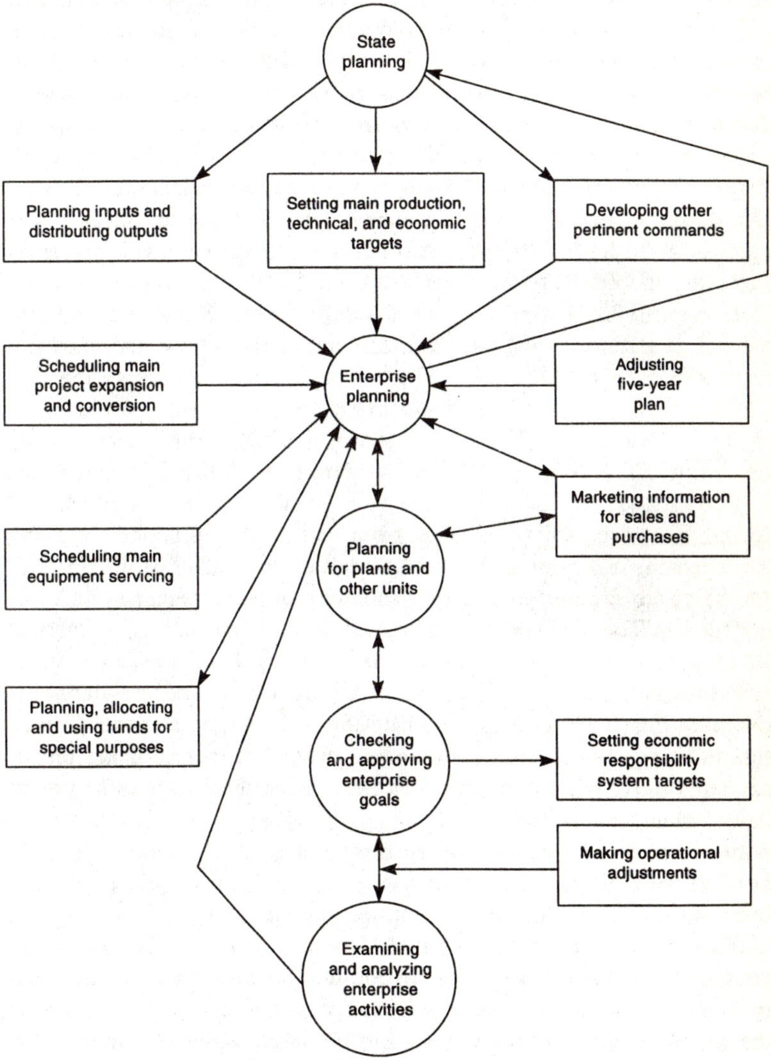

Source: Zhang Renjia *et al.* (1991) 'Application of Input–Output Method to Anshan Iron and Steel Company' in K. R. Polenske and Chen Xikang (eds), *Chinese Economic Planning and Input–Output Research* (Hong Kong: Oxford University Press) p. 275.

LINKED SYSTEM OF ACCOUNTS

China, Italy and Japan are among the few countries in which managers at the micro level and policy-makers and planners at the macro level can take advantage of an up-to-date and extensive set of national and regional input–output data to form an integrated system of accounts for policy analyses. For the purposes of illustration, we present the basic concepts required for such a network in China.[1] By late 1995, China had a 1992 national input–output table as well as regional input–output tables for all regions except Tibet and Hainan Island (29 in all), for 118 sectors (101 productive and 17 non-productive), and similar data for 1987 has been available since 1990.

These accounts are already consistent, in that both the state and provincial statistical office staff use similar methodology and identical industrial classifications as they construct the accounts. First, the provincial statistical office staff collect data from enterprises in the province and tabulate them. They store all provincial data from the enterprises on floppy disks using the Dbase III+ program, and they give the data in that form to the computer centre staff at the State Statistical Bureau (SSB). The SSB staff collect data from each of the 30 regions and sum them to obtain the national total. In addition, a number of members of the SSB staff are responsible for estimating the final demand and value added data. The SSB staff then adjust all the data to satisfy the important input–output accounting consistencies. Staff in each provincial statistical office have responsibility for the construction of the provincial accounts, using the data as provided to the SSB. At the provincial level, the staff may use the data for more, or fewer, than 118 sectors, if needed for planning purposes, and they make their own estimates of final demand and value added.

In Figure 3.2, I portray how these provincial and national data could be organized, along with enterprise and global input–output accounting data, to form a linked accounting system. The available data, of course, do not yet form a complete system of even multi-regional accounts for China. In order to complete the multi-regional system, analysts would also need to assemble inter-regional trade data, specifying the amount of each commodity shipped between regions. This will help to establish a systematic set of inter-regional linkages for policy analyses.

The next step is to make the actual link of the regional accounts with those of one or more of the enterprises. The AISC accounts would be an ideal place to start such a linked system. Those accounts already form a subsystem of accounts for the enterprise in that they are con-

Figure 3.2 An integrated system of input–output accounts

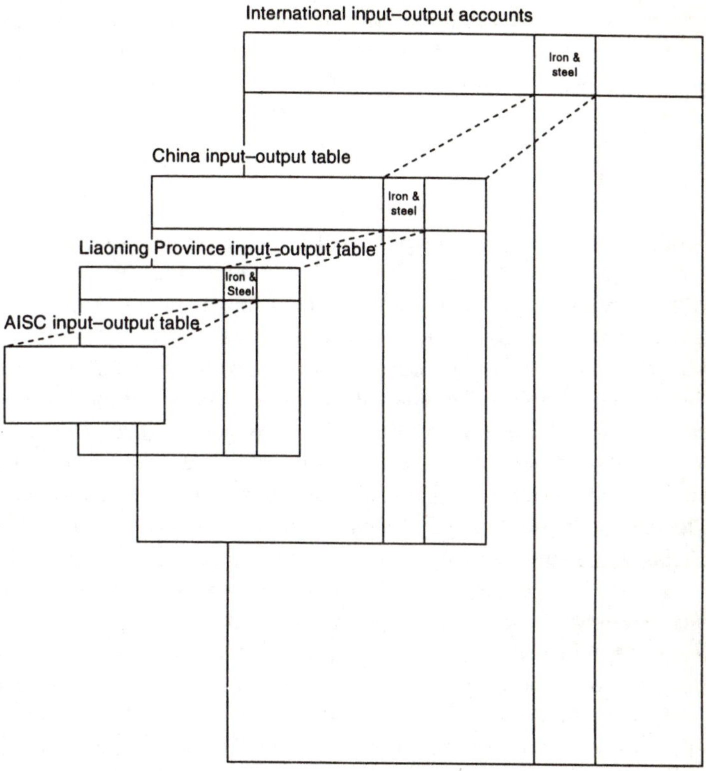

structed for each of forty plants. An input into (output from) one of those plants can therefore be specified as coming from (distributed to) either the plant itself, another AISC plant, another enterprise within Liaoning province (where AISC is located), an enterprise in one of the other provinces, or from abroad. Thus analysts in China will have available a systematic way to account for all purchases and sales by a given iron and steel firm, at local, regional and national levels.

Analysts can then use these accounts, along with updates of data from other South-east Asian countries assembled by the Institute of Developing Countries staff in Tokyo, to extend the accounting system to an international level. By using input–output data from any of the other enterprises in China, analysts can conduct a vast number of intriguing analyses concerning many important energy balances, economic and environmental impacts of policy issues, international, national, and/or provincial rules and regulations, and changes in transportation requirements. The accounts, if extended to include financial information, can start to replace some of the managerial and financial accounting tools used in Western countries.

CONCLUSION

The linked system of accounts proposed in this chapter would not have been possible to implement in the 1970s or even the 1980s. During the 1990s tremendous advances have been made in computer technology, database management systems, and availability of input–output and other data in many countries. In the mid-1990s, in at most a few hours using a microcomputer, data are processed and models constructed that used to take many hours, or even days, and required huge sums of money to be run on mainframes. New devices such as CD ROMs are making large census and other data sets more easily available to microcomputer users. China is blessed with one of the most up-to-date and extensive sets of input–output data available anywhere in the world. The concept of a linked set of enterprise, regional and national accounts, therefore, is conceivable.

The benefits of a linked set of accounts to those interested in firm, regional, national or even international policy questions are significant, because analysts can look simultaneously at the interactions of specific policy decisions at both the individual firm and global levels. Analysts still have considerably more work to do, however, to identify the types of enterprise for which such accounts can be readily constructed, the ways an input–output accounting system can be used in conjunction with revised forms of the managerial and financial accounts, and the new accounting concepts that may be needed as a linked system of accounts is developed.

Note

1. Much of the information presented here was obtained from State Statistical Bureau staff in Beijing and from discussions with various input–output analysts working in Beijing and in several of the regions (Anhui, Guangxi, Hebei, Heilongjiang, Jiangsu, Liaoning, Shanghai and Zhejiang).

References

Cooper, R. (1987) 'Does Your Company Need a New Cost System?', *Journal of Cost Management* (Spring) pp. 45–9.

Cooper, R. and R. S. Kaplan (1991) *The Design of Cost Management Systems: Text, Cases, and Readings* (Englewood Cliffs, NJ: Prentice Hall).

Davidson, S., C. P. Stickney and R. L. Weil (1988) *Financial Accounting: An Introduction to Concepts, Methods and Uses* (Chicago, Ill.: Dryden Press).

Dudick, T. S. (1987) 'Why SG&A Doesn't Always Work', *Harvard Business Review* (January–February) pp. 566–70.

Filipic, P. (1985) *Implementation of Input–Output (Structure) Models in Planning of Organizations of Associated Labor* (in Serbo-Croatian) (Split, Yugoslavia: LOGOS).

Filipic, P. (1986) 'Input–Output Model as the (Quantitative) Basis of Self-Management Planning System', paper presented at the Eighth International Conference on Input–Output Techniques, Sapporo, Japan, July 28–August 2.

Foster, G. and C. T. Horngren (1988) 'Cost Accounting and Cost Management in a JIT Environment', *Journal of Cost Management* (Winter) pp. 4–14.

Institute of Developing Economies (1982) *International Input–Output Table for ASEAN Countries, 1975* (Tokyo, Japan: Asian Economic Press Ltd).

Johnson, H. T. (1988) 'Activity-based Information: A Blueprint for World-Class Management Accounting', *Management Accounting* (June) pp. 23–30.

Johnson, H. T. (1992) *Relevance Regained: From Top-down Control to Bottom-up Empowerment* (New York: Free Press).

Johnson, H. T. and R. S. Kaplan (1987) *Relevance Lost: The Rise and Fall of Management Accounting* (Boston, Mass.: Harvard Business School Press).

Kaplan, R. S. (1984) 'The Evolution of Management Accounting', *The Accounting Review*, vol. 59, no. 3 (July) pp. 390–418.

Kaplan, R. S. (1985) 'Accounting Lag: The Obsolescence of Cost Accounting Systems', in K. B. Clark, R. H. Hayes and C. Lorenz (eds), *The Uneasy Alliance: Managing the Productivity–Technology Dilemma* (Boston, Mass.: Harvard Business School Press).

Kaplan, R. S. (1986) 'Accounting Lag: The Obsolescence of Cost Accounting Systems', *California Management Review*, vol. 28, no. 2 (Winter) pp. 174–99.

Kaplan, R. S. and A. A. Atkinson (1989) *Advanced Management Accounting* (Englewood Cliffs, NJ: Prentice Hall).

La Noce, M. and M. Latorre (1988) 'Intersectorial Table of the IRI Group 1985', Discussion Paper No. 1 (September) (Rome: Instituto la Reconstruzione Industriale (IRI) Research Department).

Lammert, T. B. and R. Ehrsam (1987) 'The Human Element: The Real Challenge in Modernizing Cost Systems', *Management Accounting* (July) pp. 32–7.

Li Bingquan (1991) 'Applications of the Input–Output Technique in Chinese Enterprises', in K. R. Polenske and Chen Xikang (eds), *Chinese Economic Planning and Input–Output Applications* (Hong Kong: Oxford University Press) pp. 257–72.

Pimpao, A. (1979) *Analyse Input–Output du Complexe Petrochemique*, Ph.D. thesis, Universidad do Algarve, Portugal.

Pimpao, A. (1990) Personal communication.

Polenske, K. R. (1989) 'System of Input–Output Accounts for Corporate

Planning', in A. Franz and N. Riner (eds), *Compilation of Input–Output Data* (Vienna: Orac) pp. 375–88.
Polenske, K. R. (1991) 'Chinese Input–Output Research from a Western Perspective', in K. R. Polenske and Chen Xikang (eds), *Chinese Economic Planning and Input–Output Applications* (Hong Kong: Oxford University Press) pp. 1–23.
Tong Rencheng (1989) 'An Enterprise Input–Output Table with Two Factors', in K. R. Polenske and Chen Xikang (eds), *Chinese Economic Planning and Input–Output Application* (Hong Kong: Oxford University Press) pp. 296–317.
Zhang Renjia, Gao Nansen and Wu Haiying (1991) 'Application of the Input–Output Model Method to Anshan Iron and Steel Corporation', in K. R. Polenske and Chen Xikang (eds), *Chinese Economic Planning and Input–Output Applications* (Hong Kong: Oxford University Press) pp. 273–95.

4 Dynamic Price Patterns in Spatial Oligopolistic Markets: The Impact of Lagged Quantity Adjustments

Richard Schuler

INTRODUCTION

It is well known that when the role of space is considered in economics, because of scale economies in production and because the costs of transporting raw materials to the production site and/or goods and services to their ultimate users are significant, most markets are oligopolistic, and not perfectly competitive. Even with relatively low-cost entry into markets and price competition, it has been shown (see Holahan and Schuler, 1988, as an example) that positive economic profits may persist in equilibrium if the spacing of existing firms does not offer a promising, underserved site. Furthermore, Beckmann (1971) has shown that in the case of mill pricing without price competition where neighbouring firms merely divide the service area between them, competition through the successful entry of a new firm located between existing producers will lead to an increase rather than a decrease, in mill prices.

And as summarized by Holahan and Schuler (1988), even when intense price competition does emerge in spatial markets, it is unlikely that price will be driven to marginal cost under Bertrand assumptions about price conjectures. A Nash equilibrium exists where competitors still earn positive economic profits, so long as the price elasticity of demand for the product declines as its price falls. Most of these spatial competition results, whether based upon price or quantity conjectures, do not, however, lay out explicitly the dynamics of the price or quantity adjustment process; although Nash equilibria conditions are usually demonstrated.

What is also true about most spatial markets is that in response to price changes, quantities supplied and/or consumed cannot change instantaneously. As an example, under uniform delivered pricing, a firm that undercuts its neighbour's price may not be able to rearrange its chain of distribution instantaneously to serve the flood of new customers, even if it can get the price information to them rapidly. And in the case more applicable to the analysis that follows, it may take customers some time to shop around to find their new, lowest-cost suppliers following a change in mill prices. Again, the cost of searching over space may lead to lagged consumer responses to new price opportunities, and this analysis describes the additional oligopolistic features introduced by that lagged response.

Extending a previous analysis, by Schuler and Hobbs (1992), this chapter illustrates the optimal dynamic pricing strategies for producers when their customers' responses, in terms of changed quantities demanded, take place slowly over a substantial period of time. Just as space can insulate producers from the effects of price competition by other firms, so too it is shown that a lagged consumer response, which may in fact be directly attributable to costs arising from distance, also insulates a producer from instantaneous retaliation by competitors and may lead to price increases (not declines) in the face of competition. A key portion of this analysis is the exploration of how space and producer location contribute to the lagged response by consumers, which in turn permits firms to engage in monopolistic pricing policies.

With the exception of an unpublished paper by Louis Phlips and Jean François Richard (1986) and a much earlier paper by Robert Barro (1972), there is little microeconomic-based theory regarding the price dynamics of individual economic agents. This lack is particularly surprising since such theories might form a natural base for constructing macroeconomic models of inflation, where lagged price adjustments are typically assumed in the aggregate (see Chapter 6 in Okun (1981) as an example). And while rational expectation models to apply microeconomic techniques to the analysis of aggregate price adjustments, perfectly competitive markets throughout the economy are typically assumed in those analyses.

Yet a substantial portion of most developed economies, and certainly in developing economies, is characterized by imperfectly competitive markets, and this obvious fact must be acknowledged when modelling the conscious price-setting patterns of some economic agents. That is precisely what Barro (1972) did for a monopolistic supplier who faces adjustment costs in reaching a new equilibrium output position; price adjustment will lag changes in triggering economic variables. What Phlips and Richard (1986) have added is an analysis of dynamic price responses in oligopolistic markets – the typical case for most economies. The need for this conceptual framework is highlighted by Dennis Carlton's empirical analysis (Carlton 1986) that provides evidence of prolonged price rigidities in the markets for many commodities in the USA.

Curiously, there has been an eruption of analyses since the 1970s concerning the observe problem: given the existence of price differentials, what is the optimal rate of adjustment of physical quantities supplied and/or demanded? These models have received special attention in the analysis of labour market movements, and their applications have been extended under the label of search theory to the explanation of lagged adjustment by consumers to out-of-equilibrium prices.

In an earlier, non-spatial analysis of dynamic price-setting by firms in oligopolistic markets, Schuler and Hobbs (1992) took the pattern of lagged quantity adjustments by consumers as a given. When those markets are oligopolistic, the natural question arises: is it ever in the profit-maximizing interest of a supplier to adjust price with a considerable lag in response to a price cut by a competitor because it is recognized that all is not lost instantaneously? The answer is 'yes', in many circumstances, and the reason can be understood by analogy to a similar result in the spatial oligopoly literature (see Holahan and Schuler (1988) for one example). Where price undercutting by a neighbouring supplier in a spatial economy does not result in the loss of all of a firm's customers, the optimal response, depending on cost and demand parameters, may be to raise prices, thereby extracting the maximum possible monopoly rents from the residual customers. So too, where customers' demand responses are lagged, for good and sufficient economic reasons, the optimal response by large oligopolistic suppliers will, in many instances, be to hold the line in response to lower prices by other firms; this result offers some conceptual support for Carlton's empirical evidence of price rigidities.

In this chapter the economic rationale is developed for a lagged response by customers buying in a spatial market, together with analytic support for particular functional forms. Two lag mechanisms are emphasized: first, possible delays in the dissemination and digestion of information about changes in product prices; and second, delays in action by individual consumers after the information is received, perhaps because of a desire to survey satisfactory experiences by neighbours and other consumers who are using the alternative supplier. In fact, both of these effects could be lumped together under the label 'information costs'; however, their separation emphasizes different spatial characteristics, different states of technology for distributing information, and different transportation cost characteristics for potential buyers. These cost components are also combined differently depending upon whether a mill-pricing (MP) or uniform-delivered-pricing (UDP) scheme is associated with the good or service in question.

MARKET SHARE ADJUSTMENT MECHANISMS IN A SPATIAL ECONOMY

Before potential buyers can act on changes in prices by different suppliers for similar products or services, they must first *become aware* of the new price situation, and second, *make a decision* to switch suppliers, perhaps after first-hand confirmation that other customers have bought from the alternative supplier at the newly quoted price and they are satisfied that the product quality is identical (or superior). As a rough rule in developed economies, the *awareness* effect occurs primarily through mass-media print and tele-information technologies, although some awareness is provided through personal travel and shopping trips. In contrast, the *confirmation* effect frequently requires some physical travel to sites where the alternative product is being used, or where its users congregate; although increasingly with an electronically-interconnected society, the confirmation of product value may also be accomplished without personal travel.

Uniform delivered pricing (UDP)

UDP is the effective spatial pricing where the supplier ships the product or service to the customer without imposing charges that are differentiated over space; utility services and express mail are two examples. UDP is also the effective pricing mechanism when customers make regular, frequent trips to a number of different markets and they buy a variety of products at each. This scenario is characteristic of much suburban, shopping-centre-related purchasing in the USA, where customers make a weekly circuit of malls with their car to buy small routine items and groceries. In that case the incremental transportation cost of picking up a product at Mall A versus the more distant Mall B is zero, so long as the trip will be made in any case and there is extra room in the car for the merchandise. In the second scenario, the transportation and search costs become routine, fixed weekly costs, and the marginal transportation cost associated with purchasing an item at alternative locations within that routine network is zero.

Logistic adjustment mechanism

Consider a modern, hi-tech, electronically-wired suburban society, like much of the USA. In this case, the UDP scenario is applicable and there may be virtually no lag between a producer's announced price change and when that news is available to each and every consumer. The question is: when does a typical consumer become *aware* of the news? Because of the scarcity of time, the consumer may sample her/his newspaper, catalogues and/or electronic devices periodically, but not continuously. Otherwise, consumers would never have time to enjoy the products they did buy. If we assume that a constant fraction of the population tunes into a TV announcement (or reads an advertisement, or opens their junk mail), then the share of the market that becomes *aware* of the new opportunity in each period is:

$$\Delta A_t^i = \mu(1 - s_t^i) \quad (4.1)$$

where ΔA_t^i = increased share of the market that becomes aware that producer, i, is offering a lower price at time, t $(0 \leq \Delta A_t^i \leq 1)$

μ = fraction of customers that received and are aware of information about price changes in each period

s_t^i = market share buying from producer, i, at time, t

Here it is assumed that consumers will continue to purchase a particular product, *so long as they do not receive unfavourable news about its price.* When, however, they receive and become aware of information about an alternative supplier who charges a lower price, they will investigate the veracity of that information before changing suppliers. The *rate* at which potential consumers seek confirmation of the better opportunity is proportional to the price difference among suppliers, but how consumers interpret the validity of the information hinges upon a number of factors. Certainly, the larger the proportion of customers they know or meet who use and are satisfied with the alternative supplier, the more likely the potential customers are to act. In a UDP scheme, the consumers may stay at home because the product is delivered to them, and they learn about other consumers' satisfaction from their immediate neighbour (a slow aggregate process) or through tele-information devices that give them wide-ranging access to other consumers. In the latter case, the proportion of the market that confirms the validity of the information is the fraction buying from the new supplier, so the market share that receives confirmation in any period is:

$$M_t^i = \lambda^*(p_t^j - p_t^i)s_t^i \tag{4.2}$$

where M_t^i = proportion of those becoming aware of price difference ($p_t^j > p_t^i$) at time, t, who will switch suppliers ($0 \leq M_t^i \leq 1$)

p_t^k = price charged by supplier, k, at time, t

λ^* = constant

This same formulation might also apply to suburban shoppers who tour many malls each week, and so they confirm the validity of competing claims by observing what other consumers are buying or have bought, either as they drive by other consumers' homes or by observing the purchases of others at the different shopping centres. In either case, each customer will have access to a random sample of the entire market and so will receive positive confirmation of the truth of the pricing claim in proportion to the market share of the alternative supplier. Equation (4.2) also applies to the opposite extreme: the ill-informed, stay-at-home member of society who waits until an adjacent neighbour switches suppliers before acting. But with UDP, if the conversions are random throughout space, then the chances of an aware customer changing are proportional to market share. In either case, the market share adjustment process is the product of the proportion of customers using other suppliers who become aware that a change might be advantageous, times the proportion that act, given their awareness, or equation (4.1) times equation (4.2), as stated in (4.3).

$$s_{t+1}^i - s_t^i = \lambda(p_t^j - p_t^i)\, s_t^i(1 - s_t^i) \tag{4.3}$$

where $\lambda = \mu\lambda^*$, a constant

This logistic functional form is exactly the lagged adjustment mechanism used in Schuler and Hobbs (1992) and it is illustrated in Figure 4.1. This relationship has the convenient mathematical property that it is symmetrical, and so as relative prices reverse ($p^1 > p^2$) the path of market shares is merely reversed.

The logistic is also the functional form implied by most partial ad-

Figure 4.1 Logistic market share adjustment mechanism for products requiring first-hand confirmation

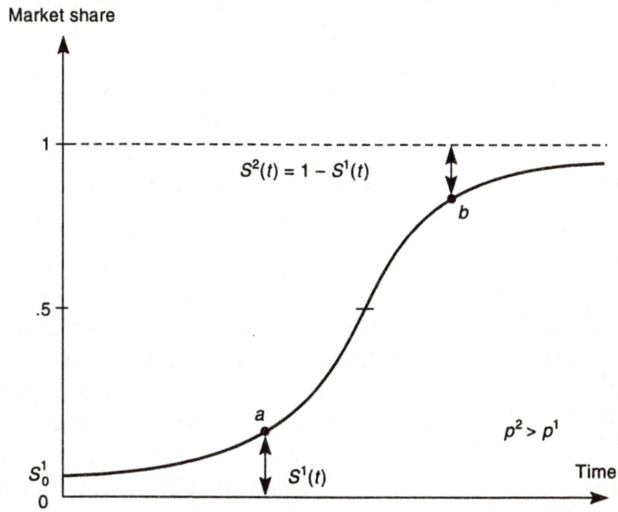

justment models that are so widely used in empirical macroeconomic analyses. As an example, a variant of the logistic function is the optimal adjustment mechanism that Barro (1972) developed in his paper.[1] Furthermore, the search theory literature dealing with potential information flows that are described by stationary stochastic processes regularly lead to optimal adjustment (transition) mechanisms that are described in terms of hazard functions[2], $f(x)/1-F(x)$, where $f(x)$ is the density function and $F(x)$ is the distribution function over some variable x, so $f(x) = F'(x)$. In fact, the logistic function of Equation(4.3) links the hazard function directly to the firm's existing market share and to the price differential, by rearranging: $\dot{s}/(1 - S) = \lambda(p^j - p^i)S$.

Concave adjustment mechanism

By comparison, as tele-information technologies are widely adopted by most consumers in developed economies, and/or catalogue shopping with assured low-cost return of unsatisfactory merchandise to suppliers becomes widespread, the 'confirmation' function may be performed at very low cost (the need for a confirmation trip is eliminated) to customers, and extremely rapidly, so the expression reflecting the proportion of customers who are aware of a lower price alternative who act may be far less dependent on the existing market share. In terms of equation (4.2), the revised form is:

$$M_t^i = \lambda^*(p_t^j - p_t^i) \tag{4.4}$$

If the information arrival rate for potential new customers retains the form of equation (4.1) the new share adjustment relationship becomes:

$$s_{t+1}^i - s_t^i = \lambda(p_t^j - p_t^i)(1 - s_t^i) \tag{4.5}$$

for $p_t^j > p_t^i$

Note that this functional form is strictly concave, as shown in Figure 4.2, and since each firm is assumed to produce identical products, then if relative prices reverse, the other firm should face an identical adjustment process. Therefore, while for $p_t^j > p_t^i$, $s_t^j = 1 - s_t^i$, as shown in equation (4.6), if the relative prices are reversed, the indices of the

$$s_{t+1}^j - s_t^j = -\lambda(p_t^j - p_t^i)s_t^j \tag{4.6}$$

for $p_t^j \geq p_t^i$

adjustment equation must also be reversed so that the firm offering the lowest prices always experiences a concave adjustment process, as shown in Equations (4.7a) and (4.7b):

$$s_{t+1}^j - s_t^j = \lambda(p_t^i - p_t^j)(1 - s_t^j) \tag{4.7a}$$

$$s_{t+1}^i - s_t^i = -\lambda(p_t^i - p_t^j)s_t^i \tag{4.7b}$$

for $p_t^i > p_t^j$

where $\lambda = \mu\lambda^*$, as before

As compared with the logistic adjustment process in Equation (4.3), for the same parameter values the initial rate of market penetration will be much greater for a supplier with a small initial market share who offers a lower price in the electronic society as shown in Equation (4.5), as compared to the adjustment process of Equation (4.3). In both cases, however, as market share becomes large, the rate of penetration saturates because there is an ever smaller residual market share to acquire.

Figure 4.2 Concave market share adjustment mechanisms for low-cost confirmation of product attributes

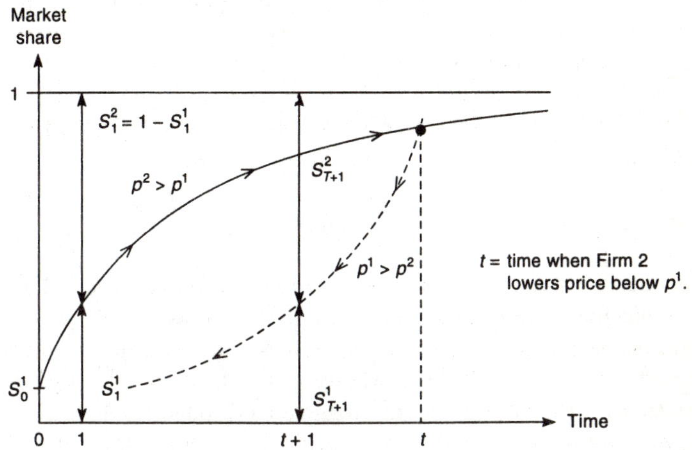

By contrast, in a fairly self-contained society where purchasers make very few shopping trips and all products are delivered to the consumer, if the customer becomes aware of the price change through the media (newspaper, radio or TV) the rate of awareness retains the functional form of Equation (4.1). But because of a lack of interactive telecommunications, the customer must wait until an immediate neighbour adopts the new, low-price supplier in order to confirm the validity of claims, then if the rate at which the conversions are propagated over space are proportional to the price savings, then starting with customers immediately adjacent to the low-cost supplier, the market share that has received confirmation will move linearly away from the supplier over time. With a uniform distribution of customers over space, this means that the functional form for the fraction converting at any time will be the same as equation (4.4), and so the complete adjustment process, in this case, is still described by Equations (4.5), (4.6) and (4.7). It is ironic that the same functional form might represent the lagged customer response in both an advanced, hi-tech society and also in a fairly remote isolated society, so long as news is transmitted by some media; the major difference is that the parameter, λ, will be much larger (faster adjustment) for the hi-tech society as compared with the widely dispersed economy.

Linear adjustment mechanism

If the relevant trading area is sufficiently remote and isolated so that information about relative prices of suppliers cannot be communicated effectively by the media, and word-of-mouth transmission from neighbour to neighbour is relied upon, then both the awareness and confirmation effects may spread linearly over time throughout the society, and the linear adjustment process used by Phlips and Richard (1986) would be relevant, as described in Equation (4.8):

$$s^i_{t+1} - s^i_t = \lambda(p^j_t - p^i_t) \tag{4.8}$$

In this case, current market shares have no effect on the speed of adjustment, and therefore on the firm's pricing decisions.

This adjustment mechanism may also have some applicability to widely spread international suppliers where, either because of language or institutional difficulties, price information and product confirmation data are not readily transmitted by the media or observed through routine shopping trips.

Mill pricing (MP)

For those purchases where customers make a separate shopping trip, either because of the importance (price) of the purchase or its physical size and weight (significant unit transport cost), or where the supplier delivers the product but assesses space-differentiated charges[3] (again, perhaps because of significant unit transport costs), the mill pricing paradigm, where each customer pays a different delivered price representing the sum of the price at the supplier's location plus distance-related transport costs, is relevant.

While the variety of price difference 'awareness' mechanisms that were discussed for UDP are equally applicable to MP, the confirmation mechanism that triggers a switch in suppliers may be somewhat different under MP, since the customer's normal shopping trips are only to her/his normal supplier. In this case, consumers in between who are observed are almost surely also buying from the same supplier, since their delivered price is even lower (they are closer to the supplier). Therefore, a special shopping trip must be undertaken in the opposite direction in order to observe consumers of the product from the alternative supplier.

As illustrated in Figure 4.3, a customer located at *A* in between two

Figure 4.3 Spatial market allocations under mill pricing

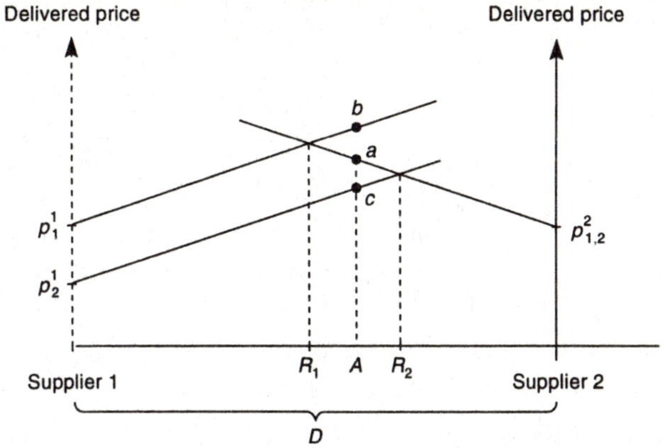

suppliers charging identical initial mill prices, p_1^1 and p_1^2, would buy from Supplier 2 because the delivered price from that supplier, *a*, is less than the delivered price, *b*, from Supplier 1. Suppose in Period 2, Supplier 1 drops its price to p_2^1, but Supplier 2 retains the same mill price as in Period 1. In this case the customer at *A* should prefer to switch to Supplier 1, since the new delivered price, *c*, is less than *a*, but how does consumer *A* confirm the product attributes of Supplier 1 if all of the shopping trips are to Supplier 2, and previously, everyone in between $(D - A)$ was also buying from Supplier 2? In a hi-tech society, confirmation is readily available through two-way telecommunications, and everyone between $R_2 - R_1$ switches as soon as they become aware of the price difference. In an isolated society, the household at *A* waits until a neighbour switches suppliers as confirmation, and then converts. In this case the confirmation moves in proportion to the *delivered price saving* at a linear rate between R_1 and R_2. In either case, the customer share adjustment mechanism is concave, but that shape is accentuated (the adjustment is stretched out) because the confirmation process is also concave, in this case because with a constant unit transportation cost, the delivered price saving decreases as market size increases. Note, only if customers at *A* confirm the quality of the product from Supplier 1 by taking a special trip in that direction, will the adjustment process become logistic; in that case, as $S^1 = (R_1/D)$ increases, the average distance between customers buying from Supplier 2 and the nearest customer buying from Supplier 1 will decrease, implying reduced transportation-related confirmation costs.

The other significant difference with MP is that the supplier offering a lower price without retaliation from the competitor still cannot hope to acquire the entire market. As an example, in Figure 4.3, Supplier 1, charging p_2^1 will eventually gain market share $(R_2 - R_1)/D$ if customers are uniformly spaced, not the entire market. And so when applying the lagged customer response mechanisms to MP cases, that dynamic process can only be applied to the maximum additional share of the market that can be supported by the change in MP.

For all of these reasons, the adjustment process under MP is likely to be slower than under UDP (λ is smaller under MP), and the chances are greater that the functional form will be concave rather than logistic.

FIRM BEHAVIOUR

For simplicity, UDP will be used exclusively in the following analysis. Each supplier is assumed to attempt to maximize the net present value of its expected profits over a fixed time horizon. For illustrative purposes, the model is established over three periods with two firms, where the last period represents the end of the firm's planning period (or at least the planned tenure of the current crop of managers).[4] A finite game is used to focus on the dynamics of price adjustment, not just on equilibrium conditions. Furthermore, the sequence of events in the spatial market-place is as follows:

- (i) the firms' initial market shares are given;
- (ii) each firm simultaneously sets a price for Period 1 and sales are consummated, given those prices and market shares;
- (iii) market shares are revised for Period 2, based upon any price spread that might have existed in the previous period; and
- (iv) prices are set simultaneously for Period 2, and transactions occur based upon Period 2's prices and market shares, and so on.

This sequence of events is consistent with the consumer behaviour in a spatial market that was described previously; given historic prices (last period's) customers form expectations about current prices (they remain the same), and, given these price expectations, customers choose a supplier. Having chosen a supplier, customers are free to vary the quantity consumed based upon the revealed price, but they must wait until the next period to change their supplier (make an additional shopping trip).

What has been described from the supplier's perspective is a standard dynamic programming problem, that may be solved recursively, starting with the last period first.

Period 3

$$\max_{p_3^1} \; S_3^1 \, \pi(p_3^1) \tag{4.9}$$

where S_3^1 = Firm 1's predetermined market share in Period 3
p_3^1 = Firm 1's price charged in Period 3, normalized in terms of its monopoly price, so $p_3^1 \in [0,1]$

Since both firms are assumed to have identical cost structures and each firm knows its own and its competitor's costs, without further loss of generality the marginal cost of production and selling can be assumed to be equal to zero. Then the optimal price in Period 3 is the monopolist's price, $p_3^1 = 1$, since that final period's market shares have already been determined. Here a nicely behaved profit function is assumed, with the following properties.

$$\pi(0) = 0 \qquad \pi(1) = \pi^M \qquad \frac{\delta\pi}{\delta p} \geq 0, \quad 0 \leq p \leq 1$$

$$\frac{\delta\pi}{\delta p} < 0, \quad p > 1 \qquad \frac{\delta^2\pi(1)}{\delta p^2} < 0 \tag{4.10}$$

Thus in a multi-period optimization process, the firm will never charge $p > 1$, since it then stand to earn less than maximum profits from its current customers and it also risks losing additional customers in the future. Under the conditions of Equation (4.10), the firm can always find a $p < 1$ that yields the same profit level from existing customers as any $p > 1$, but in addition it may also gain some market share in the next period, depending upon the price selected by its competitor. Thus in Period 3, with the end of the world at hand, $p_3^1 = 1$ and $\pi(p_3^1) = \pi^M$. The same optimal solution holds for Firm 2.

Moving towards the present by one period:

Period 2

$$\max_{p_2^1} S_2^1 \, \pi(p_2^1) + S_3^1 \beta \pi^M \equiv \Pi_2^1 \tag{4.11}$$

where, in general

S_t^i = Firm i's market share in period t
p_t^i = Firm i's normalized price in period t
β = discount factor = $1/(1+\rho)$
ρ = real interest rate
π^M = monopolist's profit per customer

For illustrative purposes, the concave adjustment process described in equations (4.5), (4.6), and (4.7), and shown in Figure 4.2, will be used here since the results under a logistic adjustment were described previously by Schuler and Hobbs (1992).

For Supplier 1, there are two alternative profit equations depending upon how its price compares with that of Supplier 2.

Where $p_2^2 > p_2^1$:

$$\frac{\Pi_2^1}{\pi_M} = \left\{S_2^1\left[\frac{\pi(p_2^1)}{\pi_M}\right] + \beta\left\{\overbrace{\lambda(p_2^2 - p_2^1) + S_2^1\left[1 - \lambda(p_2^2 - p_2^1)\right]}^{0 \le S_3^1 \le 1}\right\}\right\} \quad (4.12a)$$

Where $p_2^1 > p_2^2$:

$$\frac{\Pi_2^1}{\pi_M} = \left\{S_2^1\left[\frac{\pi(p_2^1)}{\pi_M}\right] + \beta\left\{\overbrace{S_2^1\left[1 - \lambda(p_2^1 - p_2^2)\right]}^{0 \le S_3^1 \le 1}\right\}\right\} \quad (4.12b)$$

Similarly, Supplier 2 has two alternative profit expressions.

Where $p_2^1 > p_2^2$:

$$\frac{\Pi_2^2}{\pi_M} = \left\{S_2^2\left[\frac{\pi(p_2^2)}{\pi_M}\right] + \beta\left\{\overbrace{\lambda(p_2^1 - p_2^2) + S_2^2\left[1 - \lambda(p_2^1 - p_2^2)\right]}^{0 \le S_3^2 \le 1}\right\}\right\} \quad (4.12c)$$

Where $p_2^2 > p_2^1$:

$$\frac{\Pi_2^2}{\pi_M} = \left\{S_2^2\left[\frac{\Pi(p_2^2)}{\pi_M}\right] + \beta\left\{\overbrace{S_2^2\left[1 - \lambda(p_2^2 - p_2^1)\right]}^{0 \le S_3^2 \le 1}\right\}\right\} \quad (4.12d)$$

For the purposes of this recursion, S_2^1 is predetermined, as is π^M, by economic parameters, so the firm optimizes the expression within the braces. Note that p_2^i, S_2^i, π_2^i/π^M and β all are $\epsilon[0, 1]$ unless real interest rates are negative. Here the firm is balancing optimal current profits against potential profits as a result of market share gains in Period 3, and if the profit function is differentiable, then, for Supplier 1:

$$\frac{\delta\Pi_2^1}{\delta p_2^1} = \pi^M \left\{ S_2^1 \frac{\frac{\delta\pi}{\delta p_2^1}}{\pi_M} - \beta\lambda(1 - S_2^1) \right\} \tag{4.13a}$$

where $p_2^2 > p_2^1$

or

$$\frac{\delta\Pi_2^1}{\delta p_2^1} = \pi_M S_1^2 \left\{ \frac{\frac{\delta\pi}{\delta p_2^1}}{\pi_M} - \beta\lambda \right\} \tag{4.13b}$$

where $p_2^2 < p_2^1$

Note that if either Equation (4.13a) or (4.13b) is strictly positive (perhaps because of a large market share (S_2^1), slow rate of customer disaffection (λ), or high real discount rate (small β)), the firm may also select a monopolistic price for Period 2, even without collusion!

Moving back yet another period towards the present:

Period 1

$$\max \Pi_1^1 = S_2^1\, \pi(p_1^1) + \beta\Pi_2^1$$

In this case, four different equations must be explored for Supplier 1 to reflect the four possible combinations of the relative prices between Firms 1 and 2 in each of the two periods. In these cases, the values for S_2^1 become endogenous, since they hinge on the relative prices, p_1^1 and p_1^2, and the initial market share, S_1^1.

Where $p_1^2 > p_1^1$ and $p_2^2 > p_2^1$.

$$\frac{\Pi_1^1}{\pi_M} = S_1^1\left[\frac{\pi(p_1^1)}{\pi_M}\right] + \beta\left[\frac{\pi(p_2^1)}{\pi_M}\right]\overbrace{\left\{\lambda(p_1^2 - p_1^1) + S_1^1\left[1 - \lambda(p_1^2 - p_1^1)\right]\right\}}^{0 \leq S_2^1 \leq 1} +$$

$$\beta^2 \left\{ \lambda(p_2^2 - p_2^1) + \underbrace{\overbrace{\left\{ \lambda(p_1^2 - p_1^1) + S_1^1 \left[1 - \lambda(p_1^2 - p_1^1)\right]\right\}}^{0 \le S_2^1 \le 1} \left[1 - \lambda(p_2^2 - p_2^1)\right]}_{0 \le S_3^1 \le 1} \right\} \quad (4.15a)$$

Where $p_1^2 > p_1^1$ and $p_2^2 < p_2^1$:

$$\frac{\Pi_1^1}{\pi_M} = S_1^1 \left[\frac{\pi(p_1^1)}{\pi_M}\right] + \beta \left[\frac{\pi(p_2^1)}{\pi_M}\right] \left\{ \overbrace{\lambda(p_1^2 - p_1^1) + S_1^1 \left[1 - \lambda(p_1^2 - p_1^1)\right]}^{0 \le S_2^1 \le 1} \right\}$$

$$+ \beta^2 \left\{ \underbrace{\overbrace{\lambda(p_1^2 - p_1^1) + S_1^1 \left[1 - \lambda(p_1^2 - p_1^1)\right]}^{0 \le S_2^1 \le 1} \Big\} \left[1 - \lambda(p_2^1 - p_2^2)\right]}_{0 \le S_3^1 \le 1} \right. \quad (4.15b)$$

Where $p_1^2 < p_1^1$ and $p_2^2 > p_2^1$:

$$\frac{\Pi_1^1}{\pi_M} = S_1^1 \left[\frac{\pi(p_1^1)}{\pi_M}\right] + \beta \left[\frac{\pi(p_2^1)}{\pi_M}\right] \left\{ \overbrace{S_1^1 \left[1 - \lambda(p_1^1 - p_1^2)\right]}^{0 \le S_2^1 \le 1} \right\}$$

$$+ \beta^2 \left\{ \underbrace{\lambda(p_2^2 + p_2^1) + \left\{ \overbrace{S_1^1 \left[1 - \lambda(p_1^1 - p_1^2)\right]}^{0 \le S_2^1 \le 1} \right\} \left[1 - \lambda(p_2^2 - p_2^1)\right]}_{0 \le S_3^1 \le 1} \right\} \quad (4.15c)$$

Where $p_1^2 < p_1^1$ and $p_2^2 < p_2^1$:

$$\frac{\Pi_1^1}{\pi_M} = S_1^1 \left[\frac{\pi(p_1^1)}{\pi_M}\right] + \beta \left[\frac{\pi(p_2^1)}{\pi_M}\right] \left\{ \overbrace{S_1^1 \left[1 - \lambda(p_1^1 - p_1^2)\right]}^{0 \le S_2^1 \le 1} \right\}$$

$$+ \beta^2 \left\{ \underbrace{\overbrace{S_1^1 \left[1 - \lambda(p_1^1 - p_1^2)\right]}^{0 \le S_2^1 \le 1} \left[1 - \lambda(p_2^1 - p_2^2)\right]}_{0 \le S_3^1 \le 1} \right\} \quad (4.15d)$$

The profit expressions for Supplier 2, Π_1^2, are symmetrical to those of Firm 1.

Equations (4.15) represent a two-period game in extensive form whose optimal solution is subgame perfect. Firm 1 selects a set of price strategies (p_1^1, p_2^1) over the two periods, whose consequences depend upon the strategies of Firm 2 (p_1^2, p_2^2). While it is possible to work out pure price strategies for this two-period game, where $0 \leq p_t^i \leq 1$ (the strategy for the third period is obvious), the calculations are tedious because the bounds for the market shares in each period, as shown in Equations (4.15), must be checked continually.

Instead, in order to emphasize the nature of the solution to this game and to gain qualitative insights about the impacts of economic parameters upon the nature of the solution, the possible prices that might be selected by each firm are restricted to two: the monopolists's price (p = 1), and a totally competitive price (p = 0). The Nash equilibrium solution to this two-period game, if one exists, is subgame perfect in terms of the limited price set, since the objective Equations (4.15) in extensive form are developed by backward recursion.[5]

NUMERICAL SOLUTION TO THE GAME

With each firm's possible set of prices for each period reduced to [0;1], $\pi(p)/\pi^M \in [0;1]$, the payoffs to each firm can be normalized in terms of the level of monopoly profits per customer, π^M. As in the Schuler and Hobbs (1992) analysis of logistic adjustment, it is useful to reformulate the speed of adjustment parameter, λ, slightly so that it can be related to previous demand elasticity estimates for particular commodities. In particular, let $\lambda = \lambda / P_M$, where P_M is the monopoly price for the commodity (this normalization will facilitate subsequent numerical analyses). Then, rearranging the logistic adjustment Equation (4.3):

$$\lambda = \left[\frac{\frac{dS^1}{dt} / S^1}{\left(\frac{P^2 - P^1}{P_M} \right)} \right] \div (1 - S^1) \qquad (4.16)$$

The term in brackets in Equation (4.16) has the dimensions of a dynamic price elasticity of demand, $1/t$, where the price base is its monopoly level. Here the dimension of λ is also $1/t$, a rate of change, since market share, S^1, is a pure number. Equation (4.16) can be used to estimate λ provided that all the values on the right-hand side are contemporaneous. As an illustration of the relative magnitude of this coefficient, if a supplier having a 50 per cent market share is suddenly faced with a 5 per cent price disadvantage (where the percentage base is the monopoly price, not the actual price for that commodity,) and that firm anticipates losing 5 per cent of its market share per year for every year that the price disadvantages persists, then $\lambda = 2$.

The choices and potential payoffs confronting each firm with the restricted set of prices can then be summarized as follows:

Period 3

$$p_3^1 = 1 \qquad \frac{\Pi_3^1}{\pi_M} = S_3^1 \tag{4.17a}$$

$$p_3^1 = 0 \qquad \frac{\Pi_3^1}{\pi_M} = 0 \tag{4.17b}$$

Period 2
(given $p_3^1 = 1$)

where $p_2^1 = 1 (p_2^2 = 1)$:

$$\frac{\Pi_2^1}{\pi_M} = S_2^1(1+\beta) \tag{4.18a}$$

where $p_2^1 = 1 (p_2^2 = 0)$:

$$\frac{\Pi_2^1}{\pi_M} = S_2^1 + \beta\{S_2^1[1-\lambda]\} \tag{4.18b}$$

where $p_2^1 = 0 (p_2^2 = 1)$:

$$\frac{\Pi_2^1}{\pi_M} = \beta\{\lambda + S_2^1[1-\lambda]\} \tag{4.18c}$$

where $p_2^1 = 0 (p_2^2 = 0)$:

$$\frac{\Pi_2^1}{\pi_M} = \beta S_2^1. \tag{4.18d}$$

Choose $p_2^1 = 1(p_2^2 = 1)$ where $S_2^1 > \beta\lambda S_2^2$. (4.19a)
Choose $p_2^1 = 1(p_2^2 = 0)$ where $1 > \beta\lambda$. (4.19b)

The nature of optimal price strategies and the importance of economic parameters begins to emerge in Period 2. Under the binary restriction in choices of prices, Firm 1 will also select a monopoly price in period 2 if $\lambda < 1/\beta$. If this firm's market share is larger than its competitor's, it will select $p_2^1 = 1$. Thus it is possible, in this model, with a sufficiently slow speed of customer disaffection (small λ) and a high real interest rate (small β), that even in the face of potential loss of market share, firms may choose not to compete for some period of time.

Note the role of the discount factor in Equations (4.19). As real interest rates rise, β becomes smaller, which lessens the possibility of choosing the competitive price in the current period. For a game of longer duration, the effect of higher real interest rates would be to push competitive pressures backwards into the past, and in a game of finite duration, competition will cease at an earlier date. Thus rising real interest rates appear to accelerate price increases in this kind of imperfectly competitive market. This reinforces the result obtained by Phlips and Richard (1986) in their numerical simulations.

Of course, a general solution for Period 1 requires the selection of p_1^1 and p_2^1 in Equations (4.15), and the payoff (net present value of profits for the three periods) hinges on the choices by firm 2 of p_1^2 and p_2^2. For Firm 1 there are four possible price strategies: [0;0], [0;1], [1;0] and [1;1]. Similarly, Firm 2 may select from among the same four possibilities, so a four-by-four payoff matrix is required to determine the solution to this game. In extensive form, the payoff possibilities for each player are found by solving Equations (4.15), recalling that $\pi(p_t^i)/\pi^M \in [0;1]$ as $p_t^i \in [0;1]$ and choosing a 3 per cent real interest rate, so $\beta = 0.971$. Furthermore, values of λ sufficiently large should be selected so that competition is possible in this two-period game. As an example, if $S_2^1 = 0.5$, then, by inequality (4.19) the firms are indifferent about competing, where $\beta = 0.971$, if $\lambda = 1.03$, so pick $\lambda = 2$ for numerical convenience, since it certainly insures that competition may be economical in some situations.

Numerical illustrations for the concave market share adjustment process are provided for three different structures of the market in the initial period, $S_1^1 = 0.1$, 0.3 and 0.5, which correspond to $S_1^2 = 0.9$, 0.7 and 0.5. The payoff matrices are presented in Tables 4.1a, 4.2a and 4.3a. In Table 4.4a, the speed of adjustment parameter is increased fourfold ($\lambda = 8$), with $S_1^1 = .1$. Tables 4.1b, 4.2b, 4.3b and 4.4b, represent the

Table 4.1 Payoff summary for binary choice, intertemporal pricing game ($S_1^1 = 0.1$; $\beta = 0.971$; $\lambda = 2$)

A Concave adjustment process

		Firm 2's price strategies and payoffs			
	p^1 \ p^2	0, 0	0, 1	1, 0	1, 1
Firm 1's price strategies and payoffs	0, 0	0.85 0.094	0.87 0.94	0.90 0.94	0.90 0.94
	0, 1	0.94 0.097	1.7 0.19	* 1.80 0.97	0.90 1.9
	1, 0	0.19 0.10	0.19 1.0	1.70 0.19	** 1.8 1.0
	1, 1	0.94 0.10	0.38 0.10	1.80 0.20	2.6 0.29

B Logistic adjustment process

		Firm 2's price strategies and payoffs			
	p^1 \ p^2	0, 0	0, 1	1, 0	1, 1
Firm 1's price strategies and payoffs	0, 0	0.850 0.094	1.553 0.264	1.579 0.264	1.898 0.644 *
	0, 1	0.943 0.097	1.722 0.191	1.843 0.272	2.278 0.536
	1, 0	0.943 0.100	1.914 0.100	1.749 0.194	2.453 0.364
	1, 1	0.943 0.100	1.914 0.100	1.843 0.197	2.622 0.291

Notes: * Nash equilibrium
** Pareto superior solution
NE corner: 2's payoff
SW corner: 1's payoff

payoff matrices for the same game, with the same parameter values, except that the logistic adjustment process, shown in Figure 4.1, is used to compute changes in market shares.[6]

RESULTS AND THEIR IMPLICATIONS

For all but one of the eight examples, there exist unique Nash equilibria in pure strategies that are subgame perfect. Examining the various cases with the concave adjustment process, Table 4.1A shows a Nash equilibrium

Table 4.2 Payoff summary for binary choice, intertemporal pricing game ($S_1^1 = 0.3$; $\beta = 0.971$; $\lambda = 2$)

A Concave adjustment process

	Firm 2's price strategies and payoffs				
	p^2 \ p^1	0, 0	0, 1	1, 0	1, 1
Firm 1's price strategies and payoffs	0, 0	0.66 0.28	0.68 0.94	0.70 0.94	0.70 0.94
	0, 1	0.94 0.29	1.3 0.57	1.6 0.97 *	0.70 1.9
	1, 0	0.57 0.30	0.58 1.2	1.4 0.58	1.4 1.2
	1, 1	0.94 0.30	1.1 0.30	1.6 0.59	2.0 0.87

B Logistic adjustment process

	Firm 2's price strategies and payoffs				
	p^2 \ p^1	0, 0	0, 1	1, 0	1, 1
Firm 1's price strategies and payoffs	0, 0	0.660 0.283	0.944 0.679	0.964 0.679	0.972 0.943
	0, 1	0.943 0.291	1.339 0.574	1.344 0.998 *	1.236 1.378
	1, 0	0.943 0.300	1.914 0.300	1.356 0.583	1.644 0.979
	1, 1	0.943 0.300	1.914 0.300	1.643 0.591	2.040 0.874

Notes: * Nash Equilibrium
NE corner: 2's payoff
SW corner: 1's payoff

where Firm 1, with a 10 per cent market share, competes initially, but then moves to the monopoly price for Periods 2 and 3, $p^1 = (0, 1)$; whereas, the dominant firm holds to the monopoly price in Period 1, but then competes in Period 2 to regain market share for the final period, $p^2 = (1, 0)$. So, some competition takes place, but in an oscillating manner, and neither firm falls into the prisoner's dilemma trap of static games where $p^1 = p^2 = (0, 0)$. However, there is a weak Pareto superior strategy for both players, $p^1 = (1, 0)$; $p^2 = (1, 1)$, so price competition does lead to somewhat lower average prices over time, and minimally lower profits, than would be obtained through a collusive result.

Table 4.3 Payoff summary for binary choice, intertemporal pricing game ($S_1^1 = 0.5$; $\beta = 0.971$; $\lambda = 2$)

A Concave adjustment process

		Firm 2's price strategies and payoffs			
	p^1 \\ p^2	0,0	0, 1	1, 0	1, 1
	0, 0	0.47 0.47	0.49 0.94	0.50 0.94	0.50 0.94
Firm 1's pricestrategies and payoffs	0, 1	0.94 0.49	0.96 0.96	1.44 0.97 u	0.50 1.90 u
	1, 0	0.94 0.50	0.97 1.44 u	0.97 0.97	0.99 1.40 u
	1, 1	0.94 0.50	1.90 0.50 u	1.40 0.99 u	1.46 1.46

B Logistic adjustment process

		Firm 2's price strategies and payoffs			
	p^1 \\ p^2	0, 0	0, 1	1, 0	1, 1
	0, 0	0.471 0.471	0.486 0.943	0.500 0.943	0.500 0.943
Firm 1's price strategies and payoffs	0, 1	0.943 0.486	0.957 0.957 *	0.500 1.914	0.500 1.914
	1, 0	0.943 0.500	1.914 0.500	0.971 0.971	0.986 1.443
	1, 1	0.943 0.500	1.914 0.500	1.443 0.986	1.457 1.457 **

Notes: * Nash equilibrium
** Pareto superior solution
u Unstable solutions
NE corner: 2's payoff
SW corner: 1's payoff

An increased initial market share for Firm 1, 0.3 (smaller share, 0.7, for Firm 2) with the same parameter values leads to the same Nash equilibrium price strategies in Table 4.2 as in Table 4.1, except that here there in no Pareto improvement possible for the $p^1 = (0, 1)$, $p^2 = (1, 0)$ price strategies. When we move to equal initial market shares ($s_1^1 = s_1^2 = 0.5$) as in Table 4.3A, extremely curious results emerge: *there is no set of Nash equilibrium prices.* While the (0, 0) price strategies

Table 4.4 Payoff summary for binary choice, intertemporal pricing game ($S_1^1 = 0.1$; $\beta = 0.971$; $\lambda = 8$)

A Concave adjustment process

Firm 2's price strategies and payoffs

Firm 1's price strategies and payoffs	p^1 \ p^2	0, 0	0, 1	1, 0	1, 1
	0, 0	0.85 0.094	0.87 0.94	0.90 0.94	0.90 0.94
	0, 1	0.94 0.097	1.7 0.19	* 1.8 0.97	0.90 1.9
	1, 0	0.75 0.10	0.78 1.0	1.7 0.19	** 1.8 1.0
	1, 1	0.94 0.10	1.5 0.10	1.8 0.20	2.6 0.29

B Logistic adjustment process

Firm 2's price strategies and payoffs

Firm 1's price strategies and payoffs	p^1 \ p^2	0, 0	0, 1	1, 0	1, 1
	0, 0	0.849 0.094	1.044 0.773	1.070 0.773	1.075 0.943
	0, 1	0.943 0.097	1.722 0.191	1.843 0.796 *	1.244 1.569
	1, 0	0.943 0.100	1.914 0.100	1.749 0.194	1.944 0.873 **
	1, 1	0.943 0.100	1.914 0.100	1.843 0.197	2.622 0.291

Notes: * Nash equilibrium
** Pareto superior solution
NE corner: 2's payoff
SW corner: 1's payoff

are dominated by the other three; there is no systematic way to select an equilibrium, or indeed a preferred set of prices from among the marked in cells in Table 4.3A. *The results are indeterminate!*

Table 4.4A returns to the small initial market share case for Supplier 1, but with a fourfold increase in the speed of adjustment parameters; nevertheless, the Nash equilibrium solution remains the same as in Tables 4.1A and 4.2A with p^1 = (0, 1) and p^2 = (1, 0). Here, however, as in Table 4.1A with the slower adjustment, a weak Pareto improvement is possible if the p^1 = (1, 0), p^2 = (1, 1) price strategies are adopted.

It is interesting to compare the results for the same parameter values between the concave adjustment process that may be representative of emerging high-tech, computer-interactive shopping societies with the logistic adjustment process that may reflect characteristics of current shopping mall tours in the USA. The distinguishing feature of the concave adjustment process is that for suppliers with small initial market shares, the rate of gain of share in response to a lower price is much greater than with the logistic adjustment. As might be expected, then, the logistic Nash equilibrium with $s_1^1 = 0.1$ is $p^1 = (0, 0)$, $p^2 = (1, 1)$; whereas with the more rapid initial concave adjustment, $p^1 = (0, 1)$ and $p^2 = (1, 0)$. Because of Supplier 1's rapid initial incursion into the market, Supplier 2 is forced to compete in Period 2 in order to provide some market for the final period. The offset is that Firm 1 gains market share so rapidly compared with the logistic adjustment that is no longer finds it profitable to compete in Period 2.

However, the Nash equilibrium solutions for parameter values in Tables 4.2A and 4.2B and 4.4A and 4.4B are the same for both adjustment mechanisms. Furthermore, the Nash equilibria in all cases cannot be improved upon by employing mixed strategies in this game, where both firms possess perfect information, and in the chaotic case of Table 3.1, a mixed strategy is not possible.

What is surprising in comparing the cases of equal initial market shares in Table 4.3A and 4.3B, is the indeterminate result under concave adjustment; whereas the logistic adjustment in Table 4.3B leads to fairly predictable stable results. The Nash equilibrium in the case of logistic adjustment shows intense competition in Period 1, but then reverts to monopoly pricing thereafter, $p^1 = p^2 = (0, 1)$. Still, this is better for consumers than the Pareto superior collusion strategy, $p^1 = p^2 = (1, 1)$. By comparison, the concave process with equal shares is indeterminate. Although more rapid initial rates of customer adjustment, as represented by the concave process, normally imply more intense competition, perhaps the competitive result, loss of market share, is too rapid here for stability. *Thus as market shares become more nearly equal in a world of rapid feasible consumer changes in suppliers*, the possibility of unstable market conditions may increase.

CONCLUDING OBSERVATIONS

Note that most of the results in this chapter differ from those of James Friedman's (1977) analyses of intertemporal oligopolistic games, but that should not be surprising since he is dealing with collusive games with enforceable threats over an infinite time horizon, rather than non-cooperative games over a finite horizon. Obviously, each model has its applications in different economic scenarios, and it should not be surprising that Friedman's models suggest that rising real interest rates will slow down price increases, whereas the same stimulus accelerates price changes in the model presented here.

While at first it may appear that the very different results in this analysis arise from the finite horizon of the decision-maker, recent results by Langlois and Sachs (1993) suggest otherwise. They show that in infinite horizon supergames, that a 'benefit denial' principle emerges naturally in a reaction function equilibrium and leads to Pareto superior results (for example, positive economic profits). And so, the finite period game studied here in order to gain an understanding of price dynamics can be extended infinitely by asserting that the payoff in the final period is merely the net present value of all future payoffs in a supergame. With that final period's payoff in hand, the analysis of explicit dynamic price adjustments merely walks backwards in time, recursively, to the present, as in the examples presented here.

As intended, this analysis raises more questions than it resolves, but by the introduction of a single added degree of realism to the analysis of many oligopolistic markets – non-instantaneous customer responses to price differentials among suppliers – a much richer array of outcomes is shown to be possible depending upon the values of key economic parameters. In addition, if the planning horizons of the decision-makers in firms are finite, or can be truncated for purposes of analysis, then under a variety of circumstances, non-competitive prices arise in many periods as the non-cooperative, Nash equilibrium outcome to this competitive game.

In terms of public policy, what this chapter introduces is the importance of the speed of customer response in gauging the competitiveness of oligopolistic markets. Where the cost of space or information (search costs) are high, those lags are likely to be long, and opening a market that was previously dominated by one or a few firms to competition may be no guarantee of competitive market-like prices for a long time, even if entry is quite fast and low in cost. So long as the customers are slow to learn that there are better opportunities available, or their cost of changeover is high until existing equipment wears out, the dominant firm will be glad to exploit that asymmetry in information or in lagged responses by charging higher monopolistic current prices, even though it may mean an eventual accelerated loss in market share.

Periodically, under concave-shaped market share adjustment, processes that might emerge in hi-tech, tele-information-aided purchasing, chaotic market behaviour may emerge with no equilibrium paths because the initial consumer response to price changes is too fast.

Notes

1. In Barro's model, the optimal *percentage* rate of adjustment is shown to be equal to the difference between the actual and desired levels. Thus, $\dot{x}/x = \gamma(x^* - x)$ or $\dot{x} = \gamma x(x^* - x)$, a form of logistic function.
2. See Kiefer (1988) as an example.
3. A monopolistic supplier may also use transport cost as an excuse to engage in spatial price discrimination, but that case is not analyzed explicitly here. Qualitatively, the customer adjustment mechanisms discussed for mill pricing will be relevant for spatial discriminatory pricing.
4. This model can be extended to an infinite-time-horizon, non-cooperative game using the results of Langlois and Sachs (1993). They show the existence of a reaction function equilibrium in a supergame, using the 'benefit denial principle,' that is Pareto superior. If the finite net present value of that supergame is used as the payoff in the last period, this finite game represents an infinite time horizon.
5. The Nash equilibrium set of prices over time for each firm will represent what Reinganum and Stokey (1985) have called a 'path equilibrium'; however, the solution here does not possess the seemingly restrictive 'commitment' properties Reinganum and Stokey (R & S) associate with a path equilibrium. R & S distinguish 'decision rule strategies' – Nash equilibria resulting from forming a sequence of optimal prices that is updated over time, given the outcomes of previous periods – from 'path equilibria', where they claim firms must irreversibly commit to a price path over time in the initial period. But if a set of Nash equilibria prices is developed where each firm's decision rule strategy is to set a current price consistent with maximizing the net present value of payoffs over the remaining life of the game (not just a value maximizing price for the current subperiod of the game as in R & S's illustration), then the result from applying this decision rule is identical to the subgame perfect Nash equilibrium results yielded by Equation (4.15), since that equation was developed by backward recursion of this decision rule! So, if both firms have foresight to the end of the game in each period of a game over discrete time, the consistent application of the decision rule strategy leads to the same result, as does what R & S call a Nash equilibrium in path strategies, but without the need for any mechanism to enforce commitments. The anticipation of updated rationality is a sufficient club in this non-cooperative game.
6. For computational details on the game with the logistic adjustment process, see Schuler and Hobbs (1992).

References

Barro, R. J. (1972) 'A Theory of Monopolistic Price Adjustment', *Review Economic Studies*, vol. 39, pp. 17–126.

Beckmann, M. J. (1971) 'Equilibrium vs. Optimum: Spacing of Firms and Patterns of Market Areas', *Northeast Regional Science Review*, vol. 1, pp. 1–20.

Carlton, D. W. (1986) 'The Rigidity of Prices', *American Economic Review*, vol. 76; pp. 637–58.

Friedman, J. W. (1977) *Oligopoly and the Theory of Games* (Amsterdam: North-Holland).

Holahan, W. L. and R. E. Schuler (1988) 'Imperfect Competition in a Spatial Economy: Pricing Policies and Economic Welfare', CORE Discussion Paper 8821, Université Catholique de Louvain, Louvain-la-Neuve, Belgium.

Kiefer, N. M. (1988) 'Hazard Functions and Economic Duration Dates', in *Journal of Economics Literature*, vol. 26, pp. 646–79.

Langlois, J.-P. P. and J. A. Sachs (1993) 'Existence and Local Stability of Pareto Superior Reaction Function Equilibria in Supergames', *Journal of Mathematical Economics*, vol. 22, pp. 199–221.

Okun, A. (1981) *Prices and Quantities: A Macroeconomic Analysis* (Oxford: Basil Blackwell).

Phlips, L. and J. F. Richard (1986) 'A Dynamic Oligopoly Model with Demand Inertia and Inventories', CORE Discussion Paper 8603, Université Catholique de Louvain, Louvain-la-Neuve, Belgium.

Reinganum, J. F. and N. L. Stokey (1985) 'Oligopoly Extraction of a Common Property Natural Resource: The Importance of the Period Commitment in Dynamic Games', *International Economic Review*, vol. 26, pp. 161–73.

Schuler, R. E. and B. F. Hobbs (1992) 'Price Adjustments in Oligopolistic Markets: The Impacts of Lags in Customer Response', in J. M. A. Gee and G. Norman (eds), *Market Strategy and Structure* (London: Harvester Wheatsheaf) pp. 125–42.

5 Spatial Aspects of Knowledge Networks: The Case of Scientific Collaboration at a Distance

Martin Beckmann

Scientific collaboration as revealed by joint authorship of articles appears to be growing rapidly (de Solla Price (1963) p. 88; Andersson A. E. On the one hand, the technical possibilities have improved: cheap and easy air travel and the fax machine. On the other hand, the growth of scientific activity has created more instances of individuals focusing on the same question. Rather than race each other, they prefer to collaborate, for rational reasons: in lists of publications, the articles are not always discounted for co-authorship. In fact, willingness and ability to collaborate may throw a favourable light on a scientist. A formal analysis of decision-making in scientific collaboration is made below.

Let a set of individuals, i, have the opportunity of working on their own – at a level of productivity standardized as unity – or to collaborate partially or fully with others, j. If the proportions of time spent in these pursuits are labelled x_i and x_{ij}, respectively, then total output equals:

$$\sum_i x_i + \frac{1}{2} \sum_{ij} b_{ij} \sqrt{x_{ij}\, x_{ji}} \tag{5.1}$$

where we have assumed a symmetric Cobb–Douglas production function to represent the output of collaboration; b_{ij}, the productivity coefficient, describes the joint output from a unit contribution by each partner.

Without restriction, we set:

$$b_{ij} = b_{ji}$$

Notice that these productivity coefficients must be scaled by 0.5 to allow for double counting. The time budget for individual i is

$$x_i + \sum_j t_{ij} x_{ij} \leq 1 \tag{5.2}$$

Here, t_{ij} is the actual time spent to achieve one unit of time of effective collaboration between i and j. In-house collaboration requires $t_{ij} = 1$, but interaction at a distance requires

$$t_{ij} = 1 + k \cdot r_{ij} > 1 \tag{5.3}$$

where r_{ij} is a measure of distance and the coefficient, k, depends on how often one must travel to achieve effective interaction.

Maximizing the Lagrangean

$$L = \sum_i x_i + \sum_{ij} \frac{1}{2} b_{ij} \sqrt{x_{ij}\, x_{ji}} + \sum_i \lambda_i [1 - x_i - \sum t_{ij} x_{ij}] \tag{5.4}$$

yields

$$x_i \begin{Bmatrix} = \\ \geq \end{Bmatrix} 0 <=> 1 \begin{Bmatrix} < \\ = \end{Bmatrix} \lambda_i \tag{5.5}$$

$$x_{ij} \begin{Bmatrix} = \\ \geq \end{Bmatrix} 0 <=> \frac{b_{ij}}{4t_{ij}} \sqrt{\frac{x_{ji}}{x_{ij}}} + \frac{b_{ji}}{4} \sqrt{\frac{x_{ji}}{x_{ij}}} \begin{Bmatrix} < \\ = \end{Bmatrix} \lambda_i . \tag{5.6}$$

In view of symmetry $b_{ij} = b_{ji}$, the right half simplifies to:

$$\frac{1}{2} b_{ij} \sqrt{\frac{x_{ji}}{x_{ij}}}$$

The efficiency price λ_i, to be called i's worth, measures the marginal product of i per effective time unit.

Equation (5.6) is inoperable when $x_{ij} = x_{ji} = 0$.

Using

$$\frac{x_{ji}}{x_{ij}} = \frac{\lambda_i}{\lambda_j} \tag{5.12}$$

(from below)

one has

$$\frac{1}{2}\, b_{ij} \sqrt{\frac{\lambda_i}{\lambda_{ij}}} \begin{Bmatrix} < \\ = \end{Bmatrix} \lambda_i$$

or

$$x_{ij} \begin{Bmatrix} = \\ \geq \end{Bmatrix} 0 <=> \frac{1}{2}\, b_{ij} \begin{Bmatrix} < \\ = \end{Bmatrix} \sqrt{\lambda_i \lambda_j} \tag{5.6a}$$

in agreement with Equation (5.18) from below.

In cases of collaboration, $x_{ij} > 0$, when the equals sign holds in the right inequality of Equation (5.6a), 0.5 of the productivity coefficient turns out to be the geometric mean of the marginal productivities λ_i, λ_j, of the two partners.

Proposition 1

$\lambda_i \geq 1$ and '>' if and only if i collaborates with some j. (5.7)

The motivation for collaboration is thus to raise one's worth λ_i above the unit level achieved in working alone. (Thus in the achieved collaboration, each partner rises above the unit level of productivity, even allowing for part of the success being attributed to the other partner.)

From Equation (5.6) it is seen that $x_{ji} > 0$ implies $x_{ij} > 0$. Interaction occurs as soon as one party is willing.

Writing Equation (5.6) for i and j and multiplying, we have:

$$\left(\frac{b_{ij}}{2t_{ij}}\right)^2 \equiv \frac{b_{ij}^2}{4t_{ij}^2} \leq \lambda_i \lambda_j \tag{5.8}$$

'=' if and only if $x_{ij} > 0$ and hence $x_{ji} > 0$.

This yields the following:

Proposition 2

$$x_{ij} > 0 \quad \text{if} \quad \lambda_i = \max_j \left(\frac{b_{ij}^2 / t_{ij}}{2}\right)^2 \Big/ \lambda_j \tag{5.9}$$

A partner j is chosen if and only if the resulting worth to partner i:

$$\frac{1}{4}\frac{b_{ij}^2}{\lambda_j t_{ij}^2}$$

is maximal with respect to j.

The maximiser, j, need not be unique. Thus an individual, i, may, in general, choose to collaborate with several partners. If i chooses to spend some time on his/her own, then $\lambda_i = 1$ and hence:

$$1 = \max_j \left(\frac{b_{ij}}{2t_{ij}}\right)^2 \Big/ \lambda_j \tag{5.10}$$

Corollary:
Suppose that i dominates k such that:

$$\frac{b_{ij}}{t_{ij}} \geq \frac{b_{kj}}{t_{kj}}$$

for all j,

then $$\lambda_i \geq \lambda_k$$

Proposition 3

Suppose that

$$\frac{b_{ij}}{t_{ij}} < 2$$

then i and j will not collaborate.
Proof: Assume the contrary. Then:

$$\lambda_i = \frac{1}{4}\left(\frac{b_{ij}}{t_{ij}}\right)^2 \Big/ \lambda_j < 1$$

by hypothesis and Proposition 1. This contradicts Proposition 1.

Proposition 4

Suppose that for a given i and some Partner j, $\lambda_{ji} = 1$ and $b_{ij} > 2\ t_{ij}$. then i will collaborate with some partner k.

Proof:

$$\lambda_i = \max_k \frac{\left(\frac{b_{ik}}{2t_{ik}}\right)}{\lambda_k}$$

$$\geq \left(\frac{b_{ij}}{2t_{ij}}\right)^2 > 1 \qquad (5.11)$$

Using Proposition 1, the assertion follows.

Writing Equation (5.6) for i and j and dividing:

$$\frac{x_{ji}}{x_{ij}} = \frac{\lambda_i}{\lambda_j} \qquad (5.12)$$

we have Proposition 5.

Proposition 5

The contribution of partners are inversely proportional to their worth, λ. This can be interpreted as follows. A partner of lower value, λ_j, must compensate by greater effort, x_{ji}. In fact, multiplying Equation (5.6) by x_{ij}:

$$\frac{1}{2}\frac{b_{ij}}{t_{ij}} = \lambda_i x_{ij}$$

shows that i (and hence j also) can contribute half to the value of output per effective time.

Exclusive collaboration between i and j means that:

$$x_{ij} = x_{ji} = 1 \qquad (5.13)$$

From Proposition 5 it follows that then $\lambda_i = \lambda_j$

Hence:

$$\lambda_i^2 = \left(\frac{b_{ij}}{2t_{ij}}\right)^2$$

$$\lambda_i = \lambda_j = \frac{b_{ij}}{2t_{ij}} \qquad (5.14)$$

Proposition 2 states:

$$\frac{b_{ij}}{2t_{ij}} = \max_k \left(\frac{b_{ik}}{2t_{ik}}\right)^2 \Bigg/ \lambda_k$$

$$= \max_L \left(\frac{b_{Lj}}{2t_{Lj}}\right)^2 \Bigg/ \lambda_L \qquad (5.15)$$

It is not likely that both conditions will hold simultaneously.

Now consider a large number of individuals available for collaboration. Then a full search by i for the optimal j is infeasible. Rather, i must consider b_{ij} to be a random variable and look for a j that realizes approximately the expected aspiration level L for λ_i. Assuming the same aspiration level for the potential candidates j as well, a collaboration will come about whenever

$$\lambda_i = \frac{1}{4}\left(\frac{b_{ij}}{t_{ij}}\right)^2 \Bigg/ L \geq L$$

or

$$\frac{1}{2}\,\frac{b_{ij}}{t_{ij}} \geq L \qquad (5.16)$$

To calculate the expected frequency of collaboration occuring between locations h and k, we first consider its probability for a randomly choosen pair, i, j, from these two locations.

$$\mathrm{pr}(x_{ij} > 0) = \mathrm{pr}\left(\frac{1}{2}\,\frac{b_{ij}}{t_{ij}} \geq L\right) \qquad (5.17)$$

$$= \mathrm{pr}(b_{ij} \geq 2L\ a\ r_{hk})$$

where a is the factor of proportionality in:

$$t_{ij} = a\ r_{hk}$$

Assume b_{ij} to be normally distributed and use a logistic approximation:

$$N(x) = \frac{1}{1+e^{-\alpha x}}$$

with

$$\alpha = \frac{4}{\sqrt{2\pi}} \qquad \text{(say)}$$

then

$$\mathrm{pr}(b_{ij} \geq x) \doteq 1 - \frac{1}{1 + \mathrm{e}^{-\alpha x}}$$

$$= \frac{1}{1 + \mathrm{e}^{-\alpha x}} \doteq \mathrm{e}^{-\alpha x} \qquad (5.18)$$

for large x.

Using Equation (5.18) in Equation (5.17), we have:

$$\mathrm{pr}(x_{ij} > 0) \doteq \mathrm{e}^{-mr_{hk}}$$

where m is a suitable constant.

The expected number of collaborations between locations h and k is then this probability times the number of trials, that is, of pairs ij from the two sets in h and k. Then, if N_h and N_k researchers are available in locations h and k, we have:

$$X_{hk} = \underset{\substack{i\epsilon h \\ j\epsilon k}}{E}\, x_{ij} = N_h \cdot N_k \cdot \mathrm{e}^{-mr_{hk}}$$

This is a classical gravity formula for interaction at a distance.

Appendix

Calculating the aspiration level L.

Assume $t_{ij} = 1$ (no loss of time through interaction at a distance) and a logistic distribution of the productivity coefficients:

$$\frac{b_{ij}}{2}$$

over j for given i:

$$\mathrm{pr}\left(\frac{b_{ij}}{2} \leq x\right) = \frac{1}{1 + e^{-\alpha x}}$$

where α is determined by the approximation to the standard normal distribution. Thus at $x = 0$:

$$N(0) = \frac{1}{\sqrt{2\pi}} = \frac{\alpha e^{-\alpha \cdot 0}}{(1 + e^{-\alpha \cdot 0})^2} = \frac{\alpha}{4}$$

$$\alpha = \frac{2\sqrt{2}}{\sqrt{\pi}} \doteq 1.596$$

The expected value of:

$$\frac{b_{ij}}{2}$$

in the domain

$$\frac{b_{ij}}{2} \geq 1$$

is then

$$\begin{aligned} 1 \cdot F(1) + \int_1^\infty x \mathrm{d}F(x) &= F(1) + x\,[F(x) - 1]\Big|_1^\infty - \int_1^\infty [F(x) - 1]\,\mathrm{d}x \\ &= \int_1^\infty [1 - F(x)]\,\mathrm{d}x \\ &= \int_1^\infty \left(1 - \frac{1}{1 + e^{-\alpha x}}\right)\mathrm{d}x \\ &= \int_1^\infty \frac{e^{-\alpha x}}{1 + e^{-\alpha x}}\,\mathrm{d}x \\ &= -\frac{1}{\alpha}\ln(1 + e^{-\alpha x})\Big|_1^\infty \\ &= \frac{1}{\alpha}\ln(1 + e^{-\alpha}) \\ &= \frac{\sqrt{\pi}}{2\sqrt{2}}\ln\left(1 + e^{-2\sqrt{\frac{2}{\pi}}}\right) \doteq \end{aligned}$$

The expected value of the maximum of n random variables with distribution $F(x)$ is given by:

$$
\begin{aligned}
L = E \max_{i=1,\dots,n} x_i &= \int_1^\infty [1 - F^n(x)]\,\mathrm{d}x \\
&= \int_1^\infty \left[1 - \frac{1}{(1+\mathrm{e}^{-\alpha x})^n}\right]\mathrm{d}x \\
&= \int_1^\infty \left(1 - \frac{1}{(1+\mathrm{e}^{\alpha x})}\right) + \sum_{k=1}^{n-1}\left[\frac{1}{(1+\mathrm{e}^{-\alpha x})^k} - \frac{1}{(1+\mathrm{e}^{-\alpha x})^{k+1}}\right]\mathrm{d}x \\
&= \frac{1}{2}\sqrt{\frac{\pi}{2}}\ln\left(1+\mathrm{e}^{-2\sqrt{\frac{2}{\alpha}}}\right) + \sum_{k=1}^{n-1}\int_1^\infty \frac{\mathrm{e}^{-\alpha x}}{(1+\mathrm{e}^{-\alpha x})^{k+1}}\,\mathrm{d}x \\
&= \frac{1}{2}\sqrt{\frac{\pi}{2}}\ln\left(1+\mathrm{e}^{-2\sqrt{\frac{2}{3}}}\right) - \frac{1}{\alpha}\sum_{k=1}^{n-1}\frac{1}{k}\,\frac{1}{(1+\mathrm{e}^{-\alpha x})^k}\Bigg|_1^\infty \\
&= \frac{1}{\alpha}\ln(1+\mathrm{e}^{\alpha}) + \frac{1}{\alpha}\sum_{k=1}^{n}\frac{1}{k} - \frac{1}{\alpha}\sum_{k=1}^{n}\frac{1}{k}\left(\frac{1}{1+\mathrm{e}^{-\alpha}}\right)^k
\end{aligned}
$$

Using the approximation:

$$\sum_{k=1}^{n}\frac{1}{k} \doteq \ln n$$

and

$$\sum_{k=1}^{n}\frac{x^k}{k} \doteq -\ln(1-x) = \ln\frac{1}{1-x}$$

we obtain:

$$
\begin{aligned}
L = E \max_{j=1,\dots,k} \frac{1}{2}\mathrm{b}_{ij} &= \frac{1}{\alpha}\ln(1+\mathrm{e}^{\alpha}) + \frac{1}{\alpha}\ln(1+\mathrm{e}^{-\alpha}) + \frac{1}{\alpha}\ln n \\
&= \frac{1}{2}\sqrt{\frac{\pi}{2}}\ln\left(1-\mathrm{e}^{\frac{2\sqrt{2}}{\sqrt{n}}}\right) \\
&\quad + \frac{1}{2}\sqrt{\frac{\pi}{2}}\ln n \\
&= c_0 + \frac{1}{2}\sqrt{\frac{\pi}{2}}\ln n \\
&\doteq -0.05 + 0.6267\ln n
\end{aligned}
$$

The expected value of the maximum of n logistically distributed random variables is thus roughly proportional to $\ln n$.

In conclusion, we note the following. If t denotes the normally distributed random variable with 0 mean and unit variance, then:

$$x = \mu + t\sigma$$

has expected value

$$E\,x = \mu + \sigma E t$$

and

$$E \max_{j=1,\dots,n} x_j = \mu + \sigma E \max_{j=1,\dots,k} t_i$$

References

Anderson, A., Research Communication.
Solla Price, D. de (1963) *Little Science, Big Science* (Princeton: Princeton University Press).

6 Measuring the Regional Quality of Life

Jean H. P. Paelinck

INTRODUCTION

Over many decades economists have studied the problems raised by the evaluation of 'non-merchant' aspects of human activity: euphoria aspects (in the medical sense of the term: from the Greek 'feeling well'); aspects of artistic emotion (as one of the dimensions of aesthetic activity); and security aspects. In a previous article (Paelinck, 1970) we presented a concept that transcends affluence and welfare (the 'non-merchant' elements of the quality of life) and termed it 'well-being'. From that point of view, the economic discipline has separated itself from Disraeli's 'dismal science'; but still economists keep being accused of professional reductionism. As Power (1980) writes:

> Yet economists have often been charged with knowing the 'price of everything but value of none'. Two explanations of this charge are relevant here. As pointed out earlier, economists have in the past concentrated on market or commercial values while ignoring non-market but very real and important values. This is a major failure and an important and persistent bias which this study has tried to help eliminate. Secondly, economists focus primarily on goods in relatively abundant supply and then they focus on value 'at the margin', i.e. on the value of small changes in availability. (Power, 1980, p. 86)

However, all this does not imply that the economists should refrain from integrating qualitative phenomena into their reasoning, using their own analytical tools. To quote Power (1980) once more (p. 87):

> The quality of life is productively open to economic analysis because it is in fact pursued by individuals. Such active pursuit indicates that high quality natural and social environments are scarce. They are not available in unlimited supply. That is what makes the

quality of life, at the margin, valuable. If high quality environments were available at no effort to everyone, no value would be attached to one environment compared to another. As a result of the scarcity and value of high quality environments, people commit scarce, valuable resources to their pursuit. They change their behavior and trade-off one desirable objective for another as they use their resources to improve their condition. It is this use of resources which have alternative uses in the pursuit of a particular objective that give the QOL an economic aspect.

In what follows, we shall present concepts and methods clarifying certain operational points of the debate.

CONCEPTS

Utility, satisfaction, euphoria – a human being derives these from a certain number of elements belonging to the environment. That environment can be an immediate one (the being's state of health, its domestic environment, for instance, or workplace conditions and attached income) or a rather more diffuse one (the local neighborhood, region and country, or the political system, local, regional, national or international).[1]

A first observation to be made is that 'comfort', the *appreciation* of the quality of life, cannot initially be considered as a global magnitude, but rather as a function of a series of very diverse elements[2] which, at first sight, are not mutually comparable, and certainly not additive; in mathematical terms, we are faced with a *vector*, for which we will use the symbol e.

If one wants to compare different states of the quality of life, one must compare vectors; now, if one considers two vectors e_s and e_t (two realizations of the quality of life at two different times, in two different towns or regions), for example, one will observe that the vectors differ element by element. For instance, there will be more e_{si} (index i indicating an element of vector e_s) than e_{ti}, and less e_{sj} than e_{tj}; how, then, should one judge whether the quality of life should be considered better in t than in s (or the reverse)?

The economist has solved the problem by postulating that an 'evaluator' (individual, collective; a political decision-maker, for example[3]) constructs on e_s and e_t an *evaluation function* (let us call it a 'comfort function', according to the earlier introduced terminology), of which the role is to weigh the different elements of the vectors e_s and e_t, that is:

$$a_k(e_s), \qquad a_k(e_t), \tag{6.1}$$

where k is the index[4] of the consulted 'evaluator'. From here on, different paths are open. The first path starts from the economic problem of obtaining a given level of appreciation of a life quality (expressed in terms of a_k) at least cost, c; the problem is specified as:

$$\min_e c \Big|_{a_k = a_k^*} \tag{6.2}$$

and its solution is given by:

$$\min_e c \Big|_{a_k = a_k^*} = a_k^* \lambda_k \textstyle\sum_i E_i, \tag{6.3}$$

which means that, apart from a factor of personal appreciation ($a_k^* \lambda_k$), total (minimum) cost is equal to the sum of the appreciation elasticities (the E_i), which are relative variations (in percentages) of the appreciation of the quality of life as a consequence of the variation (again relative, in percentages) of each of the elements of which it is composed. If those elements have a price, their individual cost, if at all measurable, gives an indication of their appreciation *at the margin*. So here we have a first aspect of the 'economization' of the elements of the quality of life.

The economist has, however, developed another concept – a very important one – and that is the notion of substitution; there would indeed be no economic science in an environment of scarcity of resources, if there were no possibilities of substitution: the replacement of one element by another. Implicit in (6.3) is the golden rule of economic allocation, according to which:

$$r_{ji} = {}^{p_i}\!/_{p_j} \tag{6.4}$$

or again, in terms of the elasticities defined earlier:

$$\frac{E_i e_j}{E_j e_i} = \frac{p_i}{p_j} \tag{6.5}$$

But we know that E_i are proportional to the costs of e_i, which, given those costs, the corresponding elements of the quality of life, and a price (for example, p_j), allows us to compute p_i, so as to evaluate the elements of the quality of life in terms of market prices, p_j. This is the very foundation of exercises that measure regional wage differences, or in terms of improvement costs (fighting pollution, noise, illness, for example) (Power, 1980).

The consequence of all of this is that the production of 'social indicators' is not sufficient to pronounce a judgement on the quality of life (Mukkerjee, 1989); other elements are necessary, which from the behaviour of economic agents, 'reveal', as it were, their preferences and their satisfactions.

The difficulty is that very often the elements of e are not measurable using the usual meaning of that word (that is, on a proportional scale, in miles or seconds); some of them can only be compared in plus or minus terms (degrees Celsius or Fahrenheit: for example, it is warmer today than yesterday . . .), or even only on what is called a 'nominal' scale (presence or absence of a given property: a city has or has not got a university).[5] One should thus look for an operational method to implement the concepts that have been presented in this section.

MODEL

The situation discussed above is typically a multi-criteria case, presented in Table 6.1.

The e_s (s = 1, 2, 3) are vectors of the quality of life, the m_i measures of their respective elements: m_1 in money, for instance (say, regional income per head); m_2 in 'more or less' (the greater or smaller degree of cleanliness of the environment); m_3 in 'present or absent' (the case already quoted of the university). The difficulty resides in the fact that it is difficult (though not impossible) to construct an appreciation function, a_k, starting from such a mix, whence the necessity to use other mathematical tools; one of them is a multi-criteria method, QUALIFLEX (Paelinck, 1978).

Without going into details, let it be said that, exactly as in the second section, it minimizes a distance function, in this case:

$$\min_{j\&J} \left| \; d = \sum_J w_i d_{ij} \right. \tag{6.6}$$

Table 6.1 'Mixed' multi-criteria matrix

w	$m \diagdown e'$	e_1	e_2	e_3
w_1	m_1	20	30	40
w_2	m_2	++	+++	+
w_3	m_3	1	0	0

where the d_{ij} are distances between a given ranking (j) of the three states of life quality (e_1, e_2 and e_3) and the individual rankings according to m_1, m_2 and m_3; one sees clearly that a purely quantitative measure, m_1 (regional income per head), is not sufficient to compare the 'euphoric' states e_1, e_2 and e_3, which depend on other elements (for example, a low level of m_1 does not mean 'low euphoria', and 'global euphoria' does not necessarily increase with the elements of m_1!).

As in the second section, one can 'invert' the problem: given the ranking of e_1, e_2 and e_3, one can *infer* the weights attributed to the 'aspects' m_1, m_2 and m_3, of which the next section gives an example.

APPLICATION

Let us start from Table 6.1, and suppose the 'evaluator' is able to say that:

- e_1 is preferred to e_2, and e_2 to e_3;
- the *differences* in appreciation build a ratio of 3 to 2.[6]

Applying the QUALIFLEX method in its 'inverse' version, we compute the weights relating to three quality of life elements:

$$w_1 = 0.17$$
$$w_2 = 0.33$$
$$w_3 = 0.50$$

and construct Table 6.2, showing the substitution rates between those elements.

If one considers w_1 as the (relative) price of a 'unit of money', one observes that the evaluator attaches to a 'unit of environment' a price double that amount, and three times that amount to a 'unit of university'. In this the evaluation follows completely the economic logic exposed

Table 6.2 Substitution rates

Aspects	m_1	m_2	m_3
m_1	1	2	3
m_2	0.50	1	1.5
m_3	0.33	0.66	1

in the second section, using the marginal tools that have rendered so much service in economic analysis.

CONCLUSIONS

We have tried to operationalize the problem of the 'economic valuation' of elements that build up the regional 'quality of life'.

Some authors warn – and rightly so – against the inconsiderate generalization of the concepts used; they argue that the economist reasons in terms of 'atomic' independent agents (excluding externalities, but in a way these were taken into account: pollution, congestion, for example); of static exogenous preferences (but we mentioned that they were variable through space and time); of differences between needs and aspirations (a real problem, but from a point of view of personal judgements only impressions *experienced* matter, whatever the degree of information); and, finally, of the classical tools of mathematical economics (but they can be refined, as we have shown). We quote Power (1980) one last time:

> What is required is an abandonment of the mathematics which economists rather slavishly borrowed from physics and which physics long ago abandoned, the differential calculus, functional analysis, and simultaneous equations, for the mathematics of set theory, lexicographic orderings, and simultaneous inequalities. Although mathematics is a sort which underlines the qualitative, non-mechanical character of rational choice.

It is essentially therefore that we wanted to contribute to the development of a tool that – to be perfected later on – allows a better approach to understanding the important problem of the 'measurement' of the regional quality of life.

Notes

We would like to thank Niek Mares for bibliographical assistance.

1. For different aspects of the quality of life, see: Campbell et al. (1976); Durand and Harff (1977); Economic Planning Centre (1973); Frossard (1979); Katzner (1979); Lefèvre (1977); Scheer (1972); Szalai and Andrews (1980); UNPD (1990); Ventafridda et al. (1986); Zautra (1975).
2. Bailly (1981) p. 196, mentions that, as a result of factor analyses, they may be regrouped in five categories: space, socioeconomic level, family, employment and institutions.
3. We shall not go into the aggregation problem; see Arkhipoff (1974).
4. k is the marginal cost attached to an increase in the appreciation of the quality of life.
5. One can 'have' a university 'with a certain intensity'; the spatial analyst should not forget to mention the problem of accessibility to regional infrastructural elements. This should, however, not be confused with a fuzzy subset approach.
6. If the evaluator cannot give this precise information, a result can still be obtained, but it will of course be more 'fuzzy'.

References

Arkhipoff, O. (1974) 'Le problème de l'agrégation dans le mesure de la qualité de la vie: reformulation de généralisation du théorème d'Arrow', Etude no. 495/940 (Paris: INSEE).

Bailly, A. S. (1981) *La géographie du bien-être* (Paris: Presses Universitaires de France).

Campbell, A., Ph. E. Converse and W. L. Rodgers (1976) *The Quality of American Life – Perceptions, Evaluations and Satisfactions* (New York: Russell Sage Foundation).

Durand, M. and Y. Harff (1977) *La qualité de la vie* (Paris: Mouton).

Economic Planning Centre (1973) *Quality of Life – Social Goals and Measurement* (Helsinki).

Frossard, M. (1979) *Qualité de la retraite de vie active* (Thèse: Université de Grenoble).

Katzner, M. (1979) *Choice and the Quality of Life* (London: Sage).

Lefèvre, Ch. (1977) *Qualité de la vie, vie de qualité* (Toulouse: Privat).

Mukkerjee, R. (1989) *The Quality of Life, Valuation in Social Research* (New Delhi–London: Sage).

Paelinck, J. H. P. (1970) 'De Verenigde Staten van America – De Verdeelde Staten van Europa, 2–1 of 1–1, Praeadvries voor de Accountantsdag', *De Accountant*, vol. 77, no. 1, pp. 6–14.

Paelinck, J. H. P. (1978) 'Qualiflex, A Flexible Multicriteria Method', *Economics Letters*, vol. I, no. 3, pp. 193–7.

Power, Th. M. (1980) *The Economic Value of the Quality of Life* (Boulder, Col.: Westview Press).

Scheer, L. (1972) *Quality of Life* (Vienna: Schriftenreihe der Arbeitsgemeinschaft für Lebensniveauvergleiche).

Szalai, A. and F. M. Andrews (1980) *The Quality of Life – Comparative Studies* (London: Sage).

UNPD (1990) *Human Development Report 1990* (New York–Oxford: Oxford University Press).

Ventafridda, V., F. S. A. M. van Dam, R. Yancik and M. Tanburini (eds) (1986) *Assessment of Quality of Life and Cancer Treatment* (Amsterdam: Excerpta Medica).

Zautra, A. (1975) *Quality of Life: The Communication of Satisfaction*, Ph.D. thesis, University of Utah.

7 Innovative Environments: Concept and Application

Marc-Urbain Proulx

Even though the term 'environment' has been used for a long time by the natural sciences and in the area of community development, several social science analysts have given it a wide audience since the 1970s. The concept has acquired pertinent multi-disciplinary conceptual elements. In addition, the empirical research has generated numerous facts that allow the anchoring and measuring of many variables of the environment. At the turn of the 1990s, the results accumulated from the research of Aydalot (1986), Aydalot and Keeble (1988), RIPME (1989), RERU (1991), Benko and Lipietz (1992), Maillat and Perrin (1992), Ratti (1992), RCSR (1992) and Maillat *et al.* (1993), with other works by GREMI,[1] formed a corpus that was sufficiently important to allow us to formulate a theory on environments[2] (*milieux* in French) that we sometimes quality as local, regional, entrepreneurial, fertile and so on – i.e. generally innovative.

Correlating the theoretical construction, the numbers, the richness and the diversity of the contributions makes the process of synthesis an ambitious project. Nevertheless, efforts in this direction are inevitably welcomed as much by scientists and academics as by the practitioners of socioeconomic development. Part of this section has been written from the perspective of attempting to synthesize the theoretical corpus on innovative environments. Because the isolated factors in the literature influence the quality of innovation in the environment, they will be investigated according to a general model with eight main components. No attraction will be spent on any particular component or indicator; our specific concern will be the articulation of the general planning process of an innovative environment in a local or regional territory.

CIRCUMSTANCES FAVOURABLE TO THE NEW THEORY

There are many important trends in the recent evolution of the social sciences. Consequently, the theory of innovative environments is in

Figure 7.1 Circumstances favourable to the new theory

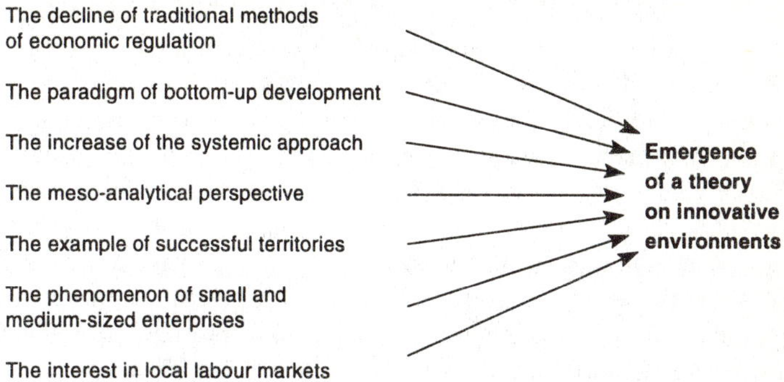

fact emerging within the framework of a certain number of major sociological trends. In this regard, we shall consider seven major circumstantial trends that favour the elaboration of this new development theory (see Figure 7.1).

Given the decline of the Fordist model of production – mass consumption on the one hand, and the financial crisis of the interventionist (Keynesian) state on the other, several analysts of the contemporary economy, which has become more and more globalized, are looking for the appropriate formula for a new model of socioeconomic regulation adapted to the interests and new tendencies of tomorrow. Through this research, a number of topics[3] provoke discussion among specialists in favour of the essential role that must be played by the territorial foundations in relation to the living environment of the population, to the workers and to the organizations. A strengthening of the community at its core has been proposed in order to ameliorate the wide and turbulent changes currently taking place. In this sense, the arguments most often referred to are certainly those of Piore and Sabel (1984) concerning the quality of spatial forms of small size that they call 'district', with reference to the works of Marshall (1890, 1919). According to the Marshallian concept, the contiguity of the enterprises in a given space (district/environment) generally produces, to a certain degree, positive external effects;[4] the main interest in terms of research into innovative environments obviously exists in reactualizing this comparative benefit in the contemporary context.

The broad popularity with analytical scientists of this concept of innovative environment is, of course, dependent on the strong recovery of the paradigm of 'bottom-up development' prevalent since the turn of the 1980s (Stohr and Taylor 1981). The principal theories of regional top-down development[5] were particularly deceiving in their capacity to reduce inter-territorial inequalities. It is largely left to the forces and the dynamism of the core (individuals, organizations and communities) to create the conditions for their own development. This ascending approach, praised by certain people as neo-humanistic, becomes the new orthodoxy that in fact directs many theoretical and empirical schools of research, one of the major concerns of which is the use of analysis on a global scale at the level of base communities. In this holistic sense, development is not only measured in economic terms but is also considered in social, cultural, political and environmental terms, generally perceived as the top of the economy.

It should also be specified that the orientation towards a multi-dimensional approach to the environment is dependent on the systematic perspective that has largely influenced the social sciences since Berthalanffy (1950). The theory of the organization and the theory of the firm were profoundly enriched by this new perspective. For these two theories, the classical model of analysis (often qualified as Weberian) draws support from an alternative approach termed 'environmental'. This allows a reflection well beyond the traditional mechanism of internal efficiency. It also permits one to consider the micro-organization, such as an open system in constant interaction with the macro-environment on which it relies in its quest for entrants. To this end, since the decision-making process takes place in short, sequential steps (Planque, 1988), particularly with regard to decisions concerning operations, the immediate environment becomes essential from the viewpoint of the content of entrants (resources, abilities, information) that are necessary for organizations. For the sake of economic science in general and of the regional economy in particular, this direct focus on the spatial environment belongs to a perspective that is called 'meso-analytical'. Etymologically, mesology is recognized as the study of the environment we live in. Therefore, it is no longer necessary to spatialize the available tools (offers, demand, production, investment and so on) in an independent manner according to tradition. It is, however, necessary to start with the spatial environments and to apply systematically the micro- and macroeconomic tools in order to produce a thorough analysis of the phenomena observed. This meso-perspective offers a remarkable opportunity for regional economic renewal (Perrin, 1983). This is certainly why the emergent theory of innovative environments now causes such enthusiasm in regional science. Enthusiasm for the theory is well grounded in empirical observation. In fact, it has been demonstrated that in most occidental countries certain environments are more innovative and fertile than others, without nevertheless responding to the traditional and known criteria of growth and development. The observation and analysis of these spaces, districts, valleys, regions and niches allow the induction of a range of winning formulas; these are often novel, sometimes uncommon and are normally transposable only with great difficulty. These identified innovative environments represent a very interesting phenomenon, because they join to counter the classical theory of innovation that relies largely on the principle of diffusion from large urban centres. Defined as a new combination of entrants, innovation[6] appears then to be able to emerge in an endogenous manner in a given peripheral space. It is necessary to understand the complex structures involved in order to multiply the process where the need is felt, particularly in the underdeveloped areas of the national territories.

The effective fertility of certain environments and the desired fertility of others is often measured in terms of small and medium-sized enterprises. Small and medium-sized enterprises have become since the 1970s, an essential element of economic dynamics (Chicha *et al.*, 1985), because they create most of employment in occidental countries. It has been maintained widely that small and medium-sized enterprises do not respond to the factors of attraction that are important to the theory of localization. Hence a general postulate of research on innovative environments stipulates that activities are generated more by their immediate environment, known as the 'local environment' (Aydalot, 1984). In this regard, the fertility of the environment is related to its capacity to incubate and encourage the growth of small and medium-sized enterprises according to the appropriate conditions of its substratum and in relation to the necessities of actual and anticipated production processes.

Job creation by the small initiatives that take hold in their local context, moreover, has been proposed widely by specialists playing a pertinent political and economic game. By using the notion of 'pools of labour' or 'local labour markets', most occidental countries have at this stage launched programmes that are both concerned with the offer of work (workers) and specifically adaptable to different spatial contexts on national territories (OECD, 1982).

Since these interventions have already generated considerable consequences, particularly in the areas of the adaptation of abilities and the launching of initiatives that value local expertise, employment has become an objective that in fact justifies the decentralization of responsibilities towards smaller territorial entities. The concept of the innovative environment wins the argument once more.

Thus, this argument, tied to the seven main circumstantial tendencies described in summary, allows us to understand all the scientific interest that has been directed during the late 1980s and early 1990s towards the phenomena of innovative environments.

DEFINITION OF THE INNOVATIVE ENVIRONMENT

In the literature, the concept of 'environment' already possesses a certain number of convergent definitions. Though it definitely encompasses the concepts of territory and of quality of innovation, it must be emphasized immediately that the innovative environment has a content different from the concept of industrial parks, technology parks, science parks and so on that has been applied widely, with the reinforcement of publicity and public resources, in the early 1990s. With respect to the concepts generated by the research on the spatial condition of innovation, the first typical characteristic of the innovative environment concerns its global aspect, since it incorporates not only the enterprise, but also the population, the workers and many organizations as well as numerous social and cultural dimensions.

Considering in detail the importance of the theoretical corpus, which incidentally contains a large number of variables brought to the fore, one cannot but reach a definition that is all-encompassing. Since the concept of 'district' is often associated or confused with that of innovative environment, one must keep in mind the definition of Becattini (1992), which is 'a socio-territorial entity characterized by the active presence of a community of people and a population of enterprises in a geographic space at a historical time'. If this definition relates to the reality of the environment as it is described in the literature, it nevertheless does not insist sufficiently on the innovative character. To this Maillat (1992) gave more precision by considering that the innovative environment contains five components, namely a geographic space, a technical culture, a series of actors, a logical organization and a learning dynamic; we could quote many others.

Such very broad definitions illustrate well that we are at the dawn of research that has generated up to now only a few laws applicable in a general way. Nevertheless, it is widely agreed that the essential quality of an innovative environment affects the collective production, in a particular environment, of a genuine territorial synergy.

THE MODEL OF ANALYSIS

The innovative environment, i.e. the creator of new activities[7] that relate to the economy,[8] has spatial, social, cultural, environmental, administrative and economic dimensions. The numerous contributions combine to bring out, all in all, a large number of factors, both old and new, that influence the quality of the innovative environment in a given territory. We can classify all these factors into eight categories that consequently become the main components of the innovative environment, and this classification allows us to construct an octagonal model (see Figure 7.2).

1. Satisfying the basic needs of the population for: health, education, food, leisure, living conditions, sports, public transportation, self-improvement activities.
2. Presence of environmental amenities: recreational parks, low pollution count, quality of the natural elements, open-air sports and leisure, proximity of work and home, hours of sunshine.
3. Equipment and infrastructure in the territory: transportation and communication, grounds, buildings, industrial areas, commercial areas, hospitals, schools, daycare, community centres, sports arenas, cultural centres, business centres.
4. Education: training and perfecting skills, schools, working climate, health and safety in the workplace, technical culture, learning circles, quality of work circles, loyalty of the workers, mobility of skills.
5. Access to information on: the market, opportunities, programmes, methods of exporting, laws and regulations, the usable technologies, expertise, raw materials, semi-finished products, new commercial techniques.
6. Socio-economic drive: social climate, support and initiatives, communication between actors and eventual partners, cultural events.
7. Entrepreneurship: business climate, entrepreneurial culture, healthy competition, services that help in management, training for entrepreneurs, visibility of success models.
8. Financing: risk capital, financial aid programmes, attitude of the financial institutions, common funds, banking services.

In these eight main categories of factors, a range of private, public and collective organizations intervene for various reasons. Each of them contributes towards making a local or regional territory of intervention, an innovative environment.

Figure 7.2 The octagon of innovative environment

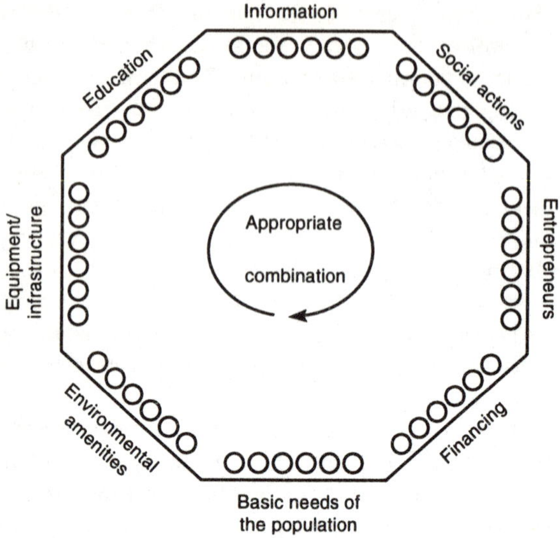

All these factors are not present equally in all every environment that qualifies as innovative. In fact, our synthesis allows us to consider that the appropriate combination of factors for a territory to become an innovative environment does, in essence,[9] differs between one area and another. It has been widely suggested that it is up to the environment to organize itself through the deciding factors (organizations), and to create specific and appropriate social, cultural, technological, administrative, political and economic conditions. These conditions should be specific and appropriate to the innovative dynamism in their actual or potential activities. It is a matter of finding, in the eight major categories of factors, the appropriate recipe for the local or regional territories that are searching for innovation and development. It can therefore be deduced that all organizations linked to these multiple potential factors can be mobilized towards researching the solution collectively.

In fact, the experiences of 'successful environments' that were 'innovative environments' or territories endowed with 'the effect of the environment' largely bring out the importance of the procedure of collective organization of the territory. On the other hand, operational methods are manifestly numerous. Various labels exist in the literature to designate this general community phenomenon and its variables, namely: collective cognitive process (Perrin, 1983); inter-organizational networks (Mulford, 1983); concerted actions (Stohr, 1985); community co-operation (Jessop and Weaver, 1987); networking (Proulx, 1989); partnership (Gagnon and Klein, 1991); system of territorial agreement (Planque, 1992); and networks of networks (Perrin, 1992).

Whatever the term used may be, one of the main aspects in the creation of an innovative environment is the collective process of inter-organizational collaboration on a voluntary basis while respecting the autonomy of the various actors. The voluntary aspect of the process is generally insisted upon, because the conditions of the organizational environment of the territory already occupied by various autonomous organizations, are incompatible with the introduction of the interventionist and rigid process of territorial integration of actions by any centralizing power.

Consequently, most territorial procedures for integration, organization or planning recommended in the literature lean on a flexible framework, capable of generating the voluntary collaboration of decision-makers in the many organizations that intervene on the territory. The ability to generate positive effects depends on this collaboration. In this sense, many specialists agree to link the quality of this inter-organizational collaboration with the state of the organizational culture (or of the planning culture) that exists in the local and regional territory (Friedmann, 1987; Blakely, 1987; Perrin, 1992). The creation of an innovative environment that is dynamic and capable of implementing local or regional development must be considered, in the first place, under the general topic of the territorial organizational culture that surrounds the population, the workers and the organization.

TERRITORIAL IDENTITY AND ORGANIZATIONAL CULTURE

If the anthropological definition of culture refers us to a system that structures ideas, significance and symbols or knowledge, then the organizational culture of an eventual innovative environment appears to be, in our sense, a system that structures the decision-making process concerning the territorial community. In this sense, the culture plays a dynamic role (Bassand *et al.*, 1985). The organizational component of the culture in a local or regional territory is associated with the endogenous capacity of individuals to take control collectively of the future of their community and of the organization of the day-to-day environment as desired by and on behalf of the community.

The scientific literature has uncovered numerous elements tied to vaues and behaviour that, in all the evidence, influence the capability to take control of the community. It has, however, proved in essence to be very difficult to measure most of these elements. Our synthesis drawn from the literature allows us to attempt to draw up an inventory of the principal elements of the organizational culture of an environment-territory:

- traditional co-operation, mutual aid and partnership
- collective abilities of community consensus
- respect and reliability of community solidarity
- institutional interdependence and confrontations
- corporatism and professional alliances
- political partnerships strategic alliances
- popular participation in the decision-making processes of the community
- presence of clans and cliques in the decision-making elite
- transferability of useful information to the decision-makers
- ability to learn collectively.

Even though these factors are more qualitative than quantitative, each local or regional territory has them to some degree. An attentive ethnological analysis can reveal the qualities of the organizational culture. Therefore the object of analysis is much less concerned with precise measurement than with the identification of various elements.

Thus, Bassand (1990) demonstrates effectively that the identification process is an essential basic element of this qualitative evolution. Therefore the territorial division of an eventual planned innovative environment must draw its inspiration from this principal of territorial identity. There exist to this effect territorial symbols that are tied to the geography, the history, the natural resources, the architecture, and the social, cultural and economic activities of the region, and these must not be neglected. However, the market areas (of management) of various organizations, particularly those linked functionally to the elements included in the octagonal model as illustrated in Figure 7.1, become very important criteria for considering in concrete terms the division by function of the territorial identity.

IDENTIFICATION AND POSITIONING OF THE ACTORS

Moreover, the notion of organizational culture forces us also to focus on the dynamics between the actors (the decision-makers of the organizations). Since the character of the evolution is essential to the quality of innovation, it is the organizational or structuring process that proves to be important for the innovative environment and not for any institutional structure established a priori or a posteriori. In this sense, Blakely (1987) defines local and regional development as a continual cultural process of institutional construction of the territory. The decision-makers of the organizations are thus directly called as actors in the continual creation process of an innovative environment in the identified territory.

These are,[10] at first glance, very numerous and very diverse. It is a matter of identifying them, of qualifying them, and positioning them in the organizational environment of the particular territory. In order to do this, the model proposed by Friedmann (1992) appears to be entirely appropriate. Friedmann differentiates the four main spheres of social practice:

1. The state: legislative machinery, executive and judiciary.
2. The civilian society: citizens, owners, households, families, clans, ethnics, social classes.
3. The incorporated economy: private corporations and their collective interests.
4. The community: social movements and independent political organizations.

These four main spheres of activity do not allow a completely final and precise classification in a territory of organizations that can potentially work to produce an innovative environment. Many of these belong to two spheres at a time, while others come under three spheres. Thus our spheres intersect with one another (see Figure 7.3).

The application of this general model to a defined local or regional territory necessitates, of course, a certain quantity of information on each organization in order to be able to be located in a good zone in the quadraspheric diagram. The unidimensional organizations are relatively easy to position. However, the bidimensional or tri-dimensional organizations necessitate a little more attention. To this effect we must know certain minimal characteristics, such as:

Figure 7.3 The actors of the innovative environment

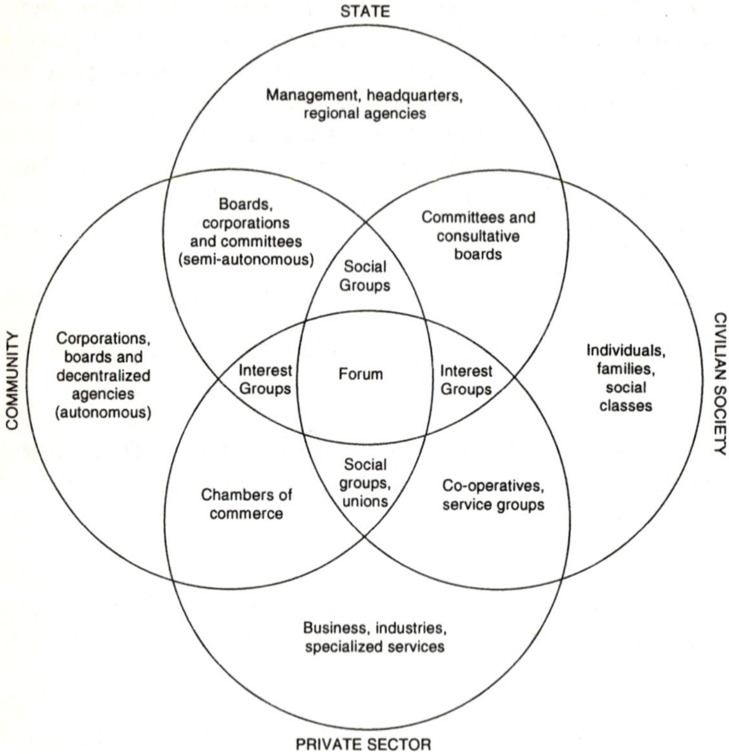

- the status of the organization
- the territoriality (territory in management; market area)
- the internal structural organization
- the sources of financing
- the mission and the practised functions
- the objectives and orientations
- the decision-making process and the autonomy.

On the basis of the information that is to be obtained on each organization, it becomes possible to locate each one of them on our model of analysis. In order to do this, it is a matter of taking an inventory of the present private, public and collective organizations, of analyzing the characteristics of their profiles, and of positioning them in the proper area in to model. Figure 7.3 illustrates our efforts at localizing organizations in regional territories of Quebec, Canada.

Besides the complete inventory of organizations who use the investigated territory in their management, this procedure of positioning and classifying the various organizations allows us to consider the functions carried out according to the elements in our octagonal model of the innovative environments, illustrated in Figure 7.2. Thus, by knowing better the organizations that are present on the territory, we shall be able to identify and sensitize those that are more apt to collaborate closely in the collective process of creating an innovative environment.

ESTABLISHING A TERRITORIAL FORUM OF COLLECTIVE REFLECTION

The area of intersection between the four spheres in the Friedmann (1992) model proves to be, given all evidence, a privileged area of occupation, since it touches all four spheres of social practice, that is to say, all the decision-makers of the territory. To this effect, the eventual occupation mode of this territorial crossroads must be specially adapted to the complexity of interests at work, to the autonomy of the many decision-makers, to the institutional structures in place, and to the state of the organizational culture in the territory.

The private, public and collective organizations already in place make it very difficult to introduce interventionist planning for an innovative environment on a selected territory. We advocate the implementation of a territorial forum in order to initiate and activate an intelligent collective process. During the early 1990s, a great number of local and micro-regional territories in most occidental countries have already experimented successfully with a concept capable of generating dialogue and exchanges between various decision-makers (OECD, 1985–92). In the particular framework of the small regions of Quebec (Proulx, 1991), we have noticed that the implementation of such a forum endows the territory with a brain and collective decision-making process that unites rationality and democracy in a global vision of the future of the community. It must be made clear that the territorial forum recommended is not a heavy structure but a simple area for communication between decision-makers. Thus everybody can express themselves freely, find out about collective interests, and defend opinions and principals as well as take part in the collective priorities. Some initiatives of territorial organization can be piloted through this forum, particularly the procedural steps of planning an innovative environment.

DEFINITION OF THE ROLE FOR THE ENVIRONMENT

Through the action of a territorial forum capable of gathering all the interested decision-makers, without distinction, the community in question inevitably debates the values, the function and the community goals. The superior intelligence that is created through this process must also be able to:

- identify the progressive values at the dawn of the twenty-first century
- identify the great social, cultural and economic interests of the late twentieth century
- develop information files on pertinent themes
- explore possible and desirable future scenarios for the territory
- argue systematically for the elements of the territorial society
- explore the feasibility of action that would structure the innovative environment.

Such a process of collective and systematic reflection on the future of the territory must necessarily lead to the determination of a role for the eventual innovative environment as desired and anticipated by the community. In this regard, the literature teaches us that such a selected role generally proves to be sector-based (textiles, microelectronics, cultural, farm produce, tourism and so on) but it can also be intersector-based on the interest holders, such as: maritime, rural, exports, diplomacy, high technology, commerce and so on.

IMPLEMENTATION OF A TERRITORIAL DATA BASE

Even though many of the components appear inevitably in the framework of the establishment of the role of an innovative environment, the building of a global portrait of the territorial situation (assessment, diagnostic profile) is a specific step in the planning of an innovative environment. Once conceived, such a portrait must be enriched and reactualized constantly in order to take the concrete form of a real territorial data base. This method of treatment and stocking of information clarifies the various decision-makers by pertinent and reliable identifiers[11] on an environmental and socioeconomic basis, of which the main components are the following:

- elements of the natural environment
- demography and human resources
- constructed environment (built framework)
- general economic characteristics
- problematic and sector-based analysis (competitive forces)
- endogenous and exogenous institutional systems
- community factors.

Each of these components contains a certain number of elements that must be ideally measured by an array of identifiers. The completed database thus built and reactualized becomes a source of information accessible to all the decision-makers of the innovative environment that is emerging. If we consider the uncertainty in which the decision-makers live when they lack pertinent information, the strategic usefulness of such a database for the territory in question is unequivocal.

ESTABLISHMENT OF STRATEGIES FOR THE INNOVATIVE ENVIRONMENT

From the moment the territory has defined a role for itself and has all the information on the global portrait of the situation, it is now a matter of equipping itself with strategies capable of directing the future of a true innovative environment. In fact, the strategies allow the assembling, co-ordinating and framing of the various fragmented actions of the many organizations towards aims and collective goals that are to be achieved.

The strategic fields of intervention on the planned territory are at first very numerous, especially if we use the traditional division by sectors (health, education, leisure, agriculture, steel and so on). In the case we are concerned with, the octagonal model presented in Figure 7.2 indicates eight main strategic themes that correspond to the major interests tied to the capacity of innovation. For each of these themes, it becomes essential to initiate a collective reflection table concerned with the eventual elaboration of a common strategy for the various contributors in the field in question.

With regard to this, the strategic reflection tables can refer to many sources of information in order to enrich the debate:

- strong foreseen tendencies in the medium
- components of the development theory
- role, aims and goals of the territory
- portrait of the territorial situation and sector-based problematic
- international contexts and conjectures
- inventory of available equipment for development
- inventory of action projects that can potentially be done in the environment
- strategies, policies and programmes of the public sector (all levels)
- strategies of private organizations
- strategies and policies of collective organizations
- strategies and implementation in other similar territories
- previous strategies implemented in the territory.

On the basis of this strategic information, each table must acquire a problem that will bring out the strengths, weaknesses, opportunities, constraints, and needs of the debated themes. The contributors then examine the creation of the main objectives, such as diversification, purification, growth, valorization, development, structure, reduction, concentration, dispersion, conservation and so on. These objectives must be measurable to the triple plan of anticipated outputs (jobs, investments, production, added-value, induced effects and so on) of the necessary outputs (natural, human, building and financial resources) and of the available inputs for concrete realization. Since resources are limited, the reduction, growth or elimination of an objective provokes the adjustment of the available inputs for other objectives. Thus the many combinations of inputs–outputs become arguments to consider in the comparative evaluation of the feasibility of different strategic options proposed by the decision-makers. For each thematic table, the necessary prioritization of one or a few strategies by consensus between the contributors then has a strong base of rational criteria.

ASSEMBLING OF STRUCTURING ACTIONS

Among the parameters of evaluation of the strategic options that aim at the transformation of a territory into a true innovative environment, the opportunities for action must necessarily be considered. Therefore, the analysis of the pre-feasibility of the eventual structuring actions (production, equipment, infrastructures, services and so on), becomes essential.

In order to do this, a dossier of opportunity must be established; that is, preparing the document that describes not only potential action but also the various components (costs, benefits, impacts, constraints) of the project. Thus the classical procedure foresees three main elements:

1. Identification and measurement of the necessary inputs in terms of resources.
2. Identification and measurement of the anticipated outputs on the level of structuring effect.
3. Establishment of multicriteria feasibility (technical, environmental, administrative, financial, social, political, economic) of the opportunity.

With this material, the person responsible for each file can put together the presentation of the opportunity as well as the systematic argumentation in order to confront the project at its different stages of production, leading to the agreement of the partners on the concrete realization.

RESEARCH OF TACTICAL EXECUTION

Tactics are generally defined as the art of using means available in order to execute actions according to well-known strategies. From then on it is a matter of using them in an opportune fashion (through ruse, quickness, spontaneity initiatives, demonstrations and so on) the fluctuations arising from economic conditions that present themselves when faced with the opportunity of action. In their desire to operate the concrete action strategies which aim at the transformation of a territory into an innovative environment, the tacticians must in this regard consider certain essential tasks systematically:

1. Establishing an articulated plan for the development of the territory:
   - values, goals, aims and role of the environment
   - global portrait of the location of the territory (synthesis)
   - elaborated and prioritized strategic orientations
   - files of structuring actions for the environment.

2. Making an inventory of the disposable means for the territory:
   - private market (investments, loans, stocks)
   - public-sector programmes of all grades
   - community sector
   - popular funds
   - international organizations that help development.

3. Considering the field conditions:
   - field (decision-makers in place, population, climate, social, economic fluctuations)
   - atmosphere (power, competition conflicts, partnership, traditional alliances)
   - solidarity (sensitization, mobilization, collective consensus)
   - context (procedures, demonstration, pressure, direct action, media).

4. Presenting the projects in a systematic way:
   - formal designation of the file holder
   - complete dossier of feasibility
   - engaged partnership
   - marketing
   - establishment of a billbook.

It goes without saying that tacticians work on specific tasks that are limited and short term. It is a matter of executing these actions. In an innovative environment progress in this regard is often tortuous.

CONCLUSION

After setting out the theoretical model of the innovative environment, we have proposed an articulated procedure capable of generating the process of the creation of such models in local and regional territories. It is imperative that these possess the prerequisite qualities from the point of view of collective identity, organizational culture and dynamics between the organizations. Controlled by a collective think-tank which sits on a regional forum, the offered procedure integrates the recent theoretical and empirical contributions of territorial planning and foresees the use of modern techniques for its operation. Thus the definition of the role in the eventual innovative environment, the setting-up of a database, the elaboration of strategies, and the establishment of structuring actions as well as the research of tactics to execute all this become, in the various components, the organizational elements for the concrete application of the concept of innovative environment in a local or regional territory.

It goes without saying that not all the territories that use this procedure will obtain the same level of success in their systematic transformations into innovative environments, because they do not all have the same resources, the same needs, the same opportunities and the same constraints at the beginning of the exercise. However, the endowment of a collective think tank and of an articulated procedure of territorial planning favours the emergence of a synergy that generates not only hope but also real activity in most cases. In this regard, many authors attach more importance to one or another step of the procedure, particularly the elaboration of appropriate strategies. From our point of view, we believe that it is the quality of the global procedure that counts. The planning must be implemented in a continuous manner; that is to say, we must define a long-term role but also reactualize and re-evaluate the options (strategies–policies–actions) regularly according variations of the territorial database. In our opinion it is through a continual collective process of learning that we shall discover the secrets of the future of innovative environments.

Notes

1. The European Research Group on Innovative Environments has organized many colloquiums on the various aspects of the subject since 1984.
2. It is to be noted that certain researchers work in the same direction by using different terms such as industrial district, spatialized production systems, support areas, spatial incubation structures, niches, etc.
3. Weakening role of the state; sociocultural diversity; local division of production; necessary flexibility of production; and industrial redeployment.
4. The externalities of the district (industrial atmosphere; technical culture; mobility of skills; formal and informal exchanges; atmosphere of professionalism; etc.) would be an important asset for acquiring the necessary flexibility that is now present in industrial production.
5. The base theory of exporting; industrial location theory; principal of the cumulative circular process; and theory of polar growth.
6. New technology; new production methods; new products; improvement of existing products; new marketing techniques; new management practices; new markets; etc.
7. Of a social, cultural, administrative, forest, agricultural, industrial etc. nature that generates investments, new jobs or added value.
8. Investments, jobs, production or added value.
9. The resources, the economic base, the potentiality, the need, the opportunities and the constraints vary from one territory to another.

10. We can also find the potential decision-makers: that is, individuals who do not represent an organization but who are in search of responsibilities in this sense.
11. Qualitative and quantitative data on the resources, needs, problems, weakness, opportunities and constraints.

References

Aydalot, P. (1984) 'Technologies nouvelles et développement territorial', Rapport préliminaire et projet de recherche, Groupe Technologies Nouvelles et Espace, La Sorbonne, Paris.

Aydalot, P. (ed.) (1986) 'Milieux innovateurs en Europe' (Paris: Groupe de Recherche Européen sur les Milieux Innovateurs).

Aydalot, P. and D. Keeble (eds) (1988) *High Technology Industry and Innovative Environments* (London: Routledge).

Berthalanffy, L. (1950) 'The theory of open system in physics and biology', *Science*, vol. 3.

Bassand, M. *et al.* (1985) *Innovation et changement social* (Lausanne: Presses Polytechniques Romandes).

Bassand, M. (1990) *Culture et régions en Europe* (Lausanne: Presses Polytechniques Romandes).

Becattini, G. (1992) 'Le district marshallien: une notion socio-économique', in Benko and Lipietz (1992).

Benko, G. and A. Lipietz (eds) (1992) *Les régions qui gagnent* (Paris: P.U.F.).

Blakely, E. J. (1987) *Planning Local Economic Development* (London: Sage).

Camagni, R. (ed.) (1992) *Innovation Networks – Spatial Perspectives* (London: Belhaven Press).

Chicha, J. *et al.* (1985) *La PME dans un monde en mutation* (Sillery, Québec: Presses de l'Université du Québec).

Faludi, A. (1987) *A decision-centred view of environmental planning* (London: Pergamon Press).

Friedmann, J. (1987) *Planning in the Public Domain: From Knowledge to Action* (Princeton, NJ: Princeton University Press).

Friedmann, J. (1992) *Empowerment* (Cambridge, Mass.: Blackwell).

Gagnon, C. and J. L. Klein (1991) 'Le partenariat dans le développement local', *Cashiers de Géographie du Québec*, vol. 35, no. 95.

Jessop, J. and C. M. Weaver (1987) 'La coopération communautaire: une stratégie pour le développement local', *Revue Internationale d' Action Communautaire*, vol. 13, no. 53.

Maillat, D. (1992) 'Milieux et dynamique territoriale de l'innovation', *Revue Canadienne de Science Régionale*, vol. XV, no. 3.

Maillat, D. and J. C. Perrin (eds) (1992) *Entreprises innovatrices et développement territorial* (Neuchâtel: GREMI, EDES).

Maillat, D. *et al.* (1993) 'Réseaux d'innovation et milieux innovateurs: un pari pour le développement régional', Groupe de Recherche Européen sur les Milieux innovateurs, (Neuchâtel: EDES).

Marshall, A. (ed.) (1890) *Principles of Economics* (London: Macmillan).

Marshall, A. (ed.) (1919) *Industry and Trade* (London: Macmillan).
Mulford, R. (ed.) (1983) *Interorganizational Relations* (New York: Human Sciences Press).
OECD (1982) 'Programme ILE: étude préliminaire des activités' (Paris: OECD).
OECD (1985–92) 'Les Cahiers des ILES' (Paris: OECD).
Perrin, J. C. (1983) 'Contribution à une théorie de la planification décentralisée', in B. Planque (ed.), *Le développement décentralisé*, (Paris: GRAL, LITEC).
Perrin, J. C. (1992) 'Pour une revision de la science régionale: l'approche en terme de milieu', *Revue Canadienne de Science Régionale*, vol. XV, no. 3.
Piore, M. and Sabel, C. (1984) *The Second Industrial Divide: Possibilities for Prosperity* (New York: Basic Books).
Planque, B. (1988) 'La PME innovatrice: quel est le rôle du milieu local', *Revue Internationale PME*, vol. 1, no. 2.
Planque, B. (1992) 'Les milieux innovateurs en PACA, France', *Revue Canadienne de Science Régionale*, vol. XV, no. 3.
Proulx, M. U. (1989) 'Activité résillière et organisation économique de l'espace', *Revue d' Economie Régionale et Urbaine*, no. 3.
Proulx, M. U. (1991) 'Espaces locaux, réseaux utilitaires et dynamique économique', *Revue Canadienne de Science Régionale*, vol. XIV, no. 1.
RCSR (1992) Numéro thématique de la Revue Canadienne de Science Régionale sur la 'Creation de milieux innovateurs', vol. XV, no. 3.
RERU (1991) Numéro spécial de la Revue d'Economie Régionale et Urbaine, no. 3–4.
RIPME (1989) Numéro spécial de la Revue Internationale P.M.E., vol. 2, no. 2–3.
Stohr, W. B. (1985) 'Le rôle stratégique de la concertation', in M. Boisvert and P. Hamel (eds) 'Redéploiement industriel et planification régionale', University of Montréal.
Stohr, W. B. and D. R. F. Taylor (eds) (1981) *Development from Above or Below* (London: John Wiley).
Weaver, C. M. (ed.) (1984) *Regional Development and the Local Community* (New York: John Wiley).

8 Intergenerational Transfers in a Framework of Fused Regional Accounts

Stan Czamanski

INTRODUCTION

Traditional social accounts do not meet the needs of economists and decision-makers dealing with development, especially at the regional level. Of the five types of social accounts, the most widely used are income and product accounts. The major aggregates of these accounts, such as gross domestic product (GDP), national income, or personal income, are of lesser concern within the context of long-run planning. Increases in their value may tell little of whether the economy being studied enhances its future growth potential or uses up its irreplaceable resources at a fast rate. Similarly, impact studies, which form the focus of input–output accounts, or changes in money supply, studied with the help of money flow accounts, are of greater interest for short-run macroeconomic policies. In the long-run, attention centres on changes in key stock variables, many of which have some or all of the characteristics of public goods. Future growth of an economy and increase in the welfare of its inhabitants depends, of course, not only – and perhaps not even primarily – on quantifiable economic factors, but on sociopolitical determinants.

There has been renewed interest recently in constructing social accounts that will partly address themselves to the needs of development planning (United Nations, (1979, 1992), Alarcon *et al.*, (1990), European Commission (1992). One line of approach, lumped together under the name of social accounting matrices (SAMs) was initiated by E. Thorbecke at Cornell University (Keuning and Thorbecke, (1992), Keuning and de Ruijter (1988), Pyatt (1988), United Nations (1992). Independently, there have been renewed efforts at constructing systems of accounts incorporating environmental factors (Keuning (1992), United Nations (1992)).

The purpose of the present study is slightly different and limited to developing a fused system of economic accounts highlighting the long-term growth potential of the economy. Of main interest are variables recording changes in invested capital, in human capital, in natural resources, in infrastructure and in environmental factors. Sociopolitical aspects, dealt with in Social Accounting Matrices, are evaluated only indirectly. The term 'intergenerational transfers' used in the title is in this context slightly misleading, since the time range of the changes considered does not conform to a life-span of a human generation but varies in longevity. Needless to say, like all social accounts, the system presented is not a simple summary of statistical data, but it does not purport to be an econometric model either. The dividing line is not clear-cut but, like all social accounts, the fused system should be useful for a variety of purposes, some of which are hard to specify in advance.

STATIC ACCOUNTS

The accounts described in this study are cast in the convenient form of a set of interlocking matrices. The master matrix presented in Figure 8.1 summarizes the main flows and changes in stock variables, and displays the major aggregates.

Each entry in the matrix represents two flows, namely, the real flow of goods or services, or the equivalent in terms of value reverse flow of money. The rows are sectors supplying goods or services and receiving payments, while the columns are sectors receiving the goods or services, in which the money flows originate. The designation of flows refers sometimes to goods and services, and sometimes to financial instruments. For example, the entry in the first row, *Personal Consumption*, describes the flow of goods and services from the sector Business to the sector Households and at the same time the flow of payments from Households to Business. On the other hand, the entry *Wages, salaries and other labour income* describes the flow of labour inputs from Households to Business and the flow of money from Business to Households, although the designation refers to the flow of money rather than of real services.

The matrix is divided into three parts. The first part in the upper left corner summarizes the flows of intermediate goods and services between business firms. In the supporting matrix disaggregated by sectors it corresponds to the main body of an input–output table. The part

Figure 8.1 Master matrix

	Business	*Households*	*Governments*	*Rest of the world*	*Intergenerational transfers*		
					Investments	*Regional endowment*	
Business	Intermediate goods and services	Personal consumption	Current government purchases of goods and services	Exports minus imports Dividends and interest from rest of the world	Net domestic private investments Public investment	Technical progress Depletion of: non-renewable resources, renewable resources, soil resources; Degradation of the environment	Adjusted NRP (net regional or national product)
Households	Wages, salaries, other labour income Net personal interest Proprietor's income Rental income Business transfers		Net interest paid by governments Transfer payments less: social security contributions			Increase in human capital	
Governments	Corporate taxes Social security taxes Indirect taxes Surplus of government enterprises less subsidies	Personal taxes Local taxes				Increase in value of subsoil resources	
Rest of the World			Transfer payments		Net investment or disinvestment in the rest of world		
Savings	Retained earnings NRP (net regional or national product	Personal savings Personal income	Governments' surplus or deficit on current account				
Changes in wealth					Net increase in assets	Net increase in endowment	Net increase in wealth

of the matrix framed by heavy lines covers flows between three sectors, namely Households, Governments, and Rest of the world (RoW). Definition of sectors is based, as far as possible, on grouping of entire decision-making units, according to their role in economic processes. In the Business sector, comprising corporate and unincorporated enterprises and some activities of Households, the income side, or column, contains the various services received from Households and Government, described as payments (or as retained earnings of corporations). Their sum is one of the major aggregates, namely *Net national or regional product*.

The income of Households, which includes some non-profit organizations, includes *Wages, salaries and other labour income Dividends, Net personal interest, Proprietors' income, Rental income, Business transfer payments, Net interest paid by governments*, and *Transfer payments less contributions to social security*. The expenditures comprise *Personal consumption, Personal taxes*, and *Local taxes* (Czamanski, 1973). The balancing item is *Personal savings*. The total yields another major aggregate, namely, *Personal income*, which is an important measure of well-being. The various entries largely follow actual flows, with the notable exception of *Rental income*, which includes imputed value of owner-occupied dwellings and passes through the Business sector.

Governments comprise all kinds of jurisdictions and the bulk of non-profit organizations, notably those having substantial enforcement powers. The income side covers *Corporate taxes, Social security contributions of employers, Indirect taxes, Personal and local taxes*, and *Surplus of government enterprises less subsidies*. The expense side is limited to exhaustive expenditures and embraces *Current governments' purchases of goods and services, Net interest paid by governments, Transfer payments to households less their social security contributions*, and *Transfer payments to the rest of the world*. The balancing item is *Governments' surplus or deficit on current account*. It differs from budget deficits of governments, which include non-exhaustive expenditures.

Rest of the world embraces in principle foreign firms, individuals and governments, but in fact there are considerable difficulties in defining RoW, particularly at the regional level. The income side is composed of *Transfer payments from governments* (which can be negative), while expenditures cover *Exports minus imports*, and *Dividends and interest payments to and from the rest of the world*. Since investments are outside of the flow part of the matrix, there is no balancing item.

INVESTMENTS

In order to analyse dynamic processes taking place in the economy, it is essential to consider changes in stock variables. Some of these are a result of flows of goods and services which are neither used up in production nor consumed. These are summarized as Investments, and their counterparts are financial flows, which may or not be of equal size, identified as *Savings*. But beyond investments, representing diversions of goods from consumption, of equal and sometimes even greater importance are changes in stock variables forming part of regional wealth but not, or only partly, man-made. These stocks, collectively called *Regional endowment*, comprise the store of useful knowledge, human capital, natural non-renewable and renewable resources, and broadly defined quality of the environment.

Investments are usually classified into private and public. The market value of the former reflects expected future income flows discounted to the present. In the context of long-run development, of significance are net investments, which alone represent additions to productive capacity. Depreciation of tangible man-made assets, forming a major part of capital consumption allowance, refers to replacement of assets used up in production. Operationally, the division of gross investments into net investments and capital consumption is not always easy to make, since reported depreciation follows the changing rules of taxation.

Investments differ greatly in terms of such characteristics as capital–labour ratio, type of labour employed, contributions to exports, and ancillary infrastructures required – all of which are major considerations in long-run development planning. Housing, for example, is extremely capital intensive and because of its magnitude has, except at the most aggregate level, to be singled out. In the present study the data needed for calculating those ratios are provided in the supporting tables. Many investments, such as owner-occupied housing, private cars or durable household utensils, do not generate income flows but utility. Their market price reflects partly the value that households place on future as opposed to present consumption.

The treatment of public investments is beset by formidable data problems. Government expenditures frequently are reported without separating current outlays from investments, often simply for budgetary convenience. Moreover, many government investments are pure public goods, while most have some characteristics of non-exclusion and joint consumption. The life-spans of government investments differ greatly and their contributions to welfare and economic growth are as a rule difficult to assess.

In the present study, five major categories of public investment are singled out:

1. Productive facilities, typically built in order to provide employment or stimulate economic growth. Their value may be analogous to similar private investments.
2. Public housing, usually evaluated either by its cost, or by comparing it with prices of private housing within the same neighbourhood, or by imputed streams of competitive rents.
3. Public amenities, comprising a wide variety of facilities, such as schools, hospitals, sport and recreation buildings, as well as elements of physical infrastructure. As a rule they are estimated according to their costs, although this involves the rather strong assumption that the decisions of public officials reflect correctly their marginal values to society.
4. Technical infrastructure, comprising transportation and communication facilities, provision of power, water and sewage, and industrial parks. Some of these may be provided by private companies, regulated to various degrees by governments.
5. Economic infrastructure, including stock and goods exchanges, technology transfer institutes, trading, and venture capital companies. The importance for development of the last two categories may not be directly, and almost certainly not linearly, related to government investment outlays.

The various types of investment are recorded concisely in the master matrix shown in Figure 8.1, in the column labelled 'Investments'. In the row referring to Business they are divided into *Net domestic private* and *Public investments*. While the flows of goods and services they summarize originate in the Business sector, their character and sources of funds obviously differ. Another category of outlays shown in the column is *Net investment or disinvestment in the rest of the world*, composed of ownership of real assets and balance of indebtedness. The sum of this column yields an important aggregate *Net increase in assets*.

The row labelled 'Savings' records the counterpart of Investments and shows the origin of funds. The savings are disaggregated into *Retained earnings*, or undistributed corporate profits; *Personal savings*, originating in households; and *Governments' surplus or deficit on current account*. The balancing item is *Net investment or disinvestment in RoW*.

REGIONAL ENDOWMENT

Among the key stock variables of interest to development economists a prominent role is played by regional endowment, to the discussion of which we now turn. Changes in the variables of which it is composed are only partly due to investments.

Technical progress is the result of outlays on Research and Development (R&D) and of what has been called 'learning by doing'. The effects of technical progress are both direct (measured by the efficiency with which goods and services are produced) and induced (raising the quality of essential infrastructure). There are various ways of measuring technical progress, but the simplest is via total factor productivity, that is, increases in productivity, after removing contributions of labour and capital. Rigorously, one should deduct from the total recorded in the column Regional endowment outlays on R&D which have already been accounted for in the column Investments, but these represent relatively minor components and may perhaps be disregarded.

Human capital plays a central role in regional development. In many studies it often turned out to be the single most important explanatory variable. Attempts to quantify or to put dollar values on human resources have a long history, dating back to Petty and the classical economists. They are beset by a number of conceptual and practical difficulties. Human assets in a non-slave economy lack one of the basic attributes of a good, namely transferability. Moreover, the manifold activities of humankind are not limited to, and perhaps not even primarily, economic in character. In the total absence of market prices, value estimates can be based on either the cost approach or the income approach. Either of the two approaches can be on a net or a gross basis.

In the net cost method, the worth of human capital is equal to the sum of outlays on education. On a gross basis, consumption expenses during the period of training are added, and sometimes even income forgone during education as well. In the income method, anticipated future income streams during the remaining active life are added up, while in the less frequently used net income method, consumption is deducted. Each method has its advantages and drawbacks. In the present study, focusing on changes in the economic value of human capital, the cost approach would fail to account for its appreciation that was not as a result of formal training (learning by doing). In addition, the increased productivity of an individual generates positive externalities by raising the efficiency of others.

In the income approach, the population is divided into relatively homogeneous groups by age, sex, education and occupation, and their anticipated discounted future income streams over the remaining active life are added up. Using this method one has to assume either constancy or specific future changes in some key parameters, such as death rates, labour force participation rates, occupational structure, migrations, and average earnings. Even larger looms the problem of a 'social' discount rate for converting future earnings into present values, which affects the final result in an major way.

Natural resources, or gifts of nature, are classified into non-renewable (or depletable), and renewable (living populations). To the former belong subsoil assets, and to the latter, forest and aquatic resources. Natural resources can be further grouped into privately and publicly owned.

The first category, namely subsoil resources, comprises metal ores, minerals, building materials and fossil fuels. Variations in their value are caused by changes in estimates of recoverable quantity and in unit prices. Recoverable quantity is a function of the level of exploitation, new discoveries, changes in mining technology, and last, but not least, world prices of the resource, affecting profitability and use of poorer deposits. Anticipated additions to the stock of existing sediments (future new discoveries) are obviously hard to predict. Existing models used by geologists such as McKelvey, Hubbert, Ahrens or Skinner, while yielding generally acceptable results, use little more than time, or sometimes volume of current explorations, as independent variables.

Setting a unit price on unrecovered deposits is hardly less intricate. As far as privately owned resources are concerned the issue has been debated by the accounting profession, regulatory agencies, industry groups and others. Three methods have been recommended at one time or another. The first one, suggested by the United Nations, is based on the present value of the future stream of revenues. The second is based on estimates of the market value of resources in situ. The obvious difficulty is that transactions are rare and that we are dealing here with heterogeneous commodities. The third is based on net price of the resource at pithead equivalent to current revenues per unit, less production costs, multiplied by estimated available quantity. Some economists claim that all three methods are equivalent, assuming that prices of subsoil resources behave in accordance with long-run competitive equilibrium. This presupposes that owners of resources arbitrage between periods by holding stocks.

But revenues from exploitation of non-renewable natural resources cannot be all considered as forming part of the Net national or regional product, since they involve using up an irreplaceable asset. Hence it is necessary to calculate that part of the revenues from mining depletable resources which can be consumed without reducing the national wealth. In other words, the current revenues have to be decreased by savings which ought to be invested in other activities so as to insure a permanent income stream. The rather obvious formula recommended (Serafy (n.d), see also Peskin (1989), Repetto *et al.*, (1989)) is:

$$C = R\left(1 - \frac{1}{(1 + r)^T}\right),$$

where

C = maximum current consumption with a permanent long-term income stream

R = current net revenues

r = current interest rate on 'reasonable' long-term investments

T = estimated time until the end of economically viable exploitation.

It might be added that the value of recoverable subsoil deposits may change because of fluctuations in market prices, improvements in mining techniques, or reduced transportation costs.

Valuation of renewable resources, of which forest and aquatic are the most important (although not the only) ones, appears at first view to be less problematic. In principle, as long as one is not over-cropping, the resource may last forever. One might thus compare data on annual harvests with estimated natural reproduction rates and take the differences are representing additions to or subtractions from regional wealth. Two complications have, however, to be faced. The first stems from the fact that ownership of some living, especially marine, populations is often controversial. A possible solution is to consider only coastal waters, but even this is problematic. Another, and even more challenging problem, is the fact that eco-systems comprise many species and are usually highly complex. It may be misleading to consider reproduction and harvesting rates of one species at a time. Even in a simple prey–predator system the results of human intervention may in fact be beneficial (see Lotka (1956), and Keyfitz (1977)). Ideally, one would have to consider and evaluate the effects of human activities on an ecosystem as a whole.

Finally, for most renewable resources one would have to appraise the aesthetic value of living populations, both to local residents and as a tourist attraction or a regional asset.

Land can be grouped roughly into four major categories, namely urban land, parks and green spaces, agricultural land, and forests. The value of the last category is distinct from forest resources, such as timber. Changes in land values over time may be caused by change in use (since the differences between the major land-use categories are very substantial), changes in accessibility, in intensity of use, and in fertility. Fertility of land changes slowly and arises from an interplay of physical and chemical characteristics of soils, and type and intensity of land use. Some micro- and even macroclimatic influence (for example, acid rain) are sometimes of importance. Soil erosion is estimated by comparing soil classification, available from land inventories, with land-use data. Valuation of urban land is usually based on adjusted estimates made for tax purposes or on sales records in land registry.

Increases in total value of land in a region have to be singled out and analyzed separately from other elements of regional wealth, since their significance for future development differs from increases in value of other tangible assets. Because, unlike serendipitous increases in subsoil resources, or in human capital, they may not attract other factors of production. Total value of regional land resources may rise sharply due to an increase in urban populations, so that land in central locations becomes far more valuable because of transition to a more capital intensive agriculture.

ENVIRONMENT

The growing concern with the physical environment has led since the 1970s to a good deal of research into both its technical and economic aspects. It has also resulted in some significant policy measures. The numerous facets of deterioration of the environment can perhaps be grouped into three major categories, namely, water pollution, air pollution, and a rather heterogenous group related to industrial activities and urban congestion. The last category comprises (while not being limited to) solid and toxic waste accumulation, high noise levels, fire danger, pests, and urban blight.

Water resources. Fresh water constitutes only about 3 per cent of all available water, but it is crucial for sustaining human populations, especially in arid and semi-arid areas. The accessible quantity is usually measured as a balance between inflows and outflows. The inflows or additions comprise precipitation, surface and underground streams, and desalination of sea water. The subtractions or outflows consist of evaporation, flows of both surface and underground streams, and human uses, the latter composed of, in order of decreasing magnitude, irrigation, industrial and urban consumption.

Available quantity of fresh water is only one aspect of water supply. In most countries an equally critical problem is water quality. There are several methods of measuring the degree of pollution of flowing water. A very simple, but usable as an approximation method, is a count of the number of living species. As a stream becomes more polluted the number of species decreases, until the water becomes dead or an open sewer. Pollution of water resources is caused by discharges of degradable, and even more significantly, non-degradable, substances into water streams. Some of these originate in households, but the majority emanate from industrial activities and some, like DDT and other pesticides, from agriculture. This last category especially may find its way into food chains and constitute a health hazard.

There are very few regions left in the world in which naturally available water can be put directly to urban or even industrial uses. In most regions water has to undergo various degrees of treatment. In some regions, such as, for example, the Ruhr Valley, water is used and processed fifteen times before being discharged into the sea. The cost of water treatment or of augmenting the available quantity through desalination processes (of which several exist) is included in *Current governments' purchases of goods and services*. Part of these outlays represent intergenerational transfers. Insufficient treatment of effluent has negative long-run consequences. Even more ominous for the future may be excessive use of underground aquifers, resulting in their increased salinity.

The total value of available water resources is hard to estimate. For while payment for water is usually exacted from users, its price is not the result of an interplay of supply and demand, and except for agriculture, is far too low to affect consumption. In fact, water conservation measures have to be based on government regulations and not on the price mechanism. Hence, of necessity, valuations of available water resources have to be based on costs and not on marginal productivity. Similarly, the negative value of depletion of underground aquifers has to be arrived at by considering the cost of alternative sources, such as desalination of sea water.

Air pollution is an externality associated mainly with industrial activities and transportation. It is classified into local and regional, according to its geographic extent. The major air pollutants having detrimental health effects (and sometimes causing damage to property) are: sulphur dioxides (SO_2), nitrogen oxides (NO_2), carbon oxides (CO), hydrocarbons (CH_4 and C_2H_4), aerosols, ozone and lead. It might be added that natural air pollution often far exceeds, both in quantity and intensity, pollution due to human activities. For example, the eruption of Krakatoa in 1883 had worldwide effects, and the aerosols generated by desert storms often drift across entire continents.

A formula often used for measuring the concentration of pollutants is

$$l_i^r = \sum a_i^{rs} q_i^s + \beta_i^r; \; (i = 1, 2, \ldots 7)$$

where
l_i^r = concentration of pollutant i at receptor sites r
a_i^{rs} = transfer coefficient, or rise of concentration at target r, if emission increases by one unit
q_i^s = emission of i at source s
β_i^r = background concentration of i at target r

Generally, one has to distinguish pollution at industrial plants, where employees are exposed to it during working hours, from pollution in residential areas, where people, including elderly people and children, are exposed to it round the clock. Another concern are rare catastrophic events, such as poisoning of whole populations of cities in which chemical plants are located.

Several methods are employed by authorities in order to improve air quality. One of the most common is command and control (CAC), in which maximum emission or reduction levels are allocated to each source. Another method used in, among other countries, France, Germany and the Netherlands, relies on emission charges, although their amount is often determined by the need to raise funds. In the USA, the Environmental Protection Agency has used for several years so-called Transferable or Marketable Emission Permits. These permits allow owners to discharge into the air a specified pollutant and can be traded between plants, although the quantity to which a plant acquiring one unit of TEP is entitled depends upon its location. Up to 1994 there had been some 12 000 transactions involving TEPs.

The value society places upon clear air is difficult to ascertain. Direct surveys, sometimes making use of ingenious questionnaires, fail to reveal unambiguously the price people would be willing to pay for clean air. Of equally uncertain merit are studies using various forms of hedonic regressions, trying to measure the influence on the value of real estate of local air pollution, which is at best a minor explanatory variable.

A different approach is based on assessment of the costs of preventive measures, although obviously outlays on avoiding generation at source are not equivalent to the damage that can be caused by pollution. In order to assess the harm caused by air pollution, or alternatively to put money value on clean air, it is proposed in the present study to make use of parametric programming. The primal may be defined as

$$\max \sum q_i^s \cdot c_{ij} \qquad (i = 1, 2, \ldots, 7)$$

subject to

$$q_i^s \cdot a_i^{sr} \leq (l_i^r - \beta_i^r);$$

and the dual as

$$\min v_i^r (l_i^r - \beta_i^r)$$

subject to

$$v_i^r \cdot a_i^{sr} \geq e_i^s,$$

where c_s^i = cost to plant of emitting a unit of polluter i
l_i^r = maximum level of concentration of pollutant i at location r
v_i^r = value of concentration of pollutant i at receptor r

The instrument variable is q_i^s and by maintaining the values of l_i^r, and c_i^s, one can read off the values of v_i^r. Changes in v_i^r following changes in l_i^r give the value of clean air.

The trouble with this approach is that, as far as industrial pollution is concerned, the cost of even sophisticated preventive measures (such as scrubbers) generally represents less than 3 per cent of the value of output and is far too small to affect production profiles or industrial location decisions. Yet industrial locations are the real long-term effects of anti-pollution measures, because pollution originating in industrial activities may be quite harmless in the absence of spatial concentration of sources of contamination. The acceptable size of an industrial agglomeration depends obviously upon the nature of the industries locating and local microclimatic conditions. Here lies the second important factor concerning valuation of clean air, namely that it is eminently a local or small region problem. Extending it and thus broadening Accounts dealing primarily with development issues to the national economy, or even to very large regions, while feasible, involves additional assumptions and may be quite laborious.

Congestion encompasses most other types of pollution or degradation of the environment, such as solid and toxic wastes, fire hazard, noise, pests, or urban blight. These are all functions of spatial organization, or more precisely urban congestion. There is here a basic discrepancy between economic efficiency and public well-being.

With increasing density the cost of building and operating a city decreases, at least up to a point. In several studies it has been found that the cost of construction of housing per square foot of floor area decreases with increasing height up to about twenty floors and then starts to rise again. Services such as water, gas and electricity supply, sewage or telephone lines are obviously significantly cheaper with increasing urban density. Against the economic advantages have to be set the negative aspects, such as scarcity of green spaces and general deterioration of the urban environment.

The issue of congestion is separate although related to urban size. Larger cities provide a number of amenities (some of which defy quantification) missing from smaller centres, such as specialized hospitals, universities or theatres. Congestion and urban size are obviously basically long-run issues and form part of intergenerational transfers. Their effects can be assessed only indirectly.

AGGREGATES

In the master matrix (see Figure 8.1) the entries in the column 'Regional endowment' are grouped in a slightly different order from that in which they have been discussed, and reflect, albeit imperfectly, the sectoral ownership. In the first row dealing with Business appear five entries, namely: *Technical progress*, *Depletion of non-renewable resources*, *Renewable resources*, *Soil resources*, and *Degradation of the environment*. The sum of this row yields a major aggregate, of considerable importance for assessing economic progress: *Adjusted NRP* (net regional or national product). In the second row, corresponding to Households appears a single entry: *Increase in human capital*. The third row, corresponding to Governments, records *Increase in value of sub-soil resources*, even though some may be the property of Business or Households. The entry obviously refers not only to price changes, but above all to exploitation of existing deposits and to new discoveries. It may clearly be negative.

The sum of the column yields one of the important aggregates: *Net increase in endowment*. The corresponding row – Changes in Wealth – contains three major aggregates, namely *Net increase in assets*, *Net increase in endowment*, and finally, *Net increase in wealth*. Changes in all three are of fundamental importance for assessing the progress of the economy and its development potential.

DETAILED ACCOUNTS

So far, the discussion has been limited to the master matrix cast in terms of summary data. By itself the matrix yields several aggregates of interest to development economists and enables them to follow changes in key stock variables. In addition, however, it is usually necessary to consider the components of the various entries in the matrix, or the database from which these were derived. The more detailed statistics are displayed in three supporting matrices, namely: the sectoral flows matrix (Figure 8.2), the income and consumption matrix (Figure 8.3), and the governments' programmes and investments matrix (Figure 8.4). The matrices obviously do not exhaust the wealth of data usually assembled in order to compute the accounts, but they summarize those necessary for making decisions affecting development and for constructing regional models.

The sectoral flows matrix (Figure 8.2) presents current flows between Business, Households, Governments and Rest of the world, but unlike the master matrix, most of the flows (framed by heavy lines) are disaggregated by 2–3 digit SIC sectors, while wages and salaries are shown by wage levels. Other entries are aggregates and repeat simply for the sake of clarity, the corresponding entries in the master matrix. While it is not the purpose of this chapter to discuss sources of data, suffice it to indicate that in most regions these are available from secondary sources without recourse to field surveys (see Czamanski and Ablas, 1977).

The main purpose of the income and consumption matrix (Figure 8.3) is to show personal consumption by sectors and, even more importantly, by income level. The necessary data can usually be derived from statistics compiled as a by-product of ongoing cost-of-living sur-

Figure 8.2 Sectoral flows matrix

	Business by 2-3 digit sectors	*Households*	*Governments*	*Rest of the world*
Business by 2–3 digit sectors	x_{11} x_{12} x_{13} x_{14} x_{21} x_{22} x_{23} x_{31} x_{32} x_{41} Intermediate goods and services	c_1 c_2 c_3 c_4 Personal consumption	g_1 g_2 g_3 g_4 Current governments' purchases of goods and services	e_1 e_2 e_3 e_4 Exports minus imports
Labour income	w_{11} w_{12} w_{13} w_{14} w_{21} w_{22} w_{23} w_{31} w_{32} w_{41} Wages and salaries by wage level group			
Other household's income	Dividends Net personal interest Proprietor's income Rental income Business transfers		Net interest paid by governments Transfer payments less social security contributions	
Governments	Corporate taxes Social security taxes Surplus of government enterprises less subsidies	Personal taxes Local taxes		
Rest of the world			Transfer payments	
Savings	Retained earnings	Personal savings	Governments' surplus or deficit on current account	

Figure 8.3 Income and consumption matrix

	Business	*Households by income level*	*Governments*
Business by 2–3 digit sectors	Σx_{1i} Σx_{2i} Σx_{3i} Intermediate goods and services	c_{11} c_{12} c_{13} c_{14} c_{21} c_{22} c_{23} c_{31} c_{32} c_{41} Personal consumption by industry and income level	g_1 g_2 g_3 Current governments' purchases of goods and services
Labour income	Σw_{1i} Σw_{2i} Wages and salaries by wage level group		
Other households' income	Dividends Net personal interest Proprietor's income Rental income Business transfers		Net interest paid by governments Transfer payments less social security contributions

veys compiled in order to ascertain the level of inflation. The transition from commodities to sectors is achieved by an iterative process (Czamanski, (1973) and Czamanski and Ablas (1977)).

The governments' programmes and investments matrix (Figure 8.4) simply shows components of current governments' purchases of goods and services (divided into Defence, and Other) and of investments. The net domestic private investments are divided into: Housing and Other, while public or governments' investments are divided into: Productive facilities; Public housing; Public amenities; Technical infrastructure and Economic infrastructure. The division simply reflects the totals most frequently used in development planning and for deriving various multipliers.

Figure 8.4 Governments' programmes and investments matrix

	Current governments' purchases of goods and services		*Investments*							
	Defence	*Other*	Net domestic private investments		Public investments					
			Housing	*Others*	*Productive facilities*	*Public housing*	*Public amenities*	*Technical infrastrucure*	*Economic infrastructure*	*Total Governments' Investments*
Business by 2-3 digit sectors										

CONCLUSION

The accounts presented in this chapter provide a convenient format for use by development economists. The variables and aggregates displayed in the master matrix and in the supporting tables provide many of the quantitative estimates needed in order to estimate progress or directions of development.

The entries in the matrices are also sufficient to compute most if not all of the major multipliers on which economists rely for assessing the effects of various government programmes. More specifically, one can compute the input–output multipliers, investment multipliers, employment–income–consumption multipliers, and housing and public services construction multipliers (Czamanski and Ablas, 1977). Obviously, summary data may have to be supplemented by statistics used in their compilation.

References

Alarcon, J. V., J. van Heemst, S. J. Keuning, W. de Ruijter and R. Vos (1990) *The Social Accounting Framework for Development* (Aldershot: Gower).

Czamanski, S. (1973) *Regional and Interregional Social Accounting* (Cambridge, Mass.: Lexington Books, DC Heath).

Czamanski, S. and L. A. Ablas (1977) 'A Model of Multiplier Effects in Maturing Economics: The Case of Sao Paulo', *Papers, Regional Science Association*, vol. 38.

European Commission (1992) *Towards Sustainability: A European Community Programme of Policy and Action in Relation to the Environment and Sustainable Development* (Research Paper: European Commission).

Keuning, S. J. (1992) 'National Accounts and Environment: The Case of a Systems Approach' (Amsterdam: National Accounts Research Division, Central Bureau of Statistics of the Netherlands; mimeo).

Keuning, S. J. and W. A. de Ruijter (1988) 'Guidelines to the Construction of a Social Accounting Matrix', *The Review of Income and Wealth.*

Keuning, S. J. and E. Thorbecke (1992) 'The Social Accounting Matrix and Adjustment Policies: The Impact of Budget Entrenchment on Income Distribution', in E. Thorbecke *et al.*: *Adjustment and Equity in Indonesia* (Paris: Organization for Economic Co-operation and Development).

Keyfitz, N. (1977) *Introduction to the Mathematical of Population* (Reading, Mass.: Addison-Wesley).

Lotka, A. J. (1956) *Elements of Mathematics Biology* (New York: Dover Publications).

Peskin, H. M. (1989) *Accounting for Natural Resources Depletion and Degradation in Developing Countries* (Washington, DC: World Bank; mimeo).

Pyatt, G. (1988) 'A SAM approach to Modelling', *Journal of Policy Modelling*, vol. 10, no. 3.

Repetto, R., W. Magrath, M. Wells, C. Beer and F. Rossini (1989) *Wasting Assets: Natural Resources in the National Income Accounts* (Washington, DC: World Resources Institute).

Serafy, S. El (n.d.) *The Proper Calculation of Income from Depletable Natural Resources. United Nations Environment Programme – World Bank Symposium.*

United Nations (1979) *Future Directions for Work on a System of National Accounts* (New York: United Nations).

United Nations (1992) *Revised System of National Accounts, Provisional Version* (New York: United Nations).

9 Uncertainty as a Management Evaluation Tool for Infrastructure Projects

Kingsley E. Haynes, Fred Y. Phillips and Rajendra K. Srivastava

INTRODUCTION

Infrastructure policy is implemented through the planning for individual projects. Initial infrastructure planning is based on the simple calculus of rate of return on investment (ROI) or cost benefit (C/B) analysis, while infrastructure capacity expansion is a function of assessing existing capacity and forecasting future demand levels (Manne (1961; 1967), Meier (1977), Smith (1980), Freidenfelds (1981), Liebermann (1989)). However, the parameters of this calculus are embedded in substantial and pervasive uncertainty (Haynes and Li Qiangsheng, 1993). On the supply side, the future costs of existing infrastructure technology are made uncertain by volatility in the capital markets which affects interest rates and assumptions about appropriate discount levels (Haynes and Krmenec (1989), Haynes *et al.* (1984)). On the demand side, the increased reliance on user charges and their impact on the elasticity of demand increases uncertainty in forecasting usage levels. Further complicating uncertainties in supply and demand is the rapid pace of technological innovation, particularly in the telecommunications and transportation sectors, and the consequent impact on technological obsolescence and substitution. Witness the impact of telefax technology on the overnight letter delivery service and the effect of e-mail on both. Planning for periodic capacity expansion must assess stochasically growing demand with feedback effects in an environment of dynamic technological change (Srinivasan (1967), Kydland and Prescatt (1982), Bean *et al.* (1992)). These sources of uncertainty are complicated by public–private partnerships that have often been framed where the private

Figure 9.1 Infrastructure project evolution

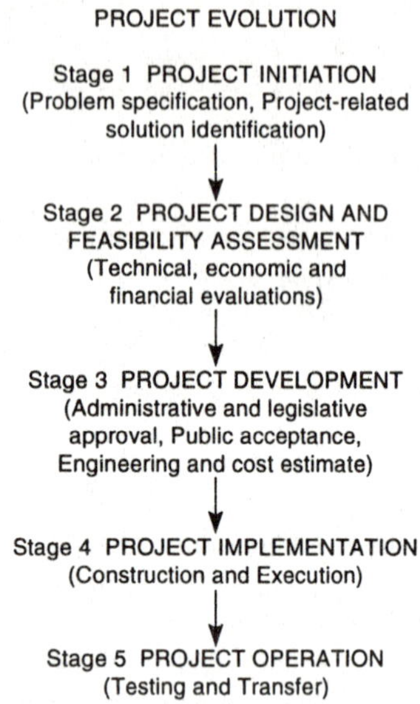

role is investment and profit and the public role is lowered cost of capital and risk reduction (Berthouex and Polkowski, 1970). Decision-making in this uncertain environment has been politically difficult, with elected leadership being overly timid about presenting infrastructure options to a tax-sensitive public (Peterson, 1991).

An infrastructure project generally goes through five classic stages of development (see Figure 9.1). The concept or the initiation of a project may come from a variety of sources including public sector planners and private entrepreneurial developers whether the project is a public investment, a private commercial venture or an industrial activity. Public and/or private demand is the main driving force behind such initiatives. Market assessment drives private investment while the public sector initiates projects on the basis of public demand and social, municipal or institutional needs (that is, larger societal considerations).

Each stage involves certain cost commitments and specific expenditures and at each stage there is a risk of stopping the project (Erlenkotter *et al.*, 1989). Changes are made throughout the process, and these are evaluated at each stage of the project's evolution. However, the irreversibility issue is of central concern at each stage of analysis (Henry (1974) Arrow and Fisher (1974), Baldwin (1982) and Bernanke (1983)).

EVALUATION

Evaluation research has become a fundamental part of planning and policy analysis and has evolved with the latter (Haveman, 1987). The role of evaluation research as part of policy analysis dates back, at least, to the planner Stuart Chapin (Chapin, 1947), who suggested that systematic serial experimentation was the only means open to gauge scientifically the impact of public policy intervention intended to affect human behaviour. This was an attempt to use social science methodology to provide guidelines for normative policy practice.

From the early 1900s onwards, through the Depression Era and the Second World War, the evaluation of public policy outputs has become an increasing part of policy analysis in the USA. Although experimentation and its consequent social evaluation procedures reached their height in President Lyndon Johnson's War and Poverty and Great Society Programs, they were not alone: economic evaluation procedures were also widely utilized as part of the system used by the Department of Defense during the same period. Since then, evaluation in general has become embedded in US government programmes first required by the executive branch and later institutionalized by Congress as part of new programme legislation.

Operationally, this has meant the design and articulation of an evaluation component associated with most federally funded projects. Although it is often unclear as to the impact of such evaluation requirements, they are now a specified element of most programmes. It is interesting, however, that although such evaluation requirements exist and are designed into most projects from the beginning, they are almost invariably executed ex-post facto (that is, purposively executed at the end of a project). This means that the results of the evaluation, if used at all, will only be relevant to a follow-on project or a very similar project carried out in a very similar circumstances (social, economic, geographic and so on) at a later point in time. Given the dynamism and complexity of the real world, this is a major limitation on the usefulness of evaluation research in public policy.

With the increasing sophistication of evaluation research and the predisposition to its inclusion in project design, it is curious how little evaluation is included in actual project execution or as an aid in project management and implementation. This appears to be partly a function of the social science methodology within which the paradigm of evaluation research developed. Such a paradigm generated a detached 'scientification' based on the hypothesis-testing paradigm of the scientific method, which is more tuned to reproducible clinical assessment with a primary focus on minimizing contamination through real-world interaction. This is in contrast to an interactive management (Warfield and Cardenas, 1994) or action theory (Haynes and Stubbings, 1987) paradigm interested in correcting the process and using evaluation information as a continuous feedback mechanism for project adjustment. This latter process of evaluation incorporates new information on a continuous basis in order to inform decisions. One of the most important decisions that needs to be informed effectively in real time are the Go/No Go decisions associated with the project evolution stages for large, irreversible capital investments of the infrastructure variety.

Project life cycle

It has been observed that in most new project developments (from initiation through operations) that costs are committed ahead of actual expenditures. Further, cost commitments rise most rapidly in early stages of project selection as design alternatives are discarded and options reduced. Although expenditures usually lag behind cost commitments in the early phases, they catch up at the final phase, where project implementation or facility construction is undertaken. Commitments and expenditures come together with project completion, hopefully balancing each other (Figure 9.2).

At each phase of a project's development cycle, management should attempt to reduce uncertainty by obtaining increasingly accurate estimates of costs and increasingly accurate measures of desired outcomes (McDonald and Siegel (1986), Majd and Pindyck (1987)). Clearly, a manager should not commit to costs at a rate that exceeds the rate of reduction in uncertainty. This is precisely why information is important and why each new commitment of costs is a Go/No Go decision. Further, we know that large past expenditures should not condition future commitments, especially when it is increasing certain that the future project will be unsuccessful.

Evaluation needs to be a continuous process in project development. It is not simply a post-project assessment exercise. Although great strides have been made in public management to incorporate evaluation mecha-

Figure 9.2 Commitments vs. expenditure

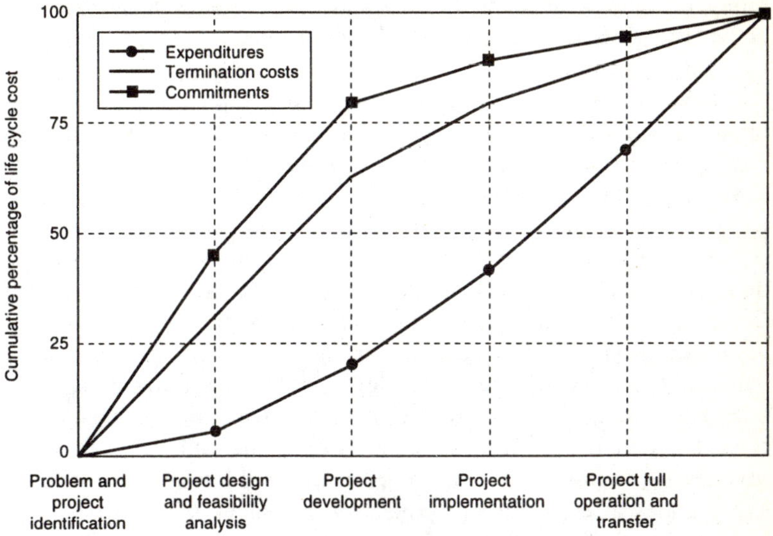

nisms, these are often set in a 'post-mortem' frame of reference. Such an evaluation process should not be abandoned. This is the 'ex-post' experiment mentality which dominates public-sector project thinking and is closely aligned with ensuring that the 'learning' part of 'learning by doing' is captured and made part of the record. However, it is equally important to utilize evaluation procedures as a fundamental part of the continuous process of project management. The fundamental purpose in such a process is uncertainty reduction.

The Go/No Go decision

The uncertainty to be reduced often centres around a specific goal or criteria, usually operationalized through such assessments as cost benefit (C/B) analysis or rate of return on investment (ROI) analysis. In cost benefit terms, a project usually requires a positive surplus of discounted benefits over discounted costs at a target level greater than one and greater than the cost–benefit ratio of alternative investments. In ROI terms, the returns must exceed a hurdle rate which is usually set at least as high as returns on alternative public – if not private – investments. When projects are first conceived and even after feasibility studies are executed there is usually considerable uncertainty (± 10 per cent) related to some elements in the analysis. When the uncertainty in various elements of a C/B assessment or ROI analysis are chained together, the resulting aggregate uncertainty can be very great (± 30 per cent to 40 per cent).

Over time, as a project becomes increasingly precise, these uncertainties are reduced by such steps as limiting goals, settling on a fixed design, and fully assessing levels of utilization. At each phase in project development these uncertainties should decrease until the C/B ratio or ROI are increasingly certain. Such certainty generates a decision point (Go/No Go) which relates committed costs to future costs and benefits or returns on investment. Even if the uncertainty around the expected C/B ratio or ROI drops to zero, it does not mean that the project should go forward. This is especially true if the uncertainty collapses to a mean C/B ratio or ROI below that of alternative investments (that is, below the hurdle rate). However, it is this reduction in uncertainty around a sufficiently high C/B ratio or ROI that allows us to move forward in creating new cost commitments and authorize continuing expenditures at each stage of project development. Classically, it has been observed that no risk-averse manager should commit funds faster than the rate of uncertainty reduction.

THE VALUE OF INFORMATION

At each phase, the decision-maker attempts to reduce project uncertainty by pursuing increasingly accurate estimates of life-cycle cost and the likelihood of success in the marketplace. Below we formalize this observation by elucidating the nature of committed costs and clarifying the associated terminology. We develop a measure of uncertainty that is pertinent to the Go/No Go decision for a project.

Some elements of committed costs (including leases and so on), are non-recoverable if the project is stopped. Other elements of committed costs (materials and so on) are possibly recoverable, but they are irreducible if the project proceeds. If we trace the sources of committed costs and expenditure in Figure 9.2 we find that this distinction is meaningful in terms of termination or 'bail out' costs.

Freezing designs and costs makes 'downstream' tasks more efficient, because engineers and managers know what it is that must be designed, built and linked to an existing system, and under what conditions these tasks must be executed. Contingency plans dealing with other design alternatives can be discarded. On the other hand, of course, committed costs reduce flexibility. They make less cash available for alternative analyses on investments that might come to light. If market estimates or consumer requirements change, costs sunk into the wrong design are not recoverable. Managers ask, 'What would it cost to terminate or bail out of this project?' The answer to this question is, 'The present value of all nonrecoverable costs.' This quantity, together with speed of response, are components of the project's flexibility.

Under sequential engineering, a prototype could be designed and tested before beginning the search for the best project production method. The costs of prototyping include not only the cost of designing, testing and economic analysis of the prototype. The prototyping activity includes looking ahead to implementation; the cost of investigating and deciding the mode of production is also part of the cost of prototyping. Under concurrent engineering, there is a pressure towards rapid building of the project, hence uncertain investigations and design 'lock in' occur early, therefore costs become committed and possibly expended earlier. If the project is terminated, these costs are not recovered. At all additional stages of the project development process, bail-out costs increase.

Clearly, maximum flexibility would result from holding design alternatives open as long as possible, and operating on a cash-and-carry basis, making the two curves of Figure 9.2 converge. But this strategy would eliminate the benefits of early cost commitment that were noted above, and is certainly unrealistic in almost all cases of investment for infrastructure development.

Postponing cost commitments

What is the relationship of cost commitment to uncertainty reduction? We shall argue that the prospect of reduced uncertainty is the only justification for postponing cost commitments. In other words, if no further uncertainty reduction is expected, all project cost could be committed at the earliest possible moment.

At many stages in the new project development process, data are collected and estimates made regarding demand management, infrastructure performance, building costs and alternatives, project schedule, alternative investments, and user response at different pricing levels. Such intelligence is critical to the management of the project development process. At each decision point the project manager may specify a value for the fraction of remaining project costs to be committed at that point. Committed costs as defined above are a different quantity from the expenditures management authorizes at each decision juncture. In the event of a subsequent project shutdown, some authorized monies that have not been committed or expended may be recoverable. Four additional choices are made at each decision point:

(i) 'Go', proceed directly to roll out of the project with no further analysis;
(ii) 'On' to the next study and evaluation point;
(iii) 'Skip' the next study and evaluation point and proceed directly to the final analysis but one, that is, conditions are identified under which a test may be bypassed (Urban and Katz (1975)); or
(iv) 'No Go', stop the project (for an expanded discussion of this, see Charnes *et al.*, 1966).

The first three alternatives imply continuing with all scheduled production, and other 'non-test' activities. Of course, for the fourth alternative, no further costs should be committed. For the purposes of analysis, we assume that no unscheduled tests or decisions are made. These conditions, plausibly reflecting management practice, justify the assertion that all remaining project costs may be committed immediately if no further intelligence is anticipated. Moreover, if the aforementioned benefits of cost commitment are significant and success is assumed, all remaining costs can be committed immediately. Figure 9.3 summarizes the possible trajectories of committed costs from a decision point 'i.' In the case of the 'On' decision, an additional decision on committed costs must be made at stage (i) +1. Other decision options determine the path of committed costs for longer time-spans.

UNCERTAINTY ANALYSIS IN PROJECT DEVELOPMENT

Rigorous and unambiguous measures of information and uncertainty have been available since the 1940s for dealing with events that are characterized by one or more probability distributions. What may be at issue in the analysis of a particular problem is the definition of the appropriate random variables and their distribution functions.

The problem addressed here is that of describing the rate at which an organization commits funds, relative to the rate at which it reduces uncertainty. The preceding section established informally that these two rates should be linked in some way. We note that the proposition is

Figure 9.3 Impact of Go-On–Skip–No-Go decision on committed costs

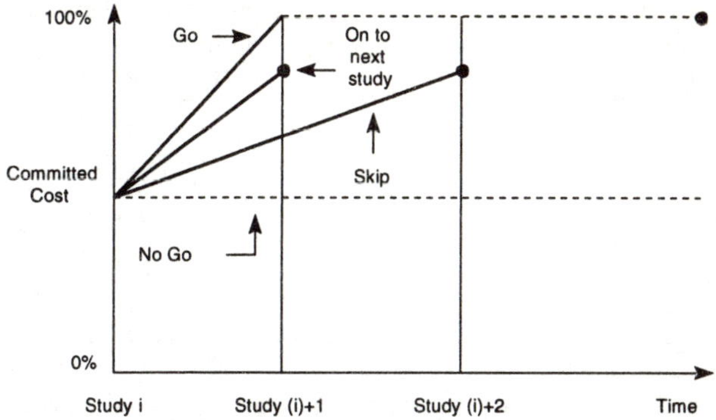

Source: Following Zirger and Maidique, 1990.

implicit in Akaike's (1973) construction of a decision-theoretic loss function from Kullback's (1959) information measure.

The entropy measure

'Committed cost' means money that must be expended at the scheduled (future) time, even if the project is cancelled today. In the language of project management or decision analysis, the level of committed cost at time t or stage n is the 'termination penalty' or 'bail-out cost'. In reality 'committed cost' is the maximum estimate of 'bail out costs' with real cancellation penalties being located between the two curves. (Figure 9.2)

Most public and private organizations maintain project histories from which the probability of bail-out at stage n can be computed, namely, as the proportion of projects that survive the stage n review. Table 9.1 displays an attrition pattern for a set of 116 new projects (from a Booz, Allen study cited by Cunningham and Cunningham, 1981). It may be read, for example, 'After economic analysis, 14 of the original 116 projects will have survived.' In the third column, the quantity q represents the updated probability of failure. The column on the far right of the table gives the entropy of the probability law, as defined in Equation (9.1):

$$H(q) = -q \ln q - (1 - q) \ln (1 - q) \qquad (9.1)$$

Table 9.1 Attrition pattern for 116 new projects

Development stage	*Number of surviving projects*	*q = probability of success, or of surviving this stage*	*H(q)*
Start	116	0.009	0.050
Project evaluation	24	0.042	0.173
Economic analysis	14	0.071	0.257
Project development	6	0.167	0.451
Implementation	2	0.500	0.693

We augment the table by assuming that, of the two projects that survive the final analyses and go to full designed and cost accounting, only one will later be built.

The entropy measure given in Equation (9.1), is often taken as an estimate of the uncertainty inherent in such a probability law (see Shannon, 1948). A simple illustration will demonstrate the use of $H(q)$. Suppose a completely prescient and truthful being tells us, at the prototyping stage, whether each given project will succeed or fail to be built. The average information content of this message is $H(q) = 0.050$. This small number means the message will almost always be, 'the project will fail and hence should not be built.' This is usually unsurprising and hence relatively uninformative. Contrast this with the higher information content of a perfect forecast delivered at the time of project execution, when prior success and failure probabilities are more equal (0.693).

Although we might regard the development process intuitively as decreasing uncertainty at each stage, Table 9.1 shows that, on the contrary, uncertainty increases. Prior experience tells us that 114 of every 116 project proposals will fail or will be rejected prior to building. Therefore, for an arbitrary project, we are almost certain that 'this won't work'. As we work to increase the odds of success for a particular project, uncertainty increases.

The above is a consequence of the fact that the graph of $H = p \ln p$ is concave over the range $0 \leq p \leq 1$, reaching a maximum when $p = 0.5$. We must look further for an information function that increases monotonically as the odds of project success progress from very small to very high.

ROI variance measure

Intelligence will be gathered at each stage shown in Table 9.1, making the project development process a multi-stage decision problem under uncertainty with recourse. That is, the Go/No Go decision is made repeatedly, using the latest updated intelligence information. Where the historical data of Table 9.1 refers to the aggregate of past projects, these updated intelligence data pertain to a particular project. It is important to note that whereas the $(q, 1 - q)$ law describes the binomial random variable 'success/failure', the project-specific intelligence refers to a different random variable, a measure of success that for the purpose of this illustration we shall assume is return on investment (ROI), the criterion could as well be cost–benefit ratio, payback rate or another traditional measure. Although advances in measurement such as data envelopment analysis (Charnes *et al.*, 1978) are now available for the multi-criteria evaluation of projects, here we stay with a single-criterion measure for simplicity of exposition and to clarify the relationship between cost commitment and uncertainty reduction.

The Go/No Go decision is made according to whether the ROI forecast exceeds a target value, possibly with a confidence margin. Each forecast may be stated as a point estimate with a variance, so that the Go/No Go decision can be conceptualized as in Figure 9.4 under a suitable assumption on the distribution of the ROI estimate. The probability of project survival, immediately prior to a test producing data like that of Figure 9.4, is the expected area of the distribution representing the shaded portion to the right of the RIO target probability. This is taken as the updated probability of success.

Each successive item of intelligence should reduce the variance of the expected ROI distribution. If this distribution is normal (Gaussian), its entropy is uniquely determined by its variance (Hastings and Peacock, 1975):

$$H(\text{ROI}) = -\ln\sqrt{(2\sigma^2\pi e)} \qquad (9.2)$$

As σ^2 decreases, H decreases, indicating a reduction in uncertainty. However, this uncertainty is uncertainty about ROI, not about the project success/failure question *per se*. The Equation (9.2) measure is therefore not suitable as a guide for scheduling the commitment of costs. To continue the illustration, suppose the ROI variance collapses to zero around a mean that is less than the target ROI. Uncertainty has been reduced maximally, yet it is clear that no further funds should be

Figure 9.4 ROI probability estimate

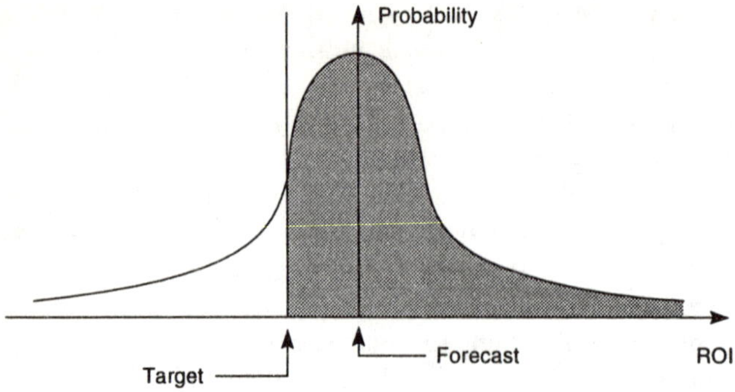

committed, that is, the decision-maker is certain that the rate of return will be less than that which is desired.

Directed divergence

Using the q from Table 9.1 as a prior distribution, and p as the updated probability of project success, the reduction in uncertainty provided by intelligence at stage n may be written as:

$$I(p : q) = p \ln (p/q) + (1 - p) \ln [(1 - p)/(1 - q)] \quad (9.3)$$

where p and q refer to stage n. This measure, $I(p{:}q)$, is from Kullback (1959), and is a generalization of the entropy measure in Equation (9.1), which represents the directed divergence of p against q.

Equation (9.3) may be interpreted as the information gain from an updated sample relative to a baseline sample. Akaike's (1973) principle, however, holds that the loss function should equal the directed divergence of the sample against the true distribution. For a single development project, there is no 'true' distribution; or, we might say, the distribution collapses to Prob{success} = 0 or Prob{success} = 1 when the decision response is known. This situation violates the 'absolute continuity' assumption of the directed divergence measure (see Kullback, 1959). More simply, for a discrete distribution, this means there will be zeros in the denominator.

Equation (9.3) highlights the fact that uncertainty is not reduced in an absolute way; it is reduced relative to some prior state of knowledge. Without bringing in additional considerations, we have no guidance as to how to specify the prior state of knowledge. For example, to measure reduction in total project uncertainty, must we use as a baseline only the 1-in-100 odds given at the top of the Table 9.1, or is there a way to use all the information given in Table 9.1? The odds of project success are not 1-in-100, and it does not relate directly to the odds of success. Thus, Equation (9.3) alone cannot be used to guide cost commitment.

Discriminant functions

Balachandra (1984) uses discriminant analysis in a retrospective study of 100 new development projects, and translates the result of the analysis into qualitative guidelines ('red light, yellow light, and green light' signals) for the Go/No Go decision. Zirger and Maidique (1990) also use discriminant analysis to find the organizational factors conducive to success of the development process. In this section we use the discriminant technique, with increased intelligence as independent variables, for a different purpose. This purpose is to arrive at an information function that will yield quantitative guidelines for the commitment of project costs.

Suppose that successful projects, in the past, have returned ROIs distributed as the density function $g(.)$, and failed projects have had a distribution of ROI $h(.)$. The latter distribution is constructed using the best estimated ROIs of projects that have been terminated prior to execution, and the actual ROI performance of projects that have failed after being built (that is, did not mean target returns). The specific functional forms of these distributions are immaterial at present.

According to Morrison (1976), the log likelihood ratio:

$$\lambda = \ln [g(\cdot)/h(\cdot)] \tag{9.4}$$

is a sufficient function for discriminating between the two distributions, based on an observation vector x of study results. In the Kullback (1959) theory, λ is equal to the information provided by x favouring the hypothesis $H_1 : x \sim g(x)$ over the hypothesis $H_2 : x \sim h(x)$. That is, the discriminant function in Equation (9.4) is the optimal way of classifying a project either as a member of the population of 'projects that will succeed' or as a member of the population of 'projects that will fail'. The decision rule is, 'x was generated by a member of the successful population if $\lambda \leq 1$'.

The usual assumption that g and h are continuous density functions over the interval $(-\infty, \infty)$ implies that, for example, a member of the 'successful' population may have an ROI less than the target value. In reality, projects may succeed or fail for reasons other than ROI performance. Thus this representation is not unreasonable.

CONCLUSIONS

Joint consideration of the three curves 'committed cost', 'expenditure' and 'information gain' can illuminate the relationship between flexibility and risk. The relationships drawn in this paper can elucidate the risk behaviour of organizations, aid the comparison of new project development procedures, and provide operational (normative) guidelines on how managers should commit project costs.

The above mathematical formulation addresses committed costs, and does not deal explicitly with the wider category of determined costs. Costs are 'determined' in this wider sense when design decisions lock in materials and project production technologies. The issue associated with 'determined costs' is that changing materials costs, market requirements, alternatives, and technologies may reduce the acceptability of a current design. By including technological scanning within the scope of project intelligence, and by including technology assessment in the ROI estimate for a current design, the mathematical model offered by this chapter can address technological risk without modification.

The overt problem in new project development is to increase the 'hit rate', that is, the proportion of infrastructure projects that become successes in terms of meetings their service or ROI goals. A collateral problem, no less important, is reducing the cost of failures. It is the latter problem to which the present research is most applicable. This chapter has discussed the nature of committed and determined costs, and quantified their relationship to the reduction of project uncertainty. We have emphasized the role of project intelligence for considering marketing and production factors jointly in project evaluation. We have shown that the ideas developed can indicate the relationship between cost commitment and risk behaviour of the organization and provide guidance for operational decisions within a project management situation. We close with a call for the careful collection of project-specific data for further analysis of these ideas.

Finally, it seems that the lesson for developing countries is that information matters, and that reduction in uncertainties is critical to good project decisions as well as to management. Hence investment in new and better data has important payoffs, for public and private sector investors.

References

Akaike, H. (1973) 'Information Theory and an Extension of the Maximum Likelihood Principle', in B. N. Petron and F. Csaki (eds), *2nd Annual International Symposium on Information Theory*, pp. 267–81 (Budapest: Akademiai Kiado).

Arrow, K. J. and A. C. Fisher (1974) 'Environmental Preservation, Uncertainty and Irreversibility', *Quarterly Journal of Economics*, vol. 88, pp. 12–319.

Balachandra, R. (1984) 'Critical Signals for Making Go/No Go Decisions in New Product Development', *Journal of Product Innovation Management*, vol. 1, no. 2.

Baldwin, C. Y. (1982) 'Optimal Sequential Investment when Capital is Not Readily Reversible', *Journal of Finance*, vol. 37, pp. 763–82.

Bean, J. D., J. L. Higle and R. L. Smith (1992) 'Capacity Expansion Under Stochastic Demand', *Operations Research*, vol. 40, pp. 5210–5216.

Bernanke, B. (1983) 'Irreversibility, Uncertainty and Cyclical Investment', *Quarterly Journal of Economics*, vol. 98, pp. 85–106.

Berthouex, P. M. and L. B. Polkowski (1970) 'Design Capacities to Accommodate Forecast Uncertainties', *Journal of Sanitary Engineering Div ASCE*, vol. 96, pp. 1183–210.

Blanchard, B. S. and W. J. Fabrycky (1990) *Systems Engineering and Analysis* (2nd edn) (Englewood Cliffs, NJ: Prentice Hall).

Chapin, F. S. Jr. (1947) *Urban Land Use Planning* (Urbana, Ill.: University of Illinois Press).

Charnes, A., W. W. Cooper, J. K. DeVoe, and D. B. Learner (1966) 'DEMON: Decision Mapping Via Optimum Go/No Go Networks – A Model for Marketing New Products', *Management Science*, vol. XII, no. 11.

Charnes, A., W. W. Cooper and E. Rhodes (1978) 'Measuring the Efficiency of Decision Making Units', *European Journal of Operations Research*, vol. 2, pp. 429–44.

Chenery, H. B. (1952) 'Overcapacity and the Acceleration Principle', *Econometrica*, vol. 20, pp. 1–52.

Cunningham, W. H. and I. C. M. Cunningham (1981) *Marketing: A Managerial Approach* (Cincinnati, Ohio: South-Western Publishing Co.).

Erlenkotter, D., S. P. Sethi and N. Okada (1989) 'Planning for Surprise: Water Resources Development Under Demand and Supply Uncertainty, I: The General Model', *Management Sciences*, vol. 35, pp. 149–63.

Freidenfelds, J. (1981) *Capacity Expansion: Analysis of Simple Models With Applications* (New York: North-Holland).

Hastings, N. A. J. and J. B. Peacock (1975) *Statistical Distributions* (London: Butterworth).

Haveman, R. H. (1987) 'Policy Analysis and Evaluation Research After Twenty Years', *Policy Studies Journal*, vol. 16, no. 2, pp. 191–218.

Haynes, K. E. and A. Krmenec (1989) 'A Sensitivity Assessment of Uncertainty in Infrastructure Expansion', *Annals of Regional Science*, vol. 31, pp. 301–15.

Haynes, K. E. and Li Qiangsheng (1993) 'Policy Analysis and Uncertainty: Lessons from the IVHS Transportation Development Process', *Journal of Computers, Environment and Urban Systems*, vol. 17, pp. 28–35.

Haynes, K. E. and R. G. Stubbings (1987) 'Planning and Philosophy: The Anthropology of Action', *Journal of Planning Education and Research*, vol. 6, no. 2, pp. 75–85.

Haynes, K. E. *et al.* (1984) 'Planning for Capacity Expansion: Stochastic Process and Game Theoretic Approaches', *Socio-Economic Planning Sciences*, vol. 18, pp. 195–205.

Henry, D. (1974) 'Investment Decisions Under Uncertainty: the Irreversible Effect', *American Economic Review*, vol. 64, pp. 1006–12.

Kullback, S., (1959) *Information Theory and Statistics* (New York: John Wiley) pp. 196–207.

Kydland, F. E. and E. G. Prescatt (1982) 'Time to Build and Aggregate Fluctuations', *Econometrica*, vol. 50, pp. 1345–70.

Lieberman, M. B. (1989) 'Capacity Utilization: Theoretical Models and Empirical Results', *European Journal of Operational Research*, vol. 40, pp. 155–68.

Majd, S. and R. S. Pindyck (1987) 'Time to Build, Option Value, and Investment Decisions', *Journal of Financial Economics*, vol. 18, pp. 7–27.

Manne, A. S. (1961) 'Capacity Expansion and Probabilistic Growth', *Econometrica*, vol. 29, pp. 632–49.

Manne, A. S. (1967) *Investment for Capacity Expansion: Size, Location, and Time-Phasing* (Cambridge, Mass.: MIT Press).

McDonald, R. and D. Siegel (1986) 'The Value of Waiting to Invest', *Quarterly Journal of Economics*, vol. 101, pp. 707–27.

Meier, P. M. (1977) 'Game Theory Approach to Design Uncertainty', *Journal of the Environmental Engineering Div ASCE*, vol. 103, pp. 99–111.

Morrison, D. F. (1976) *Multivariate Statistical Methods* (2nd edn) (New York: McGraw-Hill).

Munnel, A. H. (1990) 'How Does Public Infrastructure Affect Regional Economic Performance?', *New England Economic Review*, September, pp. 11–23.

National Science Foundation (1990) 'International Workshop on Concurrent Engineering Design', IC^2 Institute, University of Texas at Austin.

Peterson, G. E. (1991) 'Historical Perspectives on Infrastructure Investment: How Did We Get Where We Are?', Conference on Infrastructure Needs, Project Report, The Urban Institute, Washington, DC.

Robert, K. and M. L. Weitzman (1981) 'Funding Criteria for Research, Development and Exploration Projects', *Econometrica*, vol. 49, pp. 1261–88.

Shannon, C. E. (1948) 'A Mathematical Theory of Communication', *Bell System Technical Journal*, vol. 37, pp. 10–21.

Smith, R. L. (1980) 'Optimal Expansion Policies for the Deterministic Capacity Problem', *Engineering Economics*, vol. 25, pp. 149–59.

Srinivasan, T. N. (1967) 'Geometric Rate of Growth of Demand', in A. Mannel (ed.), *Investments for Capacity Expansion: Size, Location, and Time-Phasing* (Cambridge, Mass.: MIT Press) pp. 151–9.

Urban, G. L. and G. M. Katz (1975) 'Pre-Test-Market Models: Validation and Managerial Implications', *Journal of Marketing Research*, vol. 20, pp. 221–34.

Warfield, J. N. and R. Cardenas (1994) *Handbook of Interactive Management* (Ames, Iowa: Iowa State University Press).

Weitzman, M., W. Newey and M. Robin (1981) 'Sequential R&D Strategy for Synfuels', *Bell Journal of Economics*, vol. 12, pp. 574–90.

Zirger, B. J. and M. A. Maidique (1990) 'A Model of New Product Development: An Empirical Test', *Management Science*, vol. 36, no. 7, pp. 867–83.

10 Simulating Regional Systems: A System Dynamics Approach

Colin Lee

INTRODUCTION

The use of quantitative models to develop understanding, prepare forecasts and explore policy options in the context of urban and regional development remains a popular activity, although rather more so in the academic community than in the planning profession. However, the history of the application of formal models to policy problems does not produce great confidence. Objective evaluation of the use of models in policy-making is complicated by the fact that, as a former colleague once said, computer models are like children: most people tend to like their own better than others', some look a lot better than they behave, and when they are bad they are horrid! This chapter starts from the perspective that computer modelling, simulation and policy analysis promise to realize their greatest potential when they are combined with understanding and application of the concept of feedback. It discusses a particular approach to the modelling and simulation of systems that is based on this concept, and which appears to have much to offer, both to the academic investigator and to the practising professional. System dynamics is a methodology for creating models or representations of real-world systems, in order to study their behaviour with a view to controlling or improving system behaviour. The system dynamics approach has been summarized as 'observing and identifying problematic behaviour of a system over time and creating a valid diagrammatic representation (or model) of the system, capable of reproducing (by computer simulation) the existing system behaviour and of facilitating the design of improved system behaviour' (Wolstenholme (1990) p. 2). The method was originally developed by Forrester at the Massachusetts Institute of Technology, as a means of analysing complex problems in industrial management (Forrester, 1961, 1969). Although the original applications were largely industrial, the subject area has widened considerably, to the extent that it is now claimed that 'the scope of application has become extremely wide, covering most traditional academic disciplines of study, but with a strong emphasis on socio-economic areas' (Wolstenholme, 1990). System dynamics now has its own international society and journal (the *System Dynamics Review*), and the range of applications continues to expand.

THE CHARACTERISTICS OF URBAN AND REGIONAL SYSTEMS

One of the most important considerations in developing or selecting a model for use in a planning context is the ability of the model to reproduce the phenomena or problems in which the planner is interested. As a preliminary to the discussion of the system dynamics approach, it is therefore appropriate to start with a review of the major characteristics of regional systems, in order to be aware of the requirements that a model of regional systems should be capable of satisfying. A region can be regarded as a complex socioeconomic system. The essential characteristics of such a system, in so far as they affect our ability to reproduce their behaviour in a simulation model, are:

1. They contain a large number of variables, many of which must be preserved in disaggregated form if the essential interrelationships among them are to be preserved.
2. Many of the variables and subsystems are connected by feedback relationships, and it is these interconnections which give rise to the dynamic behaviour of regional systems. Decisions and events cannot be considered in isolation, for the sequence of individual, corporate and public decisions changes the environment, which then provides the information for future decisions and actions. It is unlikely that any attempt to reproduce (model) the behaviour of regional systems which does not incorporate the important feedback mechanisms can ever be more than partially successful, because the system as a whole will behave in ways that cannot be deduced from an examination of the parts separately.
3. Not only do the components of regional systems interact, the interaction and feedback operate over time, and the way in which they operate is likely to change with time; moreover, there are invariably delays, or lags, in the ways in which the system components

react to change. A basic requirement of a realistic simulation therefore must be the ability to incorporate time as a variable within the structure of the model, in order to be able to trace the performance or behaviour of the system over time.

4. The majority of relationships in social and economic systems are non-linear. Whereas it is possible in some cases to make linear approximations to non-linear behaviour, the restrictions of such approximations impose severe limits on the ability of models to reproduce accurately system behaviour, as much of the system behaviour that is important will be the result of non-linear phenomena. The ability to handle non-linearities must therefore be regarded as an important requirement of a regional systems model.

To summarize the discussion, the desirable characteristics of a model of socioeconomic systems – including regions – are:

(i) the capacity to handle large numbers of variables;
(ii) the ability to deal explicitly with the interactions between variables, and the feedback characteristics of real-world relationships;
(iii) the ability to reproduce dynamic behaviour and incorporate time-varying relationships; and
(iv) the ability to deal with non-linear relationships.

SYSTEM DYNAMICS

There are four key characteristics of the system dynamics approach:

1. As the name suggests, the approach is dynamic, not static. It is concerned with the behaviour of complex systems, and the way this behaviour varies with the passage of time. The approach recognizes, and makes explicit provision for, delays in the transmission of information or material between the elements of a system.
2. The basic element of a system dynamics model is the feedback loop. It therefore not only recognizes the importance of feedback in systems: the modelling approach is in fact based on this concept.
3. The system dynamics approach is essentially concerned with system behaviour in as full a way as is necessary to describe a particular phenomenon. Where subsystems are modelled, they are explicitly related to one another within a 'systems' framework.
4. Because system dynamics models depend on simulation rather than

on analytic solutions, they are capable of dealing with large numbers of variables, and with non-linear relationships, without exceeding the capabilities of readily-accessible computers.

There are numerous definitions of system dynamics. Forrester, in his original formulation of the methodology, describes it as: 'The investigation of the information-feedback character of industrial systems and the use of models for the design of improved organizational form and guiding policy' (Forrester (1961) p. 13). A review of system dynamics and its relevance to urban and regional planning describes it as 'a simulation methodology which has been specifically developed for studying the dynamic behaviour of complex social systems' (Newcastle System Dynamics Group. (1973) p. 4). Recent workers in the field emphasize that there has been a move away from an obligatory use of quantified simulation models towards an increasing recognition of the usefulness of the diagramming phase of the methodology (Wolstenholme (1982, 1990), Wolstenholme and Coyle (1983), Morecroft (1988)). Although qualitative system dynamics is undoubtedly a useful tool for understanding aspects of system structure with a minimum investment of time and effort, the development of quantitative system dynamics models provides a more rigorous (and perhaps more useful) tool for exploring system behaviour and testing alternative policies, and it is the use of quantitative system dynamics models that is the focus of this paper.

The distinction between structure and behaviour

There are two important concepts in relation to system dynamics models, namely *structure* and *behaviour*. The distinction – and the relationship – between the two is important. Structure is concerned with the arrangement and interrelationships between the elements of a system at a given point in time. Behaviour is concerned with the way in which elements of the system interact and change over time. Fundamental to the system dynamics approach is the view that system behaviour is primarily determined by system structure. In system dynamics terms the structure of systems is described by feedback loops. The concept of feedback lies at the heart of the system dynamics approach. The proponents of system dynamics argue that one of its greatest strengths is its ability to capture the important feedback relationships that many other approaches cannot easily incorporate.

Figure 10.1 Feedback loops in a simple system

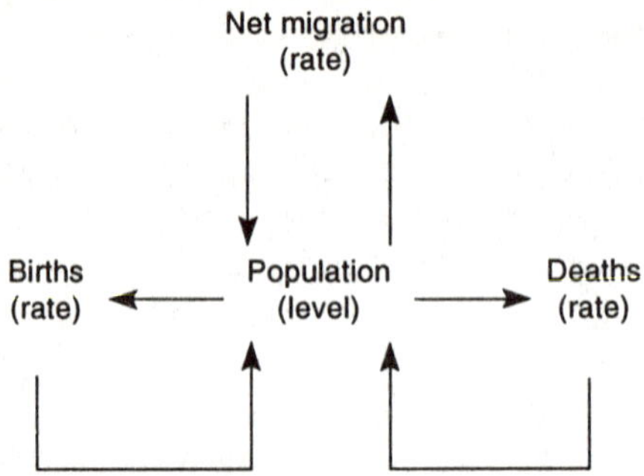

The importance of feedback

Most succinctly, 'feedback is the transmission and return of information' (Weiner (1961) p. 96). A *feedback loop* is a closed sequence of causes and effects, a closed path of action and information. An interconnected set of feedback loops is a *feedback system.* In terms of socioeconomic systems, feedback loops are typically responsible for determining the nature of system behaviour. Population growth, for example, can be described in terms of feedback loops between population and births, deaths and net migration (see Figure 10.1). The larger the population, the more births there will be; and the more births there are, the more people there will be. Similarly, the bigger the population, the more deaths there will be; and the more deaths, the smaller the population.

In system dynamics there are two basic types of variable within a feedback loop – *levels* and *rates*. Level variables describe the condition of the system at one point in time – the state of the system. Rate variables describe the flows that cause the levels to change (this is directly analogous to the economists' distinction between stocks and flows). For example, in the simple population system shown in Figure 10.1, the state of the system is represented by population, a level, which changes in response to three rates – births, deaths, and net migration. It is the mutual interaction between the feedback loops which determine changes in the state of the system, that is, the level of population.

Although the simplest type of feedback system includes only one level and one rate, realistic models of social and economic systems will consist of a very complex multiple-loop structure, with information from many levels determining action at several points within the system. One of the strengths of the system dynamics approach is that it enables complex relationships to be described and incorporated in dynamic models. The degree of complexity with which system dynamics models can cope is illustrated in the regional system dynamics models that are reviewed later.

Model formulation

To operationalize a model requires a precise statement of relationships, which, in a typical system dynamics exercise involves two stages – the construction of a flow diagram and the formulation of equations that allow the dynamic behaviour of the model to be simulated.

The advantages of representing models in this way are:

(i) the flow diagram is a useful means of understanding and communicating the detailed structure of a model; and
(ii) because each element in the flow diagram is directly equivalent to an equation, it eases the process of developing formal equations.

The equations in system dynamics models describe the processes by which rates of change lead to the accumulation or depletion of quantities stored in levels. In mathematical terms, it is based on calculus, and levels are the integration of rates over a period of time. However, system dynamics uses simulation based on difference equations to calculate the changes in levels as opposed to using analytical methods of solution based on calculus. Changes in levels are calculated simply by multiplying the rates of change by the elapsed time:

$$\text{LEVEL}_{\text{now}} = \text{LEVEL}_{\text{past}} + (\text{intervening time}) * (\text{rate of change})$$

The special-purpose simulation languages that have been developed for system dynamics deal with this process of change by the use of subscripts representing time periods. For example, a simple population model incorporating only natural change (births and deaths) would be represented as:

$$\text{POP} \cdot K = \text{POP} \cdot J + DT * (\text{BIRTHS} \cdot JK - \text{DEATHS} \cdot JK)$$

where

POP · *K*	=	population now
POP · *J*	=	population one time interval ago
DT	=	length of intervening time period
BIRTHS · *JK*	=	births over the time interval *JK*
DEATHS · *JK*	=	deaths over the time interval *JK*

To simulate the behaviour of a dynamic feedback system over time, the program calculates the value of each equation in the model, one time interval at a time, for the whole of the simulation period.

Model validation

Model validation has been one of the most controversial areas of debate in relation to the system dynamics approach. Obviously, once output has been produced from a simulation model, the modeller – and certainly the client – will want to know how much confidence can be placed in the model output. Not surprisingly, therefore, model validation is regarded as one of the key stages (perhaps the most important) in the model development process. Unfortunately, it is also perhaps the most difficult, with different schools of modelling even disagreeing about what good validation is or ought to be. One view is that 'No model has ever been or ever will be thoroughly validated. . . . "useful", "illuminating", or "inspiring confidence" are more apt descriptors applying to models than "valid" (Greenberger *et al.*, 1976). There are clearly general difficulties in attempting to validate any kind of formal model. In the case of system dynamics models these are compounded by the conventional (and controversial) system dynamics view of validation, and it is undoubtedly the system dynamicist's approach to model validation that has been the cause of so much hostility towards the methodology. For example, the best-known examples of system dynamics models outside the business/management area are *Urban Dynamics* (Forrester, 1969), *World Dynamics* (Forrester, 1971) and the *Limits to Growth* study (Meadows *et al.*, 1972). All these attained extremely high levels of exposure, and none made any attempt at formal validation. They relied instead on the 'traditional' system dynamics point of view that the main test of validity for a model is whether or not it is capable of reproducing the 'general mode of behaviour' of the situation being studied.

The majority of modellers from other traditions regard this approach as cavalier, to say the least, and it is not surprising that many have been reluctant to consider the potential of the system dynamics approach because of what they regard as a totally inadequate approach to model validation.

However, some system dynamicists have begun to adopt a more rigorous approach to model validation, without sacrificing the traditionally broad perspective of their discipline. One of the foremost practitioners in the field, for example, emphasizes the importance of comparing the results of model simulations with historical data (perhaps the biggest single bone of contention between the system dynamics and other modelling schools):

> We now routinely engage in extensive comparison of simulation results with historical times series, applying demanding standards of accuracy. . . . We are increasingly confident in our models as forecasting tools. I now believe that it is unnecessary and counter-productive to make excuses for our methodology with statements such as 'System dynamics models are not developed for forecasting, they are tools for understanding problems.' Our models can serve both purposes. (Weill, 1980)

This dramatic change in posture on the part of system dynamics practitioners is long overdue, and has been partly a response to overwhelming criticism, and partly a function of the development of appropriate statistical methods for the validation of complex dynamic models (Peterson (1980), Sterman (1984), Wolstenholme (1990) p. 60). It is particularly welcome because if it becomes more widely accepted, it will help to remove perhaps the strongest theoretical and practical arguments against the use of the methodology for policy analysis.

A REVIEW OF SOME APPLICATIONS

The purpose of this section is to review a number of applications of system dynamics methodology for regional analysis and planning. The focus of the review is less on the models themselves than on the illustration of key points relevant to the practical application of the system dynamics method. The selection of models for review has been limited to practical applications that demonstrate clearly the usefulness and potential of the methodology. The objectives, the causal structure, the level of detail and the ultimate use of each model are described first. This is followed by a brief commentary on the utility and validity of the models.

Susquehanna River Basin Model

This was a pioneering study, the first attempt at using system dynamics outside the industrial management field for which it had been developed. The Batelle Memorial Institute at Cleveland was commissioned to undertake a study of the Susquehanna River Basin by ten local electric power companies. The terms of reference were to study the economy of the area and to help define the role that water resources might play in the development of this economy. The study was intended to aid the formulation of development plans by the sponsors, and to assist in the appraisal of the plans of other agencies. For these purposes, economic and water-use projections were required under a variety of alternative assumptions. The model that was developed therefore had a dual role – to produce forecasts for planning purposes, and to simulate the effects of policy decisions on the river basin. An additional objective of the study was to consider alternative methods of model-building that might be used for these purposes, and to select and develop the most suitable approach.

Model description

A review of regional projection methods led to the choice of a continuous simulation approach because of its ability to handle many different forms of relationship and variables, especially those with dynamic and feedback properties. It was considered that this approach 'placed least restrictions on problem representation' (Hamilton *et al.* (1969) p. 92).

The boundaries of the river basin were defined, for modelling purposes, according to hydrological criteria, subject to the constraint of maintaining a homogenous economic region. Eight subregions were defined, so that the Susquehanna River flowed through each one, and so that they were relatively independent labour markets and trading areas, based on population census data, and retail and wholesale trade statistics. The main sectors of the model and the links between them are shown in Figure 10.2. The demographic and employment sectors are connected by feedback loops, but are connected to the water and income sectors without feedback. Both the demographic and the employment sectors are considerably disaggregated.

Population is divided into six age groups, each affected by births, deaths and migration, but, curiously, no distinction is made between males and females. Population in the working age groups provides the labour

Figure 10.2 The structure of the Susquehanna River Basin Model

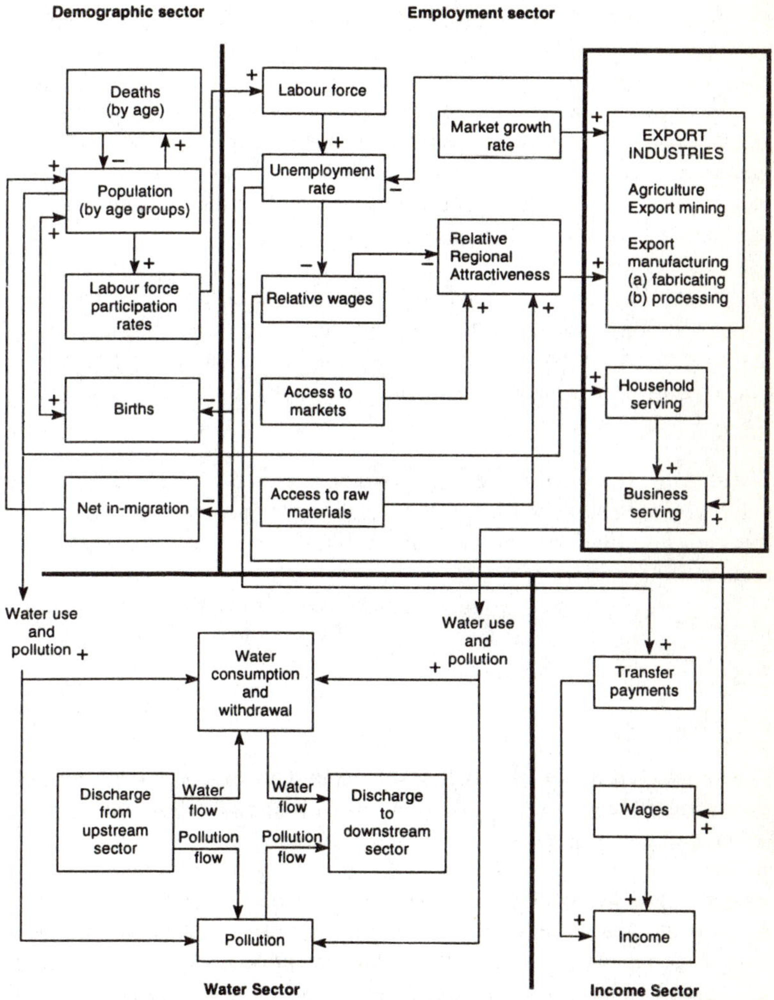

force, the size of which is determined by the application of labour force participation rates. These in turn are influenced by unemployment rates. The latter also influence migration, thereby providing two strong feedback loops between the demographic and employment sectors. A further, perhaps more questionable, link is provided by the impact of unemployment rates on births.

Economic activity is represented by employment, which is disaggregated into twelve categories, each of which falls into either an export or a service grouping, in the terms of economic base theory. Export industries grow in relation both to exogenous forces and to the relative attractiveness of the region. Relative attractiveness depends upon accessibility to markets and raw materials, and upon local wage rates. Wage rates are assumed to decrease as unemployment rises and, in an important feedback loop, increase as the proportion of export industry employment rises. Employment in service industries depends on both population levels and other employment.

The water sector is concerned with the volume and purity of the water flowing through each subregion. These features are related to the quantity and quality of discharge upstream, and to the consumption and pollution arising from subregional demand for water from both householders and employers.

The income sector adds transfer payments to wages derived from the employment sector. Neither the water nor the income sector includes feedback to other sectors. In addition, there are small sectors for recreation and power.

The complexity of the model structure and the degree of disaggregation combine to make a very large model – the final version of the model contained 1800 equations.

Use of the model

The model builders claimed that the modelling exercise was successful, in that it was used by its sponsors to assist in policy formulation in the following ways:

(i) Projections for fifty years ahead, to assist the sponsors in understanding and auditing the reports of others concerned with the river basin's economy. The projections provided information about population, employment, migration and unemployment rates, and per capita income.
(ii) The analysis of the impact of alternative systems of river works. The model was used to test three programmes for waterworks construction, and the model output was used to help in the choice between them.
(iii) The study and definition of the role of water in the development of the local economy.

The model was used to test the adequacy of water resources, both overall and at critical points, under a wide variety of assumptions concerning economic growth and water consumption rates, and to examine the effects upon water quality. In addition to meeting its objectives in this way, the model proved very flexible and easy to use, despite its size. Over 200 simulations were carried out. It is also worth noting that the model was fairly soundly based in terms of data, as extensive efforts went into data collection and validation. Also, unlike Urban Dynamics and World Dynamics, attention was given to model validation, both in terms of parameter estimation and the testing of model output against historical data, although the planned range of tests had to be curtailed because of the lack of relevant historical data.

Regional utility simulation model

This case study is concerned with a regional utility simulation model (RUSIM) developed by Development Analysis Associates to examine long-term water and power demands in Saudi Arabia (Development Analysis Associates, 1978). The work was carried out for the Saline Water Conversion Corporation (SWCC), the government agency responsible for the provision of desalinated water supplies to Saudi Arabia's rapidly growing towns and cities.

Because of the rapid growth in national income following the quadrupling of the price of crude oil in the early 1970s, major changes in economic structure and the distribution of population were expected. In a country with no rivers and limited groundwater supplies, availability of water is a major constraint to economic and urban growth. The principal strategy adopted to tackle this problem is the development of large-scale desalination plants to provide for industrial and urban development. It was to help in the forecasting and planning of the demand for desalinated water that the SWCC commissioned the development of a regional forecasting model.

Model description

The causal loop structure of the model is illustrated in Figure 10.3. The regional structure of the model is based upon the recognition of separate 'demand clusters' based on three settlement categories – cities and growth centres, towns, and villages, reflecting the different growth patterns of each of these types of settlements. Figure 10.3 shows the structure of a single region. The region's connections with the rest of

Figure 10.3 The structure of the Regional Utility Simulation Model

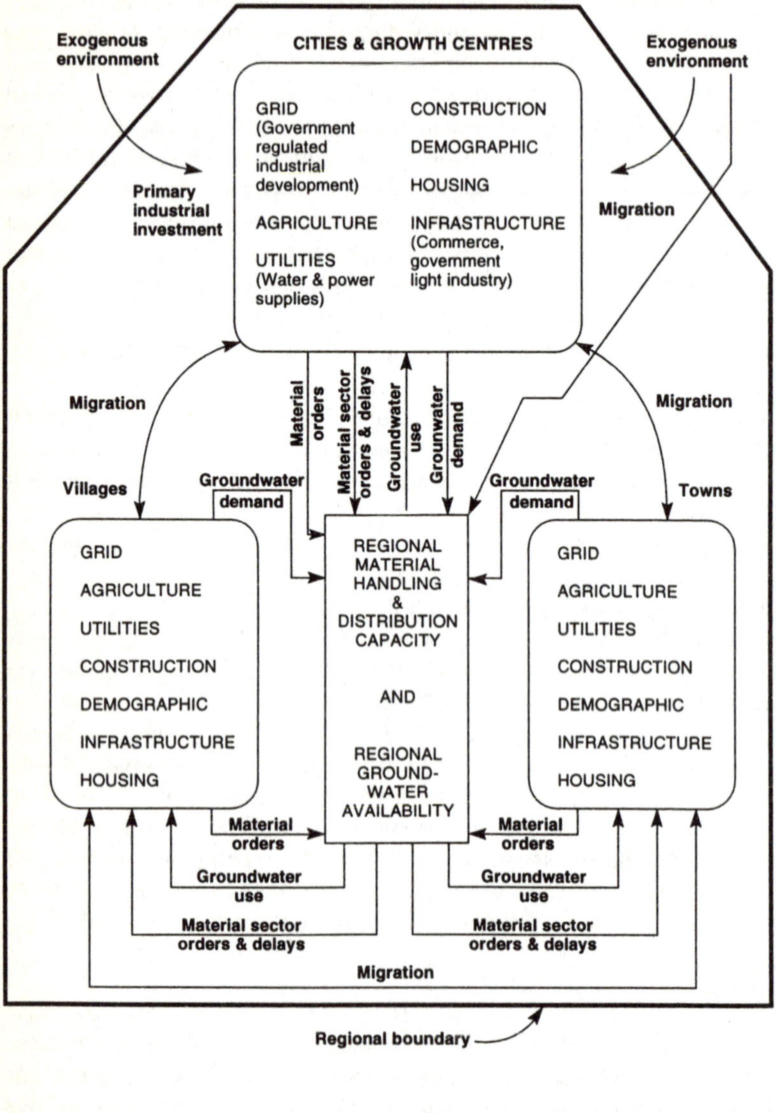

the country (and the world!) take place through flows of people (migration), materials and government funds for development. Within the region, the model recognizes three types of 'demand clusters' – cities and growth centres, towns and villages. The settlements in each type of cluster interact with each other through flows of migration and information.

Some of the key interactions within the region take place via a regional sector which is concerned with regional materials handling and distribution, and with regional groundwater supplies. These sectors are modelled separately because they represent services/resources that cannot easily be divided between the clusters. The material handling sector, for example, typically includes ports, airports and roads, which provide a service for the region as a whole rather than individual settlements. Similarly, the groundwater resources are not confined to single settlements.

Each settlement cluster within the model has a similar structure, comprising seven sectors:

1. Agriculture.
2. Housing.
3. Construction.
4. Demographic (population).
5. Infrastructure.
6. Primary industrial development.
7. Utilities.

Although each settlement cluster has the same seven components, their relative importance differs, reflecting the differences in economic structure between the clusters. These sectors are connected by flows of information and materials, for example, orders for construction, labour, services, housing, and water and power requirements. The model structure recognizes explicitly the delays that occur between the placing of orders and the flow of goods, equipment and people.

The demographic sector provides for changes in population increase arising from natural change and migration. It has three age groups, which are subject to age-specific rates for mortality, fertility and migration. Migration rates depend on the relative attractiveness of the cluster based on the assessment of seven 'quality of life' indicators:

(i) job availability;
(ii) perceived business opportunities;
(iii) availability of housing;
(iv) adequacy of water supply;
(v) adequacy of electricity supply;
(vi) utility distribution networks; and
(vii) availability of government and private sector services.

The housing sector simulates the processes of construction, utility connection, ageing and demolition. Information on the housing stock is combined with demographic information to determine residential water and power demand. Similarly, the demands on the infrastructure, construction and material handling sectors are influenced by changes in population and housing.

The Government Regulated Industrial Development (GRID) sector provides the main stimulus to growth and change within the model, in recognition of the key role of government in the promotion of industrial and economic development. It includes the planning, construction and operation of government-financed industrial complexes as well as individual projects. The development of public-sector projects in turn stimulates the general economy of the settlements and regions that are the beneficiaries of public investment.

The agriculture and groundwater sectors are closely linked, and are designed to generate information about the competition for limited groundwater supplies between agriculture and urban and industrial development. This information is used to develop alternative policies for the development of desalination capacity to supply non-agricultural demands. In the absence of supplies of desalinated water, it is assumed that non-agricultural users have priority. The availability of water supplies has a significant effect on the patterns of migration between settlements.

Use of the model

The RUSIM model was used by the consultants to generate regional water and electricity demand projections over a 20-year period. It was also used to explore the effects of a wide range of government policies affecting urban and industrial growth, and therefore influencing the demand for water and power. Among the most important of the policies tested were planned industrial growth; the location, scale and timing of housing development; foreign worker migration and settlement; the provision of public services and infrastructure; groundwater extraction and the timing, location and scale of the provision of desalination plants.

The output from the regional simulation model is used as the input to a supply optimization model which determines the least-cost way to meet the projected demands. Together, the suite of models provide the basic information for one of the major capital expenditure programme in the country.

Although it was not possible to attempt comparison of the model forecasts with historical data (because there was no historical data!), the model-building exercise was notable for the effort that went into data collection so that the model parameters could be soundly based. A series of household and industrial surveys were carried out over a two-year period in order to provide knowledge about water and electric power consumption, as well as the economic, demographic and sociological characteristics that influence consumption patters. Moreover, the study recognized the need to update this information on a regular basis, because of the dynamic characteristics of Saudi society in the face of rapid economic and urban development.

Modelling for population and sustainable development (ECCO)

The third and final case study is of a different character, but is of sufficient interest in terms of current and future concerns to merit inclusion. It is not a single case study, but a general approach to the modelling of population and development problems which has been applied in a number of case studies. The approach is known as Enhancement of Carrying Capacity Options (ECCO) and it has been developed since the early 1980s by staff at the Centre for Human Ecology at the University of Edinburgh (principally Dr M Slesser and Dr J King), with a view to providing a tool to guide policy-making towards more sustainable development (Gilbert and Braat, 1991). Support for the approach has been provided by UNESCO, the UN Population Fund (UNFPA) and the UN Food and Agriculture Organization (FAO). Case studies using the methodology have been carried out in the United Kingdom, Mauritius, Thailand, Zimbabwe and China.

The ECCO approach

ECCO is a dynamic simulation model which quantifies feedback among the different sectors of the national system in physical resource terms. Specifically, it is based on the concept of energy accounting, with resources quantified through the energy required to release them and to produce any good or service in the economy. The principal features of the ECCO approach have been described as follows:

> It links in a dynamic manner population issues and development concerns, considering population growth in relation to the available resource base. It draws attention especially to 'carrying capacity', that is the capacity of a given territory to sustain its population. . . . Four key concepts – population, resources, environment and development – are thus linked, and projected over a relatively long-term time scale, that is, within the context of sustainability. (Gilbert and Braat (1991) p. xv)

The major inter-relationships within the ECCO model are shown in Figure 10.4. The model has been designed to be as simple as possible while containing the primary feedback mechanisms. The model provides explicitly for the incorporation of policy decisions, and once they have been defined the model runs endogenously. ECCO has been described in detail in a number of publications (FAO/UNESCO, (1985), Slesser (1987), King (1987), and its use in development planning discussed by King and Slesser (1988). An extensive review of the theoretical basis of ECCO, together with a description of a number of case studies, is provided by Gilbert and Braat (1991).

It is acknowledged that data availability is a problem for the validation of ECCO, but attempts have been made to validate the model for the United Kingdom (Slesser, 1985). Slesser reports that the largest error occurring in the statistical testing of ECCO using UK data for 1974–84 was a Theil's inequality coefficient of 0.045 for the forecast value of Capital Stock in Investment Goods. This compares with a best value of 0.29 for the same variable in the UK Treasury's forecasting model (a perfect forecast gives a coefficient of zero, with larger values indicating a progressively poorer fit).

The applications in developing countries recognize the problem of data availability and quality, and in the short term have tried to bypass it by using data from other countries – a pragmatic but unsatisfactory approach, except in the very early stages of model development. How-

Figure 10.4 Influence diagram for ECCO

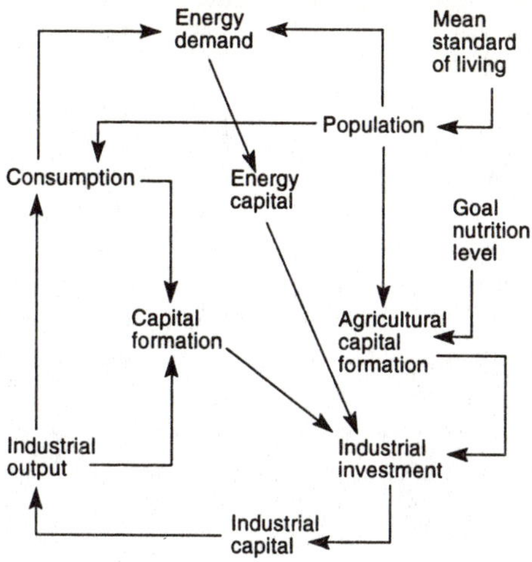

Source: After Slesser (1991).

ever, it is acknowledged that data collection must be an important priority if potential users of the model are to have confidence in its results.

One of the main conclusions to emerge from a recent workshop to review the future of the ECCO approach was the need to develop a regional version of the model. This was based on the recognition that many of the factors which influence development decisions are regional in nature, and that the impacts of development vary spatially. It seems likely therefore that the development of a regional dimension to ECCO will represent one of the major areas of future modelling activity. Work is already under way in the United Kingdom, and the report of the China case study in Gilbert and Braat (1991) suggested that a regional focus was considered to be important there.

THE UTILITY AND VALIDITY OF SYSTEM DYNAMICS MODELS

The discussion above has been concerned with two aspects of system dynamics – the method itself, and a number of individual models. This concluding section draws on both general and specific discussions to assess the utility and validity of system dynamics as a tool for the analysis of regional problems.

Representing social systems

The comparison of the structure of system dynamics with some of the underlying characteristics of social systems showed the method in a favourable light. The level-rate concept seems well suited in principle to represent the structure and process of systems in an integrated manner, and to capture the dynamic feedback character of their behaviour. Against this, it must be acknowledged that, in common with other methods, system dynamics does not permit the kind of adaption of system *structure* observed in the real world, and which may lead to fundamental changes in system behaviour. In other words, system dynamics models cannot guarantee the constancy of the relationships embodied in their structure (Lee, 1973). They do, however, have greater robustness than have static descriptive models, in so far as they are able to embody cause-and-effect relationships which permit the adaptation of the *behaviour* of systems in the face of change.

The utility of system dynamics

The potential strength of system dynamics in being able to provide a valid representation of some of the key characteristics of social systems is well matched by its flexibility, and thus utility, as a tool for model building. The inherent simplicity of the level-rate concept in representing feedback loops, the ability to use this simple concept to develop complex structures, and the flexibility of the simulation approach in handling non-linear relationships and delays is beyond dispute.

The models examined amply demonstrate this potential. They exhibit a breadth of treatment through the integration of subsystems, and a wide range of subject matter treated at many levels of detail. Moreover, the simple basic structure and the availability of special-purpose software allow the development of complex models with relative ease. Once developed, the causal loop and system dynamics flow diagrams are invaluable tools for communicating their structure and assumptions, while the flexible graphic and tabular output is an invaluable aid to the effective presentation of results.

However, attempts to apply system dynamics are not without their problems, particularly with regard to the questions of spatial disaggregation and interaction, and model validation.

Spatial considerations

Very few of the system dynamics models developed to date deal adequately with spatial disaggregation and interaction. Although both the case studies presented in this chapter recognize different spatial levels, the degree of interaction between them is extremely limited. The extent to which spatial disaggregation is important is, of course, primarily a function of the model's purpose. There are undoubtedly a number of important issues in regional development that do not need to be addressed in terms of spatial disaggregation. However, there are an equal number of issues concerned with transport, the spatial development process and the spatial impact of policies where the ability to incorporate a spatial dimension is of critical importance. There are some research (as opposed to applied) system dynamics models that have attempted to incorporate spatial disaggregation, but the level of spatial detail included is strictly limited.

A more fundamental problem is the complexity to which the inclusion of spatial interaction may give rise. Given their potential for representing dynamic and non-linear behaviour, system dynamics models have a built-in tendency towards complexity – witness the 1800 sets of equations in the Susquehanna model. Were the interactions between a large number of zones to be superimposed upon this, the resultant complexity might stretch the bounds of comprehensibility.

Problems of validation

There are a number of critical issues related to model validation. The first is the 'traditional' approach to the validation of system dynamics models, which argues effectively that formal validation is not appropriate, because the purpose of a system dynamics model is not to produce precise values, but to identify general models of behaviour. This is quite simply not an acceptable point of view for models designed to aid policy-makers. One of the key tests of confidence that policy-makers expect is the ability to reproduce historic performance within accepted limits. Although, as we have seen, there are now methods for attempting formal validation of system dynamics models, these are still not widely used. Until the system dynamics community accepts the relevance of these methods and makes use of them, it is unrealistic to expect the potential of the system dynamics approach to be realized.

Another aspect of the difficulty of model validation is related to the question of the availability of suitable time-series data. Clearly, without such data, the ability of a model to reproduce historic patterns of change is severely limited. Thus model-builders are forced to apply very partial validation tests, restricted to the few elements in the model for which historic data are available.

CONCLUSION

This chapter has suggested that system dynamics has considerable potential as a tool for the development of models for use in regional analysis and planning. The a priori suitability of the method to represent social systems, coupled with its flexibility in use, make it a powerful tool in real applications for this purpose, as demonstrated by the review of a number of case studies. However, the ability of the method to represent many of the complexities of the real world can make it a complex tool to use. Attempts to use it have emphasized the deficiencies in our theoretical and empirical knowledge of urban and regional systems. The problem of combining the complexity of interaction between variables over both time and space is one that may be difficult to resolve, if comprehensibility of model structure is to be maintained.

These problems are inherent in any serious attempt to model the world realistically, and as such are not restricted to system dynamics. The emphasis of the approach on the importance of model structure may provide some insurance against some of these problems, though even this must be qualified by the need for a sound theoretical basis for model structure. In order to advance the case for system dynamics, more applications of the method are needed, and increasing interest in issues related to sustainable development may provide a fertile area of application.

References

Development Analysis Associates (1978) *Water and Power Requirements for Saudi Arabia: Technical Volume 1* (Cambridge, Mass.: Development Analysis Associates).

FAO/UNESCO (1985) *Carrying Capacity Assessment: With a Pilot Study of Kenya* (Rome: FAO; Paris: UNESCO).

Forrester J. W. (1961) *Industrial Dynamics* (Cambridge, Mass.: MIT Press).

Forrester J. W. (1969) *Urban Dynamics* (Cambridge, Mass.: MIT Press).

Forrester J. W. (1971) *World Dynamics* (Cambridge, Mass.: MIT Press).

Gilbert, M. and G. Braat (eds) (1991) *Modelling for Sustainable Development* (London: Routledge).

Greenberger, M., M. A. Crenson and B. L. Crissy (1976) *Models in the Policy Process* (New York: Russell Sage Foundation).

Hamilton, H. R. *et al.* (1969) *Systems Simulation for Regional Analysis: An Application to River-Basin Planning* (Cambridge, Mass.: MIT Press).

King, J. (1987) *Beyond Economic Choice* (University of Edinburgh: Centre for Human Ecology).

King, J. and Slesser, M. (1988) 'Resource Accounting for Development Planning', *World Development*, April.

Lee, C. (1973) *Models in Planning* (Oxford: Pergamon Press).

Meadows, D. M. et al. (1972) *Limits to Growth* (New York: Universe Books).

Morecroft, J. D. W. (1988) 'A Critical Review of Diagramming Tools for Conceptualising Feedback System Models', *Dynamica*, vol. 8, pt. 1.

Newcastle System Dynamics Group (1973) *System Dynamics Modelling Methods in Urban and Regional Planning* (University of Newcastle upon Tyne).

Peterson, D. W. (1980) 'Statistical Tools for System Dynamics', in J. Randers (ed.), *Elements of the System Dynamics Method* (Cambridge, Mass.: MIT Press).

Richardson, G. P. and A. Pugh (1981) *Introduction to System Dynamics Modelling with DYNAMO* (Cambridge Mass.: MIT Press).

Slesser, M. (1985) *Resource Accounting in Development Manning: A Validation Study of the UK* (Glasgow: University of Glasgow Resource Use Institute).

Slesser, M. (1987) 'Net energy as an energy planning tool', *Energy Policy*, June.

Slesser, M. (1991) 'Planning for Sustainable Development', in Gilbert and Braat (1991).

Sterman, J. D. (1984) 'Appropriate Summary Statistics for Evaluating the Historic Fit of System Dynamics Models', *Dynamica*, vol. 10, pt. 11.

Weill, H. B. (1980) 'The Evolution of an Approach for Achieving Implemented Results from System Dynamics Projects', in J. Randers (ed.), *Elements of the System Dynamics Method* (Cambridge, Mass.: MIT Press).

Weiner, N. (1961) *Cybernetics: Or Control and Communication in the Animal and the Machine* (Cambridge, Mass.: MIT Press).

Wolstenholme, E. F. (1982) 'System Dynamics in Perspective', *Journal of the Operational Research Society*, vol. 33.

Wolstenholme, E. F. (1990) *System Enquiry: A System Dynamics Approach* (John Wiley).

Wolstenholme, E. F. and R. G. Coyle (1983) 'The Development of System Dynamics as a Methodology for System Description and Qualitative Analysis', *Journal of the Operational Research Society*, vol. 34.

11 Applied Spatial Informatics as a Framework for Natural Disaster Mitigation

George G. van der Meulen

INTRODUCTION

A number of computer programs for training have been developed for decision-makers involved in disaster reduction, particularly in natural disaster reduction.

This activity is based on and was started during the final stage of compilation of the so-called UNDRO manual, published in 1991. The main author of that manual, acting in the capacity of chairman of the foundation Compuplan, approached me in 1987 with a general question concerning the feasibility of the development of personal computer programs for the training of planners and decision-makers involved in natural disaster mitigation. Although the text of the UNDRO manual was not at that time available, the main idea was clear. During the years since then, that general idea of translating natural disaster phenomena into disaster reduction training programs has been developed, using a methodology and technique called 'applied spatial informatics'. This approach in connection with natural disaster mitigation will be discussed in this chapter. A number of examples are included, in particular using screen dumps of the prototype training programs developed.

CONCEPTS AND OPERATIONS

First, a general conceptualization of the phenomenon which places disaster reduction in a spatial framework, simulating the disaster spatially and calculating its effects both in terms of attributes and costs, executing disaster-reduction strategies, followed by resimulation and an evaluation of costs and benefits of such strategies. Second, an operationalization of these conceptual choices allowing a transformation and translation into software algorithms. The major decision during the process of operationalization concerns the introduction of geographical information system tools for database handlings. The data sets included are geographical data organized as vectorized layers, attribute data organized in grid layers (data rasters), and cost parameters for attributes and physical elements under risk. The grid-based attribute database is an on-line database allowing direct change of attribute data. Placing the 'action', that is, the disaster event, in its spatial environment, allows the simulation of the disaster according to the mathematical model included. The results of such a simulation concern the effects shown both cartographically and quantitatively. Assuming that implementation of an intervening policy can reduce the hazard of those effects, the simulation is repeated after a mitigating device has been chosen.

The costs generated by the simulation, with and without the implementation of an effect-mitigating device, are compared during evaluation. Being aware that financial resources are limited, the decision-making process will focus only on the elimination of a part of the total risk.

SOFTWARE PROGRAMS

Several software prototypes have been developed, covering, for example, river flooding, seawater level rising, cyclone on volcanic eruption. Futhermore, training prototypes have also been developed for some more or less human-made disasters, for example, explosion and toxic cloud (simulating Bhopal's Union Carbide accident). A number of these approaches have been described in international publications (Meulen, van der, 1989, 1991, 1993 a, b and c).

PROGRAM STRUCTURE

The PC software programs developed for training of planners and decision-makers involved in (natural) disaster risk mitigation are built up as explained below. Their approaches should be been to be within the framework of 'applied spatial informatics', integrating geographical information and decision-support system tools. Applied spatial informatics has been defined as: 'application oriented scientific and professional approaches for the support of decision and policy making,

making use of both geographical and attribute information, aided by computer hardware and software combined through special user interfacing, as much as possible aided by knowledge based systems' (Meulen, van der 1993c).

The main menu structure of these programs is:

0 Front page with program title and illustration or animation.
1 General program information, sometimes with a map offering an overview of the subject concerned in a geographical context.
2 Geographical layers of the study area.
3 On-line Attribute data handler available for inspection as well as updating (data change).
4 Parameters, and especially cost parameters, set-up module.
5 Thematic analysis.
6 Vulnerability, risk-setting and event simulation, with results in tables and map images.
7 Intervention strategy choice.
8 Resimulation and evaluation by ante – post evaluations.

The general structure of these operations, worked out as bar and pull-down menus, are shown in Figure 11.1, '>' indicates that a further, more detailed, submenu exists.

The following figures (Figures 11.2; 11.3; 11.4; 11.5) show a selection of examples concerning several disaster-mitigating training programs mentioned above, using fictitious data.

EVALUATING THE BENEFITS OF THE UNDECAD UMBRELLA APPROACH

The programs developed under the UNDECAD umbrella are prototypes for training purposes, mainly focusing on spatial planners and decision-makers involved in the reduction of hazardous (natural) disasters. Nevertheless, while being used for training, these programs are also applicable to real world situations, and in principle suitable for anywhere in the world, because the approaches developed allow any study area to be included, both geographically and relation to its relevant attribute data. Furthermore, several international institutions working as disaster preparedness centres, for example, the Disaster Management Center, University of Wisconsin, and the Asian Preparedness Center, AIT, Bangkok) have expressed interest in these software approaches, particularly as training programs.

Figure 11.1 General program structure

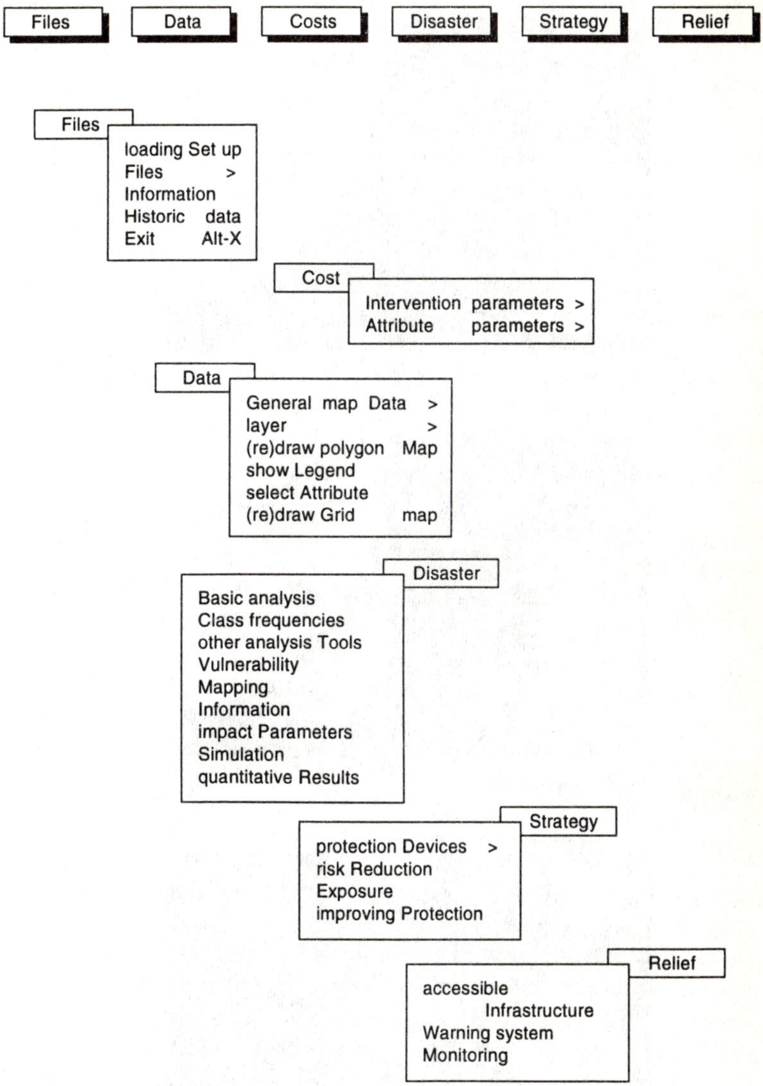

Figure 11.2 Animation and elaboration of a cyclone disaster by applied spatial informatics

(a) Animation 1

(b) Animation 2

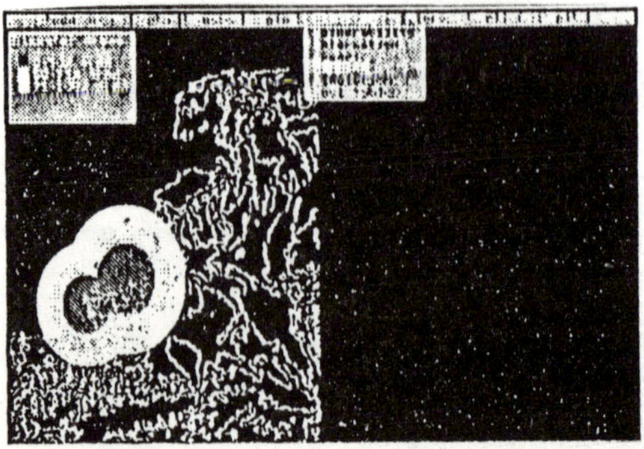

(c) Elaboration

Figure 11.3 Elaboration of global seawater level rising by applied spatial informatics

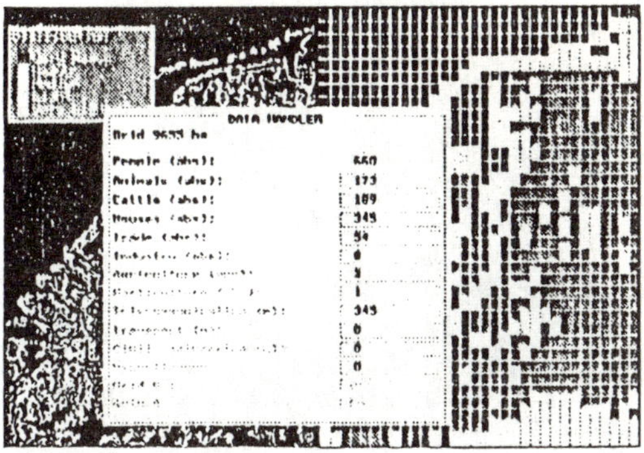

(a) on-line data handler

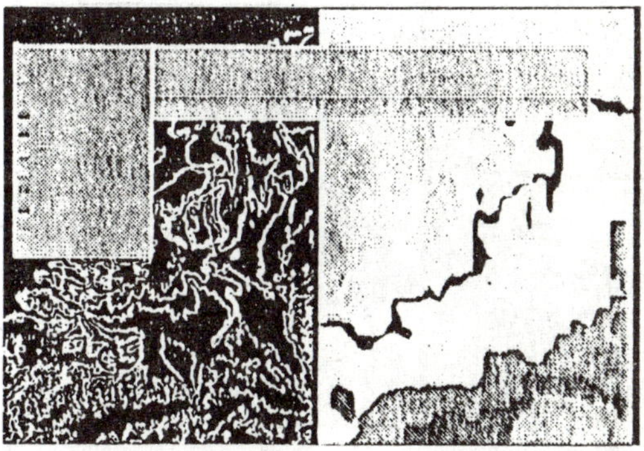

(b) Height assumption

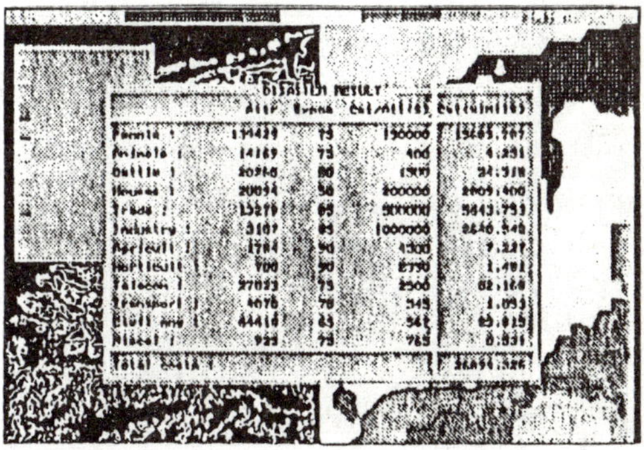

(c) Quantitative effect of simulated flooding line

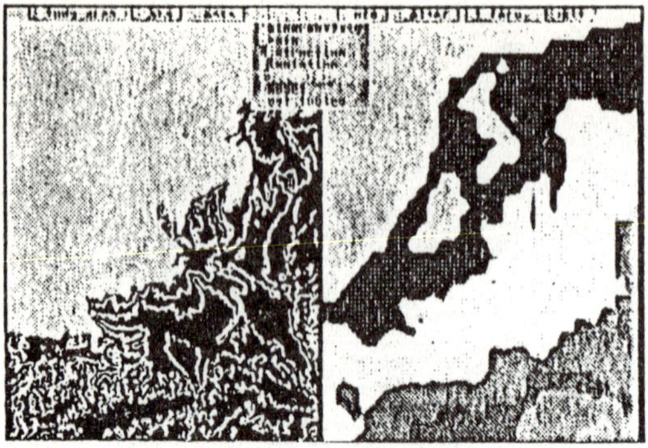

(d) Flood plain assumed according to sea level

(e) Accessible infrastructure

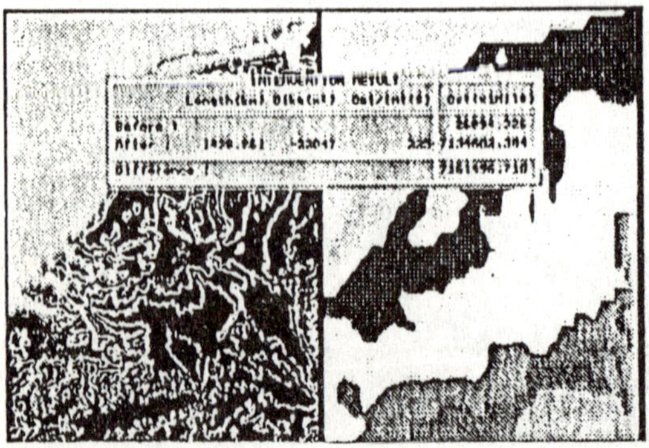

(f) Quantitative disaster results

Figure 11.4 Data elaborated by applied spatial informatics

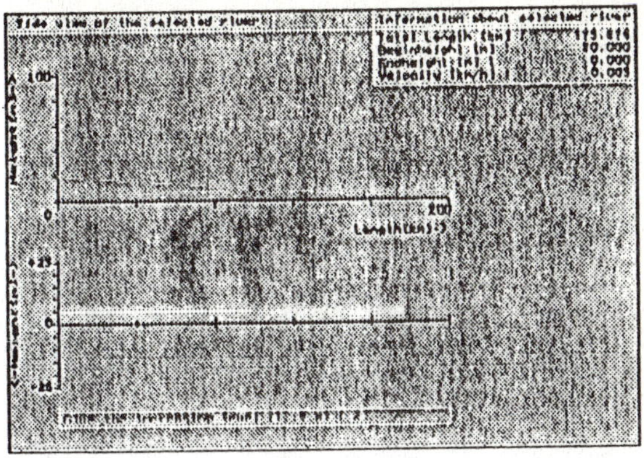

(a) Water table

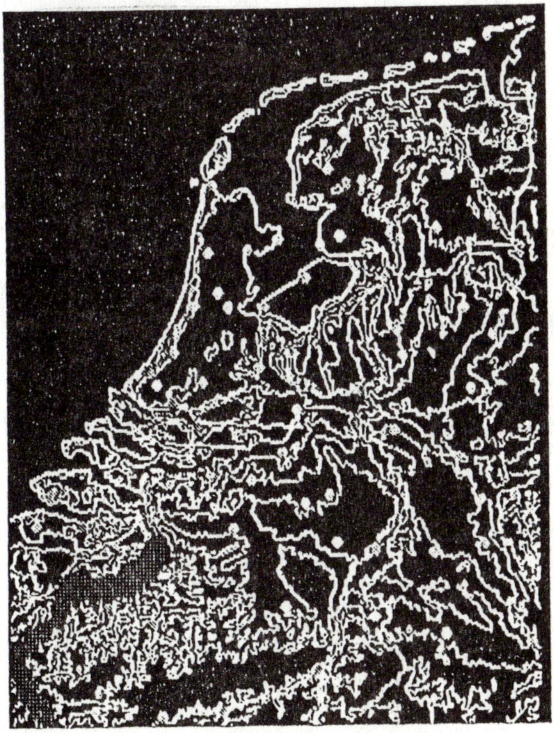

(b) Flood plain of a river flooding disaster

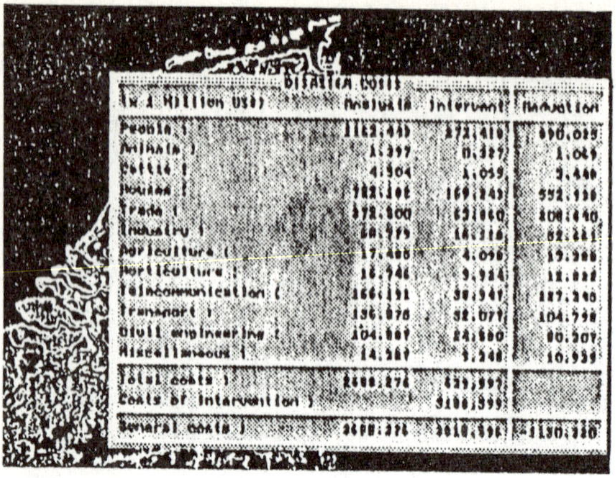

(c) Cost table (ante)

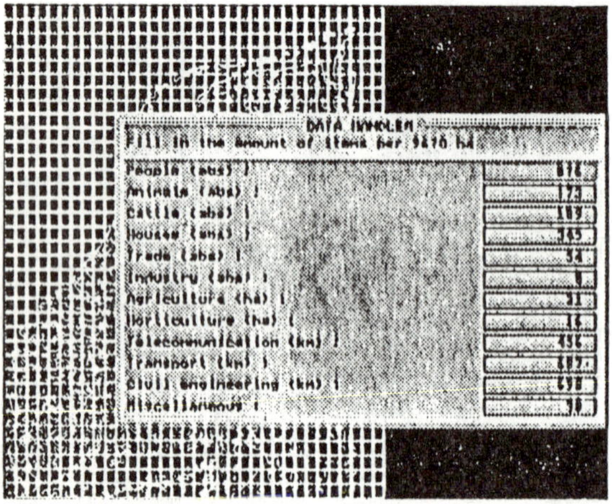

(d) Cost table (post)

DEVELOPMENT AND ENVIRONMENT

Disaster mitigation is not only a matter of implementing intervention strategies such as effect-reducing devices, the removal of people and/or buildings (human habitat), and/or the reallocation of water cultures (ecological habitaat).

Figure 11.5 Animation and elaboration of a volcanic eruption disaster by applied spatial informatics

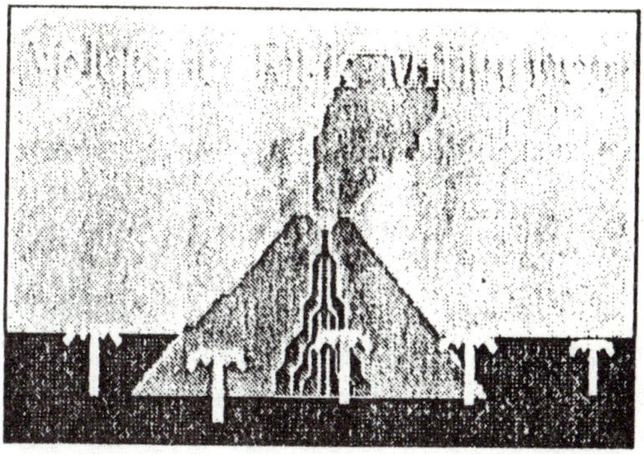

(a) Animation 1

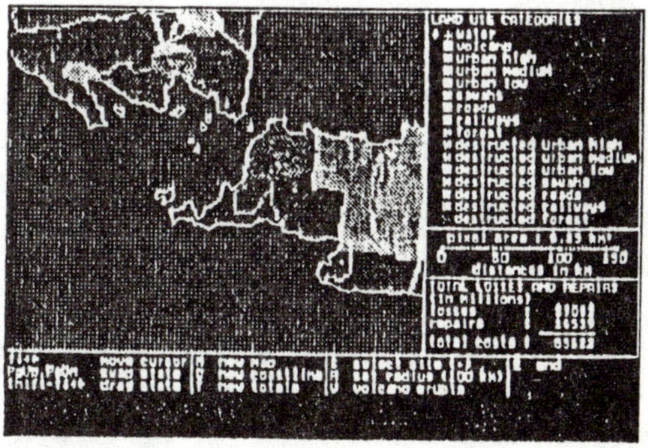

(b) Animation 2

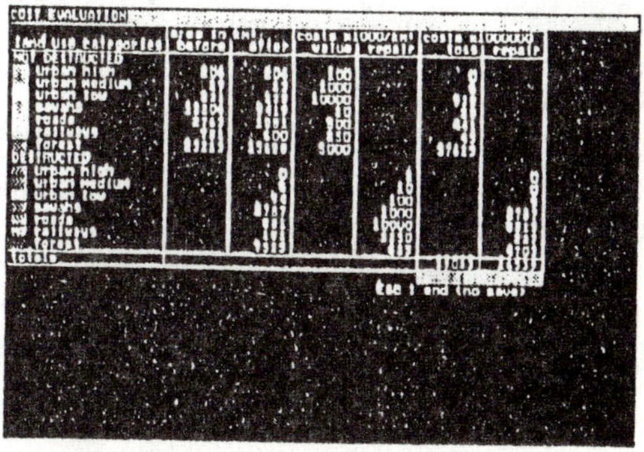

(c) Elaboration

The process of disaster mitigation is also highly dependent on spatial planning and decision-making. A connected special activity concerns spatial plan design. In particular, land-use zoning is obviously important for steering spatial developments while reducing risk in case of certain disastrous events. Developing countries in particular are confronted by a large number of (natural) disasters, but these countries do not have enough skilled spatial plan designers; furthermore, partly as a consequence, they cumulated arrears in the production of spatial plans (Meulen, van der, 1992). The general effect of such arrears is that much more serious in areas under risk from any natural disaster.

A change in this situation is only possible if more capacity can be built or supportive tools can be used. For that reason, AUTOPLAN has been developed by Compuplan as an integrated spatial plan design tool for land-use planning relation to structure and specific plans. AUTOPLAN is a PC software package, using GIS tools, integrating knowledge concerning geographic analysis, spatial plan regulations, legal rules for land usage, and related case law. The package has been developed as a highly user-friendly system to be optimally useful in the circumstances of a developing country. The three screen dumps shown in Figure 11.6 are examples of a specific plan developed by this package.

RELIEF AND ROUTING

Another very relevant approach is provided by distance minimalization if the traffic network should be used in case of emergency (See Figure 11.7), and it may be assumed that only part of this network is accessible and available (see Figure 11.3(e)).

If emergency announcements are to be made by, for example, a police patrol car touring around, these approaches can be simulated by shortest route and shortest path algorithms. Compuplan's program AUTOROUT has been developed for this purposes.

While AUTOROUT uses a methodological approach, CPPOLDER contains applications on both emergency announcements and shortest routing for evacuation in case of polder flooding. CPPOLDER has been developed with the Dutch Ministry of Transport, Public Works and Water Management. The screen dumps, shown in Figure 11.7 represent some examples of a polder flooding evacuation decision support approach.

Figure 11.6 Comprehensive land use and spatial planning design images

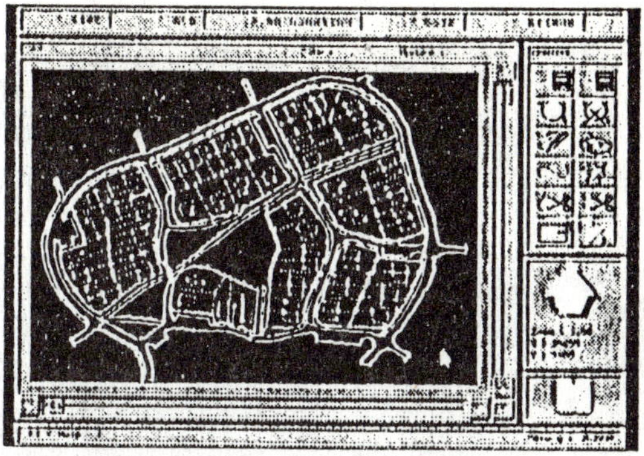

(a) Housing area zoning plan (parcellation)

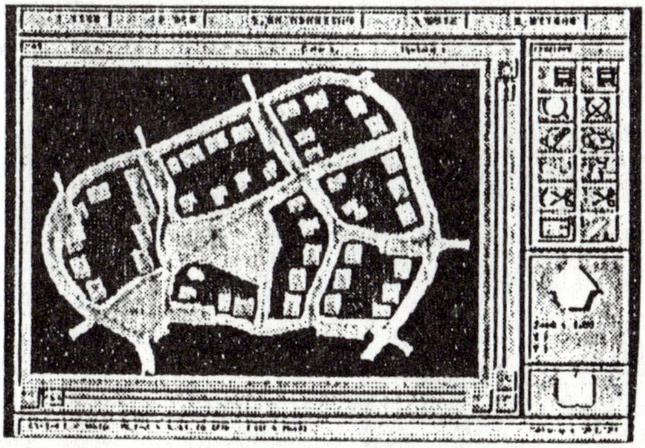

(b) Housing area zoning plan (regulation)

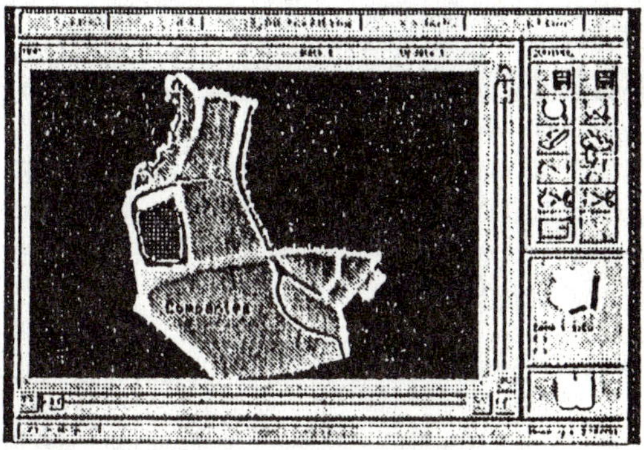

(c) Structure plan for an industrial zone

Note: Introduced as a model in RPD (1990).

Figure 11.7 Simulated emergency announcements and evacuation of inhabitants of a flooding polder

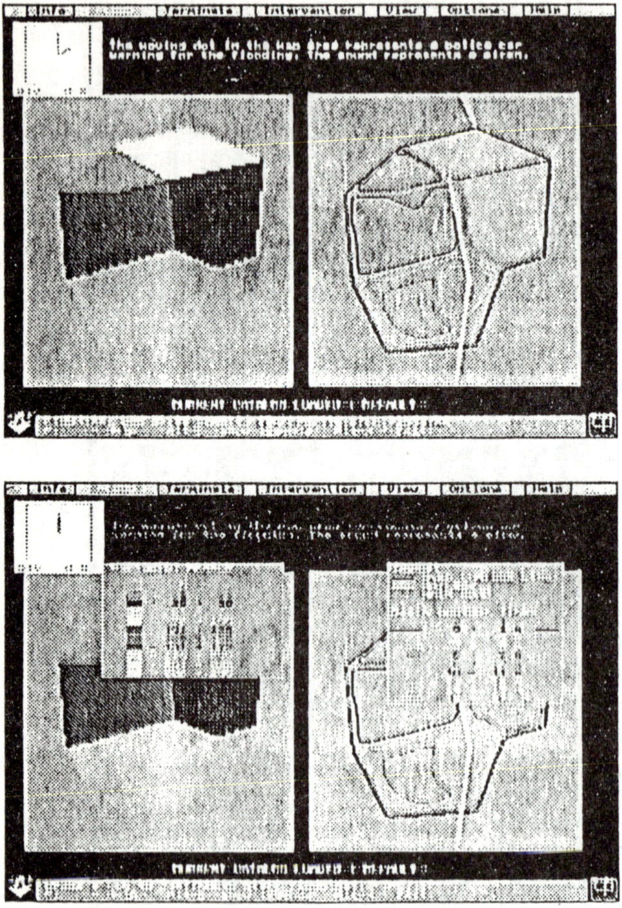

INSTITUTION BUILDING

Disaster reduction depends greatly on the institutions involved such as: governmental organizations; disaster preparedness centres; relief agencies; and research and training centers (Wolters and van der Meulen, 1993). In the current United Nations' Decade for Disaster Reduction, the need for adequate and effective policies to support disaster management is obvious, at both an international and a national level. Action to be undertaken in this context is the formulation of National Disaster Management Plans, to provide and to ensure a disaster management framework; Mitigation Programmes at both national and local levels, to establish risk monitoring and control systems; and Information Management Systems, for disaster information and communication.

Such institution-building and related action require support by available advanced methodologies and techniques. The training-orientated software approaches described above may offer a contribution to both a good understanding of the disaster processes concerned, and risk monitoring, decision-making and risk mitigation.

CONCLUSIONS

Natural disaster reduction needs both an institutional framework and useful methods and techniques to support decision-making at supranational, national and local level. The widely disseminated personal computer supported by adequate software dedicated and tailored for decision support to prevent and to mitigate natural disaster effects, can help in many ways, understanding, information, monitoring and early warning being only a few of these.

The examples shown in this chapter concern a variety of natural disasters, including several intervention approaches, based on so-called applied spatial informatics and knowledge engineering. Their usability as training programs will be obvious; for their applicability as real field approaches a great deal more work has to be carried out in the future.

References

Meulen, G. G. van der (1989) *Spatial Planning Software and Knowledge Engineering Handbook with Adapted Approaches for Urban and Regional Planners in Developing Countries* (Bangkok: Chulalongkorn University).

Meulen, G. G. van der (1991) 'Flood-risk Simulation, A Disaster Mitigating Training System', in *Proceedings of the International Workshops, Storm Surges, River Flow and Combined Effects STORM '91*, a contribution to the UNESCO-IHP Project H-2-2, Hamburg, 8–12 April, pp. 245–55.

Meulen, G. G. van der (1993a) 'PC Global Seawater Level Rising, General Effects on the World Hatibat, Using a PC', in *Proceedings of the International*

Workshop SEAWATER '93, Noordwijkerhout, The Netherlands, April, p. 10.

Meulen, G. G. van der (1993b) 'UNDECAD PC Umbrella Disaster Mitigation Training Programs. Compuplan's Involvement in (Natural) Disaster Reduction', paper presented at an expert meeting 'Rampen, Noodhulp, Ontwikkeling en Millieu', Ministry of Foreign Affairs of the Netherlands, The Hague, 6 April p. 12.

Meulen, G. G. van der (1993c) *Applied Spatial Informatics, A Handbook* (Bangkok: Asian Institute of Technology).

RPD (1990) *Bestemmen met Beleid* ('s-Gravenhage: RPD)

RNDRO (1991) *Mitigating Natural Disasters. Phenomena, Effects and Options. A Manual for Policymakers and Planners* (Geneva: RNDRO).

Wolters, T. M., and G. G. van der Meulen (1993) 'Disaster Management and Institution Building', in *Proceedings of the International Conference 'Urban Environment in Developing Countries; Futures, Ideas, Directions'*, Eindhoven University of Technology, Eindhoven, The Netherlands, 16–18 June p. 10.

12 Climate Change and the Social Sciences: Global and Regional Issues

Peter Nijkamp and Celeste Wilderom

THE TYRANNY OF THE 'HIDDEN FOOT'

In past years the notion of ecologically sustainable economic development, vigorously advocated in the Brundtland Report published by the World Commission on Environment and Development (1987) has gained much popularity in the Western world. The awareness has grown that environmental degradation and poverty cannot be addressed sufficiently by simple recovery measures; it requires proactive strategies by both governments and the business sector. It has often been tempting to resort to the development of new technology, to solve problems, but, increasingly, it is being recognized that technological progress as such cannot alone cure environmental decay (leaving aside the point that technology may also be the source of much evil). Clearly, a number of fundamental causes of these problems lie in the organization and function of society itself.

In a fully operating market system, where all actors incur all costs of activities undertaken by them, the 'hidden hand' (*á la* Adam Smith) would ensure the attainment of a balanced production and consumption system, where all external costs and benefits would be internalized. In the absence of a market for environmental goods and in the absence of a democratic system where the interests of future generations or distant nations would also be fully incorporated, a distorted outcome is likely to occur. Thus, if the 'hidden hand' fails, a biased result will emerge, where the decisions are no longer based on 'real' prices for scarce commodities. This new driving force will create an overconsumption of unpriced goods (for example, the environment). The driving principle towards a distortion of socially desirable goods is sometimes called the 'hidden foot'.

The 'hidden foot', which operates mainly outside the realm of the price mechanism, may endanger our ways of decision-making even more, as it may also intensify – as a consequence of market failures – the occurrence of policy failures. Governments – charged with the task of servicing the public interest, which includes ecological sustainability – are often misinformed about the causes of, or actors in, environmental decay, especially those with an effect on the long run. Public interventions may sometimes even intensify environmental problems. Various examples of this can be found in Barde and Button (1991). For example, several urban parking restrictions imposed to discourage vehicle traffic generated eventually even more car kilometres!

It is clear that the 'hidden foot' problem cannot be overcome solely by technical measures or by responsive governments. It also requires new institutional frameworks supporting the generation of environmental benign strategies, insights and new attitudes, based on a deeper awareness of cultural and ethical dimensions of sustainability. This requirement demands intensified research into the backgrounds, consequences and responses of the environmental problem, not only in the 'hard' sciences, but even more so in the social sciences.

The issue has recently become even more important, as it have been recognized that the human impact on nature may cause dramatic and irreversible changes in the environmental condition. Thus the compatibility of our current production and consumption system with current and future environmental conditions can no longer be guaranteed: the co-evolution of humans and nature has become rather a problem (see also Archibuchi and Nijkamp, 1989).

An illustrative case in this respect is climate change. This case will be used as the main focal point of interest in this chapter.

GLOBAL ENVIRONMENTAL CHANGE

The size and intensity of human activities leading to devastating impacts on the Earth's physical, chemical and biological systems have increased dramatically since the nineteenth century. By the turn of the century it seems plausible to assume that all areas on our planet are under severe environmental threat. This holds for both the geosphere and the biosphere. Clearly, these two systems are interlinked, as is, for example, illustrated by global change phenomena such as deforestation, desertification, ozonization and so on.

It is generally taken for granted that natural physical systems are never static, but always in a state of flux. This also holds for biogeochemical cycles connecting the geosphere and biosphere and for the climatic system. The climatic system varies in accordance with solar radiation or losses of energy from the Earth. In recent decades especially belief has grown that 'greenhouse' gases play a critical role in keeping the lower atmosphere and the Earth's surface relatively warmer. This effect has been a 'normal' phenomenon in the history of our planet, but it has led to intensified greenhouse effects during the twentieth century, thought to be caused by anthropogenic stimuli emerging from the large-scale emissions of carbon dioxides and other gases. The biogeochemical cycles are unable to encapsulate the drastic increase in these greenhouse gases. As a result, the climate on Earth may gradually change. This has implications for all regions and cities on earth. For example, coastal areas in Bangladesh may be permanently at risk, agricultural areas in Siberia or North Canada may show drastic changes, and so on.

Climatic change is not the only global change. Other examples are stratospheric ozone depletion, worldwide acidification, and loss of biodiversity (see also Jacobson and Price, 1990). All such changes are directly or indirectly related to the consumption of fossil fuel, biomass fuel consumption, land use changes, population change, urbanization, industrialization, agricultural activities and so on.

It is clear that research on such long-term changes needs a considerable effort in the field of climatology and related disciplines. And significant progress has recently been made in understanding such long-term processes. But at the same time it is recognized that thus far the social sciences have not yet built up any research tradition in the area of global change, notably climate change. Yet it should be noted that – as far as global change is caused by anthropogenic factors – it is of extreme importance to investigate their driving forces as well as stimuli to change these forces. Even if the assumption of anthropogenic climate (and global) change is not universally accepted, it is evident that social science research would be needed into ways of coping with the negative impact of such global changes on the man-made and natural systems of the Earth. There is thus a need for an action agenda for social science research on global change (including climatic change).

A first example of such increased interest in social science research can be found in the USA, where the National Academy of Sciences carried out a study on the human sources of global change (see Kates *et al.*, (1990), Clark (1990)). This study revealed the need for integrative models, process studies and data sources at the edge of social sciences and global change. In particular, it was suggested to give priority to the following research initiatives:

1. To develop integrative models of human sources of emissions and land cover change for earth systems models:
   - global agriculture;
   - global greenhouse gas emissions; and
   - regional land cover conversion: tropical forests and wetlands.
2. To support the model development with key studies of important processes:
   - fertilization in agriculture;
   - biomass burning; and
   - intensity of energy and materials use.
3. To provide critical data for model development and process studies:
   - population/land cover – use – capability; and
   - global historical energy and materials use.

The interest in regional and spatial issues in this list is evident. This impressive research agenda does not give much detail on the type of methodological approach to be adopted in such social science studies. Furthermore, alternative policy responses would need to be investigated in more detail. Thus, despite the recognition of the increasingly important role of social science research, a more thorough exploration of the direction of research and policy is necessary. This will be discussed in the next section.

SOCIAL RESEARCH AND POLICY STRATEGIES

Widespread concern about environmental degradation on a global scale leads to the need for a better understanding of the causes of global environmental change, its foreseeable impacts and the policy implications of new pathways towards sustainable development (both adaptively and proactively). The drastic negative effects of global warming thus require an intensified effort of the social sciences in order to respond adequately to the great many uncertainties and challenges posed by the environment.

The British Economic and Social Research Council (ESRC) (1991) has formulated in this respect an initiative programme, encouraging:

1. International research collaboration (for example, in the area of agricultural policy and decision-making, risk and uncertainty, energy and the greenhouse effect, and industrial/technical change and the environment).

2. Research on international policies (for example, protection of the 'global commons', international opinion formation and policy-making processes, and new technology and the global environment).
3. Case studies of regions of the world particularly susceptible to environmental change (for example, tropical forest areas, Sahel and Sub-Sahelian Africa, and Arctic studies).

These focal points are all relevant and require a further assessment in terms of the costs and benefits involved. In other words, environmental and global change science policy would require a targeting on problems that threaten us most (see Pearch and Steinhardt, 1990/91). This question might be answered by means of cost-effectiveness analysis. Such analysis would require an assessment of risks involved in the existence of each of the global change components, an assessment of all costs involved in coping with these problems, and a specification of target levels for an ecologically sustainable economy. However, in view of the great many uncertainties characterizing global change processes, such a cost-effectiveness assessment is very hard to carry out, so that new research directions in this field will necessarily include subjective expert and *ad hoc* political opinions.

A brief clarification of the above choice problems may be offered by using a payoff matrix (shown in Figure 12.1) which incorporates two possible actions (active policy vs. passive policy) *vis-à-vis* two states of nature (a further climate change in the case of continuation of current emission trends vs. no further climate change in the case of continued emission trends).

The entries in the payoff matrix would then represent net benefits. It will then depend on the risk behaviour of policy-makers as to which action is selected (for example, a max – max strategy *vis-á-vis* a min – max regret strategy). This will then eventually have an impact on the direction and size of research efforts in the area of global change. For the time being, it seems as though many policy-makers have become aware of the high risks involved in many irreversible processes in global environmental change phenomena. Hence there is an increasing tendency for a 'no regret' strategy. This means that – even though all impacts of global change are not precisely known – the perceived risks are so high that an active and proactive environmental policy is warranted, especially in those cases where an intensified policy initiative would lead to benefits in other sectors/areas (for example, an active CO_2 policy would also reduce energy consumption and hence favour industrial competition) (IPCC, 1990). The previous observations illus-

Figure 12.1 A payoff matrix

Actions	*Further change in climate*	*No further change in climate*
Active policy		
Passive policy		

trate once more the dilemma of social science research in the field of global and climate change: there is a need for a rigorous research initiative, but the prevailing uncertainties lead to a situation of 'groping in the dark' (see Tennekes, 1990). This problem will be discussed further in a subsequent section.

THE ROLE OF SOCIAL SCIENCES

In the present section we take for granted that the climate problem is – via the intermediate greenhouse gases such as CO_2 and CFCs – directly and indirectly connected with the functioning of the world's industrial and economic system, notably the use of energy and raw materials, production, consumption, demographic growth and land use. The latter elements also form in most countries the heart of their growth efforts and, therefore, it is evident that policies coping with climate changes have to induce a behaviourial change which concerns almost all aspects of human life. Thus the social sciences fulfil a critical role in this context, even though the precise nature of this research is not exactly known in advance. Nevertheless, some guidelines for meaningful research can be expressed in the form of a minimum requirements strategy which would have to be followed in any case, given the above considerations on the links between global change and human behaviour.

The essence of social science research questions in the area of global environmental changes is the so-called 'social dilemma'. Awareness of the social costs of global change does not automatically generate a behaviourial change compatible with the ecological paradigm, even though the consequences may be severe, long-lasting and global in nature. Which are the appropriate incentives to induce a needed change, and who would be responsible for such incentives? Clearly, the answer to these questions requires a broad, interdisciplinary research effort, in which integration of existing knowledge may be as effective – at least in the short run – as creation of new knowledge.

In a recent document of the Dutch Social Science Council (Social Science Council, 1991) it was suggested that the above-mentioned research question be approached from four substantive angles, which might bring to light the necessary social science knowledge regarding the global change problem. These thematic angles comprise the following elements.

The impact of humans and society on global change

This theme concerns in particular the anthropogenic aspects of global change and includes the following two research fields.

Key factors of global change

As far as global environmental change has an anthropogenic background, social science research in this field has to focus attention on human needs and attitudes, conditioned by psychological, cultural, economic, political and historical factors as well as institutions and structures influencing human behaviour. In this context, an important but unresolved research question is whether sociopsychological and socioeconomic determinants are crucial for current and future needs and activity patterns, or whether global and local sociodemographic evolution is a key factor in analyzing the climate question. Strategic exploratory research into the relative size and contribution of such critical factors is thus of primary importance. Systems-analytic research – as an interplay of economists, demographers, geographers and historians (and, of course, natural scientists) – would then be extremely fruitful, in order also to identify the main causes of the global change problem (for example, demographic growth, industrial development, economic growth, spatial mobility or agriculture) and their geographical distribution on the planet.

Social impact analysis

Despite the important cumulative effects of human behaviour at large on global change phenomena (that is, significant integral externalities), it should be recognized that the impact of one individual actor is usually negligible (that is, approximately zero individual externalities). Thus the complex chain of individual action to global change is hardly traceable, which causes great difficulties in increasing the awareness of the greenhouse effect and of the need for reorientation and drastic changes in human behaviour.

In this vein, there is a need for new social impact studies (for example, sociopsychological stimulus–response techniques, qualitative impact analysis, and attitude–behaviour relationships with intervening factors). Particular attention would have to be given to social experimentation: to identify barriers and potentials in the transition towards sustainable development paths (for example, measuring effectiveness of individual behaviour responses; acceptance of combined group and individual responsibility; individual cost–benefit assessment of changes in behaviour). All such methods would try to cope with the 'hidden foot' question. The resulting knowledge would need to discourage 'free rider' behaviour. From a pedagogical perspective, modern geographic information systems (GIS) and related expert systems would have to be developed to generate global, tailor-made information on the need to reorientate current ways of producing, consuming and decision-making.

Perception and assessment of climatic change

Global environmental change covers a time–space span which falls beyond the horizon within which decisions are normally take, either individually or collectively. Thus, rather than standard 'social engineering' methods, multi-generational trade-off problems and long-term pro-active strategies have to be considered. This leads to various research tasks for the social sciences.

Uncertainty and risk

Despite insufficient insight in the natural sciences on the precise causes and impacts of global environmental change, the social sciences face the problem of assessing the expected consequences of behavioural changes. For example, a sudden stringent CO_2 policy may generate extremely high costs to the current generation, which might perhaps not be justified from the viewpoint of opportunity costs. Thus elimination of as much uncertainty as possible, and risk assessment – from the viewpoint of ecologically sustainable economic development, are necessary items on the research agenda. Traditional scenario experiments (ranging from 'business as usual' scenarios to 'doomsday' scenarios) can certainly be helpful in this respect, while resort could also be taken to recently developed mathematical models for treating unpredictable dynamics (for example, chaos theory or fractal theory). Such approaches might be supplemented with sociopsychological risk perception analysis and socioeconomic evaluation analyses. In this framework also, the above-mentioned 'no regret' strategies could be more satisfactorily designed and used.

Flexibility and behavioural change

The 'social dilemma' alluded to previously causes the need to develop incentives to change human behaviour, even though the direct impacts of such changes are not immediately observable. This lack of direct visibility requires social research methods which would be able to demonstrate convincingly the relevance of a drastic reorientation in attitudes and behaviour. In this context, new environmental education systems – design and implementation – are a major challenge for the social sciences. This would need to focus on the motivation and objectives of individuals and groups, as well as on stimuli that induce behaviourial responses, taking into consideration psychological, economic, cultural, anthropological and historical factors. It might also be interesting to investigate which driving forces have in the past been able to generate resilience in human behaviour, to remove inertia and to overcome major developmental barriers to individuals, groups and societies (including the role of institutions). Thus identification of critical success factors for far-reaching attitudinal and behavioural change would be an important research theme in the context of global environmental change.

Technology assessment and global change

Technology plays a double role in the global change discussion: it acts as a cause of environmental deterioration and it may help cope with the problems inherent in global change. Since the mid-1980s the belief has grown that technological dynamics are not developing at random, but can be influenced by social, economic, psychological, cultural and institutional factors. Such factors appear to be of decisive influence on technology trajectories. The identification of technology trajectories that ensure in the long run a more environmentally benign outcome is extremely difficult, as it requires knowledge on ecologically sustainable technology trajectories and on ways to influence technology decisions. Thus motives for innovation have to be investigated from the viewpoint of environmental sustainability. Next, action-orientated research on diffusing new technological knowledge – taking into account global environmental change as an orientation point – would also be needed. This means that the case of environmentally sustainable pathways requires a specific technology assessment with an important behaviourial colour.

Response strategies and attitude change in global change policy

Previous observations have clarified that a social science focus on global change phenomena requires a behaviourial orientation at three levels (micro, meso, macro). The types of strategy for coping with these phenomena is, however, not immediately clear. It is obvious that preventive (or proactive) strategies are needed, but the shape, content and implications of such strategies are as yet unknown. The following streams of research are important here.

Institutions and regulations

Inert human behaviour may cause the solution to the global change to be long-lasting. Two contextual factors play a role here. First, the role and impact of established institutions and existing regulations with regard to rigidity or flexibility in human behaviour regarding consumption patterns, resource use or space consumption needs further scientific research, especially from the viewpoint of the 'tragedy of the commons'. Here is a clear case for socioeconomic research into market and government failures. Second, the question emerges of which new cultural, social, economic and political structures, institutions and value systems would be needed to induce a flexible behaviourial change, taking into account also the role of environmental education. This would need research at the interface of political science, management science, pedagogy, demography, law, sociology, psychology and economics.

Contingency studies

If we look at the environment and the climate as a 'collective' good, then it is necessary to consider also ownership rules to be imposed as restrictive measures by public bodies. Such measures will demand a high degree of social acceptance. Therefore, effectiveness studies of such measures are a *conditio sine qua non*. In such acceptance and evaluation studies, 'free rider' behaviour would also be a central component. An additional problem may be that unforeseen changes in the external environment may also generate new attitudes, intentions and behaviour, which might sometimes be at odds with an environmentally benign policy. In this context, strategic contingency studies may be a very helpful tool in social science research.

Market solutions for a global change policy

The 'tragedy of the commons' (including the global environment and the climate) is caused by the fact that the high social costs of global change are not borne by the source of the evil. Is it possible to develop market incentives to induce behaviourial change? Our current way of economic thinking and evaluating prevents us from taking into account a very long-term time horizon caused by a myopic use of the social rate of discount. Multigenerational evaluation studies would then need to be developed from the viewpoint of an ecologically sustainable pathway. The way such incentives might influence our current behaviour requires new analytical tools, where, especially, experimental economics may provide new contributions. This would need a merger of economics, social psychology, law, political science and management science.

Compatibility of local and global policy

Global environmental change manifests itself both globally and locally, which its driving forces also comprise interwovenness of local and global phenomena. This would need further analysis, as the link between local and global dimensions is not always clear and is always changing. Systems-analytic models and geographic information systems (GIS) may provide useful assistance here. Especially the risk assessment of local stimuli on global responses – and in turn upon local conditions – needs further attention (NSF, 1991).

This leads to two intriguing problems. The first concerns the coordination and maintenance of an international climate change policy, which is now still in its infancy (although the Montreal Protocol on CFCs is a promising development). Also in this context, the problem of 'free riders' among nations has to be coped with effectively.

The next problem is how a globally orientated but locally focused technology policy, resource policy, land use policy and environmental policy can be favoured, for example, via international institutions (in the form of an international climate fund, internationally accepted critical loads, strict application of local/national 'bubbles' or tradable emission rights, to give some examples). Clearly, the compatibility of local/regional policies with international trade policy is also at stake here.

The previous questions are not mainly technical in nature, but have a strong human science background, in which the 'hidden foot' principle leading to the above-described 'social dilemma' plays a key role.

Methodology of social science research on global environmental change

The social sciences have developed a rich analytical tradition, for example, in economics, demography or psychology. A synergy of the research traditions from different disciplines would undoubtedly create a high surplus value for the methodology regarding the analysis of global-change phenomena. Several elements can be mentioned briefly here.

Information systems and effect analysis

Tailor-made information systems (for example, based on panel or longitudinal approaches) would provide more insight into backgrounds of global change problems and solutions. Next, a climate impact analysis (CIA) would be meaningful in which economic, demographic, agricultural, ecological and geographical causes and effects would be monitored systematically. This would also require remote sensing and GIS techniques.

Experimental studies

The range of global change problems is so wide and diverse that a uniform research strategy is not feasible at the time of writing. Nevertheless, it would be interesting to start with a set of carefully selected pilot and experimental studies in which knowledge from different research centres would be pooled. Interesting candidate areas might be delta-areas (in relation to sea-level rise) or health effects (in relation to climatic change). Such experimental studies could easily be undertaken as a collaborative effort of research institutes, where a strong tradition in the area of social science analysis of environmental problems already exists.

The conclusion from the previous sketch of the new role of social sciences in the area of global environmental change is that this area provides an overwhelming set of intriguing research questions and options which would definitely provide for creative and interdisciplinary, policy-relevant social science research. Whether or nor these challenges will be taken up by the field depends on an important critical success factor, namely, the marketing of the social science product. This will be discussed in the final section (see Freudenburg, 1989).

GLOBAL CHANGE AS A MARKETABLE COMMODITY

The above shopping list is ambitious and needs considerable policy support. The image of the social sciences has unfortunately not always been impressively good. Policy-makers especially (for example, in the European Community) have often felt that social science research was sometimes frustrating policy-making rather than substantiating it. It has to be admitted that the marketing of social science research has never been a strong point (see Lawler (1985), Van de Vall (1987, 1990)). Extra marketing efforts seem to be needed so that the various products of social scientists are better valued and utilized.

The potential contribution of the social sciences toward reducing the 'hidden foot' is likely to be maximized when done in an interdisciplinary fashion. Given the extreme high degree of complexity involved in global change, an interdisciplinary formulation of the relevant issues (for example, by making use of multivariate and graphically-depicted conceptual models) is needed. In other words, the chances that social scientists frustrate or delay rather than help or advise policy-makers are higher when the research approach taken is not of an interdisciplinary nature. 'Interdisciplinarity' with respect to global change would also involve the natural sciences: the more environmental concerns are translated into various desired or required behavioural change modalities, the more likely that the role of the social sciences will be policy-relevant and used.

Finally, there is one crucial (marketing) task of persuasion involved in the interplay of environmental threats and research-driven behaviourial solutions or options. We expect that the more certain people are of a long-term, complex and distant negative environmental effect, the more likely they will change their, often habitual, behaviour. Yet, most people underestimate the negative effect of own environmentally damaging behaviour (the 'social dilemma'). However, the more environmental threats are shown to be facts, the lower the barriers for desired or required behavioural change. This hypothesis would need serious testing. Only educational programmes that are carefully evaluated, including quasi-experimentation (or assessing the effect of interventions in real-life field settings), will tell. That is where the tools of the social scientists will come into play. Hence, their efforts could have a lasting effect on an object that they, on purpose, always avoided: the precious natural world. Especially in areas or countries where lack of prosperity leads to a low priority profile for the environment, severe problems are to be expected. Such regional aspects of global change – with a particular emphasis on developing countries – will be discussed in the final section.

REGIONAL SUSTAINABLE DEVELOPMENT IN THIRD WORLD COUNTRIES

The situation in many developing countries demonstrates convincingly that since the Second World War mankind's capacity to destroy the Earth's habitat has increased significantly, partly as a result of radical technological changes (generating huge amounts of air, water and soil pollutants, including many toxic materials), partly as a result of the rise in world population (and its subsequent rise in consumption and mobility patterns). Consequently, the character of the interest in environmental problems has changed substantially. For example, the international scale of economic processes, North–South relationships and global environmental phenomena have all acquired a more central position in the environmental debate. The global environmental problems most alluded to in the 1990s are the rise in CO_2 concentration in the atmosphere, depletion of the ozone layer, deforestation, and the exploitation of the common seas.

Meanwhile, an increasing political interest has developed regarding the disruption of the Earth's natural resources and environmental decay. Despite many efforts, local, national and international policy bodies have been unsuccessful in ensuring a viable economic development trajectory that is compatible with environmental quality. For example, the UN Conference on the Human Environment held in Stockholm in 1972 has not nearly achieved the high goals that were set for the planet.

Despite the global nature of many environmental problems, it is noteworthy that a major problem is caused by the local scale environmental externalities, in terms of both causes and effects. For example, global problems such as acid rain, sedimentation, desertification, ozonization, eutrofication, ocean pollution and resource extraction are the result of a great many small-scale and local activities (without being controlled by an environment-watchful costituency), while far-reaching environmental impacts can be observed most clearly at a local or regional scale. Consequently, the local/regional problems of land use (interpreted in a broad sense, including landscape, 'cityscape', soil quality and marine environments) are of central importance in environmental management.

The issue of sustainable development calls also for closer attention to some of the critical concepts in regional planning, namely, allocative efficiency and distributive equity. The Brundtland Report illuminated the rise of a third challenge, namely, the need to cope with environmental decay. Considering the strong linkages between income, distribution and the environment, sustainable development requires that the present generation limits its use of ecological resources. Consequently, it makes sense to include – besides efficiency and equity – sustainability as a third key criterion in regional planning. In Van den Bergh (1991) the concept of regional sustainable development has been introduced in order to do justice to the necessary geographical scale involved in sustainable development strategies.

Clearly, the use of regions as a focal point for sustainability policies also evokes various research problems. For example, there may be considerable variation between different regions, making quantitative reliable indicators necessary for a proper analysis of differences between regions of a compound system.

Furthermore, a spatial (that is, multi-regional) system is usually not closed, but is facing various spatial (economic and environmental) interactions. Economic interactions may refer to trade flows, migration, transport and so on, while environmental interactions may refer to diffusion of pollutants, migratory birds and so on.

It is noteworthy that goals of sustainable development cannot be left vaguely at the meso scale of a region, but have to be specified as precisely as possible. This may require rather painstaking and time-consuming data collection and retrieval based on detailed fieldwork.

The advantage, however, of a meso scale approach is that policy measures can be taken much more concretely in a limited area at the interface of economy and environment facing sustainability problems.

This may imply that sustainability initiatives should be induced and instigated from a global or (supra-)national level (thus supporting the necessary change in policy orientation in developing countries), but that policy implementation should be advocated at a regional or local level, where environmental actions are much more effective. This means that the notion of 'sustainable city' and 'sustainable region' is a necessary complement to global change policy initiatives.

References

Archibuchi, F. and P. Nijkamp (eds) (1989) *Economy and Ecology: Towards Sustainable Development* (Dordrecht: Kluwer).

Barde, Ph. and K. Button (eds) (1991) *Transport Policy and the Environment* (London: Earthscan).

Bergh, J. C. P. M. van den (1991) *Models for Regional Sustainable Development*, Thesis published Amsterdam.

Clark, W. C. (1990) *The Human Ecology of Global Change* (Cambridge, Mass.) J. F. Kennedy School of Government (Harvard University).

ESRC (1991) *Global Environmental Change Programme, First Phase* (Swindon, ESRC) March.

Freudenburg, W. R. (1989) 'Social Scientists' Contributions to Environmental Management', *Journal of Social Issues*, vol. 45, no. 1, pp. 133–52.

Jacobson, H. K. and M. F. Pirce (1990) *A Framework for Research on the Human Dimensions of Global Enviromental Change* (Paris: International Social Science Council, UNESCO).

Kates, R. W. and W. C. Clark, V. Norberg-Bohm and B. L. Turner III (1990) *Human Sources of Global Change* (Cambridge, Mass.: J. F. Kennedy School of Government, Harvard University).

Lawler, E. E. (1985) *Doing Research that is Useful for Theory and Practice* (San Francisco: Jossey Bass).

NSF (National Science Foundation) (1991) *Economics and Global Change*, Workshop Report (New Haven, Conn.: NSF).

Pearch, J. D. and B. Steinhardt (1990/1) 'What We Have Learned since Earth Day', *The G. A. O. Journal*, vol. 11, Winter, pp. 29–35.

Social Science Council (1991) *Advies Sociaal-Wetenschappelijk Klimaatonderzoek* (Amsterdam: Social Sciences Council).

Tennekes, H. (1990) 'Climate Research: Hubris, Ecology, Humility', *Weather*, vol. 45, no. 2, February, pp. 67–8.

Vall, M. van de (1987) 'The Value Context of Data-based Sociological Practice: A Professional Paradigm', *The American Behavioral Scientist*, vol. 30, no. 6, pp. 644–60.

Vall, M. van de (1990) 'De Structuur van Ongestructureerde Problemen: Een Rationele Methode tot Effectuering van Beleid', in H. J. van de Braak (ed.), *Rationaliteit en Beleid: Hoofdstukken uit de Rotterdamse Sociologie* (De Lier: Academisch Boeken Centrum) pp. 279–312.

World Commission on Environment and Development (1987), *Our Common Future* (Harvard, USA: Cambridge University Press).

13 Regional Planning Implications of Climate Changes

Antoine S. Bailly

Two years ago, a book written by L. K. Caldwell, *Between Two Worlds: Science, the Environmental Movement and Policy Choice*, was published by the Cambridge University Press. It dealt with the relationship between science and the world of people. Caldwell shows how science can help shape new relationships between people and environment when information is clearly transmitted . . . which is not always the case. He reminds us that when the popular environmental movement was looking to science for guidance, most sciences, including regional science, were unprepared to explain the interactions between regional growth, economic evolution and environment changes in a way that people could understand to have an effect on public behaviour and decisions. The fundamental question of environmental policies in the late 1990s is how to use knowledge about the evaluation of environmental conditions in regional planning terms. The principal purpose of this chapter is to make basic issues and planning implications of climate changes accessible to regional scientists and to a broad public.

The chapter is concerned first with environmental perception, an aspect that many climate researchers would regard as non-scientific, since it deals more with the concept of 'climate sensitivity' than with those of climatology and meteorology. The idea of 'climate sensitivity' considers the behavioural approach as the basis for the analysis of the decision-making process: we deal here with the diffusion of information about climate change and its impact on human behaviour. One of the main questions for economic practices – tourism in mountain environments being one of these practices – concerns not climatic change as a meteorological process, but the way people perceive it. The cognition process is too often ignored, even if people need to be more informed on the implications of past, present and future climate changes when making socioeconomic decisions.

One of the questions to be raised is how, in a given climate, individuals construct their own reality in linking together the functional and the symbolic; then how perception of climate is related to experience, and how the imaginery and the real are connected for each decision in space. W. Maunder (1986) identifies three levels of sensitivity: 'how much variation is needed before it becomes significant . . . in affecting decisions; are such significant . . . climate variations the same . . . from one season to the next; and what specific effect does a significant . . . climate variation have on particular activities' such as tourism?

PERCEPTUAL SITUATIONS

The classical conception of regional science – based on Cartesian percepts of evidence (for example, the observer's independent certainty); reductionism (that is, a breaking down into sets of simple elements); causality (that is, the presupposition of an order connecting up of linear causalities) and exhaustiveness (that is, the certainty that nothing essential has been omitted) – has been thrown into question by the research on representations, for how can our scientific practices be separated from our interior existence, with its affective and emotional aspects? Must not the researcher – even of climate change – above and beyond the observation of facts, also understand the subtle and complex links which unite the real and the imaginary (Bailly and Debarbieux, 1991)?

To the precept of evidence, one must oppose that of subjectivism, allowing us, as it does, to account for human irrationality; the precept of reductionism must be replaced by that of complexity, for the more a phenomenon studied is reduced, the more complex it is, and the greater the number of dimensions one finds; probabilism opposed to causalism, as it is impossible to foresee everything (except in random terms). Exhaustiveness must be replaced by the ideological, that is, the partial representation of phenomena based on our explicit and implicit choices.

All researchers in the human sciences find themselves faced with a fabulous and complex world, a chaotic swirl of existential experiences. Should they want to understand its creation and evolution, and find order in the chaos, they will have to accept the random character of change and the apparent irrationality of human behaviour. They will also have to take an interest in the symbolics of phenomena, in their subjective connotations. In this sense, the study of climate is not only a collection of empirically observable facts, it is also the study of their meanings. It is only after understanding these symbols that we can deal with the planning implications of climate changes.

This approach is based on the theories of cognitive psychologists (Piaget and Inhelder, 1974); we know from these experiences that humans perceive and respond rapidly to highly significant events (Vernon, 1962). The greater and more sudden the change in the environment, the more likely it is to attract attention. Any situation, such as an extreme of climate, which may be potentially dangerous (drought, floods and so on) will stimulate both the observer and the planners. Conversely, peaceful and slow changes are considered apathetically even by planners; people do not maintain a prolonged awareness of a relatively slow change. Expectations and decisions are related to the probability of the occurrence of events belonging to one of these two subjective categories. A great deal is yet to be done to make people more aware of the importance of some types of event (climate changes) and some perceptual situations (for example, tourism in mountain environments, as mentioned previously).

HOW TO MEASURE OUR RESPONSES TO CLIMATE CHANGES?

The disastrous effects of climate modification, such as floods, were in the past often called 'acts of God'. In modern times, since we have learned about hazards, the main questions are: how to evaluate the risks, how to judge the acceptability of the risks, and to integrate these into spatial planning? As W. Lowrance writes, 'a thing is safe if its risks are judged to be acceptable' (Lowrance, 1976).

This approach results from studies of environmental hazards and human responses, engaged by geographers from Chicago and Boulder, Colorado, the pioneer work being by G. White. Recent studies involve a broad array of people, participating in different fields of investigation, from human to natural and technical hazards.

The search for the measurement of human responses to hazards, by I. Burton, R. Kates and G. White (1978), allows us to define an event by using seven dimensions: the magnitude; frequency; duration; areal extent; speed of onset; spatial dispersion; and temporal spacing. To list information from these authors:

- The *magnitude*: occurrences exceeding some common level; for climate it can be the maximum temperature reached during a cold wave.

- *Frequency* asserts how often an event of a given magnitude may be expected to occur in the long-run average. Thus a snowstorm of a given magnitude (depth of snow accumulation in cm) may occur only once in ten years (but not, of course, *every* ten years).
- *Duration* refers to length of time over which a hazard event persists; thus an unexpected frost may cause much damage in a few hours.
- *Areal extent* refers to the space covered by a hazard event. A snow storm's areal extent may be a short and narrow swath, while a drought may cover thousands of square kilometres.
- *Speed of onset* refers to length of time between the first appearance of an event and its peak. Drought is slow-onset hazard, whereas avalanches are of fast onset.
- The first five of these are measures of the aggregate of separate events. *Spatial dispersion* and *temporal spacing* refer to the distribution of a population of events over space and time.

How do people react to these dimensions? Since it is rare that individuals have access to full information, their responses are related both to perception of the event and to awareness of opportunities to make adjustments. In Figure 13.1, on a diagram drawn from I. Burton (1978), we show the theoretical range of responses. These may range from immediate actions to long-term ones.

Most researchers on human reactions to climatic changes have been working with violent hazards such as floods or cyclones. Non-extreme events, which are not immediately hazardous to people, are not often the object of a behavioural approach. However, a basic bibliography of publications in the social and political sciences is given by G. Dürrenberger and C. Jaeger (1992). The authors show that the range of responses depends on regional adaptation, absorptive capacity and economic constraints. People imagine, in their region, not only probable outcomes, but also develop subjective views of such probabilities. Expected utility and experience are basic to the understanding of the process of coping with risk in an uncertain environment. It is essentially a process of information and interpretation which leads to hazard appraisal and perceived alternatives. The case of Venice, and the 'aqua alta' phenomenon has often been used as an example to show the slow adaptation of local people to a phenomenon, and the desire of exterior planners to control it.

Research carried out on climatic changes in mountainous environments, such as the Alps, are often linked to future planning. Some

Figure 13.1 Human reactions to natural hazards

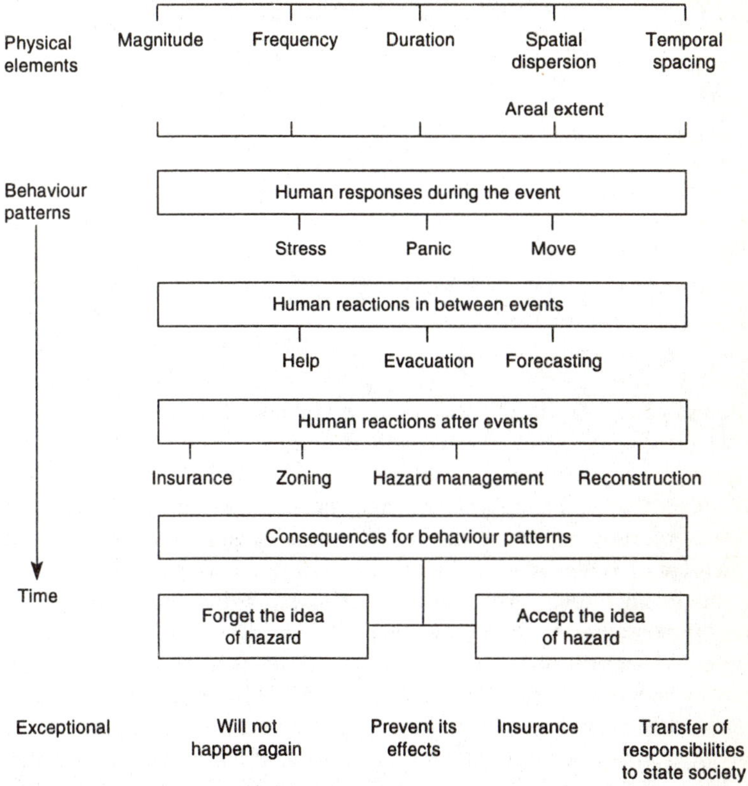

Source: Adapted from Burton (1978).

useful studies from the Grenoble Alpine Institute should be mentioned: J. P. Guérin (1984), H. Gumuchian (1984) and special issues of the *Revue de Géographie Alpine* on *Homo turisticus*, as researchers linked to PROCLIM in Switzerland. As a bibliographical base we can also use man-environments MAB publication (Messerli, 1989) and the image of mountainous environments by P. Auchlin and P. Vietti-Violi (1983). Those works have to take into account the climatological environment, such as cold waves, avalanches and floods. They make up the basis of a better knowledge of human reactions to climatic changes in the Alps in an historical perspective.

Figure 13.2 The relationship between climate change and human choices

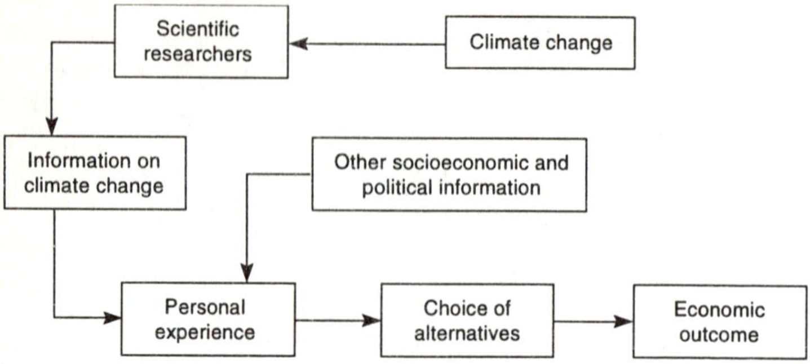

RELATIONSHIPS BETWEEN CLIMATIC CHANGE INFORMATION AND HUMAN PRACTICES

Information on climatic changes, and the climate that is expected at a specified time in the future, is now fundamental for tourism and the choice of future investments (ski lifts, snow-making machines and so on); for example, an image of a previous Christmas without snow will orientate some holiday-makers towards destinations other than Alpine ski resorts. Conversely, an early snowfall, even if the snow cover is not thick enough at low altitude to allow ski practice, will reverse this trend. All this information, summarized in Figure 13.2, with other non-climatic information (economic trends, world crisis, war, risk and so on), will lead to a choice of various alternatives, with economic outcomes for tourist regions, since they can then plan other types of activity.

The cognitive process is linked to climatic information, which has to be in the most useful form if it is to be relevant for decision-making processes. Only then will the return exceed the cost of diffusing the information. For example, to solve the question of the purchase of ski lifts, equipment and snow-making machines as an investment for the economic future of ski resorts.

The information has to answer practical questions, and to clarify the trends, causes and effects of climatic change in mountain environments for predictive purposes. Tourism planning emphasizes the relationship between climatic change and leisure practices, especially since there is an evolution through time of the perception of climatic changes.

The global environment is subject to drastic changes; what is still in doubt is the scale of change, especially in mountainous environments, where all human activities (particularly activities linked to outdoor leisure) depend on these changes. Since the duration and persistance of these changes cannot be forecast, it is still difficult to ask people to adjust now to a possible situation in the future; people living in mountainous areas are engaged in activities that may be viewed as a game with capricious nature. Regional scientists have to make people aware of the probable evolution of the climate, and give them ways to cope with possible alterations by reorganizing society. These adjustments involve new agricultural and tourism activities, more in tune with nature, and more adapted to warming trends in the climate.

However, most regional authorities still do not deal with the social aspects of climatic changes, except by rapid interventions in extreme situations. They have, however, to prepare society for probable changes and publicize the advantages of diversity and flexibility, the way to plan a future adapted to climatic change. In this direction, more behavioural studies have to be carried out, for a better understanding of human reactions. A simple model proposed by P. Bartelmus for future planning (Bartelmus, 1986) gives an idea of participative planning that is aware of environmental perceptions (Figure 13.3).

CONCLUSIONS

We presented in this chapter one issue in the environmental perception of climatic changes, but others could be studied to enable societies to face environmental realities, such as:

- erosion and soil deterioration in rural areas;
- devegetation by deforestation, desertification in dry environments; and
- destruction of natural habitats and pollution in urban regions.

Regional science needs to be used more to inform about environmental perception, human practices and their consequences for private and public decisions. The history of humanity shows that, despite errors of human behaviour, people have an inmate capacity to learn and to evaluate their experiences. But this capacity is often insufficiently shared, and environmental deterioration can affect the welfare, health and quality of life of many regions.

Figure 13.3 Major stages of the planning process

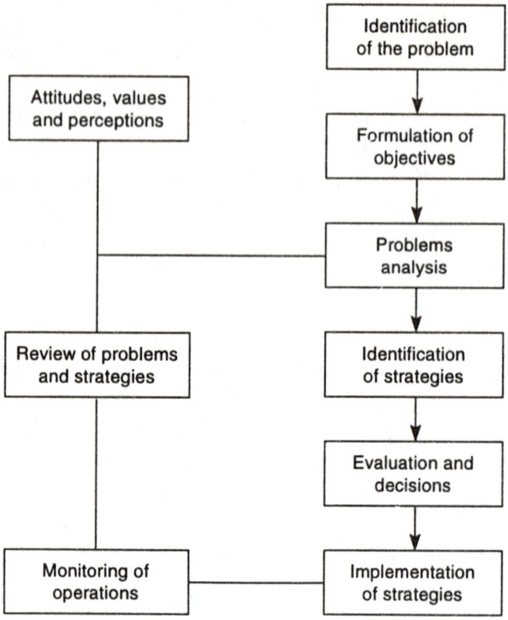

Source: Bartelmus (1986).

Notes

The term 'representation' is widely used in Francophone social science, but is not commonly employed in English. This concept refers, according to J. Piaget, to the manner in which human beings experience: how they perceive experiences, and how their perception of these is based upon an accumulated set of experiences and memories; how they represent it, imagine it and value it in verbal, written, mental or graphical form.

References

Auchlin, P. and P. Vietti-Violi (1983) 'Perception du Pays-d'Enhaut par ses touristes (1980–1981)', *MAB–Schlussbericht*, no. 3.

Bailly, A. (1974) 'La perception des paysages urbains. Essai méthodologique', *L'Espace Géographique*, vol. III, no. 3, pp. 211–17.

Bailly, A. (1984) 'Probabilités subjectives et géographie humaine. Fondements, méthodologie et applications', in *Géographes aujourd'hui; mélanges offerts en hommage à François Gay* (Nice: Universite de Nice, Departement de Geographie).

Bailly, A. (1991) 'La géographie des risques naturels', in A. Bailly *et al.* (eds), *Les concepts de la géographie humaine* (2nd edn) (Paris: Masson), pp. 181–6.

Bailly, A. and B. Debarbieux (1991) 'Géographie et représentations spatiales', in A. Bailly *et al.* (eds), *Les concepts de la géographie humaine* (2nd edn) (Paris: Masson), pp. 153–60.

Bartelmus, P. (1986) *Environment and Development* (London: Allen & Unwin).

Bridel, L. (1986) 'Gestion des dangers naturels, théorie et étude de cas', *Cours postgrade*. Planification et projet, nouvelles démarches, EPFL, Département d'Architecture Paris.

Brunet, R. (1974) 'Espace, perception et comportement', *L'Espace géographique*, vol. III, no. 3, pp. 189–204.

Burton, I., R. W. Kates and G. F. White (1978) *The Environment as Hazard* (New York: Oxford University Press).

Burton, I., R. W. Kates and R. E. Snead (1969) *The Human Ecology of Coastal Flood Hazard in Megalopolis*, Research paper 115 (University of Chicago, Department of Geography).

Caldwell, L. (1990) *Between Two Worlds: Science, the Environmental Movement and Policy Choice* (Cambridge University Press).

Claval, P. (1974) 'La géographie et la perception de l'espace', *L'Espace géographique*, vol. III, no. 3, pp. 179–87.

Dürrenberger, G. and C. Jaeger (1992) 'Klimaänderung und Risikodiskurs', NFP 31, *Schlussbericht Vorstudie*, vol. 42, unpublished, Amsterdam.

Eddy, A. *et al.* (1980) *The Economic Impact of Climate*, Vol. I (Oklahoma: Norman).

Geipel, R. (1977) 'Friaul. Sozialgeographische Aspekte einer Erdbebenkatastrophe', *Münchener Geographische Hefte*, no. 40.

Grunder, M. (1984) 'Ein Beitrag zur Beurteilung von Naturgefahren im Hinblick auf die Erstellung von mittelmassstäbigen Gefahrenhinweiskarten (mit Beispielen aus dem Berner Oberland und der Landschaft Davos)', *Geographia Bernensia*, vol. 23.

Gunder, M. and Kienholz, H. (1986) 'Gefahrenkartierung', in O. Wildi and K. Ewald (eds), *Der Naturraum und dessen Nutzung im alpinen Tourismusgebiet von Davos*, Ergebnisse des MAB–Projektes Davos, Birmensdorf, EAFV, *Bericht*, vol. 289, pp. 67–86.

Guérin, J. P. (1984) *L'aménagement de la montagne. Politiques, discours et productions d'espaces* (Gap: Ophrys).

Gumuchian, H. (1980) 'La montagne française vue par l'enfant', *Revue de Géographie Alpine*, Special issue, pp. 35–68.

Gumuchian, H. (1984) *Les territoires de l'hiver ou la montagne française au quotidien* (Grenoble: Editions des Cahiers de l'Alpe).

Gumuchian, H. (1988) *De l'espace au territoire. Représentations spatiales et aménagement* (Grenoble: Collection Grenoble Science, Université Joseph Fourier).

Kates, R. W. (1967) 'The perception of storm hazard on the shores of Megalopolis', in D. Lowenthal (ed.), *Environmental Perception and Behavior*, Research paper 109 (University of Chicago, Department of Geography) pp. 60–74.

Kates, R. W. (1975) *Risk Assessment of Environmental Hazard* (Chichester: John Wiley).

Knoepfel, P. (ed.) (1988) *Risiko und risikomanagement* (Basle: SAGUF).

Lieberherr, B. (1981) 'Système écologique et conflits d'affectations dans les régions de montagne; recherche méthodogique', *MAB-Fachbeitrag*, vol. 8.

Litaudon, C. and N. Noth (1990) *Représentation des catastrophes naturelles: le cas de Nîmes* (University of Geneva, Department of Geography).

Lowrance, W. (1976) *Of Acceptable Risk* (Los Altos, Calif.: Kaufman).

Lynch, K. (1960) *The Image of the City* (Cambridge, Mass.: MIT Press).

Maunder, W. (1986) *The Uncertainty Business: Risks and Opportunities in Weather and Climate* (London: Methuen).

Messerli, P. (1989) *Mensch und Natur im Alpinen Lebenstraum. Risiken, Chancen, Perspektiven*, Zentrale Erkentnisse aus dem Schweizerischen MAB-Program. (Bern: Haupt).

Pellegrino, P. *et al.* (1983) *Identité régionale et représentations collectives de l'espace*, PNR, 'Problèmes régionaux en Suisse', no. 25. (unpublished).

Piaget, J. and B. Inhelder (1974) *La représentation de l'espace chez l'enfant* (Paris: PUF).

Pfister, C. (1985a) 'Klimageschichte der Schweiz 1525–1860. Das Klima der Schweiz von 1525–1860 und seine Bedeutung in der Geschichte von Bevölkerung und Landwirtschaft', *Academica Helvetica*, vol. 6 (Berne: Haupt).

Pfister, C. (1985b) *Climhist. Banque de données pour l'histoire du climat*, (Berne: Meteotest).

Rebetez-Beniston, M. (1993) *Perception du climat en Suisse romande*, Doctoral thésis, University of Lausanne.

Saarinen, T. F. and J. L. Sell (1980) 'Environmental Perception. Progress reports', *Progress in Human Geography*, vol. 4, pp. 525–48; and vol. 5, pp. 525–47.

Saarinen, T. F., D. Seamon and J. L. Sell (1984) *Environmental Perception and Behavior: an Inventory and Prospect*, Research paper no. 209 (University of Chicago, Department of Geography).

Schneider, S. (1990) *Global Warming: Are We Entering the Greenhouse Century*? (Cambridge: Lutterworth Press).

Vernon, M. D. (1962) *The Psychology of Perception* (Harmondsworth: Penguin).

Whyte, A. V. and I. Burton (1982) 'Perception of Risks in Canada', in I. Burton *et al.* (eds), *Living With Risks: Environmental Risk Management in Canada*, Environmental monograph no. 3 (Toronto, Institute of Environmental Studies) pp. 39–69.

14 Economic Geography with Division of Labour and Amenity Difference

Wei-Bin Zhang

INTRODUCTION

It may be said that two approaches have dominated the literature of urban and regional economics since the 1970s. The first approach is mainly related to location of firms with exogenous spatial distribution of demand (see, for example, Isard (1956), Greenhut *et al.* (1989)). The second text is mainly related to the economic geography of residential areas with endogenous income and production structures (see, for example, Alonso (1964), Beckmann (1957), Wingo (1961), Muth (1969), Fujita (1989)). There are a few spatial equilibrium models which deal with decision-making by households and producers within a compact framework. This chapter provides a model that bears on problems inherent in economic geography, with interactions of demand and supply of various commodities, price structure and spatial divisions of labour with given preferences, territory, labour force and locational amenities.

The remainder of the chapter is organized as follows. The second section represents the basic model; the third section provides conditions for the existence of equilibria; the fourth section examines the effects of changes in the urban amenity on spatial economic structure and the fifth section concludes the study. An appendix proves the results given in the third section.

THE MODEL

This chapter is concerned with an isolated system. There are no exchanges of ideas, no goods or money flows, and no migration between the system and the outside world. The system consists of two sectors,

Figure 14.1 The one-city and one-farm system

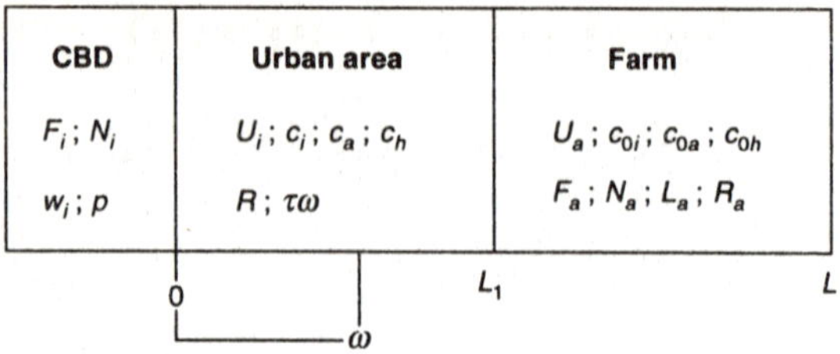

agricultural and industrial. Similar to the Alonso model, it is assumed that urban product activities are concentrated at the central business district (CBD), and workers are housed in the urban area. The possible internal complexity of the CBD is neglected and it is assumed that the CBD is a line.

This study features a linear system on a homogeneous plain whose width is unity. For simplicity, the CBD is assumed to be single-sided, as shown in Figure 14.1. Urban workers can travel in one direction only. The urban area is located between the CBD and the farm. It is assumed that farmers' dwelling and farming sites have the same location. Possible costs for professional changes and transportation costs for commodities are neglected. The labour markets are assumed to be perfectly competitive. The population is assumed to be homogenous and people are assumed to be freely mobile between the two professions. The agricultural good is selected to serve as numeraire, with all other prices being measured relative to its price.

To describe the system, one defines:

L and N = the given territorial size and the population of the system;
L_1 = the boundary between the urban area and the farm;
ω = the residential location of a worker, $0 \leq \omega \leq L_1$;
$R(\omega)$ = the land rent at location ω in the urban area;
R_a = the land rent of the agricultural area;
N_i and N_a = the employment of the industrial and agricultural sectors, respectively;
F_i and F_a = the output of the industrial and agricultural sectors, respectively;
p = the price of the urban product; and
w_i and w_a = the wage rates of the workers and farmers, respectively.

The agricultural sector

There are two inputs, labour and land, in agricultural production. The agricultural production function is specified as follows:

$$F_a = L_a^{\alpha} N_a^{1-\alpha} \qquad 0 < \alpha < 1 \tag{14.1}$$

where L_a is land employed by the agricultural sector. The production function is homogenous of degree one with respect to its two inputs.

The profit maximization yields the following conditions:

$$R_a = \alpha F_a / L_a \qquad w_a = (1 - \alpha) F_a / N_a \tag{14.2}$$

Let C_i and C_a denote total consumption of agricultural product by the workers and the farmers, respectively. The balance of demand for and supply of agricultural product is given by:

$$C_i + C_a = F_a \tag{14.3}$$

The industrial sector

For simplicity of analysis, it is assumed that industrial commodities are produced by a single input factor – labour. Other possible inputs, such as natural resources and capital, are omitted at this initial stage, A linear production function of the industrial sector is specified as follows:

$$F_i = zN_i \tag{14.4}$$

The parameter, z, measures the productivity of the industrial sector.

Perfect competition in the labour and land markets results in zero profits in the industrial sector. That is,

$$pF_i = w_i N_i,$$

or,

$$zp = w_i \tag{14.5}$$

The balance of demand for and supply of industrial commodities is given by:

$$C_{ii} + C_{ia} = F_i \tag{14.6}$$

where C_{ii} and C_{ia} are the total consumption levels of industrial commodities by the workers and farmers, respectively.

The behaviour of consumers

It is assumed that the utility level of a typical household is dependent on locational amenity and consumption levels of industrial commodities, agricultural goods and housing. Here, a household's housing is measured simply by its dwelling size. The utility function of an urban household at location ω is specified as follows:

$$U_i(\omega) = \theta_i c_i(\omega)^{\xi_i} \; c_a(\omega)^{\xi_a} \; c_h(\omega)^{\xi_h} \quad \xi_i, \xi_a, \xi_h > 0, \; 0 \leq \omega \leq L_1 \tag{14.7}$$

where $c_i(\omega)$, $c_a(\omega)$ and $c_h(\omega)$ are respectively, consumption levels of industrial commodities, agricultural goods and dwelling size of the household at location ω.

Similarly, the utility function of a typical farmer is specified as follows:

$$U_a = \theta_a c_{0i}^{\xi_i} \; c_{0a}^{\xi_a} \; c_{0h}^{\xi_h} \qquad \xi_i, \xi_a, \xi_h > 0 \tag{14.8}$$

where c_{0i}, c_{0a} and c_{0h} are, respectively, consumption levels of industrial commodities, agricultural goods and dwelling size of each farmer.

The two parameters, θ_i and θ_a, are called amenity levels of city and countryside, respectively. As life-styles, and 'professional amenities' may be different between the city and the countryside, it is reasonable to assume that even if the components of consumption are identical between a worker and a farmer, they may have different utility levels. The parameters, θ_i and θ_a, take into account differences in amenities caused by professional, locational and other factors. Although amenity levels are treated as parameters in this study, it is not difficult to determine θ_i and θ_a endogenously as functions of population and production scales in the ways as suggested, for instance, in Kanemoto (1980) and Fujita (1989).

The urban consumer problem is defined by:

$$\max \; U_i(\omega)$$

$$pc_i(\omega) + c_a(\omega) + R(\omega) \; c_h(\omega) = y(\omega) \tag{14.9}$$

where $y(\omega) = w_i - \tau\omega$, $0 \le \omega \le L_1$. Here, the parameter, τ, is travel cost per unity of distance, and $\tau\omega$ is the total travelling cost per household between the dwelling site ω and the CBD.

The optimal problem has the following unique solution:

$$c_i(\omega) = \xi\xi_i y(\omega)/p \qquad c_a(\omega) = \xi\xi_a y(\omega) \qquad (14.10)$$
$$c_h(\omega) = \xi\xi_h y(\omega)/R(\omega)$$

where $\xi = 1/(\xi_i + \xi_a + \xi_h)$.

The rural consumer problem is formulated by:

$$\max U_a$$
$$pc_{0i} + c_{0a} + R_a c_{0h} = w_a$$

The unique optimal solution is given by:

$$c_{0i} = \xi\xi_i w_a/p \qquad c_{0a}(\omega) = \xi\xi_a w_a, \qquad c_{0h} = \xi\xi_h w_a/R_a \qquad (14.11)$$

Denoting $n(\omega)$, the residential density at location ω, one has:

$$n(\omega) = 1/c_h(\omega) \qquad 0 \le \omega < L_1 \qquad (14.12)$$

As the number of the workers is equal to the sum of the urban residents over the urban area, and the total population consists of workers and farmers, the following equations are held:

$$\int_0^{L_1} n(\omega)\mathrm{d}\omega = N_i \qquad N_i + N_a = N \qquad (14.13)$$

The total land of the agricultural area is utilized for farmers' housing and agricultural production, that is:

$$L_a + c_{0h}N_a = L - L_1 \qquad (14.14)$$

As the system is isolated, agricultural and industrial products are consumed by all the households in the system. The conditions, (14.3) and (14.6), can be expressed in the following forms:

$$\int_0^{L_1} n(\omega)\, c_i(\omega)\mathrm{d}\omega + (L - L_1)c_{0i} = F_i$$
$$\int_0^{L_1} n(\omega)\, c_a(\omega)\mathrm{d}\omega + (L - L_1)c_{0a} = F_a \qquad (14.15)$$

The model has thus been completed. It has twenty variables: N_i, N_a, F_i, F_a, c_i, c_a, c_h, c_{0i}, c_{0a}, c_{0h}, w_i, w_a, p, L_1, L_a, R_a, $R(\omega)$, $n(\omega)$, U_i and U_a, and it contains the same number of equations.

THE EXISTENCE OF EQUILIBRIA

As the population is homogenous, the utility level is identical among the households, irrespective of dwelling location and professions. Using (14.7), (14.10) and $U_i(\omega) = U_i(0)$ for $0 \leq \omega < L_1$, one has:

$$R(\omega)/R(0) = \{y(\omega)/w_i\}^{\lambda} < 1 \qquad 0 \leq \omega < L_1 \qquad (14.16)$$

where $y(\omega) \leq w_i$ and $\lambda \equiv 1/\xi\xi_h > 1$. It is clear to see that the urban area's land rent declines the further it is from its CBD. As the urban households have identical utility function and wage rates, the conclusion is obvious.

Substituting (14.7), (14.8), (14.10) and (14.11) into $U_i(L_1) = U_a$ and $U_i(0) = U_a$, respectively, yield:

$$y(L_i)/w_a = \theta^{1/\lambda} \qquad R(0)/R_a = \theta(w_i/w_a)^{\lambda} \qquad (14.17)$$

where $\theta \equiv (\theta_i/\theta_a)^{\lambda\xi}$. If the rural amenity level is much lower than that in the city, the farmers' wage rate may be higher than the workers'. This is as a result of the assumed homogenous population. The following proposition shows that the system always has equilibria.

Proposition 1

The wage rate, w_i, of workers is determined by the following equation:

$$\Phi^*(w_i) \equiv \tau w_i\{Z(w_i)^{-\lambda} - 1\} - \theta_i\{\tau L - w_i + w_i Z(w_i)\} = 0 \quad (14.18)$$

where $Z(w_i)$ is a continuous function of w_i (defined in the Appendix). The equation (14.3) has at least one positive solution. Moreover, for any solution, $w_i(>0)$, all other variables are uniquely determined as functions of w_i).

The above proposition is proved in the Appendix. Here, the existence of equilibria is guaranteed. But the system may have either a unique or multiple equilibria. It should be noted that for any solution w_i of (14.18), the equilibrium values of all other variables are uniquely determined (as functions of w_i and the parameters).

AMENITIES AND ECONOMIC GEOGRAPHY

This section examines the impact of changes in the urban amenity level, θ_i, on production structure and economic geography. Taking derivatives of (A14.14) and (A14.17), with respect to θ_i, yields:

$$(1/w_i)\, dw_i/d\theta_i + a_1 dZ/d\theta_i = a_2$$

$$(\theta_1 \tau L/w_i^2)\, dw_i/d\theta_i - (\lambda Z^{-\lambda-1} + \theta_1)\, dZ/d\theta_i$$
$$= 2/\theta_i \xi_h (Z^{-\lambda} - 1) > 0 \quad (14.19)$$

in which Z, θ_1 and θ_2 are defined in the Appendix, and:

$$a_1 \equiv \alpha\lambda/Z(1 - \alpha)(1 - Z^{\lambda}) + (\xi_i Z + \xi_a \theta^{1/\lambda})/$$
$$Z\{\xi_i Z + (1-\alpha)\, \xi_a \theta^{1/\lambda}\} > 0$$

$$a_2 \equiv (2\alpha/\xi_h + \xi - \xi\alpha)/(1 - \alpha) + \alpha\xi\xi_a \theta^{1/\lambda}/$$
$$\theta_i\{\xi_i Z + (1 - \alpha)\, \xi_a \theta^{1/\lambda}\} > 0 \quad (14.20)$$

From (14.19) one gets:

$$(\lambda Z^{-\lambda-1} + \theta_1 + a_1 \theta_1 \tau L/w_i)\, dZ/d\theta_1 = a_3$$

$$(\theta_1 \tau L/w_i^2)\, dw_i/d\theta_i = (\lambda Z^{-\lambda-1} + \theta_1)\, dZ/d\theta_i + 2/\theta_i\, \xi_h (Z^{-\lambda} - 1) \quad (14.21)$$

where $a_3 \equiv a_2 \theta_1 \tau L/w_i - 2/\theta_i \xi_h (Z^{-\lambda} - 1)$.

If $a_3 > 0$, $dZ/d\theta_i > 0$ and $dw_i/d\theta_i > 0$. As $Z = 1 - \tau L_1/w_i$, in the case of $a_3 > 0$ one has $d(\tau L_1/w_i)/d\theta_i < 0$. This implies that the travel cost of urban residents from the CBD to the boundary of the urban area is reduced in terms of the city's wage rate. If $a_3 < 0$, then $dZ/d\theta_i < 0$ (that is, $d(\tau L_1/w_i)/d\theta_i > 0$), but $dw_i/d\theta_i$ may be either positive or negative. As a_3 is determined by so many parameters it is not easy to interpret the sign of a_3 explicitly.

Taking derivatives of $L_1 = w_i(1 - Z)/\tau$ with respect to θ_i yields:

$$(w_i/L_1)\, dL_1/d\theta_i = dw_i/d\theta_i - \{w_i/(1 - Z)\}\, dZ/d\theta_i \quad (14.22)$$

One sees that $dL_1/d\theta_i$ may be either positive or negative. It is obviously not easy to interpret the condition (14.22). From $p = w_i/z$ one sees that $dp/d\theta_i$ has the same sign as that of $dw_i/d\theta_i$. When the city's amenity level is increased, the price of industrial commodities will be expanded as the city's wage rate is increased.

Taking derivatives of (A14.10) with respect to θ_i yields:

$$dL_a/d\theta_i = -\{\alpha_0/(\alpha_o + 1/\lambda)\}\, dL_1/d\theta_i \qquad (14.23)$$

If the urban area is expanded because of improvements in the city's amenity level, the land employed by the agricultural sector will be reduced, and vice versa.

From:

$$w_a = y(L_1)/\theta^{1/\lambda} \qquad N_a = \{(1 - \alpha)/w_a\}^{1/\alpha}L_a \qquad N_i = N - N_a$$

one gets:

$$\theta^{1/\lambda}dw_a/d\theta_i = dw_i/d\theta_i + \tau(1 + 1/\lambda a_0)\, dL_a/d\theta_i - \xi y(L_1)/\theta_i$$

$$(1/N_a)\, dN_a/d\theta_i = -(1/\alpha w_a)\, dw_a/d\theta_i + (1/L_a)\, dL_a/d\theta_i$$

$$dN_i/d\theta_i = -dN_a/d\theta_i \qquad (14.24)$$

The sign of $dw_a/d\theta_i$ is jointly determined by three terms, $dw_i/d\theta_i$, $\tau(1 + 1/\lambda\alpha_0)\, dL_a/d\theta_i$ and $-\ \xi y(L_1)/\theta_i$. One may call them, respectively, effects of changes in city's amenity level on city's wage rate; the land employed by the agricultural sector; and rural attractiveness. If an improvement in the city's amenity level results in increases in the city's wage rate and agricultural land use, the wage rate of the agricultural sector is increased. If the wage rate of the agricultural sector is increased and the land use of the agricultural sector is reduced, the employment of the agricultural sector is reduced.

Taking derivatives of $R_a = \alpha(N_a/L_a)^{1-\alpha}$ with respect to θ_i, one obtains:

$$\{1/R_a(1 - \alpha)\}\, dR_a/d\theta_i = (1/N_a)\, dN_a/d\theta_i - (1/L_a)\, dL_a/d\theta_i \qquad (14.25)$$

Substituting the second equation in (14.24) into (14.25) yields

$$dR_a/d\theta_i = -\{R_a(1 - \alpha)/\alpha w_a\}\, dw_a/d\theta_i \qquad (14.26)$$

The sign of $dR_a/d\theta_i$ is the opposite to that of $dw_a/d\theta_i$. From $R(0) = \theta(w_i/w_a)^{\lambda}R_a$, the first equation in (14.24) and (14.26) one gets

$$\{1/R(0)\}\ \mathrm{d}R(0)/\mathrm{d}\theta_i = 1/\xi_h\theta_i + (\lambda/w_i)\ \mathrm{d}w_i/\mathrm{d}\theta_i - \{(1-\alpha)/\alpha w_a + \lambda/w_a\}\ dw_a/d\theta_i \qquad (14.27)$$

If the wage rates are not much affected by changes in the city's amenities, that is, $\mathrm{d}w_i/\mathrm{d}\theta_i$ and $\mathrm{d}w_a/\mathrm{d}\theta_i$ being very small, the land rent at the CBD is increased as the city's amenity is improved.

Taking derivatives of $R(\omega) = R(0)(1 - \tau\omega/w_i)^\lambda$ with respect to θ_i yields:

$$\{1/\lambda R(\omega)\}\ \mathrm{d}R(\omega)/\mathrm{d}\theta_i = \xi/\theta_i + \{\tau\omega/(w_i - \tau\omega) + 1/w_i\}\ \mathrm{d}w_i/d\theta_i - \{(1-\alpha)/\alpha\lambda w_a + 1/w_a\}\ \mathrm{d}w_a/\mathrm{d}\theta_i \qquad 0 < \omega < L_1 \qquad (14.28)$$

If city's wage rate is increased but the rural wage rate is reduced because of improvement in the city's amenities, then land rent at any location in the urban area will be increased. But if $\mathrm{d}w_a/\mathrm{d}\theta_i$ is positive, the impact on the urban rent may be either positive or negative.

From (14.10), (14.11) and (14.12) and the above results, one can directly see the impact of changes in θ_i on $n(\omega)$, and the consumption components of the farmers and urban workers.

Although we can give the effects of changes in city's amenity on the rest variables in the system explicitly, it is not easy to interpret the conditions similarly.

CONCLUDING REMARKS

This study developed a one-city and one-farm spatial equilibrium model with endogenous spatial patterns in a linear system. The study emphasized the impact of amenity difference between cities and division of labour on economic geography. The system is described by the twenty variables of spatial division of labour, urban and rural outputs, wages, land use and land rent distribution, and consumption components of the farmers and urban workers over space. It was shown how these variables can be expressed explicitly as functions of the parameters in the system. The study also examined the effects of changes in the city's amenity level on the variables. As it is not easy to reach explicit conclusions, the comparative analysis was not represented in detail.

The model may be extended in different ways. For example, it is necessary to introduce certain mechanisms to include amenities and productivity as endogenous variables in a long-run dynamic analysis.

It is not difficult to introduce endogenous technology and capital accumulation. There are many factors for scale and scope economies that are important for explaining urban centralization and decentralization (see, for example, Zhang, 1992, 1993a, 1993b, 1993c, 1994). The significance of introducing scale and scope economies is important when dealing with economic systems consisting of multiple regions and nations. It is also necessary to relax some strict assumptions on the geographical structure designed in this study.

Appendix

Proving Proposition 1

First, by (14.10), (14.13) and (14.16) one has:

$$n(\omega) = 1/c_h(\omega) = \{y(\omega)/w_i\}^{\lambda}\,\lambda R(0)/y(\omega) \tag{A14.1}$$

Substituting (A14.1) into (14.14) yields:

$$1 - \{y(L_1)/w_i\}^{\lambda} = \tau N_i/R(0) \tag{A14.2}$$

Substituting (A14.1), (14.11) and (14.12) into (14.16) yields

$$G = pF_i/\xi_i = F_a/\xi_a \tag{A14.3}$$

where:

$$G \equiv \xi[w_i^{1+\lambda} - y(L_1)^{1+\lambda}]\,\lambda w_i^{-\lambda}R(0)/\tau(\lambda + 1) + \xi w_a(L - L_1) \tag{A14.4}$$

From (14.2) one has $L_a = \alpha_0 w_a N_a/R_a$, where $\alpha_0 = \alpha/(1 - \alpha)$. Substituting this equation and $c_{0h} = w_a/\lambda R_a$ into (14.14) yields:

$$(\alpha_0 + 1/\lambda)\,w_a N_a/R_a = L - L_1 \tag{A14.5}$$

From (A14.3) one gets: $F_a = \xi_a pF_i/\xi_i$. From this equation and $w_a = (1 - \alpha)\,F_a/N_a$, the following equation is held:

$$w_a = (1 - \alpha)\,\xi_a pF_i/\xi_i N_a \tag{A14.6}$$

Substituting (14.17) and $zp = w_i$ into (A14.6) yields:

$$N_i/N_a = \xi_1 y(L_1)/(1 - \alpha)\,\xi_a \theta^{1/\lambda} w_i \tag{A14.7}$$

From (14.17), (A14.2) and (A14.5), the following equation is held:

$$N_i/N_a = \theta^2\{w_i/y(L_1)\}^{\lambda}(\alpha_0 + 1/\lambda)\,y(L_1)[1 - \{y(L_1)/w_i\}^{\lambda}]/(L - L_1)\,\tau\theta^{1/\lambda} \tag{A14.8}$$

From (A14.7) and (A14.8) one gets:

$$w_i\{w_i/y(L_1)\}^{\lambda}[1 - \{y(L_1)/w_i\}^{\lambda}] = \theta_1(L - L_1) \qquad \text{(A14.9)}$$

where $\theta_1 \equiv \lambda\tau\xi_i/\xi_a\theta^2(1 - \alpha)(\lambda a_0 + 1)$.

From $w_a N_a/R_a = L_a/\alpha_0$ and (A14.5) one has:

$$L_a = (L - L_1)\, \lambda a_0/(\lambda a_0 + 1) \qquad \text{(A14.10)}$$

From $w_a = (1 - \alpha)(L_a/N_a)^{\alpha}$, (A14.10) and $y(L_1)/w_a = \theta^{1/\lambda}$, one gets:

$$N_a = \alpha_0\{\theta^{1/\lambda}(1 - \alpha)\}^{1/\alpha}(L - L_1)/(\alpha_0 + 1/\lambda)\, y(L_1)^{1/\alpha} \qquad \text{(A14.11)}$$

From $N_i = N - N_a$ and (A14.7), N_a is given by:

$$N_a = (1 - \alpha)\, \xi_a\theta^{1/\lambda}w_iN/\{\xi_i y(L_1) + (1 - \alpha)\, \xi_a\theta^{1/\lambda}w_i\} \qquad \text{(A14.12)}$$

From (A14.11) and (A14.12) one gets:

$$L - L_1 = \theta_2 w_i y(L_1)^{1/\alpha}/\{\xi_i y(L_1) + (1 - \alpha)\, \xi_a\theta^{1/\lambda}w_i\} \qquad \text{(A14.13)}$$

in which:

$$\theta_2 \equiv (\alpha_0 + 1/\lambda)(1 - \alpha)\, \xi_a\theta^{1/\lambda}N/\alpha_0\{\theta^{1/\lambda}(1 - \alpha)\}^{1/\alpha} > 0$$

The two equations, (A14.9) and (A14.13), contain two variables, w_i and L_1. It is now shown that the two equations have solutions. Substituting $(L - L_1)$ in (A14.9) into (A14.13), the following equation is held:

$$\Phi(w_i, Z) \equiv w_i^{1-1/\alpha}\,(\xi_i Z + (1 - \alpha)\, \xi_a\theta^{1/\lambda})(1 - Z^{\lambda}) - \theta_1\theta_2 Z^{1/\alpha+\lambda} = 0 \qquad \text{(A14.14)}$$

where $Z \equiv y(L_1)/w_i$. We now show that for any positive w_i there is a unique Z, $0 < Z < 1$, such that $\Phi(w_i, Z) = 0$. As:

$$\Phi(w_i, 0) = (1 - \alpha)\, \xi_a\theta^{1/\lambda}w_i^{1-1/\alpha} > 0 \qquad \Phi(w_i, 1) = -\theta_1\theta_2 < 0 \qquad \text{(A14.15)}$$

There is, at least, one Z, $0 < Z < 1$, such that $\Phi(w_i, Z) = 0$. As the second partial derivative of Φ with respect to Z is negative for $w_i > 0$ and $1 > Z > 0$, the solution is unique. Let $Z(w_i)$ denote the unique solution of $\Phi(w_i, Z) = 0$. It should be remarked that it is easy to check that $dZ(w_i)/dw_i$ may be either positive or negative, depending on the parameter values. As $Z(w_i) = y(L_1)/w_i$, L_1 can be expressed as a unique function of w_i as follows:

$$L_1(w_i) = w_i\{1 - Z(w_i)\}/\tau \qquad \text{(A14.16)}$$

Substituting this relationship into (A14.9) yields (14.18).

It is now shown that the equation, $\Phi^*(w_i) = 0$, has solutions. It is easy to check that $\Phi^*(0) < 0$ and $\Phi^*(w_i) > 0$ are held for sufficiently large w_i. This implies that $\Phi^*(w_i) = 0$ has positive solutions. Although it is not easy to find out under what conditions $\Phi^*(w_i) = 0$ has a unique solution, it is now shown that for any positive w_i the other nineteen variables can be determined as unique functions of w_i. By (A14.16), L_1 is given as a unique function of w_i. The price of industrial commodity, p, is given by $p = w_i/z$. From (A14.10) one gets L_a as a function of L_1. From (A14.11) and $N_i = N - N_a$, the labour distribution, N_i and N_a, are determined as functions of w_i and L_1. The outputs, F_i and F_a, are directly given by $F_i = zN_i$, $F_a = L_a^{\alpha}N_a^{1-\alpha}$. The land rent of the rural area and wage rate in the agricultural sector, R_a and w_a, are given by $R_a = \alpha F_a/L_a$ and $w_a = (1 - \alpha) F_a/N_a$, respectively. From (14.11) one gets c_{0i}, c_{0a} and c_{0h} as functions of w_a, R_a and p. One gets U_a and U_i directly. The land rent at the CBD, $R(0)$, is given by $R(0) = \theta(w_i/w_a)^{\lambda}R_a$. The land rent, $R(\omega)$, at any location in the urban area is determined by $R(\omega) = R(0)(1 = \tau\omega/w_i)^{\lambda}$ for $0 \leq \omega < L_1$. From (14.10) one can determine the consumption components, $c_i(\omega)$, $c_a(\omega)$ and $c_h(\omega)$ of an urban household at location ω as functions of p, w_i, ω and $R(\omega)$. The residential density, $n(\omega)$, at location ω is given directly by $n(\omega) = 1/c_h(\omega)$. It has thus been shown that the nineteen variables can be expressed explicitly as functions of w_i.

The proof of Proposition 1 has thus been completed.

References

Alonso, W. (1964) *Location and Land Use* (Cambridge, Mass.: Harvard University Press).

Beckmann, M. J. (1957) 'On the Distribution of Rent and Residential Density in Cities', Paper presented at the Interdepartmental Seminar on Mathematical Applications in the Social Sciences (Yale University).

Greenhut, M. L., G. Norman and C. S. Hung (1987) *The Economics of Imperfect Competition – A Spatial Approach* (Cambridge University Press).

Fujita, M. (1985) *Urban Economic Theory – Land Use and City Size* (Cambridge University Press).

Isard, W. (1956) *Location and Space Economy* (Cambridge, Mass.: MIT Press).

Kanemoto, Y. (1980) *Theories of Urban Externalities* (Amsterdam: North-Holland).

Muth, R. F. (1969) *Cities and Housing* (Chicago: University of Chicago Press).

Wingo, L. Jr (1961) *Transportation and Urban Land* (Washington, DC: Resources for the Future).

Zhang, W. B. (1992) 'Trade and World Economic Growth – Differences in Knowledge Utilization and Creativity', *Economic Letters*, vol. 39, pp. 199–206.

Zhang, W. B. (1993a) 'Wages, Service Prices and Rent – Urban Division of Labor and Amenities', *Seoul Journal of Economics*, vol. 6, pp. 97–113.

Zhang, W. B. (1993b) 'Trade, Knowledge and Government Research Policy', *International Review of Economics and Finance*, vol. 2, pp. 103–14.

Zhang, W. B. (1993c) 'Knowledge, Economic Geography and Growth in a Two-Group Island-Economy', *Technological Forecasting and Social Change*, vol. 44, pp. 405–18.

Zhang, W. B. (1994) 'Capital, Population and Urban Pattern in an Isolated State', *Regional Science and Urban Economics*, vol. 24.

15 Comparative Analysis of Intercity Agglomeration

Tatsuhiko Kawashima, Iwan Azis and Michael Tane

URBAN CHANGES

Urban areas[1] are, in general, inclined to change dynamically: there is no question about that. An interest in this would lead us to examine the wonder of the dynamic processes of urban growth and decline. The primary purpose of this chapter is to obtain an exploratory insight into this wonder, through the window of the analytical method used in the ROXY Index and the theoretical framework of the spatial-cycle hypothesis.[2] With this intention, we first examine the spatial redistribution processes of population in approximately thirty of the largest cities in Japan, Indonesia, Sweden and the USA. Second, based on the results of the above examination, we investigate the chronological time-lags appearing to exist among the four countries with respect to spatial-cycle stages observed concerning their city systems.

In this chapter, cities are employed as spatial units. In this connection. Table 15.1 would give us useful clarification of the fundamental concepts of four technical terms that are closely associated with our investigation. The table is constructed in the form of a two-dimensional matrix. One dimension is dichotomously divided into intra-city (that is, within a city) and inter-city (that is, among cities) elements. Another is dichotomized into agglomeration (that is, convergence) and deglomeration (that is, divergence) elements. As can be explained through the position of each cell in the 2 × 2 matrix shown in Table 15.1, the term *centralization* would imply the spatial agglomeration of the population within a city towards its inner ring zone,[3] while the term *decentralization* would imply the spatial deglomeration of population within a city from its inner-ring zone towards its outer-ring zone.[4] The term *concentration* would imply the spatial agglomeration of population in a system of cities towards larger cities in terms of population size, while the term *deconcentration* would imply the spatial deglomeration

Table 15.1 Two-dimensional matrix for analysis of spatial redistribution of city population

Dimension composed of agglomeration and deglomeration elements / *Dimension composed of intra-city and inter-city elements*	*Spatial agglomeration (i.e., spatial convergence)*	*Spatial deglomeration (i.e., spatial divergence)*
Intra-city phenomena (i.e., phenomena within a city)	Centralization	Decentralization
Inter-city phenomena (i.e., phenomena among cities)	Concentration	Deconcentration

Table 15.2 Spatial-cycle framework for a system of cities: four stages in the process of spatial concentration and deconcentration of population

Spatial redistribution of population	*Four stages appearing along spatial-cycle path*	
Concentration towards larger cities	Stage 1	Accelerating concentration
	Stage 2	Decelerating concentration
Deconcentration from larger cities	Stage 3	Accelerating deconcentration
	Stage 4	Decelerating deconcentration

Source: Constructed from Kawashima and Hiraoka (1993a).

of population in a system of cities from larger cities towards less-large cities.[5]

SPATIAL-CYCLE PATH AND ROXY-INDEX VALUE

The spatial-cycle hypothesis, originally conceptualized by Klaassen,[6] argues the existence of cyclical tendencies underlying the phenomena of urban growth and decline. Table 15.2 shows the basic skeleton of an outgrowth-version[7] of the original spatial-cycle framework for the study of inter-city analysis. This framework shows the spatial-cycle

Figure 15.1 Definition of the ROXY Index for inter-city analysis (city population used as weighting factor)

$$\text{ROXY Index} = \left(\frac{WAGR_{t,\,t+1}}{SAGR_{t,\,t+1}} - 1.0 \right) \times 10^4$$

$$= \left\{ \frac{\sum_{i+1}^{n} (x_i^t \times r_i^{t,\,t+1})}{\sum_{i=1}^{n} x_i^t} \times \frac{n}{\sum_{i=1}^{n} r_i^{t,\,t+1}} - 1.0 \right\} \times 10^4$$

where:

x_i^τ = population of city i in year τ

$r_i^{t,\,t+1}$ = annual growth ratio of population in city i for the period between years t and $t+1$, which is defined as the kth root of x_i^{t+k} / x_i^t

n = number of cities

$WAGR_{t,\,t+1}$ = weighted average of annual growth ratios of population in n cities for the period between years t and $t+1$, which is equal, in the case where population level of each city is used as the weighting factor, to:

$$\sum (x_i^t \times r_i^{t,\,t+1}) / \sum x_i^t$$

$SAGR_{t,\,t+1}$ = simple average of annual growth ratios of population in n cities for the period between years t and $t+1$, which is equal to

$$\sum r_i^{t,\,t+1} / n$$

path, which is composed of four recursively transmuting stages. They are accelerating concentration, decelerating concentration, accelerating deconcentration, and decelerating deconcentration.

One of the indicative instruments to trace the course quantitatively along the spatial-cycle path followed by a system of cities, would be the ROXY Index.[8] The ROXY Index for inter-city analysis is defined as shown in Figure 15.1. In defining this type of ROXY Index, the population of each city is used as the weighting factor in the calculation of the values of the ROXY Index.

Table 15.3 furnishes us with the possible implication[9] for values of this index. As indicated by the table, the ROXY Index value would be (i) positive and increasing for the stage of accelerating concentration; (ii) positive and decreasing for the stage of decelerating concentration; (iii) negative and decreasing for the stage of accelerating deconcentration; and (iv) negative and increasing for the stage of decelerating

Table 15.3 Spatial-cycle implications of ROXY Index values for inter-city analysis (city population used as weighting factor)

A	*B*	*C*	*D*
Sign of ROXY-index value	Pattern of spatial redistribution process of population among cities	State of changes in ROXY Index value	Speed of spatial redistribution process of population among cities
Positive	Concentration	Increasing	Accelerating
		Levelling-off	Constant
		Decreasing	Decelerating
Zero	Neutrality from both concentration and deconcentration (namely, symmetrical growth or decline)[1]	Increasing	Start of ACon[2]
		Levelling-off	Continuation of neutrality
		Decreasing	Start of ADcon[3]
Negative	Deconcentration	Increasing	Decelerating
		Levelling-off	Constant
		Decreasing	Accelerating

Notes:
1. The spatial redistribution pattern of the 'symmetrical growth or decline' includes the following three subpatterns:
   (i) Balanced growth or decline (BGD): the growth-rate curve is nearly flat, reflecting the fixed share of population by cities.
   (ii) Bell-shaped growth or decline (BSGD): the growth-rate curve is bell-shaped, reflecting the 'medianization' of population over cities of different sizes of population. The 'medianization' means the increase in population share by cities of medium sizes of population and, at the same time, decreases in population share by cities of smaller and larger sizes of population.
   (iii) Cup-shaped growth or decline (CSGD): the growth-rate curve is cup-shaped, reflecting the 'bipolarization' of population over cities of different sizes of population. 'Bipolarization' means the increase in population share of smaller and larger cities and, at the same time, decreases in population share of medium-sized cities.
2. The abbreviatory notation 'ACon' stands for accelerating concentration.
3. The abbreviatory notation 'ADcon' stands for accelerating deconcentration.

deconcentration. The ROXY Index value would be at or in the vicinity of zero when the stage of the spatial redistribution process is neutral from the phenomena of both concentration and deconcentration. Based on Figure 15.1 and Table 15.3, we can construct Figure 15.2. The

Figure 15.2 Diagrammatic interpretation of spatial-cycle path by means of ROXY Index value for inter-city analysis: wavelike cyclic form

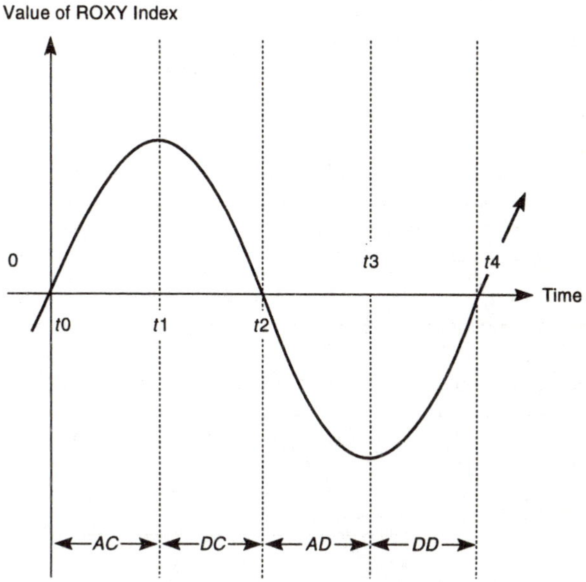

Notes: AC = Stage of accelerating concentration.
DC = Stage of declerating concentration.
AD = Stage of accelerating deconcentration.
DD = Stage of decelerating deconcentration.

wavelike cyclic curve in this table shows a diagrammatic interpretation of the stages of the spatial-cycle path by means of the ROXY Index value for the inter-city analysis.

SPATIAL-CYCLE STAGES OF FOUR COUNTRIES

For the purposes of examining the stages of the spatial-cycle path for a system of cities in Indonesia, Japan, Sweden and the USA respectively, we applied the ROXY Index approach to the inter-city data for each of the four countries. We initially tried to pick up the thirty largest cities in the year 1980 for Indonesia, Japan and the USA, and in the year 1987 for Sweden. However, because of the partial unavailability of consistent time-series data, we omitted some of the cities in

Table 15.4 Values of ROXY Index and its marginal values

(a) ROXY Index for a system of 25 cities in Indonesia: 1961–90

Period	*1961–71*	*1971–80*	*1980–90*
ROXY	75.3	34.4	−14.6
Δ ROXY	−4.3	−4.7	−5.2

(b) ROXY Index for a system of 23 cities in Japan: 1960–90

Period	*1960–65*	*1965–70*	*1970–75*	*1975–80*	*1980–85*	*1985–90*
ROXY	−52.2	−111.6	−109.0	−69.2	−22.3	−18.8
Δ ROXY	−11.9	−5.7	4.2	8.7	5.0	0.7

(c) ROXY Index for a system of 26 cities in Sweden: 1950–87

Period	*1950–60*	*1960–65*	*1965–70*	*1970–80*	*1980–87*
ROXY	−44.5	−169.7	−297.3	−99.7	1.9
Δ ROXY	−16.7	−20.2	5.6	18.7	12.0

(d) ROXY Index for a system of 29 cities in USA: 1960–80

Period	*1960–70*	*1970–75*	*1975–80*
ROXY	−51.7	−28.0	−11.7
Δ ROXY	3.2	3.2	3.3

each country. Eventually, we arranged the data, as shown in Table 15.4, for, twenty-three cities in Japan (for the period 1960–90); twenty-five cities in Indonesia (for the period 1961–90); twenty-six cities in Sweden (for the period 1950–87); and twenty-nine cities in the USA (for the period 1960–80).

We used the data shown in Table 15.4 to calculate the ROXY Index values. In this calculation, we standardized the value of the ROXY Index by employing the annual growth ratio and the level of population at the midpoint in the time segment of the data interval. An example of the calculation for the five-year span data is given by Figure 15.3, to describe our calculation method more precisely. Table 15.4 shows the computed results of the ROXY Index values as well as the marginal values of the ROXY Index.

Figure 15.3 Calculation of ROXY Index based on annual growth ratio (example for five-year span data 1980–5)

$$\text{ROXY} = \left[\frac{WAGR}{SAGR} - 1.0\right] \times 10^4$$

$$\text{where WAGR} = \sum_{i=1}^{n} \left[r_i^{\frac{1}{5}} \times \frac{X_{i,\,2.5}}{\sum_{i=1}^{n} X_{i,\,2.5}} \right] = \sum_{i=1}^{n} \left[r_i^{\frac{1}{5}} \times \frac{\sum_{i=1}^{n}\left(r_i^{\frac{2.5}{5}} \times X_{i,0}\right)}{\sum_{i=1}^{n}\left(r_i^{\frac{2.5}{5}} \times X_{i,0}\right)} \right]$$

$$= \frac{\sum_{i=1}^{}\left(r_i^{\frac{3.5}{5}} \times X_{i,0}\right)}{\sum_{i=1}^{}\left(r_i^{\frac{2.5}{5}} \times X_{i,0}\right)}$$

$$= \frac{\sum_{i=1}^{} \left\{ \left[\frac{X_{i,5}}{X_{i,0}} \right]^{\frac{2.5}{5}} \times X_{i,0} \right\}}{\sum_{i=1}^{} \left\{ \left[\frac{X_{i,5}}{X_{i,0}} \right]^{\frac{2.5}{5}} \times X_{i,0} \right\}}$$

$$\text{SAGR} = \frac{\sum_{i=1}^{n} r_i^{\frac{1}{5}}}{n} = \frac{\sum_{i=1}^{n} \left[\frac{X_{i,5}}{X_{i,0}} \right]^{\frac{1}{5}}}{n}$$

$X_{i,0}$ = Population of city *i* in 1980
$X_{i,5}$ = Population of city *i* in 1985
r_i = Five-year growth ratio of city *i* for the period 1980–5

From this table, we obtain Figure 15.4. It illustrates diagrammatically, by means of wavelike cyclic form, the course of the spatial-cycle path followed by the city system of each country. From Table 15.4, we also obtain Figure 15.5 which illustrates diagrammatically the spatial-cycle path by means of circular cyclic form. With the help

Figure 15.4 ROXY Index in wavelike cyclic form

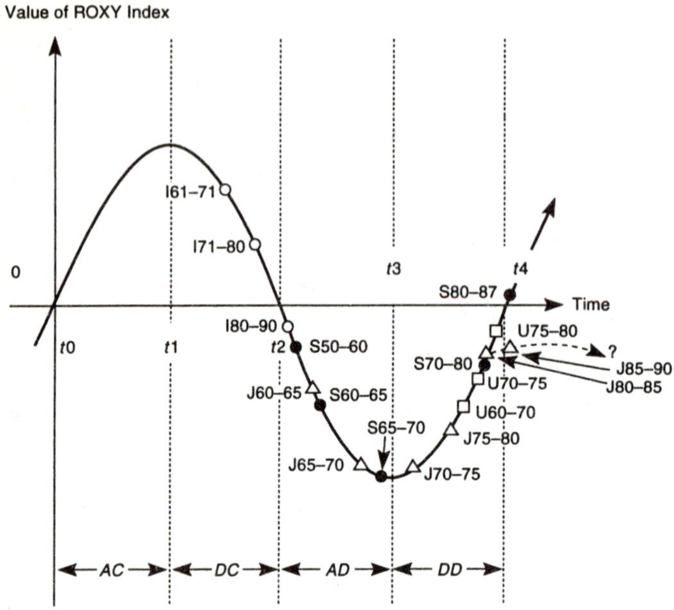

Notes: 1. *Key*:
AC = Stage of accelerating concentration.
DC = Stage of declerating concentration.
AD = Stage of accelerating deconcentration.
DD = Stage of decelerating deconcentration.
○ = Indonesia.
△ = Japan.
● = Sweden.
□ = USA.
2. The scales of vertical axis are not necessarily identical for all countries.

of these two figures, we might perhaps point out that the values of the ROXY Index in Table 15.4 would suggest the following:

1. The city system of Indonesia seems to have been deceleratingly concentrating until the middle of the 1980s. Towards the end of the 1980s, it appears to have entered into the early stage of accelerating deconcentration.[10]

Figure 15.5 ROXY Index in circular cyclic form

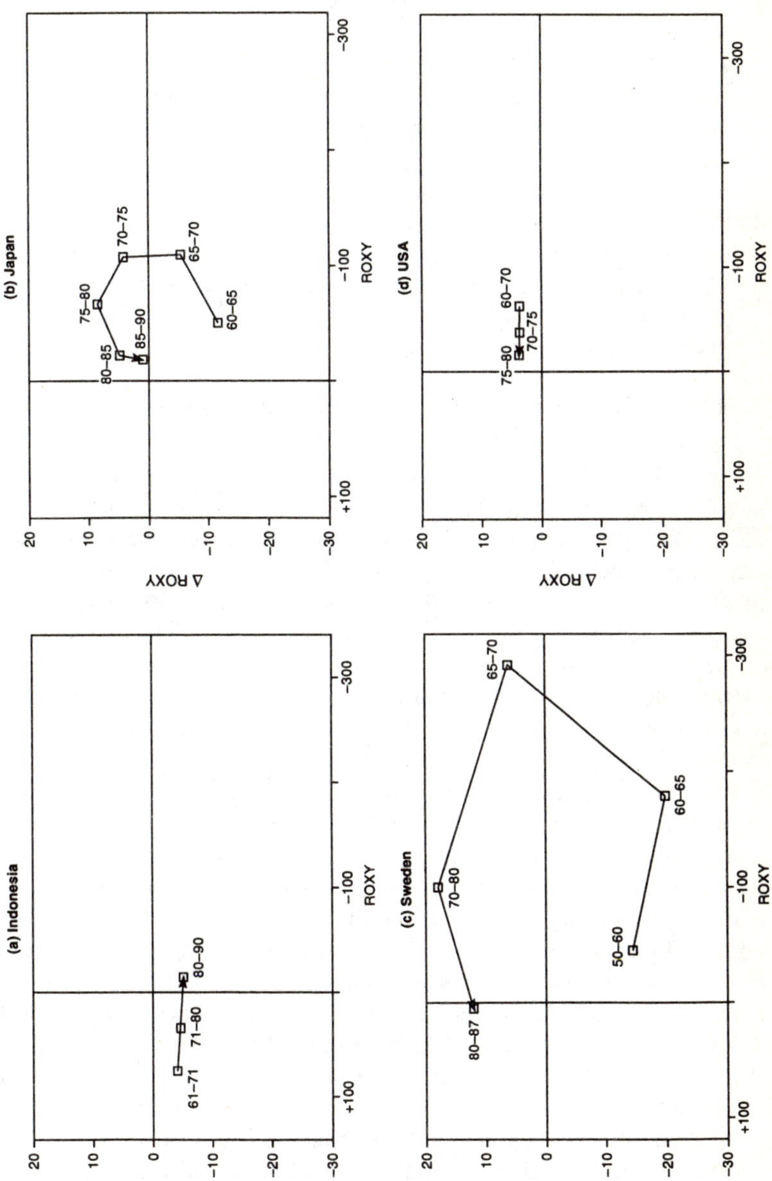

2. The city system of Japan seems to have been acceleratingly deconcentrating until around the year 1970. Towards the end of the 1980s, it appears to have been approaching the final stage of decelerating deconcentration.
3. The city system of Sweden seems to have been at the last stage of accelerating deconcentration in the second half of the 1960s. In the second half of the 1980s, it appears to have just completed the stage of decelerating deconcentration and entered into the very early stage of accelerating concentration again.
4. The city system of the USA seems already to have been at the advanced stage of decelerating deconcentration in 1960. In the late 1970s, it appears to have been very close to the start of the stage of accelerating concentration.

CONCLUSION: IS URBAN DRAMA PREDESTINED?

In light of the above investigation, the Japanese city system seems to have been behind that of the USA by approximately fifteen years along the spatial-cycle path of population redistribution, and the Indonesian city system seems to have been behind Japan by at least twenty years. Meanwhile, the city system of Sweden was somewhere between the USA and Japan. In other words, as to the course along the spatial-cycle path, there seems to be a chronological time-lag of fifteen years between the US city system and that of Japan, and perhaps a time-lag of more than thirty-five years between the US city system and the Indonesian one.

What was mentioned earlier about the time-lags over the spatial-cycle path might be of some use in urban planning. That is, urban policy-makers in less advanced countries along the course of the spatial-cycle path may be able to avoid repeating the kinds of mistake that more advanced countries along the spatial-cycle path made previously. Moreover, the less advanced countries may be able to enjoy chances to enhance and reinforce general urban necessities more timely than can the more advanced countries. This is because the less advanced countries can learn valuable lessons about effective urban policies, with the knowledge of possible time-lags, from the experiences of the more advanced countries.

The spatial-cycle hypothesis argues that the principle of the spatial-cycle path for the system of cities can hold more or less regardless of social, economic, cultural, historical or geographical differences among countries. Speaking somewhat exaggeratingly, urban policy-makers have no choice in urban planning but to move along the spatial-cycle path. They can neither stop the cyclical movement nor change the movement into reverse. They can, however, depending on the purposes and strategies of urban policies, speed up or slow down the velocity of the movement along the spatial-cycle path. Or they can manipulate the amplitude of the cyclic curve of the spatial-cycle path by making the amplitude shallower or deeper.

Metaphorically speaking, should the reader be an urban policy-maker, the title of the urban drama you are supposed to direct is destined in advance. All you can contribute to the urban drama as policy-maker is to direct the play more entertainingly and less boringly. It is as if you had to present a predetermined programme of Shakespeare's *Othello*: you cannot change the programme to *King Lear* even though you might like to. All you can do is to create an enthralling scenario of *Othello*, and to assign the parts of the play appropriately to the available actors and actresses based on your policy-making ability and prospective visions. In this sense, despite the presumed existence of the predestined path of spatial cycles you cannot avoid, you still have a chance to make urban policies in such a way that they would increase the well-being of the urban society significantly.

Notes

1. The 'urban areas' means, in this chapter, cities, metropoli, or areas of population agglomeration.
2. Among conceivable spatial units that can be used in the field of regional science would be neighbourhood communities, census tracts, villages, towns, city centres, cities, urbanized areas, suburbs, metropolitan areas, megalopolitan areas, rural areas, subnational regions, nations and subglobal areas.
3. The inner-ring zone is conceptually identical, in this chapter, to the city core or city centre.
4. The outer-ring zone is conceptually identical, in this chapter, to the suburbs or outskirt area.
5. In the case that metropolitan areas rather than cities are employed as spatial units for investigation, the interpretation of the four terminologies appearing in Table 15.1 would remain almost the same. The only minor conceptual change, however, is that the boundary line separating the outer-ring zone from the inner-ring zone within a metropolitan area tends to be delineated somewhat further out from the urban centre than the boundary-line between the two zones within a city.

6. See Klaassen and Paelinck (1979) and Klaassen *et al.* (1981) for the original concepts of the spatial-cycle framework.
7. See Kawashima and Hiraoka (1993b) for a discussion on the basic features of both original and outgrowth versions of the spatial-cycle framework.
8. The ROXY Index is in fact a comprehensive measure useful for general quantitative analyse of spatial-cycle types of redistribution processes of population and other socioeconomic variables. For more detailed discussions about this index and results of its empirical applications, see Kawashima (1982, 1985, 1986a, 1986b, 1986c, 1987, 1989) and Kawashima and Hiraoka (1983a, 1983b).
9. When we understand the implications of Table 15.3, it should be borne in mind that conditions provided in column A are *necessary* conditions for the corresponding redistribution patterns appearing in column B, and that conditions provided in column C are also *necessary* conditions for their corresponding speed-changes appearing in column D.
10. For a discussion on recent urbanization phenomena as well as on the deconcentration tendency of population and other socioeconomic activities in Indonesia, see Alatas (1992) and Azis (1992).

References

Alatas, S. (1992) 'Population Growth, Distribution, Migration, and Urbanization in Indonesia', mimeograph, The Demographic Institute, Faculty of Economics, University of Indonesia, Jakarta, January.

Azis, I. J. (1992) 'A Study of Decentralization Based on the Regional Perspective: The Application of "Analytic Hierarchy Process"', mimeograph, Inter-University Center, Economics, University of Indonesia, Jakarta, May.

Kawashima, T. (1982) 'Recent Urban Trends in Japan: Analysis of Functional Urban Regions', in T. Kawashima and P. Korcelli (eds), *Human Settlement Systems: Spatial Patterns and Trends* (Laxenburg, Austria: International Institute for Applied Systems Analysis) pp. 21–40.

Kawashima, T. (1985) 'ROXY Index: An Indicative Instrument to Measure the Speed of Spatial Concentration and Deconcentration of Population', *Gakushuin Economic Papers*, vol. 22, no. 2 (Tokyo: Gakushuin University) September, pp. 183–213.

Kawashima, T. (1986a) 'Speed of Suburbanization: ROXY Index Analysis for Intra-metropolitan Spatial Redistribution of Population in Japan', *Gakushuin Economic Papers*, vol. 22, no. 3 (Tokyo: Gakushuin University) March, pp. 243–304.

Kawashima, T. (1986b) 'People Follow Jobs in Japan? Suburbanization of Job Markets', *Gakushuin Economic Papers*, vol. 23, nos 1 & 2 (Tokyo: Gakushuin University) October, pp. 157–83.

Kawashima, T. (1986c) 'Spatial Cycle Race 1985: ROXY Index Analysis of the 1985 Population Census for Three Railway-line Regions in the Tokyo Metropolitan Area', *Gakushuin Economic Papers*, vol. 23, no. 3 (Tokyo: Gakushuin University) December, pp. 53–70.

Kawashima, T. (1987) 'Is Disurbanization Foreseeable in Japan? A Comparison between U.S. and Japanese Urbanization Processes', in L. van de Berg, L. S. Burns and L. Klaassen (eds), *Spatial Cycles* (Aldershot: Gower) pp. 100–26.

Kawashima, T. (1989) 'Basic Concepts of the Nature of the ROXY Index', *GEM Bulletin*, no. 3 (Tokyo: Gakushuin University Research Institute of Economics and Management) October, pp. 81–94 (in Japanese).

Kawashima, T. and N. Hiraoka (1993a) 'Centralization and Suburbanization: ROXY Index Analysis for Five Railway-line Regions in Tokyo Metropolitan Area', *Gakushuin Economic Papers*, vol. 30, no. 1 (Tokyo: Gakushuin University) March, pp. 203–30.

Kawashima, T. and N. Hiraoka (1993b) 'Mathematical Characteristics of ROXY Index (I): Distance and Reserved Distance Used as Weighting Factors', *Gakushuin Economic Papers*, vol. 30, no. 2 (Tokyo: Gakushuin University) July, pp. 255–97.

Klaassen, L. H. and J. H. P. Paelinck (1979) 'The Future of Large Towns', *Environment and Planning A*, vol. 10, pp. 1095–104.

Klaassen, L. H. *et al.* (1981) *Transport and Reurbanization* (Aldershot: Gower).

16 The North American Free Trade Agreement: Implications for US Regions

Niles Hansen

INTRODUCTION

On 1 January 1994 the North American Free Trade Agreement (NAFTA) came into effect, creating the world's largest free trade area in terms of population (372 million) and total output ($7.2 trillion). Over a fifteen-year period, NAFTA will eliminate nearly all the barriers to trade and investment between the USA, Mexico and Canada. In 1992, US exports to Canada amounted to $90 billion and imports to $101 billion. US exports to Mexico in that year were valued at $41 billion and imports from Mexico amounted to $36 billion; estimates of these flows in 1993 were $51 billion and $45 billion, respectively.

Although US trade with Canada is greater than that with Mexico, and will no doubt remain so, the USA and Canada already had a free-trade agreement that caused relatively little controversy in the USA. However, the possibility of free trade with Mexico provoked an emotional, divisive debate in the USA over the potential consequences for US employment, as well as for working conditions and the environment. Thus, this chapter is concerned primarily with the implications of free trade with Mexico for the USA at the regional level.

From the Mexican perspective, NAFTA will create expanded employment and exports, which in turn will enable Mexico to import the capital goods and technologies required to make the economy increasingly productive and competitive in the long run. Export-led expansion along the lines that transformed the economies of South Korea, Taiwan, Hong Kong and Singapore would also serve to reinforce free-market reforms, strengthen the basis for democratization, and curb the environmental degradation that has characterized much of Mexico's rapid industrialization.

The benefits that NAFTA supporters envisage for the USA include greater certainty and predictability for US investors in the Mexican economy; development of relatively poor US regions on the border with Mexico; enhancement of US competitive advantage in a world of emerging trading blocs; increased imports by Mexico of US products, accompanied by increased employment in US industry and agriculture; lower prices for US consumers of Mexican products; and a lessening of illegal immigration from Mexico as employment opportunities increase there. In contrast, NAFTA opponents – with labour unions, some environmental groups and H. Ross Perot in the vanguard – maintain that free trade with Mexico will affect the USA adversely by causing large-scale job losses to Mexico, declining wages and environmental degradation.

Most theoretically-grounded models designed to capture the effects of NAFTA suggest that, in fact, the overall consequences are likely to be small (Lustig *et al.* (1992), United States International Trade Commission (1992)). Mexico will gain the most, because the effects of trade liberalization will be most concentrated there. NAFTA will induce significant restructuring in Mexico, since over 70 per cent of its trade is with the USA. The incremental impact of NAFTA on Canada will be the smallest because it has little trade with Mexico and it already has a bilateral free trade agreement with the USA. In view of the large size of the US economy and the fact that it is already relatively open to trade, NAFTA will have only a modest impact in the USA as a whole. Most models estimate that as a result of NAFTA, real gross domestic product (GDP) will expand by 0.5 per cent or less; aggregate employment will increase by less than 0.1 per cent to 2.5 per cent; and there will be a rise in the aggregate real wage in the range from less than 0.1 per cent to 0.3 per cent. Although these effects are small in the aggregate, certain regions and localities are likely to experience much more important consequences, both positive and negative.

NAFTA AND US REGIONS: A GENERAL OVERVIEW

The data in Table 16.1 indicate the value of exports to Mexico in 1992 from states that were leading exporters to Mexico, the percentage change in exports in these states since Mexico began liberalizing trade unilaterally, and employment accounted for by trade with Mexico in states with the most such employment. The three highest-ranking

Table 16.1 Leading states in exports to Mexico (in billion of dollars) and in employment generated by trade with Mexico, 1992

State	*Exports ($)*	*Percentage change 1987–92*	*State*	*Employment*
Texas	18.839	191	Texas	327 075
California	6.557	190	California	150 764
Arizona	1.845	186	Arizona	50 479
Michigan	1.421	32	Illinois	32 097
Illinois	1.349	384	New York	22 895
New York	0.934	82	Pennsylvania	22 693
Louisiana	0.753	100	Michigan	22 351
Pennsylvania	0.742	310	Florida	21 267
Ohio	0.708	189	New Jersey	16 695
Florida	0.664	203	Ohio	12 520

Source: US Department of Commerce, cited in *The Dallas Morning News*, 26 December 1993, p. 10P.

exporters were the border states of Texas, California and Arizona, which also had the highest amount of employment from trade with Mexico. However, the highest rates of growth in exports were found in Illinois (384 per cent), Pennsylvania (310 per cent), and Florida (203 per cent), which are all distant from the border. Moreover, Ohio's growth rate (189 per cent) was about the same as that in the border states. The extent to which states may have lost jobs because of trade with Mexico cannot be established because such data are not available.

It might be expected that states which produce relatively large shares of goods and services in relatively high demand in Mexico would particularly benefit from NAFTA, though such factors as transportation costs, firm-specific competitive advantages, and ability to function in the Mexican business environment would also influence the regional pattern of exports. In 1991, the five largest US exporting industries to Mexico were electrical machinery, non-electrical machinery, transportation equipment, chemicals, and primary metals, which together accounted for about two-thirds of manufacturing exports to Mexico in that year (Aguilar, 1992). However, efforts to modernize the Mexican economy will no doubt modify past patterns of imports from the USA. The US Embassy in Mexico City has identified a number of products being sought by Mexican buyers (*Twin Plant News*, 1992). For example, the private sector is now playing a key role in developing Mexican telecommunications, which is creating a need for telephone and satellite communications equipment, fibre optics, data transmission, and services. Mexico's new emphasis on production for export has generated a demand for state-of-the-art producer durable goods as well as engineering and consulting services. The $300 million a year market for numerically-controlled machine tools and metalworking machinery may expand by 10 per cent annually in the few years up to the millenium. Plastics production machinery and process control equipment are also in increasing demand. New environmental goals resulting from NAFTA negotiations have created new markets for pollution-control equipment and services. And there is increasing demand for computer equipment and software; oil and gas equipment; and petrochemical, mining, and construction equipment.

Although heavily unionized areas in the industrial Middle West opposed NAFTA in Congress, in 1992 Michigan and Illinois were the leading non-border states in value of exports to Mexico; and Ohio ranked ninth. Aguilar (1992) points out that between 1987 and 1991 the five states in the Chicago Federal Reserve District increased their manufacturing exports to Mexico by 90 per cent. Machinery and transportation equipment accounted for 68 per cent of these exports, and she argues that Mexican demand for these two categories of goods should continue to increase as the Mexican economy expands. Under NAFTA provisions, Mexico's 20 per cent motor vehicle tariff was cut in half in the first year, and remaining tariffs on motor vehicles will gradually be phased out over ten years. Mexico's requirement that motor vehicles sold in Mexico have at least 36 per cent Mexican parts and labour content will also be phased out within ten years, with a rapid early reduction to 20 per cent. As a result, US auto manufacturers expect to increase US production of vehicles for export to Mexico. The US Department of Commerce estimates that 15 000 new jobs will be added in the US motor vehicle and vehicle supplies industries in the first year under NAFTA as a consequence of increases in Big Three automotive exports to Mexico (Hoglund, 1993). Although free trade will no doubt shift some motor vehicles and vehicle parts production to Mexico, industry analyses of the effects of NAFTA on the North American motor vehicle industry for the most part suggest that rationalization and consolidation into a single world-competitive level will have positive outcomes for the USA, Canada, and Mexico, with Mexico receiving the most benefit (Weintraub, 1992).

The textiles and apparel sector is the only industry for which most forecasts estimate net employment losses in the USA as result of NAFTA. Such losses would most adversely effect the Texas borderlands, the Carolinas, Georgia, Alabama and other south-eastern areas of production. It has been estimated that restrictions on apparel and textile imports have cost US consumers $1 for each cent of increased earnings of US workers (Bovard, 1991). Thus, freer trade should benefit US consumers of these items. Moreover, there are questions concerning the ability of Mexico to compete despite its production cost advantages. The Mexican clothing industry in the mid-1990s is not able to compete in its home market on the basis of either quality or fashion. Buyers in Mexico City have, as a result, turned to suppliers in New York and Los Angeles. Domestic producers have been struggling to find new markets but have been handicapped by a general ignorance of where potential markets are and a lack of familiarity with the formalities of contracting in international trade (Hinojosa-Ojeda and Robinson, 1992). A rapid response to changing fashions is critical in the apparel industry. The turnaround time of a US manufacturer from the time an order is made to the time of delivery is measured in weeks, whereas in Mexico the corresponding time is usually counted in months (Rivas, 1993). In addition, even if clothing and textile imports from Mexico do increase, a significant part may represent a shift in production from Asia and other overseas locations, which would benefit US suppliers because of the proximity of Mexico.

The contrary expected effects of NAFTA on US industrial employment at the regional level can be seen, for example, in North Carolina. The congressman from the textile centre of Greensboro opposed the treaty on the grounds that it would harm local employment, but the congressman from an adjacent district, which includes Raleigh and Chapel Hill, favoured it because his district includes IBM, AT&T and numerous other firms that expect to gain from the reduction in trade barriers (Bradsher, 1991). In much of the industrial South, espousal of free trade recognizes the interests of consumers in lower prices, but even greater emphasis is placed on the need to gain greater access to foreign markets and to lure foreign investment and technology. In the Charlotte, North Carolina area, for example, 340 foreign firms generate a great deal of local employment. In West Virginia, Corning and the Anchor Glass Container Corporation – leading glass producers – lobbied heavily in favour of NAFTA. Corning, after originally adopting a protectionist stance with respect to tariffs on glass imports, has formed an alliance with Vitro, Mexico's large glass producer, and expects to gain substantially from rising export sales as Mexico lowers its tariffs. Anchor was purchased by Vitro several years ago. Meanwhile, many of West Virginia's small firms that make glass objects by hand have already become bankrupt, often because of Mexican competition even though tariffs prior to NAFTA added 38 cents to the cost of each dollar's worth of imported glass. Many of the remaining small firms have sought to reduce costs by eliminating workers' health insurance and vacations, and by cutting wages. Although workers in these firms oppose free trade, they organized only negligible opposition to NAFTA; one reason being because of illiteracy (Bradsher, 1992).

Assessments of NAFTA-induced effects on agriculture generally agree that the US grain belt will expand exports, especially corn, to Mexico. In contrast, US producers of fresh fruits and vegetables face potentially strong competition from lower-cost producers in Mexico, although the fears of US growers were calmed to some degree by a last-minute deal in NAFTA negotiations that provides for a long transition period for trade liberalization in this area. Moreover, US health and environmental regulations also put a damper on Mexican agricultural exports (Rivas, 1993). The effects of NAFTA on Mexican and US agricultural policies cannot be isolated from such other factors as the extensive agricultural reforms being carried out in Mexico and the outcomes of GATT negotiations which could have more far-reaching implications than NAFTA. In any event, the results of most studies suggest that with increasing trade liberalization in agriculture there will be net welfare gains for both the USA and Mexico. US grain producers will gain but US consumers will experience higher prices as some of the supply is exported. In Mexico, on balance, producers will lose but consumers will gain. The net benefits from agricultural trade will be greater in the USA than in Mexico (Lustig *et al.*, 1992). However, in the fresh fruits and vegetables sector, gains to US growers are likely to exceed those to US workers as US growers compensate for competition from Mexican growers by expanding their own operations into Mexico rather than by diversifying their operations in the USA. Texas and California growers have already initiated contract arrangements or joint production ventures with Mexican growers. Thus, while many US producers can readily adapt to the new international environment, poor, unskilled farm labourers are likely to bear the brunt of the geographical reorganization of production; and these disadvantaged people and their families are particularly concentrated in California and the Lower Rio Grande Valley in Texas.

TEXAS AND THE BORDER

It is widely agreed that among all the US states, Texas will be the principal beneficiary of NAFTA. Texas is centrally located within the free trade zone, and approximately equidistant from the East and West coasts of the United States as well as between densely-populated central Mexico and Canada's industrial heartland in Ontario and Quebec provinces. In 1992, Texan exports to Canada – the state's second-largest foreign market – amounted to $3.5 billion, but this was less than 4 per cent of total US exports to Canada. In contrast, Texas has a long history of highly important trade with Mexico, and a number of major Canadian firms – for example, Systemhouse and Northern Telecom – already administer their business in Mexico from offices in Texas. Texan exports to Mexico reached $18.8 billion in 1992, which represented 46 per cent of the US total. Moreover, nearly two-thirds of the value of shipments between the USA and Mexico pass through the Texas–Mexico border.

According to DRI–McGraw Hill forecasts, US exports to Mexico under NAFTA will reach $90 billion by the year 2000. Even with a declining share, the gains to Texas would be large. A study prepared at the University of Texas by Chandler Stolp and Sidney Weintraub estimates that Texas will add 182 000 jobs by the year 2005 as a result of NAFTA. However, the study did not include services and it did not project indirect spending and employment. Estimates made by economists in the office of the Texas State Comptroller, which did include indirect effects in non-export sectors, forecast a gain of 262 000 jobs resulting from trade with Mexico in the 1990s (Alm, 1993). Of course, Texans will not benefit from NAFTA simply because they are Texans. Producers must be efficient in the face of increasing national and international competition. There is widespread recognition among state policymakers that whereas the past wealth of Texas was based on cotton, cattle and oil, in the future it will need to be based on the quality of human resources and a continuation of the shift towards a highly-skilled, highly-paid workforce. Also, unlike the past, export-led growth will be spread across a wide range of activities. The Texas sectors that would benefit most from NAFTA are those that would also benefit the most nationally: including electronics, industrial machinery, computers, chemicals, primary metals, transportation equipment, business services and franchising.

Even within Texas the benefits as well as the costs of NAFTA will differ by region. The Stolp and Weintraub study allocated expected employment gains from NAFTA over ten Texas regions. Three regions – those with metropolitan cores in Dallas, Houston and Austin – accounted for 69.5 per cent of the projected state increase because these areas are the best positioned to provide the high technology products and skilled services demanded in Mexico. Dallas alone accounted for 41.4 per cent of the growth. Since 10.8 per cent of the increase was not allocated, this means that the seven remaining regions would receive only 19.7 per cent of the state gain even though they have about half of the state population.

It is often assumed that the increasing trade flows that will be generated by NAFTA will definitely benefit the Texas borderlands, here defined as the four metropolitan areas (El Paso, Laredo, McAllen and Brownsville) and the non-metropolitan counties adjacent to Mexico. However, the Stolp and Weintraub study estimates that NAFTA will create only 15 000 new jobs – 9.2 per cent of the Texas total – in their two regions that border Mexico, even though they are generously defined to include the San Antonio and Corpus Christi metropolitan areas, both of which are 150 miles from the border. However, because their study does not include services, it fails to capture the significant employment increases that NAFTA will create in activities related to the processing and financing of international trade. It also ignores employment creation resulting from the construction of the transportation and communications infrastructure that will be required to handle the expanded trans-border movement of goods and services efficiently. Nevertheless, apart from these activities, it is quite possible that NAFTA will have adverse consequences for the Texas borderlands (which already includes some of the poorest communities in the nation) unless measures are taken to develop other aspects of the regional economy. For example, the Texas borderlands does not produce the high-technology products and sophisticated business services demanded in Mexico, but it is relatively specialized in the growing of fruits and vegetables, and in the apparel sector, both of which are threatened by imports from Mexico. Also, despite their low levels of per capita income by US standards, Texas border cities have relatively high per capita retail sales as a result of purchases by Mexicans who cross the border in large numbers to shop for what they regard as superior goods. With NAFTA, this trade is likely to decline. Once Mexican retailers can import duty-free merchandise freely, Mexicans who previously crossed the border will be able to buy just as well on their side of the border. Moreover, major US retailers which now cater to Mexicans from the US side of the border may well move to the Mexican side. In contrast, retailers of high-ticket merchandise in such interior Texas cities as Dallas, Houston and San Antonio will probably benefit from NAFTA-induced income increases in Mexico. For some time already, many wealthier Mexicans, who tend to have a high income elasticity of demand for such items, have travelled to Texas to shop in the trendier malls.

The Bracero Program, a contract labour agreement concluded in 1942 between the United States and Mexico, brought some 4 million Mexican workers to the United States for temporary employment over the following two decades. The programme induced a large northward migration of Mexicans seeking work in the USA. The number of workers who could not be accommodated by *bracero* certification and who entered the USA illegally eventually exceeded the number of legal *braceros*. The termination of the programme in 1964 and the forced expulsion from the USA of many illegal entrants created an unemployment crisis in Mexican border cities. In response, the Mexican government created the *maquiladora* (assembly plant) programme for the northern border area. *Maquiladoras* were allowed to assemble components brought in from the USA on condition that their products were re-exported to the USA. The duties that the USA imposed on entering *maquiladora* products were levied only on the value added in Mexico, essentially inexpensive labour. The system thus provided an abundant source of cheap labour for US firms, while for Mexico it provided employment as well as duties that *maquiladoras* pay to Mexico on the value added to the merchandise.

The *maquiladora* programme was originally established exclusively for the border area, but in 1989 the Mexican government announced new regulations that extended many of the benefits enjoyed by the *maquiladoras* to other Mexican industries and liberalized the conditions under which *maquiladora* outputs could be sold within Mexico. Under NAFTA, the *maquiladora* programme will essentially die out, because tariffs will disappear and within seven years of 1994 all goods produced in *maquiladoras* can be sold domestically. In 1993 there were 2150 *maquiladoras* employing approximately 600 000 workers, most of whom worked in plants on the Texas–Mexico border. Although the *maquiladoras* as such will disappear, proximity to US markets and to US sources of inputs will still make Mexico's northern border area relatively attractive for the location of many manufacturing activities of both US and Mexican firms.

It might be supposed that there would be numerous opportunities for US firms near the border to supply inputs to the *maquiladoras* and to the future Mexican border industry. Moreover, such opportunities would seem to be particularly great along the Texas–Mexico border area, where symbiotic trans-border relations are especially pronounced. The *maquiladora* programme has, in fact, often been termed the 'twin plant' programme, with the implication that there are, typically, complementary plants on either side of the border. In keeping with this notion, the Economic Analysis Center of the Texas State Comptroller of Public Accounts has maintained that growth in the Texas borderlands has been spurred by twin plants (Texas State Comptroller, 1988, 1989). But, in reality, twin plants have never really appeared to any great extent along the Texas side of the border; *maquiladora* inputs have typically come from US areas far beyond the border (Molina and Cobb, 1989). Although a substantial number of border *maquiladoras* would like to have local Texas suppliers, border manufacturing firms in Texas have not been able to handle large-volume contracts with tight tolerance and delivery-time requirements. To overcome their handicaps, Texas border firms will need to deal not only with shortages of skilled production workers, but also with deficiencies in such matters as cost analysis, financial analysis, procurement and marketing (Patrick, 1989). Inadequate education and training opportunities for the majority Mexican-American population in the Texas borderlands and a lack of business-service support networks for border manufacturing firms represent a continuing drag on the ability of Texas border firms to supply not only the *maquiladoras* and future Mexican border industry, but also their ability to participate in expanding opportunities in the US economy.

Environmental concerns voiced during NAFTA negotiations focused attention on serious problems in this regard along the border. The rapid growth of the *maquiladoras* and the increasing sophistication of the goods they produce have generated a huge array of chemical wastes, only a fraction of which are returned to the USA, as required by Mexican law. In many cases, the wastes are stockpiled at plant sites, sold to questionable 'recyclers', flushed down sewers or dumped in the desert. The dumping of industrial wastes into municipal collection systems and the inadequacy of Mexican sewage systems frequently result in toxic sewage washing across the border. Nuevo Laredo, Tamaulipas, for example, dumps 24 million gallons of raw sewage each day into the Rio Grande, a river from which communities downstream draw all their drinking water (Alm and Tomaso, 1990). In the Lower Rio Grande Valley, agricultural and industrial pollutants flow into the river from both sides of the border. Poor shanty settlements (*colonias*) take their water from the same contaminated river, and from wells which are often polluted by their untreated sewage. Chemical pollution of the air and water may be responsible for the fact that the number of babies born with severe brain damage in the Texas portion of the Lower Rio

Grande Valley is three times the US average. The adjacent cities of Ciudad Juárez and El Paso are both in violation of their respective national clean air standards (Alm and Tomaso (1990), Tomaso and Alm (1990)).

On paper, Mexico has impressive legal regimes for environmental protection, but, as in many developing countries, the government accepted high levels of pollution as part of the price that had to be paid for economic development. However, the opposition of many environmentalists to NAFTA has prompted unprecedented Mexican and US efforts to clean up the border. In 1992, the Mexican Government pledged to spend $460 million over three years on border projects to deal with waste water and solid waste. Environmental co-operation between the USA and Mexico has also increased dramatically. Just weeks before the NAFTA vote in Congress the two nations created a Border Environmental Co-operation Commission and outlined a plan to help generate $8 billion for border-related projects. The funds were to come from existing state and local programmes, the Mexican and US Federal Governments, the World Bank, the Inter-American Development Bank, and a projected North American Development Bank. Details of the organization, functions and funding of the Border Environmental Co-operation Commission were to be worked out in 1994. Meanwhile, Mexico has begun vigorous enforcement of environmental standards for plants along the border. Mexico is also utilizing US expertise concerning the treatment of industrial wastes, and the United States has agreed to provide advice and money to build a waste-water plant for Nuevo Laredo.

CALIFORNIA AND MEXICAN IMMIGRATION

In 1992, the value of California's exports to Mexico was $6.56 billion, and related employment was 150 764 (see Table 16.1). The former represented 35 per cent of the corresponding value of Texas, while the latter was 46 per cent of that in Texas. However, because California's economy is much larger than that of Texas, these comparisons understate the relative importance for Texas of trade with Mexico. For example, employment resulting from such trade accounted for 4 per cent of total Texas employment, but only 1 per cent of total California employment. As Hinojosa-Ojeda *et al.* (1992) point out, Mexico accounts for only 8 per cent of California's international trade, and while Texas is mainly linked to Mexico in terms of export production and pass-through trade, California is relatively more linked to Mexico in terms of immigration.

In the 1980s, there were 1.66 million legal Mexican immigrants to the USA, more than in the three previous decades combined. Mexicans accounted for 14 per cent of all immigrants in the 1970s, but for 23 per cent in the 1980s (Pastor, 1993). In 1991 alone, 946 000 Mexican immigrants were admitted, representing 52 per cent of all immigrants. However, beginning in 1989, immigrant data include unlawful residents who were granted permanent residence under the legalisation programme of the Immigration Reform and Control Act of 1986 (IRCA). Of the 1991 Mexican immigrants, 53 per cent were in California and 18 per cent were in Texas (US Bureau of the Census, 1993). In the 1980s, the Latino population of California, which has the highest concentration of Latinos among all states except New Mexico, grew by 69 per cent, compared with 56 per cent in Arizona, 45 per cent in Texas and 21 per cent in New Mexico (Barringer, 1991). The Mexican-origin population made up 80 per cent of the Latino population in California in 1990 (US Bureau of Census, 1993). Latino immigration represented one-third of the growth of the workforce in California in the 1980s. Latinos account for 23 per cent of California's employed work force and for 30 per cent of that in Los Angeles County, which contains 46 per cent of the state's Latinos jobs (Hinojosa-Ojeda *et al.*, 1992).

Hinojosa-Ojeda *et al.* (1992) estimate that the static effect of trade liberalisation under NAFTA by itself will have virtually no impact on the wage rates of any labour market segment in California, from the highest to the lowest paid. In contrast, migration dynamics are likely to affect the real wages adversely in some labour market sectors, and particularly those of existing immigrant Latinos in California industries in which there are considerable imports. The latter industries employ a relatively high proportion of immigrants, whereas high-export industries employ relatively few immigrants. While increased immigration results in falling real wages for immigrants, it also results in increased real wages for others who consume the less expensive outputs produced by immigrant labour. The net effect therefore is increased wage inequality.

Unintended consequences of IRCA are instructive with respect to increased immigration. Although IRCA legalized the status of many illegal residents, its main purpose was to curb the flow of illegal immigrants, especially those from Mexico. In particular, it increased funding for the Border Patrol's enforcement activities, and its imposed penalties on employers who knowingly hired illegal workers. However, the evidence indicates that IRCA did little, in fact, to increase the risks or costs of illegal border crossings. Rather, it resulted in a large increase in the number of newly-legalized workers in local labour markets and created a new illegal underground economy, increasing exploitation and lowering workplace standards. Thus IRCA failed to achieve its intended goal, while at the same time undermining the economic status of legal and illegal immigrant Latino workers (Donato *et al.* (1992), Fix (1991), Massey, (1993)).

Even if the long-run development of Mexico does produce sufficient employment opportunities to reduce migration to the United States, in the short run migration pressures may be expected to increase (Martin (1993), Pastor (1993)). The reorganization of Mexican agriculture is a major factor in this regard. For example, while US corn producers will gain from NAFTA through increased exports to Mexico, some 2.5 million poor Mexican maize farmers, who will lose protection and subsidies, represent a major potential source of increased migration to the USA. Migration to the USA may also be encouraged by rising economic expectations that exceed the capacity of the Mexican economy to meet them. Moreover, Los Angeles and other local California labour markets that receive disproportionately large numbers of legal and illegal immigrants are likely to be especially affected.

SUMMARY AND CONCLUSIONS

Although NAFTA will be mutually beneficial to the partners involved, and especially to Mexico, the aggregate effects in the USA are likely to be small. Nevertheless, there will be differential impacts, depending in part on whether, and to what extent, various states and localities are exporters of products in demand in Mexico and/or importers of Mexican products that reduce US employment. Among all the states, Texas will receive the most benefit. However, Texas communities on the border with Mexico, while gaining from the processing of trade, may also be affected adversely. Mexican shoppers have accounted for a large proportion of US retail sales at the border. With NAFTA, Mexican retailers can sell duty-free merchandize on the Mexican side, and some major US retailers may move across the border. Moreover, employment in the Texas borderlands is relatively concentrated in activities that are threatened by lower-cost Mexican imports. The border area on both sides suffers from environmental degradation, but NAFTA has induced unprecedented efforts on the part of both countries to address the major problems.

After Texas, California has the most linkages with Mexico, but the effects of NAFTA on California will come less through trade than through immigration from Mexico, which is likely to increase before the long-run development of Mexico creates ample employment opportunities there. Legal and illegal immigrants will lower costs of production in the sectors in which they concentrate, but they will also affect wages and working conditions adversely, especially for Latino immigrants. While NAFTA will benefit California as a whole, the net benefits will go to those residents employed in sectors that are not affected by immigration.

The threat that inexpensive Mexican labour represents to some segments of the US labour force is a legitimate concern, but a more fundamental long-term issue is that of international competitiveness. This is not simply a question of jobs. What is required is higher-productivity employment, which is the source of higher real incomes for workers. If cheap labour were the most important factor of production, US plants would be moving to Haiti and similar places, where labour is even less expensive than in Mexico. Most US trade is with relatively high-wage countries, in some cases higher than in the USA. European experience indicates that even such traditional goods as textiles, apparel and furniture can be produced efficiently with expensive labour if other favourable conditions are present (Hansen, 1991). In the information age, international competitiveness depends on the quality of the workforce, a well-developed social and economic infrastructure, sophisticated business services, fluid information diffusion, a steady stream of process and product innovations, and flexible production organization. In all these respects, the USA has clear advantages over Mexico. It should not be surprising that while trade with Mexico has been liberalized in recent years, the USA has moved from a trade deficit with Mexico to a surplus, implying a net gain in US jobs.

Empirical findings from Western Europe suggest that sustained economic development is primarily a local or regional, rather than a national, phenomenon. It results from milieux characterized by information richness and entrepreneurial vitality (Maillat and Lecoq (1992), Sweeney (1987)). Porter (1990) argues that the nation may not be a relevant unit of economic analysis because the conditions that underlie national competitiveness are so often localized within a nation, though at different locations for different industries. Krugman (1991) similarly points out that if one wants to understand differences in national growth rates one should start by examining differences in regional growth. These observations are consistent with the Japanese International Trade Institute's conclusion that the basic answer to the trade problems of the USA is to be found not only in greater industrial growth, but also in better-balanced regional development (Silk, 1987).

References

Aguilar, L. (1992) 'The North American Free Trade Agreement: The Ties that Bind', *Chicago Fed Letter*, September.

Alm, R. (1993) 'NAFTA: Texas Builds Its Future', *The Dallas Morning News*, 26 December, p. 1P.

Alm, R. and B. Tomaso (1990) 'Dirty Water: US Must Live with Border Pollution or Aid Mexico's Cleanup', *Transboundary Resources Report*, vol. IV, pp. 3–5.

Barringer, F. (1991) 'Census Shows Profound Change in Racial Makeup of Nation', *New York Times*, 11 March, p. 1.

Bovard, J. (1991) '"Fair" Trade is Unfair', *Newsweek*, 9 December, p. 13.

Bradsher, K. (1991) 'Free Trade: No Longer Just a Case of North versus South', *New York Times*, 23 June, p. E5.

Bradsher, K. (1992) 'An Industry's Winners and Losers once a Free-Trade Pact is Signed', *New York Times*, 21 July, p. 1.

Donato, K. M., J. Durand and D. S. Massey (1992) 'Changing Conditions in the US Labor Market: Effects of the Immigration Reform and Control Act of 1986', *Population Research and Policy Review*, vol. XI, pp. 93–116.

Fix, M. (ed.) (1991) *'Employer Sanctions' Implementation, Impact, and Reform* (Washington, DC: Urban Institute Press).

Hansen, N. (1991) 'Factories in Danish Fields: How High-Wage, Flexible Production Has Succeeded in Peripheral Jutland', *International Regional Science Review*, vol. XIV, pp. 109–32.

Hinojosa-Ojeda, R. and S. Robinson (1992) 'Labor Issues in a North American Free Trade Area', in N. Lustig, B. P. Bosworth and R. Z. Lawrence (eds), *North American Free Trade* (Washington, DC: The Brookings Institution).

Hinojosa-Ojeda, R., S. Robinson and G. Wolff (1992) 'The Impact of a North American Free Trade Agreement on California: A Summary of Key Research Findings', Working Paper No. 3 (Lewis Center for Regional Policy Studies, University of California, Los Angeles).

Hoglund, W. E. (1993) 'Detroit Sees More Exports to Mexico, More Jobs at Home', *New York Times*, 20 April, p. C16.

Krugman, P. (1991) *Geography and Trade* (Cambridge, Mass.: MIT Press).

Lustig, N., B. P. Bosworth and R. Z. Lawrence (eds) (1992) *North American Free Trade* (Washington, DC: The Brookings Institution).

Maillat, D. and B. Lecoq (1992) 'New Technologies and Transformation of Regional Structures in Europe: The Role of the Milieu', *Entrepreneurship and Regional Development*, vol. IV, pp. 1–20.

Martin, P. L. (1993) 'NAFTA will Substantially Reduce Mexican Migration to the United States', *Institute for International Economics News Release*, 12 October.

Massey, D. S. (1993) 'The 1986 Immigration Reform and Control Act and Its Aftermath', *Mexico Policy News*, no. 9, pp. 45–6.

Molina, D. J. and S. L. Cobb (1989) 'The Impact of Maquiladora Investment on the Size Distribution of Income Along the US–Mexico Border', *Journal of Borderlands Studies*, vol. IV, pp. 100–18.

Pastor, R. A. (1993) *Integration with Mexico* (New York: Twentieth Century Fund Press).

Patrick, M. (1989) 'Maquiladoras and South Texas Border Economic Development', *Journal of Borderlands Studies*, vol. IV, pp. 89–98.

Porter, M. E. (1990) *The Competitive Advantage of Nations* (New York: The Free Press).

Rivas, M. (1993) 'Apparel Industry, Other Firms, Worry About Competitiveness', *The Dallas Morning News*, 26 December p. 5P.

Silk, L. (1987) 'Japanese Stress Regions in US', *New York Times*, 20 February, p. 20.

Sweeney, G. P. (1987) *Innovation, Entrepreneurs and Regional Development* (New York: St Martin's Press).

Texas State Comptroller of Public Accounts (1988) *Fiscal Notes*, November.

Texas State Comptroller of Public Accounts (1989) *Fiscal Notes*, February.

Tomaso, B. and R. Alm (1990) 'Economy versus Ecology in Mexico's Drive for Growth Eclipses Concerns about Toxic Wastes from Border Plants', *Transboundary Resources Reports*, vol. IV, pp. 1–3.

Twin Plant News, February 1992.

United States International Trade Commission (1992) *Economy-Wide Modeling of the Economic Implications of a FTA with Mexico and a NAFTA with Canada and Mexico*, USITC Publication 2516 (Washington, DC: USITC).

US Bureau of the Census (1993) *Statistical Abstract of the United States: 1993* (Washington, DC: US Government Printing Office).

Weintraub, S. (1992) 'Modeling the Industrial Effects of NAFTA', in N. Lustig, B. P. Bosworth and R. Z. Lawrence (eds), *North American Free Trade* (Washington, DC: The Brookings Institution).

17 Regional Science and New Regional Policy in Russia[1]

Alexander Granberg*

REGIONAL STUDIES IN THE FORMER USSR: ACHIEVEMENTS AND LESSONS

The development of regional studies in the former USSR was marked by a strong influence of the state and the governing ideology. The system of central control based on the domination of USSR state ownership was created and sustained in a vast country with a formal federative structure and an immense diversity of natural, geographic, sociocultural, economic and other conditions in different regions. Inherent controversy of target orientation and objective conditions of this system functioning seriously affected the state of regional studies.

The unpretentious working concept of regional studies in terms of the objects and aspects involved is equivalent to regional science. In the USSR, however, different periods and schools favoured different names referring to this field of studies (or parts of it): allocation of productive forces; economic (or socioeconomic) geography; regional economics (and sociology); and so on. Disputes over the merits and priorities of this or that term have been most unproductive, while attempts to dissociate oneself from regional science on substantive or ideological grounds are as untenable as the opposition of American soccer to European football.

The principal directions of regional studies in the USSR were closely related to the radical shifts in the location of productive forces (the advance to the East and North), the drafting and examination of regional programmes and major investment projects, the elaboration of methodological principles of the system of territorial planning, and management (particularly of new forms of territorial organization of the economy). To be fair, it should be mentioned that many ideas, problems and traditions of these studies were formulated and elaborated in a prerevolutionary period, and the Commission for the Study of Natural Productive Forces (KEPS), founded by academician V. I. Vernadskky in 1915, became the first large all-Russia research centre for regional studies. The landmarks in applied research since the 1920s have included the GOELRO plan for the development of the electric power industry in Russia, substantiation of economic regionalization, preparation of the regional component of the first five-year plan, projects of the Urals–Kuznetsk integrated works, the Angara–Yenissei programme, the Greater Volga, the Greater Donbass, and others. Specialized research groups were formed under the auspices of the USSR Gosplan (State Planning Committee) and the Academy of Sciences, as well as with institutions of higher education. Since 1930, the Council for the Study of Productive Forces (SOPS) has become the leading research organization on applied regional studies. Large-scale expeditions into insufficiently explored areas were organized regularly, as well as a scientific conference on problem regions.

Beginning with the 1960s, the studies by various organizations differing in their approach and scale were integrated in a pre-plan (forecast) document – the *General Scheme of Development and Location of Productive Forces of the USSR*. In the 1970s, preparation was initiated of another pre-plan integrated document – the *Comprehensive Program of Progress in Science and Technology* (comprising sections on the Union republics and a consolidated regional volume). The General Scheme, as the more specific document (for a 10–15-year period), was drawn up mainly by government-related agencies and their research branches (up to 500 research and development institutions were involved), whereas the effort for the preparation of the Comprehensive Program (for a 20-year period), as the more strategic document, was led by institutes within the Academy of Sciences framework. The last General Scheme had a time horizon up to 2005, and the last Comprehensive Program, up to 2010. Another significant synthetic document was the regularly updated General Scheme of Settlement of the USSR, which consolidated the schemes of regional plans (layouts) and the urban agglomeration development project.

Concurrently with the preparation of pre-plan documents, the 1970s–80s saw a surge in studies of individual regions. Scientific groundwork was accomplished for major regional programmes (the West Siberian oil and gas complexes, the economic development of the zone of the Baikal–Amur Railway), programmes of formation of resource-orientated territorial production complexes (Timan–Pechora, Pavlodar–Ekibastuz, South Tajik, a group of complexes in Angara–Yenissei region, and so on, and local programmes of administrative territorial units. Significant decentralization occurred in the very process of regional research. By the mid-1980s there was a total of over fifty institutes specializing predominantly in regional studies in all Union republics and many cities of Russia (mainly in the North and East).

On the whole, the themes of typical regional studies in the USSR conformed to the demands of the growing economy in a phase of industrialization (and, in part, early post-industrial development) with a prevalence of extensive growth factors. The diversity and quality of regional studies (and, to an even greater extent, open publications) were adversely affected by ideological constraints.

These factors were mainly responsible for the insufficient attention – compared with Western science – given by Soviet regional science to social, demographic and environmental problems, ethnic relations, the development of infrastructure and services, information environment and diffusion of innovations. Certain groups of regional scientists, being under pressure from the command system of centralized state management, advocated erroneous (socially and environmentally unsound) ideas of 'gigantomania' ('big is beautiful') in construction, narrow specialization of regional economies and relocation of large masses of population to new industrial centres. The possibilities of central planning were emphasized at the expense of economic independence of regions and enterprises. Apparently, in the 1920s, regional scientists overlooked the potential of the new economic policy (NEP), and in the late 1960s they were not active enough in promoting the shift of economic reforms to the regional level.

It is paradoxical, however, that the results of research projects carried out to 'government commission' often failed to find a practical application. This was the case primarily with recommendations on comprehensive (economic, social, and environmental) regional development. Regionalization and regionalism were foreign to the laws of operation of a centralized command economy whose interests were represented not so much by the government and its Gosplan, but rather by sectorial departments (ministries) which had turned into gigantic state monopolies with vertical administration. Efforts by regional scientists to find an acceptable 'combination of sectorial and territorial management' were doomed to failure, even if it had been possible to avoid mistakes, and to act more purposefully and in a more organized way. The main faults in the location of productive forces and regional development within the territory of the former USSR did not arise from fallacious recommendations of scientists but rather from a consistent disregard of those recommendations.

Still, the 1980s witnessed the accrual of positive changes in the structure of Soviet regional science: the study of social and environmental aspects was appreciably expanded, as was the research in economic mechanisms of regional development and interregional relations. The transformations that have occurred and are in progress in the area of the former USSR have given rise to dramatic changes in regional studies. The dominance of centralized directive planning and the pressure of official ideology are now things of the past. Which elements of the heritage should be preserved, then? We believe that a few items must be maintained.

Our considerations are the following. As for the objects of research, the system of regional and inter-regional forecasts, the preparation of programmes for the development of the problem regions, substantiation of regional economic and social policies should be maintained. In the sphere of methodology, to continue with the elaboration of the system of economic, social and ecological balances, methods of modelling and systems analysis, and sociological monitoring. As for the organization of research, basic regional institutes and the core of regional scientists (economists, geographers, sociologists, political scientists and mathematicians), science co-ordination councils, and field trips to insufficiently explored regions should be supported.

Thus we are convinced that strong continuity needs to be maintained. Basing this on scientific and personnel potential it would be easier to adjust to the new situation.

INTERNATIONAL AND SOVIET REGIONAL SCIENCE: THE INTERACTION

For a long period (after the 1920s) social sciences in the former USSR evolved practically in isolation from the trends of international science. The situation began to change in the late 1950s, however. The general revitalization of society in the USSR was attended by an expansion of international contacts and growing interest in the achievements of international science. However, the rules of the 'ideological game' envisaged periodical warnings 'from above' of the incompatibility of domestic and Western science, and statements on the absolute superiority of the Soviet practice of regional development.[2]

The impact of world regional science on research practices in the Soviet Union was the most pronounced in the least ideology-dominated fields: the application of mathematical modelling and computer technologies. Russian translations have been published only of the main works by I. Tunen (1926), A. Weber (1926), A. Losh (1959), and W. Isard (1966). This fact is relevant as the language barrier still constitutes a major constraint for a large proportion of Soviet regional scientists. Hence the importance of works expounding the basic provisions of popular regional science theories is large. In recent years it has not been possible to arrange regular publication of fundamental works by Western scholars, nowadays for financial reasons. Thus a Russian translation of the regional economics handbook edited by P. Nijkamp was submitted to a publisher in 1992 and is still awaiting publication.

The activities of the Regional Science Association International were from the very beginning in the field of vision of Soviet specialists. Collected abstracts of papers of international congresses of the Association, published by the Institute of Economics and Industrial Organization and SOPS, contributed to it greatly. According to colleagues' opinion and my personal impression, the knowledge of works by Soviet (Russian) regional scientists in the West is even more limited. The obvious reason is the language barrier, but this is not the only cause.

Publications in English have included monographs on the territorial organizations of the Soviet economy,[3] the theory and practice of location of productive forces,[4] formation of territorial production complexes,[5] the Siberian experience of regional studies,[6] and a number of others as well as quite a large number of articles in international regional science journals, and the Soviet *Geography* magazine. But the influence of all these publications on Western studies is hardly seen.

The peak of international recognition of Soviet regional scientists is associated with the activities of the International Institute for Applied Systems Analysis (IIASA) where for a number of years Professors M. Albegov and B. Isayev co-ordinated regional development projects whose teams comprised many authoritative scholars including future leaders of the International and European Regional Science Associations. In 1976 the IIASA carried out a case study and held a conference on the problem of the Bratsk–Ust–Ilimsk territorial production complex, drawing on the experience of the complex creation for systems analysis of planning and management in the USSR.[7]

It would also be appropriate to mention Professor S. Menshikov's widely recognized work in the UN Secretariat on forecasting the development of world regions which initiated W. Leontief's project 'The Future of the World Economy' and its extension based on the use of inter-regional models, developed at the Institute of Economics and

Industrial Organization (Novosibirsk).[8] I am pleased to note Professor W. Isard's valuable participation as an expert in this project.

We trust that a substantial number of research projects implemented in the USSR, and since 1993 in the new independent states, deserve consideration by foreign colleagues. In certain areas, aspects, or scales, these studies have advanced further than similar projects in other countries. The leading fields include, in our view, the application of optimization methods to the location of production, the construction of chronological series of input–output tables for all union republics (from 1966 to 1987), the analysis of inter-regional economic interactions based on a set of optimization and equilibrium models, the development of systems of multi-level models, and methods of devising regional programmes. This list is not exhaustive. The Moscow Congress offered the regional scientists of the states of the former USSR an auspicious opportunity for a broader presentation of their projects and results.[9] The extent of international contacts of Soviet economists has always been inadequate. For obvious reasons, closer collaboration was maintained with regional scientists of socialist countries. Between 1971 and 1979 annual meetings were held of regional scientists representing that group of countries, and joint research projects were carried out. In addition, since early 1970s a series of bilateral seminars has been conducted on the methodology of modelling regional systems and regional planning in conjunction with scientists of the USA, West Germany, the Netherlands, Bulgaria, Poland and Czechoslovakia. Participation in meetings organized by the International Geographic Union followed a more regular pattern.[10]

The first 'appearance' of Soviet regional scientists at a European congress of the RSA took place in 1966; this continued periodically over subsequent years. Only beginning with the 28th Congress of the ERSA and the 2nd World Congress of the RSA did the participation of Soviet (Russian) delegation, and then only small ones, became a regular feature.

TRANSFORMATION OF THE FORMER USSR: THE EFFECTS ON REGIONS AND REGIONAL SCIENCE

By the middle of the 1980s the Soviet Union had a highly integrated economy ('the single national economic complex')[11] based on state ownership and centralized state administration. The peak of inter-regional (inter-republican) exchange was reached in 1987. This was followed by an increasing tendency towards economic disintegration, its most characteristic features being barter-orientated trade, administrative prohibitions on exporting goods beyond the region, a growing gap between public and market prices, the rationed distribution of consumer goods according to regional regulations, and the introduction of regional ersatz-money.[10] The progress of political sovereignization of union republics gave this trend a major boost, and ultimately brought about the break-up of the USSR into fifteen independent states.

However, in 1992–3 the process of dissociation of the economics of post-USSR republics continued. The volume of inter-republican exchange of goods shrank at least twice, and various forms of customs and non-customs regulations were brought in by all republics, and since the middle of 1992 the division of public monetary systems has taken place.

Within the framework of the Commonwealth of Independent States (CIS) efforts have been made to stabilize economic relations and achieve economic reintegration on the basis of political independence without a governing centre. Consulting and co-ordination bodies of the CIS have been established, and hundreds of multi-lateral economic agreements have been concluded. An agreement on the Economic Union has been prepared and signed. Within the CIS, attempts are being made to set up closer economic coalitions (for example, Russia + Ukraine + Byelorussia; Kazakhstan + 4 republics of Central Asia). Trans-republic production, trade, and financial associations are being formed, on a 'bottom-up' initiative.

Other aspects of the division of the USSR have serious social and economic implications. Suddenly, millions of 'aliens' materialized. These are primarily Russians who for decades, or even centuries, have been settled throughout the Russian empire and later the USSR. The new foreign states' (that is, 14 post-USSR republics) have a total population of 25 million Russians, and if we include in that number the so-called 'Russian-speaking' residents, mixed marriages and so on, the Russian diaspora in the new states will amount for not less than 30–35 million people. Complicated problems have also been raised by the division of the formerly unified Soviet armed forces, and withdrawal and relocation of troops.

Studies of the economic consequences of the transformation of the USSR and the possibility of new forms of economic relations among the republics of the former USSR are conventionally subdivided into strategic and tactical. Tactical research aims at short-term decision-making for stabilization and regulation of economic relations, drafting of normative documents (accords, agreements and so on). Strategic studies set the objective of formulating a long-term policy of economic co-operation among the new states.

The papers at the 31st and 32nd European Congresses outlined the results of the analysis of the economic interactions of the republics of the former USSR, based on a set of regional and multi-regional models. The main effects of inter-republican interaction, qualitative estimates of republics' 'contributions' to the end product of every republic, multitudes of efficient states of economic co-operation (Pareto optimum, the core of the economic system, efficient republic coalitions, for example), and states of economic equilibrium were exposed.

The earlier results proceeded from the condition that the foreign economic relations of the republics (that is, ties with states outside the USSR) were exogenous. This corresponded of real centralization and monopolization of foreign trade in the USSR. The main conclusion was that all the 15 republics have an objective economic interest in co-operation.

In the new series of model experiments, the foreign trade of the republics with 'third' countries was described by means of endogenous variables. The main results are mentioned in the special paper by A. Granberg and V. Suslov to the 33rd European Congress. Research on the effects of inter-republican economic interactions and the implications of different forms of regulation will be pursued further. Unfortunately, the deterioration of information on inter-republican trade presents increasing difficulties. This is also a consequence of the break-up of the USSR.

REGIONAL POLICY OF RUSSIA IN TRANSITION PERIOD

Large diversity of natural, sociodemographic, economic, political and other conditions in many regions of Russia doom to failure unified approaches to the reform implementation, orientated to some average conditions. It was not demonstrated even once in the process of previous attempts to reform centralized command-administrative economy of the USSR, or since 1993 – in Russia. Real reform cannot be limited to the programme of measures and actions for Russia as a whole.

Local governments implement various options for reform and adaptation to the universal and specific difficulties of the transition period. In effect, the variations of socioeconomic policy at the regional level are reducible to a combination of four models:

1. Forcing economic change. It is assumed that the inevitable social costs will be minimized because of rapid stabilization and normalization of regional economies. This strategy involves speedy privatization, conversion, attraction of foreign investment (for example, the cities of Moscow, Saint Petersburg and Nizhni-Novgorod).
2. Exploiting the market benefits of the present stage of reforms, first and foremost the difference in world and domestic prices of primary materials. Export-orientated regions strive to protect their hard-currency revenues from transfer to the federal budget, using them partly for providing social support to the population (Kemerovo and Tyumen provinces, Komi republic, for example).
3. Obtaining benefits and preferences for one's region from the federal government and their use for social assistance to the population (this is the orientation of most regions with below-average levels of development).
4. The preservation of a centrally planned economy at the local level – controls over prices, producers, distribution of consumer goods, bans on exports, subsidies for production of certain goods, guarantee of minimum standards of consumption to the population (the most graphic example is the Ulyanovsk region).

The objective differences in pre-reform staging positions were complemented with differences brought about by the diversity of reform options. Similarly, changes occurred in the differentiation of regions in terms of latent social tensions, which will inevitable surface in the course of further transformations. The most pronounced aggravation of tension is to be expected where local governments follow mainly the fourth model, that is, precisely in those regions which at the time of writing appear the most stable socially.

A positive result of the activities of regional scientists, different branches of power and various social political movements is the recognition of the need for a strong regional policy. That is, in fact, one of the rare examples of national consensus in Russia.

The regional differentiation of conditions and factors of continuation of economic reforms rules out the possibility of any single 'pure' option. Reforms are bound to combine different options, with their overall strategy being adjusted to the specific features of a number of regions. For the same reason, the transition from one state of socioeconomic development to another (a crisis, stabilization or upturn) will inevitably be 'blurred', with a considerable variation in timing for individual regions.

The main principle of the concept of the new regional economic policy consists of the combination of essential regionalization of economic reforms and spatial reintegration of the Russian economy.

The regionalization of reforms comprises: an account of regional characteristics in implementation of the federal structural, investment, financial, social and foreign trade policies; the transfer of a number of reforms mainly to the regional level (especially in small business, the social sphere, environmental conservation and the use of natural resources); decentralization of control over reforms; and the need for elaboration of 'custom-made' reform programmes for regions with special conditions (regional blocks of the federal programme).

The strengthening of economic integration of Russian regions requires the streamlining of the pattern of vertical and horizontal interactions of economic and government entities, the maintenance and development of federal infrastructural systems, the stabilization of the financial and monetary systems, the mobilization of efforts for the reinstatement of territorial division of labour in Russia and the formation of a unified market area, and the elaboration of measures to counteract the disruption of inter-regional economic links, and economic and political separatism trends.

In frames of regional policy, one would provide for the solution of the following priority tasks.

Social tasks

- the provision of a minimum of conditions and living standards for the population of all the regions, and support for the most backward ones;
- the revival of the village and smaller towns in the rural districts, with the attraction of local and foreign business structures;
- averting mass unemployment in major centres and industrial regions;
- regulating population migration, the migration of refugees and the ex-service military personnel, and the creation of economic privileges for their return active civilian life; and
- assistance in the development of the major recreation zones, taking into consideration that after the collapse of the USSR many traditional resort areas were located in other states.

Economic tasks

- assistance towards effective and competitive specialization of the regional economy in the common economic space of Russia;

- participation in the economic assimilation of new regions with the involvement of foreign and private home capital;
- the creation of free economic zones and technologies as well as respecialization and reconstruction of the new frontier regions;
- the formation of effective inter-regional and inter-state economic ties;
- the support of progressive structural transformations in agro-industrial regions; and
- assistance in overcoming crises in depressive regions and regions with extreme natural conditions.

Ecological tasks

- the abolition of critical situations in the zones with a heavy load on the environment;
- the elimination of the consequence of ecological disasters (Chernobyl, Chelyabisk, for example) and so on.

Tasks in the fields of national and inter-ethnic relations

- provision for the specific interests and rights of smaller nations; revival of their specific norms of economy;
- assistance in the migration of depressed nations; and
- constant control of the military and zones of inter-ethnic conflict.

The federal state will influence regional development by different administrative and economic methods with the transfer of the main power to economic regulation. The main form of the direct participation of the state in the regulation of regional development will be state regional programmes with shared financing, extremely important structure-forming investment projects, and the competitive location of the orders for product deliveries for the public needs. We give priority to the problems of disintegration and reintegration.

The USSR has broken up. Will the Russian Federation – the largest of the former USSR republics – share the same destiny, or will the disintegration trend stop? Will the process of economic reforms be carried on within the framework of a single federal programme or will it be divided into autonomous regional processes of different orientation? What means and forms of economic reintegration may be effective and sufficient for overcoming regional separatism? What state and social institutions may lead the reintegration process and keep it within the framework of democracy? Now these issues are crucial to Russia.

The main task of the federal policy of economic reintegration of

Russia consists in the formation of a unified economic area (all-Russia market) which still benefits from territorial division of labour and inter-regional and international economic co-operation. The reintegration policy of the government is based on a system of short-term and medium-term projects where the possibilities and methods of solving the problems of socioeconomic development of the regions are being investigated. The working out is in hand of the Complex forecast of the development and location of productive forces of the Russian Federation in the period up to the year 2000. At the same time, the branch and regional schemes of the development and location of productive forces as well as the General scheme of the population settlement and regional layouts are being completed. They include the main indices of the development of major economic regions and each subject of the Federation.

Priority spheres of federal state activities must be the federal infrastructure systems (energetics, transport, communications, information and space), providing for the functioning of the unified economic space. In the field of tariffs for transport and other services of federal infrastructure, integrated policy should be taken as a guideline, it should be directed at the rational inter-regional economic ties and prevent their destruction caused by market changes in goods and services, that is, caused by the abrupt rise in prices for the transportation of goods and the transmission of electric power. In connection with the fact that the majority of the Black Sea ports belong to different republics of the former USSR, as well as the absence of direct exits to West European countries, the strategy of development for the transport network is being revaluated. There must be a new evaluation approach to BAM and North-Siberian railways, which carry out the liaison between West and East. One of the most important questions now is the construction in the Far East, the North Caucasus and the North of Russia of new ports for the development of foreign relations. The state will also give support to the further development and the increase of stability in the functioning of the Northern Sea Route.

One extremely important issue of the reintegration of Russia is the termination of the system of financial federalism. Up to the end of the 1980s the USSR had a unitary system of finance which was extremely centralized. The majority of financial resources accumulated in the union budget and were then redistributed without any stable rules. Because of these policies, the regions were not particularly interested in increasing their own income. The growth of the economic rights of the republics (within the frame of the USSR), national–state and administrative–

territorial formations (within the framework of the Russian Federation) appeared first of all in the budget and tax systems. The modern system of Russian taxation has the main features of financial federalism: (i) expenditures and revenues are divided at all levels; (ii) the rules and parameters of taxation and distribution of all kinds of taxes are in force (at least for a year); and (iii) special funds for the financial support of the regions are created. But this system is not yet stable.

The situation in 1993 convinced us of the uselessness of the regional differentiation rate, regulating taxes distributed between federal and regional budgets. All regions, via taxes paid by the corresponding physical and legal persons, must bear the proportional costs of participation in national expenditure. Along with this, special funds for redistribution of resources among the regions will be established. We are speaking here first of all of the fund for regional development and the fund subventions. The application or privileges as far as the federal taxes are concerned will bear in general a functional-target (that is to say, an ex-territorial) character. Exceptions will be made mainly for a limited range of tasks and 'special' regions (extreme North, free economic zones and so on).

The principles of economic federalism and social justice correspond to the considerable increase of the share of rent payments in the sum of income going to the federal budget (at the time of writing this share makes about 5 per cent). It will give the possibility of some reduction of other taxes (first of all the tax on value added and income).

The new organizational form that may favour the economic integration of Russia is made up of regional associations of economic interaction. These started to appear, on a voluntary basis, in 1990. At the time of writing we have eight such associations, covering practically all the territory of Russia. The geography of these associations is close to the net of major economic regions, used by the State Planning Committee of the USSR and state statistics. Associations have nothing to do with the functions of the existing subjects of the Federation. Fears that regional associations are becoming a platform for regional separatism are felt to be exaggerated. The activities of regional associations supported by federal organizations (primarily the Ministry of Economy) may be concentrated in the decision of integration tasks.

The principles of federalism in Russia are confirmed by the new Constitution, adopted on 12 December 1993. These include:

- the establishment of the equality of the subjects of the Federation in their relations with the federal authorities (art. 5);
- the guaranteed unity of economic space; the free migration of goods,

services and means of financing; the protection of competition; the freedom of economic activity not forbidden by the law (art. 8);
- the use of federal funds of regional development (art. 71.3);
- the impossibility of the establishment of inner customs borders, taxes and other obstacles for the free migration of goods, services and financial means (art. 74); and
- the banning of the introduction of any other currency in Russia other than the rouble (art. 75).

It is undoubtedly important that actions violating the unity of the economic space of the Russian Federation and its monetary system will be considered to be anti-constitutional, with all the corresponding consequences.

The regulated and spontaneous reintegration of the Russian economy is going on in a situation where the disintegration trend has not yet run its course. In large economic systems the rate of destruction exceeds by far the speed of construction. It is felt that a minimum of three to four years will be required to restore the principal integration characteristics of the Russian economy to the level of the late 1980s, while the formation of an integrated Russian market will go beyond the year 2000.

The market area of Russia will remain heterogeneous for a long time yet; individual regions will implement different models of economic reforms. The federal state cannot ensure uniformity of transition to a market economy in different types of region. At best, it will have enough strength and expertise for streamlining and ordering interregional economic relations. In order to maintain the economic integrity of the country, the federal government should specifically finance integration measures even at the cost of increasing budget deficit and inflation rate. These costs amount essentially to insurance for the future of Russia.

What is unlikely to happen?[11] It seems certain that the state integrity of Russia will be preserved. None of the republics will legitimately secede from the Russian Federation, yet this issue will be the focus of political intrigues, and uncertainties will arise with regard to the status of individual territories. On the other hand, it is highly improbable that existing administrative–territorial units will be integrated into state entities, for example the formation of republics from existing provinces – the Urals, the South Urals republic, and so on. When it comes from threats to the central effective organization, the unification will be blocked by strong resistance of the local political elite. A pause in political stand-offs is a vital condition for stabilization of the trend of economic integration.

Notes and References

* The author is the leader of teams of authors who prepare regional sections for *The Program of Economic Reforms Intensification* (1992) and the programme *Reform Development and Stabilisation of Russian Economy* (1993).

1. Owing to the fast-moving nature of events in Russia, some portion of this chapter is unavoidably outdated. Information regarding the current situation can be obtained from the author.
2. The saying of the former Chairman of the USSR Gosplan, N. K. Baibakov, made at the beginning of *perestroika*: 'The display of impressive achievements of real socialism, including a new approach to the location of productive forces, is also very important for the successful struggle against our ideological opponents – beginning from ardent imperialists to opportunists and revisionists from the right' is very typical. Planning of the location of productive forces (pursuing of the CPSU policy at the stages of socialist construction), *Ekonomika*, Moscow, pt 1, 1985, p. 8.
3. Nekrasov, N. (1974) *The Territorial Organization of Soviet Economy* (Moscow: Progress Publishers).
4. Mozhin, V. (ed.) (1988) *Distribution of the Productive Forces: Theory and Practice* (Moscow: Progress Publishers).
5. (1980) *Territorial Industrial Complexes: Optimization Models and General Aspects* (Moscow: Progress Publishers).
6. A. G. Aganbegyan (ed.) (1981) *Regional Studies for Planning and Projecting. The Siberian Experience* (Mouton Publishers).
7. Knop, H. (ed.) (1977) *The Bratsk–Ilimsk Territorial-Production Complex* (Laxenburg: IIASA).
8. Granberg, A., and S. Menshikov (eds) (1984) *Interregional Models of the World Economy* (Novosibirsk: Nauka).
9. The Program of the Congress's fifteen sections features 38 papers by scientists of the states – republics of the former USSR (including 29 from Russia). The 16th (Russian language) section – 'Regional Aspects of Contemporary Socioeconomic Policy' lists 50 papers.
10. Analysis of these phenomena is contained in the paper presented to the 31st Congress of the European Regional Science Association. See A. Granberg, *The National and Regional Science Association*, also A. Granberg, 'The National and Regional Commodity Markets in the USSR: Trends and Contradictions of the Transition Period', *Papers in Regional Science: The Journal of the RSAI*, vol. 72, no. 1, pp. 3–23.
11. These studies were summarized in the paper A. G. Granberg and V. I. Suslov (1993) *Coalition Analysis of Multiregional Systems: Theory, Methods, Results of Analysis (USSR) on the Eve of Disintegration)*, Institute of Economics and Industrial Organization of the Siberian Branch of Russian Academy of Sciences, Novosibirsk.

18 Socioeconomic Transformations in Central and Eastern Europe from the Perspective of Regional Science

Ryszard Domański

Transformational processes in Central and Eastern Europe have been set in motion by the introduction of a system of parliamentary democracy and a market economy. They have resulted in the expansion of the private sector, the privatization of state-owned enterprises, and the development of banks, stock exchanges and insurance agencies. Consequently, the number of economic agents making decisions about location, investments, business contacts, and new organizations of production and foreign trade has grown prodigiously. The increase in the number of decision-makers multiplies the impact on economic space, modifying and transforming it. Another powerful influence on the space economy is the revived system of territorial self-government. Its organs set themselves different goals from those of low-level government administration, employ different modes of operation and use resources in different ways.

The return to the market economy and territorial self-government brings about two changes which are significant in spatial-economic terms: (i) the revaluation of space on the scale of towns and regions; and (ii) a change in spatial and environmental behaviour patterns of households, enterprises, and local and central administration.

Some areas which used to be attractive to investors, entrepreneurs and migrants have lost much, if not all, of their attraction. This especially concerns towns and regions with a traditional economic structure (mining and heavy industry, for example), depreciated infrastructure and production goods, and a degraded natural environment, and, moreover, those industrial centres which until recently produced goods exported to the countries of the now dissolved COMECON, and centres of the armaments industry which have lost their markets with the dissolution of the Warsaw Pact. At the same time there are towns and regions with newly-found locational appeal: those in which the tradition of private enterprise has survived, which already have a class of entrepreneurs with some capital, however modest (usually owners of small industrial or trading firms and exchange offices), which have already established foreign economic contacts (international fair cities, places of origin of former emigrants who have managed to build up substantial capital and now intend to invest in the old country), in which the institutional infrastructure of a market economy has developed, and which have a convenient transport location and an unspoilt natural environment.

What has changed the spatial and environmental behaviour patterns of households and enterprises is the diversification of wages in the private and public sectors, and making more realistic the prices of goods, services and transport tariffs, rates for public utility services, land prices, charges for using environmental resources, and penalties for polluting the environment. The creation of new job opportunities in the private sector, usually the better paid, and a simultaneous reduction of jobs in state-owned enterprises, usually the worse paid, have changed the spatial pattern of commuting. Trade and services are those branches of the economy in which privatization has been the most rapid and far-reaching.

New owners of retail and service shops often switched to different kinds of goods and services. Thus the spatial pattern of shopping trips has changed too. A new network of supply and sales links has developed among manufacturing enterprises, which also often changed their lines of production with a view to the manufacture of articles involving a higher level of processing. This leads to a reduction in the weight of freight, but the formation of the new linkage and the search for new partners may increase the distances travelled. The partners may be foreign companies. A frequent form of co-operation is West European firms providing East–Central European industrial plants with raw materials to process. Finished products are then transported back to Western Europe. Such transactions are motivated by cheaper labour in Central and Eastern Europe, and more advanced marketing in Western Europe, which is better skilled at attracting consumers. Along with the tendency to increase the distance of transport that accompanies the formation of new economic networks, there is a tendency to cut this distance, forced by the more realistic, and hence higher, transport tariffs.

These tendencies reflect the differences in the patterns and organization of production.

The realistic prices also force households and enterprises to use resources more prudently. Before the transformation of the economic system, the prices of energy, land, water and air (the admissible level of pollution) were set by the state at a very low level which bore little relation to real costs. The absence of incentives to economize led to wasteful management. Apart from the conservation of resources, another positive effect of the revised prices is the introduction, albeit still limited, of new environment-friendly technologies of production. Rents for flats, especially in multi-family, privately-owned houses, were low too. They did not even cover the costs of routine maintenance, let alone renovation work, and so they have fallen into disrepair. Similarly, the low participation of tenants in the building costs of co-op flats tended to boost the demand for them. Raising the rents has set in motion the process of exchanging bigger flats for smaller and reduced the demand for new ones. In some towns, effective demand falls short of supply. Thus, a position of equilibrium is being reached with only partial satisfaction of housing needs. The new housing policy whose drafts are being discussed at the time of writing accommodates also social, as well as economic, aspects of the hitherto unsolved housing problem.

The transformation of the sociopolitical and economic systems has brought about radical changes in local and regional administration. Local administration has regained its self-governing character, which is considered a revolutionary change. Communal councils have acquired genuine influence on the course of local events, even though initially they could not fully exert their rights because of the limited means they had at their disposal. Now communal budgetary receipts tend to increase, because the communes are getting a growing share of the taxes paid by economic agents located on their territories, and taxes on the personal incomes of local residents. Discussion is going on concerning the expansion of the self-government system to include a second level at which supra-local matters requiring higher administrative powers would be settled. The idea of a second level of territorial self-government arouses controversy, and so its implementation keeps being postponed. It is, however, important, if not urgent, in large cities, especially the state's capital. The cities are too big for the local communities inhabiting their various quarters to reach a consensus on a single set of targets and to consolidate efforts to achieve them. In the first years of the transformation period city quarters enjoyed much independence, which made it difficult to pursue a consistent policy at the level of the city as a whole. In an attempt to counteract disintegration, a legal construction was devised in the largest cities, known as an obligatory association of communes. However, the powers with which those creations were endowed were too limited to allow them the adoption of a co-ordinated policy of urban development. The negative experiences of that period speak for a self-government reform of large cities that would ensure a more integrated urban administration.

The growing diversification of the local, that is, self-government, level of administration is accompanied by a declining importance of the intermediate level as the regional representation of government administration. A substantial portion of tasks of the regional level has been taken over by local self-governments, together with operational means. On the other hand, the transformation of the sociopolitical and economic systems requires that intellectual potential should be concentrated at the central level, and that this level should be strengthened organizationally, authorized to make decisions necessary to carry radical reforms into effect, and equipped with the means to protect the poorer strata of society against their negative effects. Thus the state administration system has polarized: the extreme ends, namely, local and central, have become reinforced. The intermediate level, enfeebled by the loss of many of its powers and operational means, has lost its former identity. The weakening of the intermediate level of state administration was connected with the fact that the initial transformation was based on the neo-liberal economic doctrine. Those who authored and then implemented the reforms believed that the inherited inefficient economic system should be subjected to the hard-and-fast rules of a market economy. These rules, they supposed, would eliminate the economically unsound structures and processes. Moreover, regional problems were also believed to be capable of being solved gradually by the market mechanisms. The belief, however, that these mechanisms could straighten out regional economies started to waver in the face of the old, difficult problems being compounded by many new ones, equally hard to solve. The weakening of the regional level is contested by social regional movements that insist on self-government being extended to this level as well. In extreme cases these movements demand a high degree of regional autonomy, especially in more advanced and wealthier regions, and also in those inhabited by ethnic minorities, which has rather sinister associations in this part of Europe.

The transformation of the sociopolitical and economic systems has thus led to the formation of two systems in place of uniform territorial organs of state administration: a local one based on self-government, and an intermediate one as the regional representation of the central government. A novelty about them is that, although interdependent, they are not hierarchical. The distinction between their scope of operation and powers is made by special acts called 'competence statutes'. However, even the best of legal regulations are helpless to prevent conflicts between these systems. Thus the period of transformation is simultaneously a period of learning the difficult art of negotiating, and working out a compromise. Self-governing authorities and territorial organs of central administration find it particularly difficult to reach an agreement on the routes of planned motorways and other infrastructural investments of a linear nature. In such cases there are many communes engaged in the negotiations. These take different views on the projects and raise various objections, sometimes blocking investments judged by regional and central authorities to be important and rational. Conflicts also arise among communes, that is, within the same (self-government) system. Relations between large towns and their surrounding communes tend to give rise to the biggest number of conflicts. Negotiating and arriving at a compromise turn out to be particularly difficult in the case of the siting of rubbish tips. They can certainly be offensive or even noxious to the environment and local communities. However, a compromise is possible if city authorities undertake to satisfy sanitary requirements and to reclaim the land after the tip has been filled to capacity. Sanitary requirements include, for example the formation of an isolating layer that prevents contamination from spreading to groundwater, and the transport of refuse from towns to tips in a way least disagreeable to the residents of settlements along access routes. Making rubbish tips less objectionable, or even using them to produce additional economic and ecological effects, will be possible when new biogas-based technologies start being widely employed.

The prospect of applying regional science in the period of transformation in Central and Eastern Europe depends largely on the level of social demand for regional policy and regional planning, and this in turn depends on the acuteness of regional problems, present and future. This prospect is now brighter than at the beginning of the transition period. Initially, the reform-minded governments, scientific circles and public opinion focused their attention mainly on transformations on a macro scale. It soon turned out, however, that their regional consequences were very grave, and often painful. Some regions, especially those better developed (with already-established wide economic contacts with foreign countries, and better prepared to adopt market and technological innovations), soon started to adapt to the new conditions created by the sociopolitical and economic reforms. In the other regions, however, adaptive processes have hardly got under way, and quite a number of them have found themselves in a dramatic situation. The neo-liberal economic policy, aimed initially at ensuring all the sectors equal opportunities for development, and basically opposed to state intervention in the course of socioeconomic processes, is now being partly revised to extend the scope of this intervention. The need for the state to interfere in regional problems has become vitally urgent, thus giving rise to the development of a new regional policy. Its new problems include: (i) unemployment, especially in industrial centres and regions whose output has lost its markets, particularly in the former COMECON countries; (ii) the diversification of the economic structure in places dominated so far by a single large industrial plant (a growth role); if a plant such as that reduces output and employment, or goes bankrupt altogether, the whole of the local community finds its livelihood threatened; (iii) fighting the recession in agricultural regions in which much land belongs to state-owned farms, now mostly near collapse because of their inability to adjust to the conditions of a market economy; (iv) stimulating structural transformations and development in poorly-developed regions dominated by obsolete agriculture, unfit for competition on the home market, let alone foreign ones; and (v) stimulating structural transformations and development in highly industrialized regions with a traditional economic structure which has already contributed, and still contributes, to the deterioration of the natural environment.

Problems of restructuring and stimulating development existed even before the systemic transformation was initiated. However, under altered sociopolitical and economic conditions they have assumed a different form. Therefore, they need to be redefined, as do many other concepts of regional science as it has developed in Central and Eastern Europe. The redefinition is made easier because of the earlier wide contacts of regional scientists from this part of the world with the main centres of this discipline in the USA and Western Europe. The East–Central European community of regional scientists has now an opportunity to create original conceptions and models generalizing their experiences of the transition from a centralized to a market economic system. This is a unique experience in the development of regional thought. It is also likely to fertilize regional science centres in Western Europe and the USA. Thus new perspectives open up for the international cooperation of regional scientists.

As the field of operation of market mechanisms expanded with the progress of the transformation of the economic system, the scope of planning kept narrowing. Making plans at the national and regional level was given up; and at the local level only physical planning was carried on, and even that not in all the communes. Apart from doctrinal reasons, the demise of planning was also caused by the instability of the economy, hardly avoidable in a transition period. It made anticipating socioeconomic development difficult. Realistic forecasts did not cover more than a few months. The annual national budgets could not be adhered to without amendments being made as the time passed.

A new way of steering the development of towns and regions is emerging. In addition to spatial plans, towns start to draw up strategic programmes of socioeconomic development in which their mission is defined, as well as their main goals, together with the steps necessary to achieve these. At the regional level, programmes of economic restructuring are prepared. Initially, they applied in regions with problems, especially those seriously threatened by structural unemployment.

The low effectiveness of planning was one of the reasons why the very idea of it has been discredited. In journalism, and even in scientific literature, the term itself tended to be avoided. To improve the effectiveness of the new programmes of regional restructuring that are being prepared, regional and central authorities strive to ensure the institutional and financial conditions for their implementation. With this aim in view, agencies and foundations for regional development are set up, financed by income from three sources: local, national and foreign. Out of foreign sources supporting the restructuring of selected regions, the most promising is the Struder project of the European Union.

New challenges for regional policy are posed by the association of the countries of Central and Eastern Europe with the European Union. Regional problems are the focus of the Union's attention. It allocates a substantial part of common funds for regional development, and, more precisely, for two main goals: stimulating the development of backward regions, and restructuring old industrial regions with an antiquated economic structure. During the association period, and before obtaining the membership status in the European Union, the East–Central European countries should undertake to adjust their regional policy standards to match West European ones. Among the steps to be taken are: the transformation of the economic structure of problem regions (through the development of the private sector, securing foreign investments, balancing the labour market and so on; the levelling out of regional differences in the population's living conditions and economic development (these discrepancies are one of the factors of political destabilization); and the development of frontier areas, including the expansion of border crossings to facilitate bilateral and multi-lateral economic contacts.

The European Union can support regional development in the associated countries of Central and Eastern Europe in a variety of ways. They can include: informing about and co-operating in the design of regional policy; initiating and building up co-operation between towns and regions; co-ordinating the development of frontier areas; and finally, improving the qualifications of the managerial staff of regional administration and helping economic employees to change their qualifications to meet new requirements. What the countries of Central and Eastern Europe expect first of all, however, is help with technical infrastructure, the development of market institutions that facilitate expansion into the markets of advanced countries, and the financing of small and medium-sized enterprises.

For the countries of Central and Eastern Europe to be able to make proper use of these various forms of assistance, they have to draw up convincing multi-year programmes of regional development, the principles of financing them, ways of raising their own means to supplement foreign assistance means, and set up an institution capable of efficient management of the adjustment process.

In what spatial shape can the economy emerge from the period of transition from a centralized to a market system? Anticipating the evolution of the spatial organization of the economy is difficult because of the complexity of the processes that shape it. Several trajectories of the economic development of regions are possible, each leading to a different state of equilibrium depending on its history, current state and the impact of its surroundings. The most probable is asymmetry between the expected revival of the economy and the recession that hit it in the period of crisis and the introduction of reforms. In other words, the path of initial growth, the path of decline, and the path of renewed growth will take different courses, and will not repeat themselves. Asymmetry will be more pronounced in economic activity, its structure and technology, than in the built-up patterns of towns and regions.

The new spatial shape will be modelled by a variety of processes. First, the regions that will be more successful in attracting new enterprises or new branches of existing ones will be those with fewer spatial and environmental limitations. They will be regions with moderately advanced urban–industrial agglomerations, offering considerable external economies and only moderate limitations.

Second, there will be increasing differences at the lower, namely, local, level of spatial organization. The factors that will contribute to them include: (i) existing differences in local potentials and their attractiveness to investors; (ii) unequal access to regional and national potentials; and (iii) the varying efficiency of local governments caused by differences in experience and qualifications of the self-government personnel, and in their ability to integrate local communities around communal projects and to attract investors from outside.

In the period of transition there will be many factors at work deforming spatial processes specific to a market economy. The most important are: a high level of monopolization of the economy; difficulties attendant on the revival of private initiative; under-development of institutions favourable to the operation of a market economy; and the resistance of those social groups whose situation will deteriorate, if only temporarily, as a result of the transformation.

Other things that will change in the transition period are the hierarchical relationships in the spatial organization of the economy. In East–Central Europe the processes of disintegration of lower hierarchical levels that are commonly taking place in European countries overlap with processes resulting from the rebirth of territorial self-government. This also leads to the formation of inter-dependent, though non-hierarchical, territorial self-government–central government system. The rebirth of territorial self-government integrates the local community, stimulates local initiatives and in many cases leads to the reconstruction or expansion of the economic base of small towns and communes constituting the lower rungs of the hierarchy. This holds back the progress of the disintegration of this level of spatial organization.

19 Integration Processes and Foreign Investment in Central Europe: A Regional Perspective

Tadeusz Marszał

The disappearance of the Communist system in the eastern part of Europe, accompanied by growing tendencies towards unification in its western part, leads to the examination of the vision of future Europe. The Maastricht Treaty gives an indication of the direction and speed of the transformations. It focuses on the transition to the next stage of European integration, but does not solve the problems of Central and East European countries, which after the Second World War were deprived of the possibility of free and rational economic growth within the European market economy.

At the end of the 1980s a new political and economic situation emerged. Democratization processes in the former Communist bloc revealed the weaknesses of a centrally-planned economy and the command system of government. The disintegration of the network of old economic connections accelerated the inevitable in such a situation of deep economic crisis which was reflected also in the social sphere.

CAUSES AND STRATEGY OF THE INTEGRATION PROCESS

The principal question for Poland and other countries in this part of Europe is how to make the transition to a market economy and work out a new strategy of international economic relations. Poland's geographical position, historical inheritance and cultural, economic, social and political factors determine the country's options for development. In view of the integration tendencies, the only practicable solution is to join the European economic system represented by the European Community (now the European Union). Attempts to realize this strategic purpose resulted in Poland undertaking steps aimed at association with the European Union (EU), this being only an introduction to a full and possibly speedy integration. The 16 December 1991 Brussels Agreement of Association was the first result of these efforts (see also Marszał, 1992).

The main strengths and weaknesses of this integration process at its present stage can be formulated as follows:

1. Although the Agreement of Association with the EU has not resulted immediately in an explosion of Polish exports to West European markets, nobody questions the thesis that if the competitiveness of Polish products increases, which is bound to happen in the new situation, after 5–10 years its growth will be evident. It is estimated that during the first stage of the implementation of the agreement, Polish exports of industrial goods may increase by 15–20 per cent, provided they meet market requirements regarding quality, packaging and marketing.
2. The integration process will force structural changes upon the Polish economy, and will entail failure of those producers who will not manage to meet the demands of competition on international markets. But this will be a gradual process, and it is not true that signing the agreement with the EU will cause instant bankruptcy of all non-competitive Polish producers, for there exists the possibility of taking advantage of protection clauses (in the case when the growth of imports could harm home or regional industry, and when imports could threaten 'new' Polish industries).
3. Acceleration of the process of transition to a market economy, especially the privatization process and the market system infrastructure creation, including the introduction of the new fiscal policy principles, accounting, statistics, economic law, the banking and insurance systems, communications and transport modernization and so on.
4. Easier access to new sources of capital, and its increased inflow.
5. The agreement between Poland and the EU leaves the problem of agriculture virtually unregulated, although partial elimination of barriers in the first stage of association should make it possible to increase Polish agricultural exports by US$150m a year.
6. The integration process places certain limitations on Poland's independence, but it is a logical and inevitable cost of all integration processes.
7. International agreements constitute vital elements stabilizing Polish

economic policy in the period of pursuing a narrow and uncertain path from a centrally-planned to a market economy. In order to achieve a certain stabilization it is also essential to secure active policy and support on the part of the state and the international community.

Association with the EU creates an opportunity for Poland as well as the Czech and Slovak Republics, and Hungary to adjust the functioning of the state, the economy and society to international standards.

In order to catch up with a united Europe an enormous effort must be made by Poland, the Czech and Slovak Republics, and Hungary. These countries, planning to open the twenty-first century as full members of the EU, have only a few years ahead of them for the adaptation of their economic structures to meet European requirements. But the sad reality is that they are decades behind the changes that have occurred since the moment of signing the Treaty of Rome in 1958. The scale of this backwardness can be illustrated by such basic facts as (see Płowiec, 1992):

- an ineffectively functioning market, both in the sphere of trade turnover and in the capital or labour markets;
- technological and organizational backwardness caused by many years of isolation; and
- the lack of full external convertibility of home currency.

Given that (a) the structure of Polish economy, consistent with the nature of the economic system imposed upon the country after the Second World War, is inefficient; and (b) pursuing Europe calls for a radical transformation of this structure, it is theoretically possible to adjust to the requirements of modern competition either (i) through applying a radical shock therapy; or (ii) in a more evolutionary way (obviously there are a number of solutions between these two extremes).

An example of the first approach, which might be called 'creative destruction', is the former German Democratic Republic (GDR) (see Herer, Sadowski, 1992). After the annexation of this territory to West Germany, a drastic collapse of production occurred, reflected in the decrease in the gross national product (GNP) in 1990 by 13,4 per cent, and in 1991 by about 20 per cent. Although the consumers' demand was highly subsidized in the former GDR (for example, unemployment benefits, and state subsidies for enterprises and investments), it turned out that this demand was directed towards the purchase of Western goods and services, and nothing could save the GDR's industry from ruin caused by the opening of the frontier. Modern production has risen from the ruins of the GDR's economy. However we must not forget that the GDR received enormous financial aid; in 1991 alone US$91 billion came from the budget, and US$15 billion from private investments, which, taken together, exceeded 4 times Poland's yearly budget (in 1992, a further US$145 billion in investments were made in the former GDR).

However, making use of the experience of Germany and building new structures on the ruins of the socialist economy is unrealistic in the case of other Central European countries. Since there is no possibility of pumping such a lot of money into the economy, it is reasonable to choose equally effective but less radical solutions. This means that the development and restructuring of the economy must be carried out by means of a gradual elimination of the protection of home producers from foreign competition. This is why the asymmetry in the adoption of trade barriers eliminated at a reasonable rate is an important form of foreign assistance for countries in Central Europe. The question of the protection of home producers in the transition stage is important not only in its economic aspect, but also in its social dimension, considering the fact that in 1993 the unemployment rate in Poland exceeded 15 per cent, and in the period 1990–2005 it is hypothesized that European productive population growth (excluding the countries of the former USSR) will be accounted for mostly by Poland (Dzienio and Drzewieniecka, 1991).

The strategy of integrating operation must on the one hand take into account long-range undertakings aimed at constructing a healthy economy, included in the European division of labour on fair principles. Such a strategy should include the following elements:

(i) defining the direction and the rate of structural changes in the economy;
(ii) formulating the principles of regional policy;
(iii) defining prospects and conditions for the introduction of full external convertibility of the currency and its relationship to the ECU and the European monetary system; and
(iv) adapting Polish banking system fully to the system of central banks.

On the other hand, though, we should not neglect taking short-term anti-recession measures, which may be a necessary condition of the realization of long-range objectives. The chief current tasks are the following:

(i) securing the present level of real incomes of the population (which has dropped drastically since 1989);
(ii) stimulating export expansion, which is a necessary condition of the growth of production and foreign debts service; and
(iii) facilitating capital accumulation and the inflow of foreign capital.

In order to realize these targets, it is essential to establish market mechanisms, privatize the economy, and actively promote the adjustment processes.

THE ROLE AND CHARACTERISTICS OF FOREIGN INVESTMENTS

When the incorporation of the economy of Poland and other Central European countries into the European and world economic systems will be practicable depends largely on the investments of foreign capital in the process of transformation. The significance of this factor can be demonstrated by the above-mentioned example of changes in the former GDR. The following analysis aims to investigate the proportion and structure of this factor in the case of Poland.

During the period of orthodox 'socrealism' foreign capital was treated as a potential threat to home production, and as a carrier of values hostile to the Communist ideology. First attempts to attract foreign investors to Poland occurred in the mid-1970s when so-called 'Polonia' enterprises came into existence. However, the scale of this phenomenon was of marginal importance and in spite of a further gradual elimination of barriers to the access of foreign capital to the Polish market, until the end of the 1980s the share of foreign capital in the Polish economy was comparatively insignificant. The 1980s were for the world economy the years of a rapid growth in direct foreign investment. Many countries of the world, especially highly-developed ones and some of the South-East Asian countries, adopted strategies aimed at bringing foreign capital to their markets. Because of such actions, the total value of foreign investment at the end of the 1980s amounted to almost US$200m, with over 80 per cent of this figure going to highly-developed countries, with less than 20 per cent to Third-World countries (a major proportion of this amount went to just a few developing countries: Singapore, Brazil, Mexico, China, Malaysia, Egypt, Argentina, Thailand and Colombia). As far as the post-Communist countries are concerned (Bulgaria, the Czech and Slovak Republics, Hungary, Poland,

Romania and the former USSR), in 1991 the value of total foreign investment in this region was estimated at US$9.5 billion, and in Poland at US$0.7 billion, which is a very modest amount.

The above comparison is an indication of the scale of activities which must be undertaken by Poland and other Central and East European countries in order to enable these countries to gain a position in the capital investment market corresponding to their economic and population potential. It is a tremendous task considering the scale and range of transformations necessary to restructure their economies in such a way as to improve their effectiveness and ensure the competitiveness of their products on world markets.

Apart from low foreign capital engagement, the lack of home capital and a poorly-developed middle class, which in many countries is a major factor stimulating economic growth, present a grave problem.

In the economic situation of Poland and other countries of Central and Eastern Europe, the inflow of foreign capital is advantageous in so far as it allows, among others:

(i) a speeding up of the process of economic restructuring;
(ii) a broader participation in international co-operation;
(iii) the transfer of modern technology as well as production and business administration techniques;
(iv) increasing exports;
(v) the growth and diversification of goods and services supply to the domestic market; and
(vi) the creation of new jobs.

LEGAL REGULATIONS RELATING TO FOREIGN INVESTMENTS IN POLAND

A fundamental change in the perception of foreign investment in Poland after the collapse of the Communist system has been reflected in the development of a completely new regulatory framework for the functioning of foreign investors.

It was essential to lay down regulations that would protect to a reasonable degree the interests of home producers while at the same time create conditions favourable to the functioning of foreign capital. Extensive activities and long-lasting discussions resulted in the passing on 14 January 1991 of the Companies with Foreign Capital Act.

The resolutions of this Act allow:

(i) the conduct of foreign capital operations without the necessity of obtaining any permission (except for sea- and airport management, real estate trade, the defence industry, imported goods traffic, and legal services);

(ii) grant tax allowances in the following instances:

- if foreign capital contribution to the business stock exceeds 2 million ECU;
- if economic activity is undertaken in areas of heavy unemployment;
- if new techniques vital for the economy are introduced; and
- if exports constitute over 20 per cent of total sales;

(iii) the transfer of all profits abroad;

(iv) the obtaining of government guarantees of compensation in case of expropriation;

(v) the purchase of land and real estates.

Some other regulatory documents also contribute towards more efficient functioning of foreign capital:

- agreements between Poland and a number of countries on preventing double taxation (many European countries, and also, among others, the USA, Japan, China, India, Canada, Malaysia and Sri Lanka); and
- agreements between Poland and a number of European countries and others (for example, China, North Korea, Israel, Japan, the USA, Canada, Kuwait and Turkey) on promoting, and the mutual protection of, investments. Under these agreements partners' investments are granted equal rights, full protection and security. Conditions under which partners' investment operations are conducted must not be worse than conditions for home or other foreign investors' activities.

STRUCTURE AND SPATIAL DISTRIBUTION OF FOREIGN INVESTMENT IN POLAND

Companies with foreign capital belong to the sector of the economy that is currently experiencing the quickest growth. During the period December 1991 to December 1992 the total number of economic entities in Poland grew by 20 per cent, while the number of private-sector companies with foreign capital increased by over 110 per cent. This means that in a period of one year the number of such firms grew

Figure 19.1 Number and ownership structure of business entities in Poland, 1992

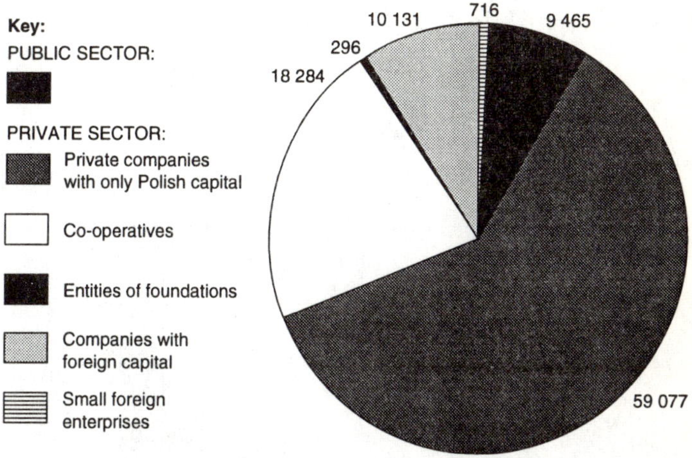

Source: Data provided by GUS (Central Statistical Office).

from 4.8 thousand to over 10.1 thousand (see Figure 19.1). At the end of 1993, foreign companies accounted for more than 10 per cent of the total number of economic entities in Poland.

Looking at the branch structure of the Polish economy we see that a sizeable proportion of firms with foreign capital are engaged in industrial production and transport (about 20 per cent of the total number of private companies functioning in these branches). It should also be noted here that industry is a branch where the rate of establishing new foreign companies is really remarkable: in the course of 1992 the number of such entities increased from 0.9 thousand to 2.1 thousand. (see Figure 19.2)

The examination of the scale of foreign capital engagement in Polish companies shows a connection between the size of a firm and the proportion of foreign capital contribution: the greater the size of an enterprise, the smaller the share of foreign capital (see Figure 19.3). This means that it is mainly small businessmen who are interested in investing in Poland, whereas big capital still tends to be cautious about investments in the country's economy.

Figure 19.4 illustrates the spatial distribution of firms with foreign capital. The most striking characteristic is the irregularity of the

Figure 19.2 Number and structure of private companies in Poland, 1991–2

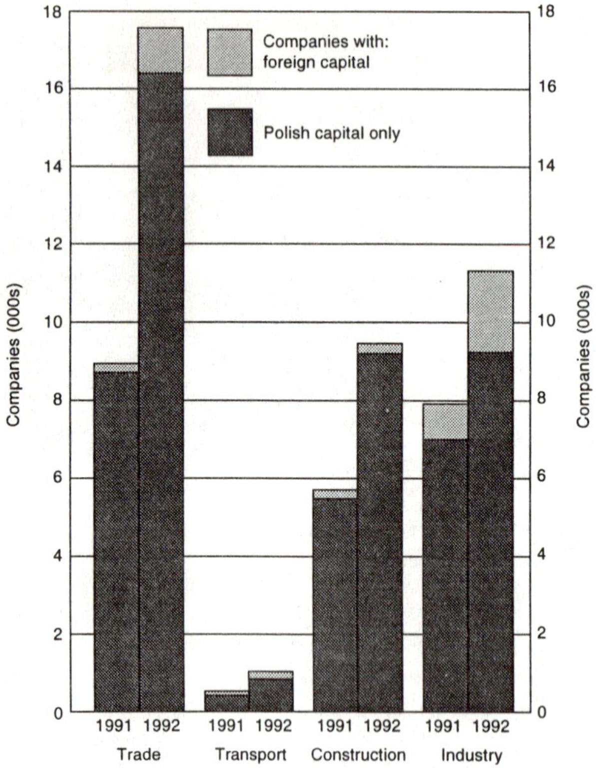

Source: Data provided by Foreign Investment Agency.

distribution pattern, with great concentration of foreign capital in some regions and an almost complete lack of it in others. The greatest concentration of foreign capital is in the Warsaw Voivodeship: in 1991 about 25 per cent of the total number of foreign companies in Poland were located there, and they accounted for a similar proportion of total employment in such firms. Other areas fairly attractive for foreign capital were the major urban agglomerations of Katowice, Poznań, Wrocław and Cracow, and the Baltic voivodeships: Gdańsk and Szczecin. There is almost no foreign investment in the poorly-developed regions in the eastern part of the country and in the agricultural voivodeships of Central Poland.

Figure 19.3 Capital structure of companies with foreign capital in Poland, 1992 (by value of equity capital)

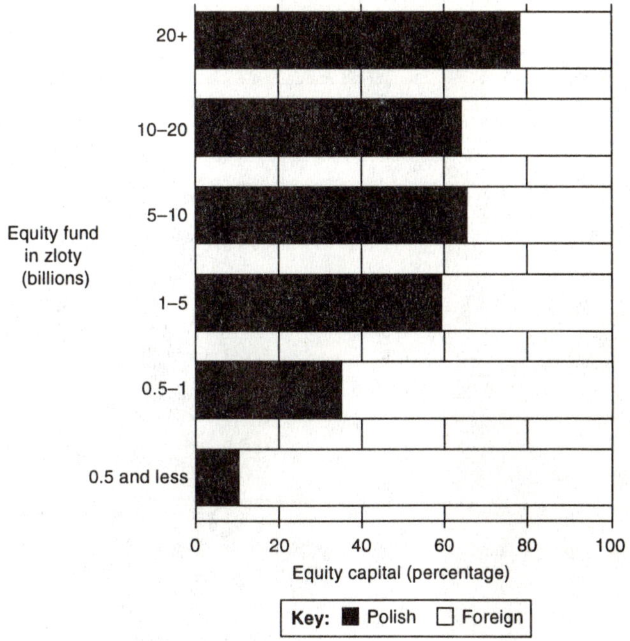

Source: Data provided by Foreign Investment Agency.

The role of foreign capital in the economy of a region is measured by the share of foreign companies in the total employment of the region. The average ratio for the whole country is 1.3 per cent; in some areas, mainly the Baltic voivodeships and the Warsaw and Poznań regions, the ratios are much higher.

Analysis of the spatial distribution leads to the following conclusion: most attractive for foreign capital are economically dynamic areas with sufficiently developed infrastructure and good transport connections, whereas underinvested and stagnant regions are, on the whole, avoided.

The value of total foreign investment in the Polish economy in 1993 amounted to almost US$3.4 billion, with over US$1 billion provided by 184 foreign investors. The largest amount of capital has been invested by Fiat (Italy) in a car-producing factory in Bielsko-Biała

Figure 19.4 Spatial distribution of employment in companies with foreign capital in Poland, 1992

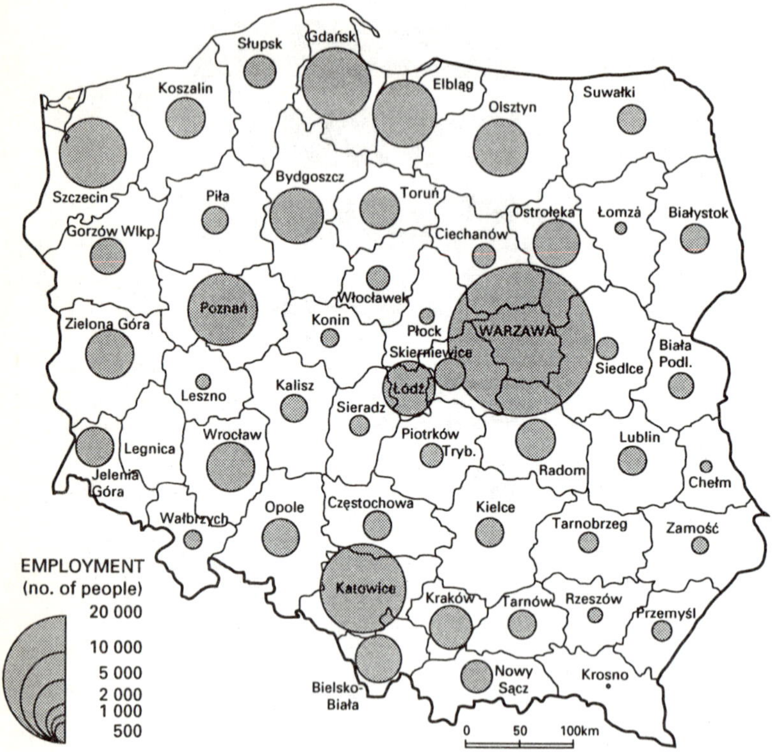

Source: Data provided by Foreign Investment Agency.

(US$260m) Among other companies that have invested fair amounts of capital are: Coca-Cola (USA) – US$180m in soft-drinks factories; International Paper Company (USA) – US$140m in a paper mill in Kwidzyń; Curtis International (USA) – US$100m in the electronics industry; ASEA Brown Boveri (Switzerland–Sweden) – US$70m in an electrical plant in Elbląg; Dolmel in Wrocław; and ZWUS in Katowice.

The branch structure of foreign investment in Poland in 1993 is shown in Figure 19.5. Electromechanical manufacturing has attracted the most capital (US$566m); next comes the food processing industry, followed by finance and banking. The degree of capital dispersion in the various branches is extremely diverse: from a very small degree in the motor

Figure 19.5 Number and value of foreign investment by branches, 1993 (investments over 1 million US$)

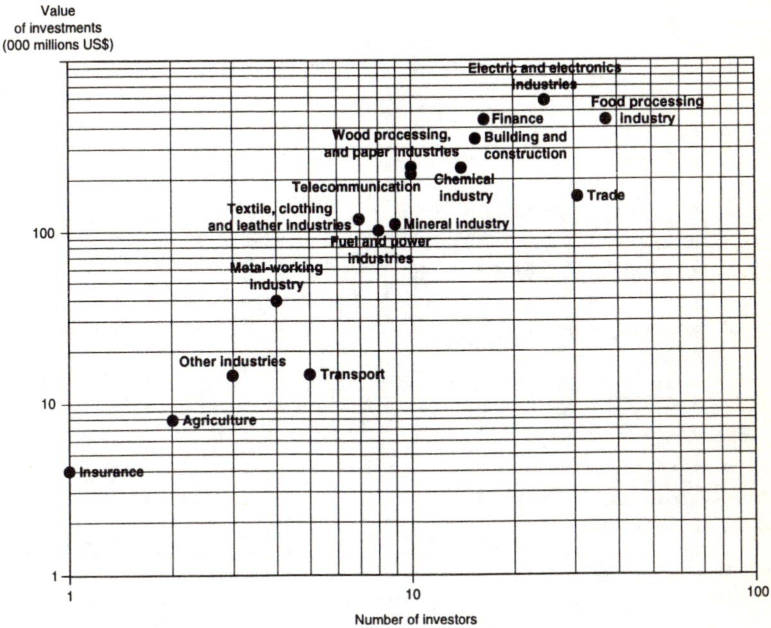

Source: Data provided by Foreign Investment Agency.

industry and metallurgy to a fairly high degree in the food-processing industry and trade. This diversity is obviously connected with the type of technological methods characteristic of different branches.

Data illustrating territorial directions of capital inflow into Polish economy in 1993 (see Figure 19.6) show the following regularities:

(i) large-scale investments in Poland were made by capital representing a limited number of countries;
(ii) only European and American investors were interested in engaging their capital in Poland. Apart from a few quite insignificant investments, bigger Japanese capital is not to be found in Poland, Hungary being its preferred country;
(iii) American capital has a dominant position, accounting for almost 40 per cent of the total value of foreign investments in Polish economy; and

Figure 19.6 Number and value of foreign investment by country, 1993 (investments over 1 million US$)

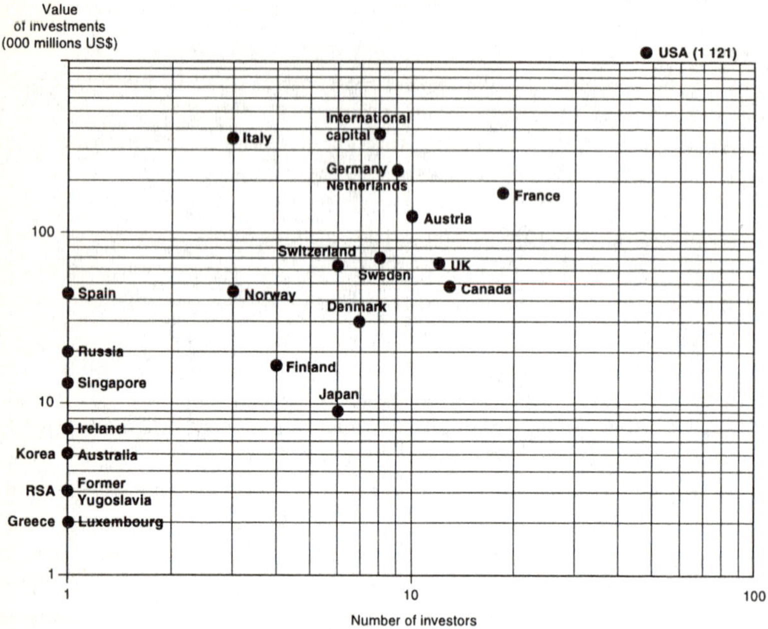

Source: Data provided by Foreign Investment Agency.

(iv) a relatively small amount of German investment was made, given the economic potential of Poland and its geographical proximity to Germany.

The explanation for the absence of Japanese investment in Poland seems to be a relatively low ranking of Poland in respect of 'country risk', a major factor influencing investment decisions of Japanese firms. As for the relatively modest value of German investment, it contradicts the opinion sometimes voiced in Poland that Polish economic independence is threatened by its German neighbour. Until 1992, 70 per cent of German capital in Poland had been provided by small-scale businesses and family firms, which is the reason why the great number of Polish–German joint ventures does not correspond to their share in terms of money. What is more, survey studies have shown that about 25 per cent of German enterprises operating on Polish territory belonged to German citizens with Polish names.

INCENTIVES AND BARRIERS TO FOREIGN INVESTMENT IN POLAND

When examining the scale of foreign capital investment in Polish industry and its future prospects it is essential to identify main strengths and weaknesses of Poland as an importer of capital.

Among the difficulties facing foreign investors in Poland, the most important are:

- a rather high level of 'country risk', although this is evidently overestimated by foreign experts, who fail to see growing political stabilization despite the country's remaining serious economic problems;
- administrative incompetence at various levels of the economy;
- a poorly developed communications infrastructure (although numerous investments in this field have been made, some of them already well advanced);
- an inefficient banking system, in spite of speedy changes and improvements taking place;
- instability in the regulatory context of the economy, especially in relation to the system of taxation;
- a significant level of inflation, estimated at about 35 per cent in 1993; and
- a shortage of solid information about Polish investment conditions and insufficient promotion of the country.

Despite the above drawbacks, Poland has many assets capable of stimulating the inflow of foreign capital:

- a large market, one of the biggest in Central Europe (40m inhabitants) with unsatisfied, and partly deferred, demand;
- cheap resources of skilled labour;
- a very advantageous geographical position on the intersection of main European transport routes;
- the immediate proximity of vast markets in the former USSR, and good knowledge of the very specific Russian or Ukrainian markets acquired during long-established trade contacts with these territories;
- easy access to the domestic market because of low effectiveness of Polish industry, which is still partly state-owned; and
- legal and economic policies adopted at both central and local levels aimed at facilitating foreign investment in Poland.

CONCLUSION

To summarize, it should be stressed that there is a clear feedback between transformation processes and foreign investments in Central Europe.

In Poland one of the weakest points of the structural transformation is the poor co-ordination of restructuring actions carried on by various institutions. From a macroeconomic perspective, this results from a number of factors:

- no clear distinction between the functions and policies of the central bank and the government;
- poor harmonization of the development strategy, across both branches and regions; and
- risk connected with a lack of social consensus.

One of the greatest achievements of Poland as regards improvement of conditions for foreign investment is a high level of foreign trade development, including:

- full liberalization of exports and considerable liberalization of imports;
- almost unlimited convertibility of the Polish currency; and
- great possibilities of profit transfer.

These weaknesses and achievements should be evaluated in relation to the processes taking place in other countries in this part of Europe. According to the findings of a survey study carried out in 1992 by the Chamber of Handicrafts from Münster (Germany), 79 per cent of the respondents stated readiness to invest, or high probability of investing, their capital in Hungary; and 68 per cent of the interviewed tradespeople expressed willingness to invest in Poland and in the Czech and Slovak Federal Republics, which gave these countries joint second position (see Figure 19.7). Only 21 per cent of respondents expressed an interest in investing in Romania or Bulgaria.

Despite these optimistic declarations, the value of foreign capital invested in Poland and other Central and East European countries is still very low in relation to the needs and expectations of these regions. The value of foreign capital engagement is different across these regions: in 1992, foreign investment in Hungary amounted to US$4.5 billion; in the Czech Republic, 1.7 billion; and in Poland, 1.3 billion. In 1993 in Poland foreign investment exceeded US$3.0 billion.

Investment commitments by foreign firms already operating in Poland

Figure 19.7 Locational preferences of German investors in Central and Eastern Europe, 1992

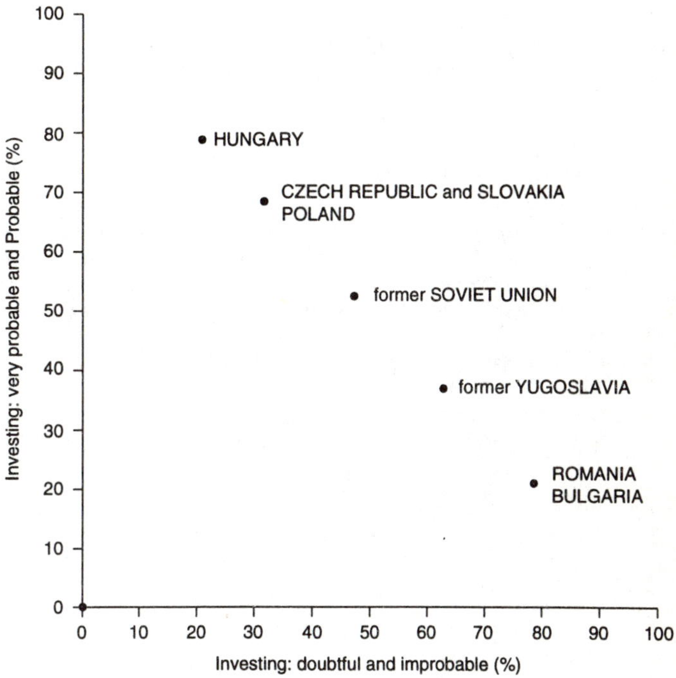

Source: Survey study in Chamber of Handicrafts, Münster, Germany, 1992.

are valued at US$4.6 billion, the biggest commitments being those of Fiat (US$1.8 billion) in the motor industry; Coca-Cola (US$0.2 billion) in the food industry; Procter and Gamble (US$0.19 billion) in the chemical industry; International Paper Company (US$0.18 billion) in the paper industry; and Lucchini Group (US$0.15 billion) in metallurgy.

But even if these commitments are realized, Poland, in a similar way to other countries of Central and Eastern Europe, will suffer from an insufficient supply of foreign capital up to the millenium. In view of their very limited domestic financial resources, these countries will undertake every effort to attract foreign capital. It would speed up and facilitate economic restructuring processes, and would stimulate economic growth in this part of Europe, which is essential for the future position of these countries in both the European and global economic systems.

References

Dzienio, K. and K. Drzewieniecka (1991) 'Sytuacja demograficzna Polski', *Raport 1991* (Warsaw: CUP).
'Funkcjonowanie inwestycji zagranicznych w Polsce', Instytut Koniunktur i Cen Handlu Zagranicznego, Warsaw, 1991.
Glisman, H. and K. Schrader (1991) 'Zur ordnungspolitischen Situation in den Laender Mittel und Osteuropas', *Die Weltwirtschaft 1991*, Heft 2.
Herer, W. and W. Sadowski (1992) 'Czy stać nas na twórczą destrukcję, *Życie Gospodarcze*, vol. 15.
'Inwestycje zagraniczne w Polsce', Instytut Kuniunktur i Cen Handlu Zagranicznego, Warsaw, 1992.
Marszał, T. (1991) 'Some Remarks on Firms with Foreign Capital in Poland: The Case of the Łódź Industrial Agglomeration', in *The Impact of Transition to a Market Economy in Countries of Central–Eastern Europe Upon the Spatial Structure of International Economic Relations* (Łódź: Wyd. UŁ).
Marszał, T. (1992) 'Association with the EEC – New Perspectives and Consequences for the Polish Economy', in *Processes and Consequences of the Changes in Production-service Sector in the Countries of Central–Eastern Europe* (Łódź : Wyd. UŁ).
Płnowiec, U. (1992) 'Najpierw strategia', *Życie Gospodarcze*, vol. 9.

20 The Trends of the 1990s: Humanity and Business Facing a World of Multiple Choices

Alain Sallez

Comparing civilized man with the state of the savage, the French philosopher, J.-J. Rousseau, wrote in 1754 in his *Address on the Origin of Inequality*, 'vous sentirez combien la nature nous fait payer cher le mépris que nous avons fait de ses leçons' (you should feel how dearly Nature makes us pay our disregard for its lessons).

Thus the value of nature is not an absolute new concern of the modern world, neither is the threat from industrial activities. For example, the first laws to insure local public safety against listed industries date back to 1809 in France. Chemical industries were targeted most, because of the danger and bad smells they brought to the local environment. But in the modern world, concern about the environment has completely changed in scale. From merely protecting neighbours' points of view, the protection of the environment has evolved towards the survival of humanity. Concern for the environment has a heavy impact on economic development and has become a major political force in many countries.

This chapter will thus recall a few facts and ask some questions about the impact of the environment at three levels of economic development: world, regions and cities.

ECONOMIC RESPONSES TO A GLOBAL DETERIORATION OF THE ENVIRONMENT

Let us recall briefly some major threats such as the earth's declining productivity, deforestation and global warming associated with the greenhouse effect and its major consequence: the risk of a rise in sea level.

According to one report on progress toward a sustainable society, such phenomena as soil erosion, shrinking forests, deteriorating rangelands, expanding deserts, acid rain, stratospheric ozone depletion, the build-up of greenhouse gases, air pollution and the loss of biological diversity are affecting food production negatively, while world population is expected to grow by 96 million people a year until 2005. Decreasing world grain production per capita is likely to occur, severely affecting the Third World (where 40 000 infants are expected to die each year). The consequences could jeopardize the international monetary system. Indeed (in order to avoid widespread starvation), Third-World governments would increase their foreign debt, while major international banks would be confronted with a wholesale forfeiture, driving interest rates upwards and thus threaten financial institutions and the international economy.

Another global threat is the shrinking of forests: in Latin America, Africa and Asia, wood-burning provides energy in the short run, inducing the creation of swamps, soil erosion and carbon dioxide emissions (CO_2), thus contributing to the greenhouse effect. In Europe, the degradation of forests caused by air pollution and acid rain ultimately reduces their photosynthetic product capacity. Equally important, the Earth's declining productivity will have severe consequences for industry, since croplands, forests and grasslands supply all its raw materials, with the exception of fossil fuels and minerals.

Finally, global warming will be discussed, which promises to be one of the central environmental issues of the 1990s. Carbon dioxide (CO_2): 25 per cent higher than pre-industrial levels; nitrous oxide; methane (100 per cent higher); and chlorofluorocarbons (CFCs) contribute to the greenhouse effect, allowing sunlight in, but trapping the resulting heat. According to computerized models, the temperature might have increased by 2.5 to 5.5°C by the end of twenty-first century. It has been estimated that a 5°C increase would raise sea level an additional six metres within 200–500 years, inundating most coastal land and coastal cities. More realistic than the long-term meltdown of the whole ice sheet (Alpine glaciers, Greenland, Antarctica), an average 4.5–17 centimetre sea level rise has been estimated by the year 2000 by the US Environmental Protection Agency.

We have to take into account that all the aforementioned forecasts are uncertain and that not all scientists agree on all the predicted effects, such as the depletion of the protective ozone layer caused by the emission of CO_2). So the question is: will the world community be ready to adopt decisions and pay for the cost, to avoid the risk of dramatic but uncertain events? One has to understand that all nations are concerned, and that their future is interdependent in the face of global environmental deterioration. However, the more severely affected countries are often the poorest, living in the Sahel zone in Africa or in Latin America, for example, while the most aware of the necessity to protect the environment are often the wealthiest. What, therefore, are the ways of co-operation?

Undoubtedly a political awakening has occurred. Concern over the future of the planet has put the environment at the heart of international organizations such as the UN General Assembly, the Council of Europe, and conferences: for example, in The Hague, twenty-four countries declared in 1989 that the right to live is the responsibility of all states throughout the world, adding that the very conditions of life on our planet are threatened by the severe attacks to which the earth's atmosphere is being subjected. Earlier, in February 1989, in Montreal, forty-six countries, later joined by thirty-one others, supported the proposition of halving the use of CFCs, the family of chemicals that may be the most damaging in the future. Many developed countries, such as the Netherlands, Norway, Sweden, the United Kingdom, the USA and Germany have adopted plans and subsequently passed bills to reduce greenhouse gases. All measures necessitated by such policies imply heavy costs for industry, which are probably more easily accepted by research orientated countries than by less developed ones. For instance, the investment in research to find substitutes for CFCs and to adapt industrial processes would amount to 4.5 billion francs for France alone. Despite the costs involved, beneficial effects are already resulting from the Montreal Protocol in many countries; for instance, in the cosmetics and drugs industries, which undertook to reduce up to 90 per cent of their consumption of CFCs in the short term.

Experts hope that the United Nations Conference on the Environment and Development in Brazil has been a landmark event. So do we. But we also know that carbon emissions from fossil fuels have grown constantly from the mid-century to twentieth century and if consumption in industrial market countries has been stabilized since the early 1970s, consumption in Eastern European and developing countries has more than doubled over the same period, accounting for half the world's consumption. So many of these countries are heavily polluted and contribute to global deterioration; but they would also be the most severely handicapped if they were obliged to use renewable energy, since fossil fuels are by far the cheapest energy sources at the time of writing. Therefore most experts anticipate many proclamations and statements but few real steps to restore the planet's health. Lester R. Brown, the Project Director of the Worldwatch Institute warns strongly that 'if the world does not seize the opportunities offered by the promise of change, the continuing degradation of the planet will eventually lead to economic decline'.

Theoretically, we know the cures. For instance, cleaning up the atmosphere and slowing down global warming imply greater energy efficiency; the reduction of motor vehicles as a means of transportation; the development of renewable energy sources; a carbon tax on fossil fuels; the reversal of deforestation in tropical countries; and the elimination of CFCs. But what are the right means to achieve these targets: commitments, regulations, tax policies, perhaps?

Economists generally agree that using tax policies is more efficient than regulation and permits the market to continue to operate as efficiently as possible while contributing to an environmentally sustainable future. As an economist, I agree with this view, but the question remains of how to convince the less-developed countries to adopt tax policies which would apparently handicap their productivity.

One proposed answer is to recalculate economic growth by depreciating the gross national product (GNP) of the used natural capital, including non-renewable resources such as oil or forests. Such a new national accounting system would certainly reflect more accurately the economic progress of nations than does the present one.

If we limit the question to Western countries and Japan, it seems that substantial improvements can occur in the coming years, from the industries themselves, either because of taxation or because they are confronted with the growing concern of their clients and the mounting pressure of public opinion. For instance, the well-known organization, Greenpeace, has developed a direct approach to denounce the heaviest polluting firms. In France, Rhône Poulenc, Atochem, ICI Francolor, Société Nationale des Poudres et Explosifs, CIBA-GIEIGY and seventeen nuclear reactors and atomic power plants are designated as the most polluting along the River Rhône, discharging between them cadmium, zinc, chrome, copper, mercury, lead, arsenic, chlorohydrocarbons and radioactive elements.

That is true, but there is also some evidence that a number of firms consider that in future they can better their image and improve their sales by devoting more R&D to developing new, less energy-intensive processes, new materials incorporating less-toxic materials, or new eco-commodities contributing to better environmental security. Technology has already reduced the enormous consumption of raw materials in Western industrialized countries. US steel consumption per unit of GNP, for example, has dropped by 30 per cent since 1974, and we know that the increasing role of information technology accounts for part of this shift, along with miniaturization and hyperminiaturization.

Still considering Western countries, the voluntary efforts of industrial firms are encouraging; large companies such as Amoco, Shell, Badilin Anische SF, Bayer and Hoechst have created co-ordinating or steering committees under the responsibility of a vice-president for health, safety and environmental conservation. In Germany, 34 per cent of industrial firms have already created such committees, integrating the concern for the environment all along the value chain of the firm, from purchasing to logistics, R&D, production, communication and distribution.

The last field of environmental concern, but also a field of economic competition for firms, is that of eco-commodities. Among the most well-known eco-commodities advertised on the market, let us mention the clean car, average-packaging, dioxine-free products, batteries without mercury and phosphate-free washing powders. These clean commodities are recognized by green labels such as the 'Blue Angel' in Germany or the AFNOR N.F. label in France. In 1994, Canada, Sweden, Norway, Finland, Japan, Denmark, the Netherlands, Great Britain and Portugal have adopted such labels. True, not all labels are of equal value, and the European Union is preparing a European label based on a multicriteria evaluation of production, elimination and recycling of eco-commodities. It is obvious that each country will help its manufacturers to impose their labels. And from this standpoint, Germany is ten years ahead of other countries, with over 3000 labelled eco-commodities, already.

In fact, we are witnessing the beginnings of a fierce commercial battle. For instance, soap and washing powder manufacturers are engaged in a gigantic competition for the market of phosphate-free products. In this battle, for instance, the brand 'Le Chat' has gained 3 points of market share in France, increasing its sales from 120 million to 300 million.

After these comments on global Environmental Deterioration, there remain two questions to be raised about global environmental deterioration:

1. What global effect can be expected if only the wealthiest countries are in a position to take effective measures? and
2. How much economic progress can be anticipated from research, development and production in accordance with environmental care?

ENVIRONMENTAL DAMAGE AT THE REGIONAL LEVEL

One major fact to come out of the decade since the mid-1980s is that pollution knows no political or national borders; consequently, international regions are concerned by air pollution, acid rain, pollution of rivers (such as the Rhine or the Danube), sea pollution and atomic risks, as demonstrated by the disasters of Chernobyl and Three Mile Island. The health of the population is often in danger, as in Eastern Europe, where specialists estimate that it will take at least twenty years to raise the quality of the environment to reasonable standards. In East European countries, figures concerning the life expectancy in industrialized regions, pollution-related illness, cancer rates (in industrial zones, as much as eight times the average of non-industrial zones in Poland, for example) and infant mortality in industrial regions are dramatic.

Not only are East European countries concerned; other regions and developing countries probably share comparable disadvantages. International programmes such as those of the United Nations, the USA or the European Union constitute an absolute necessity from a human point of view. They are also needed because regions are interdependent and international agreements have to be found, such as those run or studied for the Rhine and Danube rivers.

Lastly, regional wars are evidently adding not only to regional insecurity but also to dramatic pollution, driving down the economies of neighbours.

THE NEED OF CITIES FOR A BETTER ENVIRONMENT TO BE COMPETITIVE IN THE MODERN WORLD

Evidence shows that the biggest cities in the world are the most polluted, especially in poor countries. At the other extreme, very small cities often decline because of the lack of an economic base. What, then, is the right balance to ensure economic progress *and* a better quality of life for cities? It is clear that an attractive urban environment securing good health for the inhabitants, with sport and open-air leisure facilities and urban and architectural quality, are major factors in choosing a location for national and international investment. Clearly, European cities are now competing among themselves to attract skilled people, high-tech activities, headquarters, international fairs and modern plants, and the quality of the cities' environment is carefully considered by managers. From this point of view, the environmental policies developed by cities and states may be an asset for the future. In this field, one may wonder if the more advanced cities and states are not the more economically advanced, such as in Germany, Switzerland and Scandinavian countries. The environment constitutes a major concern for the future of mankind, but it will probably also be one of the most important factors in economic competition between firms, cities and regions for the decade up to 2005.

References

Aviam, A. M. (1990) *Entreprise et Ecologie* (Paris: Ministère de l'Environnement, December, Paris).

Bailly, A. (1991) 'Aménagement du Territoire et Environnement en Suisse: entre Libéralisme et Fédéralisme', ASRDLF – Association Allemande de Science Régionale; Nancy; June.

Comolet, A. (1991) 'La mise en place des comptes de ressources naturelles dans le bassin de la Brantos', Institut pour une Politique Européenne de l'Environnement, Paris, July.

Environment, File no. 19, May 1991; no. 20, June 1991; no. 21, July 1991; no. 22, August 1991; no. 23, September 1991; no. 24, October 1991; US Information Service, American Embassy, Paris.

Godard, O. (1984) 'Autonomie socio-économique et externalisation de l'environnment: la théorie néoclassique mise en perspective', *Economie Appliquée*, no. 2.

Godard, O. (1990) 'Théorie économique et écologie: moyens et limites d'une stratégie d'assimilation', Fondation des Services Politiques, September.

Leroy, Cl. (1990) 'La santé et l'écosystème urbain', in *L'homme et la ville* (Ligue Française d'Hygiène Mentale), July, no. 106.

Mignot, G. (n.d.) 'Huit métropoles en Europe', no. 96, Paris.

Ministère de l'Environnement (1989) 'La labellisation des Ecoproduits', Rapport du Groupe de Reflexion sur les Ecoproduits, December, Paris.

Ministère de l'Environnement et de la Prévention des Risques (1991) 'Plans municipaux de l'environnement, Etude Delphi', Délégation à la Qualité de la Vie, July, Paris.

Theys, J. and B. Kalaoara (1992) 'Les experts sont formels', *Collection Science et Société*, January, Paris (mimeo).

Vigneron, J. (1991) 'Concepts et méthodologies applicables aux éco-produits', *Les rencontres Environnement et Qualité*, Cergy Pontoise Environnement, June, Paris.

21 Dynamic Take-off: Accelerating Effects of a Continental Expressway

Hirotada Kohno, Yoshiro Higano and Yuji Matsumura

PROBLEM TO BE SOLVED – SOCIOECONOMIC EFFECTS OF LARGE PROJECTS

Apart from the microelectronics and information industries based on large-scale integrated circuits and/or optical fibres, it seems to us that the frontiers of heavy industry at present have a tendency to be stagnant. However, large projects planned for the twenty-first century, such as the second Panama Canal, the Baikal–Amur Railroad in Siberia, the Great Dam of Itaipu, the Asian Highway, the Japan-Korea Tunnel, and the Seventeen Bridges to link Shikoku Island to the mainland of Japan, are left untouched.

This is the new concept of a 'global infrastructure fund' (GIF). Such a fund should be appropriated for real physical structures such as a social infrastructure. Such large projects have a social usefulness, but not always private profitability. However, they will generate enormous socioeconomic benefits, that is, external economies. We suggest that huge facilities are founded with the intention of letting them function as 'external economies-generating apparatuses'. This will generate such benefits as spreading and scattering the economies spatially, dynamically, and globally (over entire industries).

Service yielded from them is non-marketable, and does not appreciate automatically in the market. Therefore, it is necessary to intentionally evaluate these economic effects in appraising such large projects. We aim to formulate a model based on a more economics-oriented method, the opportunity cost principle. We further intend to develop a 'dynamic multiregion, multi-industry, multi-transport mode optimal programming model' so as to evaluate the socioeconomic effects of these large projects, and appraise them using the public investment criterion based on the evaluated economic effects. This model is built as an interdisciplinary and socioeconomic planning model which combines the requisites of economics, regional science, and traffic engineering.

This model will be used to appraise the proposed Asian Expressway Network; particular emphasis will be placed on its dynamic and indirect influence on the Chinese economy. From the perspective of this dynamic programming model, we can grasp the panoramic view that the Chinese economy, by itself, is accelerating its growth process, moving from stagnation to 'take-off' proving the social meaningfulness of the large public investment in the Asian Expressway Network.

The Asian Expressway Network here proposed is slated to pass through various nodal cities such as Kita Kyushu (Japan), Pusan, Seoul, Pyongyang, Shen-yan, Peking, Shanghai, Hong Kong, Bangkok, Calcutta, New Delhi, Rawalpindi, and so on to London, or including an alternative silkroad route via Peking, Hsi-an, Lan-chou and Urumchi.

ECONOMIC EFFECTS-MEASURING MODEL FOR THE OPTIMAL DYNAMIC APPRAISAL OF INVESTMENT PROGRAMME OF THE ASIAN EXPRESSWAY NETWORK

We develop an economic effects-measuring model for the optimal dynamic appraisal of the investment programme of the Asian Expressway Network such that the objective function is maximized subject to all sorts of constraint equations: flow balance; shipment balance; export–import accumulated balance; demand–supply balances of the industrial capital, housing capital, workers, transport infrastructural facilities, and other social overhead capital; capital formations; accounts of national income and so on. We first set forth several essential characteristics of our model, and then present all of its features.

1. Fundamentally, this model is one of dynamic multisectors optimal growth;
2. The concept of a Moses-type interregional input–output programming model is incorporated (Moses (1960)).
3. We do not adopt the model building approach of the DOSSO type (Dorfman *et al.* (1958)), which allows the malleability of capital goods, but the more realistic one of the putty-clay type supposing ex post facto non-malleability; that is, the dynamic process of this model is moving on, based on the two equations of demand–supply balance of industrial capital (21.3) and industrial capital formation (21.5).

The variable of capital goods is not explicitly introduced in the DOSSO model, where there are, for example, only the goods of 'steel', the goods of 'cement', and so on. It does not need to introduce the variable of capital goods. On the contrary, the 'capital goods of the steel industry' for the production of steel, the 'capital goods of the cement industry' for the production of cement and so on are introduced explicitly in the building of our model. Once such capital goods is constructed, it cannot be transferred to the other uses without removal costs (ex post facto non-malleability).

This is because the model building allowing malleability becomes to be utterly nonsense for our model, in which the key task is to determine social capital formation such as transport infrastructural facilities, for example. Therefore, we may introduce a demolition activity of capital goods, which, however, is omitted for the time being, because the land constraint is not so limited in the present state of China, where we intend to apply our model.

4. The computational technique of 'Simulation of Traffic Assignment on the Network' (STAN) is built into our model, which makes a route search option more realistically possible and carries out demand analysis corresponding to *each link* of any route, not to the transport network as a highly ideal concept corresponding to the domestic export–import between the regions as is done in the usual 'Interregional Input–Output Programming Model' like the Moses Model of 1960, but to the more realistic, that is, detailed transport network.

   In our model, therefore, the concept of socioeconomic planning and dynamic programming has been developed, which fuses into one discipline the excellent qualities of the STAN belonging to traffic engineering and the efficient allocative qualities of the dynamic interregional input–output programming model belonging to economics. We have had experience with the application of such a dynamic model to Greater Tokyo, Kohno (1987), Higano and Kohno (1986); and with the static version, Kohno (1969).
5. Based upon the development of a model endowed with the various characteristics mentioned above, we can finally respond quantitatively to the public investment criteria of 'When? Where? How much? and What facilities?', with a focus on the *microscopic* transport link, depending on the opportunity cost principle.

OPTIMAL DYNAMIC APPRAISAL MODEL OF THE ASIAN EXPRESSWAY NETWORK BENEFITS FOR CHINA

Since the structural equations of our dynamic, multi-region, multi-industry, multi-transport mode facility, optimal programming model are very complicated and tedious to understand, they are presented in a condensed, narrative form, putting emphasis on industrial input–output relations (flow balance, shipment balance, for example); demand–supply relations of transport infrastructural facilities, and capital formation of industrial capital.

Flow balance equation I: non-service industry

This equation shows the balance of demand–supply in each period and in each zone (region) for the products of non-service industries such as agriculture, mining, light industry and heavy industry:

$$\begin{pmatrix}\text{intermediary}\\ \text{input demand}\\ \text{(all industries)}\end{pmatrix} + \begin{pmatrix}\text{investment}\\ \text{demand}\\ \text{(housing capital}\\ \text{+ transport}\\ \text{infrastructure}\\ \text{+ other social}\\ \text{overhead capital)}\end{pmatrix} + \begin{pmatrix}\text{consumption}\\ \text{demand}\end{pmatrix}$$

(including foreign zones and the zone concerned)

$$- \begin{pmatrix}\text{all the import}\\ \text{from other}\\ \text{zones}\\ (\equiv \text{suply})\end{pmatrix} \leq 0 \qquad (21.1)$$

where all the import from other regions consists mainly of domestic inflows, within which the shipment from the zone concerned is included. It is worthy to note that this formulation is much different from previous ones; for example, compare this with the Moses (1960) model.

That is, in the demand–supply balance equation there is no such term as $Y_{1l} \times 1$ in $Y_{1l}\,(1 - a^{l}_{11})$, which is the *production* of goods concerned (the 1st goods) in the region concerned (the 1st region) in the Moses formulation. However, to compensate for the deficiency of this term, the CF^{kl}_{Il} showing import of k goods from region I to region

I via '*l*' route is included in the formulation. Here, the suffixes of *I* and *II* show these to be the 1st region and 2nd region; the right-hand upper suffix *I* attached to A^I_{12} shows it to be the 1st region, the lower suffix 12 shows the transfer of goods from the 1st industry (agriculture) to the 2nd industry (manufacturing industry).

The regional input coefficients (table) are derived from the basic sources (AMA, 1984; CNSB 1983). The coefficient matrix of industrial capital formation is also derived from the same sources.

Shipment balance equation I

This equation shows the balance of the amount of shipment from all the regions in China in each period (exports to foreign countries included):

$$\begin{pmatrix} \text{total amount of} \\ \text{shipment (export)} \\ \text{of } k \text{ goods from the} \\ \text{zone } i \end{pmatrix} - \begin{pmatrix} \text{total amount of} \\ \text{production of} \\ k \text{ goods in the} \\ \text{zone } i \end{pmatrix} \leq 0 \qquad (21.2)$$

where it should be of noted that the amount of production (products) of the region concerned appears here for the first time in the explicit expression. The first term of the left-hand side of (21.2) shows exports (both domestic and foreign) from all regions.

The regional structure implies that an import to one region is equivalent to an export for the other region; this is built into the model as a system.

Demand–supply balance equation of industrial capital

$$\begin{pmatrix} \text{The amount of} \\ \text{production in} \\ \text{each industry} \end{pmatrix} - \begin{pmatrix} \text{The maximum capacity} \\ \text{of production of the} \\ \text{industry concerned under} \\ \text{the capital constraint} \end{pmatrix} \leq 0 \qquad (21.3)$$

This equation means that the product which is obtained by multiplying capital stock by the reciprocal of the capital coefficient will be the maximum capacity of production of the industry concerned, within the range of which the actual production will be done.

This balanced equation is one of the important equations which constitute the dynamic relations in our model. The data of the output-capital coefficient matrix are derived based on the original source (CNSB (1983)).

Demand–supply balance equation of the transport infrastructure facilities

$$\begin{pmatrix}\text{The load of all the}\\ \text{traffic flow using}\\ \text{the } p \text{ section of any}\\ \text{transport facilities}\end{pmatrix} - \begin{pmatrix}\text{The maximum capacity}\\ \text{of the } p \text{ section of any}\\ \text{transport facilities}\end{pmatrix} \leq 0 \qquad (21.4)$$

where the p mark of any transport facilities means the 'p section (link) concerned' defined for all transport facilities such as expressways, trunk highways, railways and so on.

It should be understood that all the traffic flow, among all the pairs of O.D. and among all the products which may potentially use this p section of any of these transport facilities is built into the model each as a separate activity (activity variable).

In connection with this matter, there is a series of tables in which the 'number of routes for each pair of O.D.' is predetermined, ranked from 1 to 4 so that the larger the rank, the greater the number of routes exogenously given to any pair of O.D. If we do not mind doing many calculations, we may as well adopt a rank of 4. However, we usually prefer a ranking of 1, at least at the beginning, to save calculation time to a small extent.

Next, if we aggregate all the routes which use the p section over all the routes set to be included in all the pairs of O.D., then this appears to be the total demand for the supply capacity of the p section of that transport facility. As it is very difficult to explain this complicated actual state, here the p section is built-in as any one of serial sections of Expressway. We introduce, as a very simple example, two routes, Route A and Route B, between the 1st region and the 2nd region, set a node at the intermediary point of each route, and form four sub-sections, Aa, Ab, Ba, and Bb.

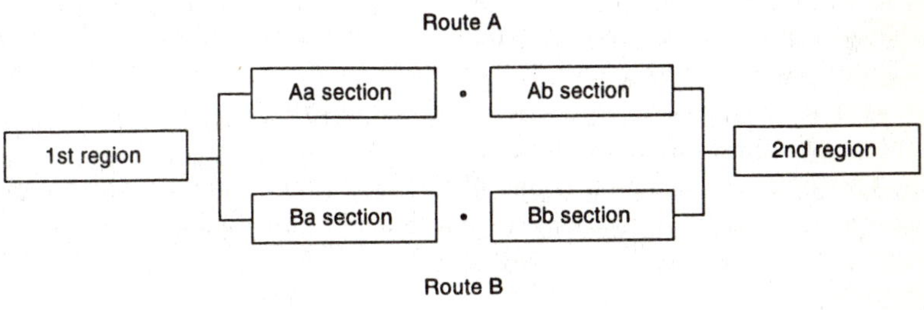

If we aggregate all the traffic flow through the p section, for example, Aa section, among all the traffic flow of CF_{ij}^{kl} which means let k goods be transported along l route from i region to j region, we can obtain the volume of the actual traffic flow.

Capital formation – industrial capital

Capital formation is an equation showing that what is invested in the period concerned without being consumed, inputted in the intermediary process, and exported, appears in the next period as an increase of the capital stock which will be available for utilization in the production of the next period and afterwards. In other words, this relates a flow variable (investment) of the present period to a stock variable on the next period and after. This is one of the structural equations which show that our model is a purely dynamic one. (See Table 21.3.)

$$\begin{pmatrix}\text{the amount of}\\ \text{capital stock}\\ \text{available in}\\ \text{period } (t+1)\end{pmatrix} - \begin{pmatrix}\text{the capital stock}\\ \text{in the } t\text{th period}\\ \text{after the allowance}\\ \text{for depreciation}\\ \text{is made}\end{pmatrix} - \begin{pmatrix}\text{investment}\\ \text{in the } t\text{th}\\ \text{period}\end{pmatrix} = 0 \qquad (21.5)$$

As shown above, the dynamic model works in the intertemporal linkage, and has a rigid and organic structure of mutual interdependency.

The detailed model described in this section will appear in Kohno *et al.* (1992).

DYNAMIC OPTIMAL PLANNING MODEL OF 12 REGIONS, 5 PERIODS, 9 INDUSTRIES, 2 HOUSES, AND 5 TRANSPORT FACILITIES

The world is divided into two parts, China and the rest of the world. China is then divided into 7 zones, and the rest of the world into 5 zones (Table 21.1).

Five transport infrastructural facilities (abbreviated as TIF hereinafter) of expressway (which constitutes the Asian Expressway Network), railway, seaway & waterway, ordinal highway, and port are set up. The set-up parameters, here, are omitted (see Kohno *et al.*, 1992).

Table 21.1 Partition into zones

Code no.	*Name of zone*	*Number of cities (node of link) belonging to the zone*	*Node of zone (centre of zone)*
1	North-East China	4	Ha-erh-pin
2	North China	8	Tianjin
3	North-West China	10	Lan-chou
4	Central China	9	Wu-han
5	East China	10	Nan-ching
6	West China	5	Ch'eng-tu
7	South China	10	Guangzhou
11	Japan	1	Tokyo
12	Korea	3	Seoul
13	Europe & former USSR	1	Rome
14	South-east Asia & Australia	1	Singapore
15	America, Canada & South America	1	New York
Total		63	

Table 21.2 Industrial classification

Code no.	*Industry*
1	Agriculture
2	Mining industry
3	Light industry
4	Heavy industry
5	Service industry
6	Truck transportation industry
7	Railway transport industry
8	Sea & waterway transport industry
9	Port physical distribution industry

Table 21.3 Planning horizon

Period	*t*	*Planning horizon*
1st	0	1985–9
2nd	1	1990–4
3rd	2	1995–9
4th	3	2000–4
5th	4	2005–9

ANALYSIS OF THE SIMULATION RESULT

Premises and case setting for analysis

Premises

(a) Asian Expressway Network (AEN) It is assumed that the AEN in the regions other than China will have been constructed completely and put to use at the expense of countries other than China by the fourth period ($t = 3$). Based upon this assumption, we can analyze the investment demand purely at the Chinese economy's expense for the part of the AEN in Chinese territory.

(b) Treatment of personal trips The load to the TIF owing to personal trips from travel activities and so on is not built into our simulation model. The setting of the capacity of the current TIF is based upon the actual freight transaction volume, and it is assumed for the Expressway that 20 per cent of section capacity is put to use for personal trips and subtracted in advance from the whole capacity.

(c) Borrowing from foreign countries Our simulation model is that of physical distribution (commodity flow) in which the money does not exist. So we cannot discriminate among the types of current trade revenue: expenditure, invisible trade, and capital transaction. Therefore, assuming that the other current items, foreign currency holdings, and capital outflow are held constant, it is assumed that the deficit in the current balance is the amount borrowed from foreign countries. (See Tables 21.4 and 21.5.)

(d) Upper limit of accumulated balance of the money borrowed from overseas supposition of a maximum limit to the growth of the chinese economy We here suppose the following three variants on the maximum permissible limit on the loan balance borrowed from overseas from the first period ($t = 1$) to the fifth period ($t = 4$).

Variant 1 shows a *natural growth* pattern of the loan balance supposed based on the past increase/decrease in the medium and long-term overseas loan balance. Variants 2 and 3 show the maximum permissible limit of another loan balance from overseas. If allowed, the amount borrowed will equal the amount of funds required to construct each AEN variant corresponding to each pattern shown in Table 21.5. Variant 2 and Variant 3 show for each case that China will,

Table 21.4 Maximum permissible limit of loan balance borrowed from overseas (US$100 million)

	$t = 0$	$t = 1$	$t = 3$	$t = 4$
Variant 1 (Var. 1)	236	489	885	735
Variant 2 (Var. 2)	266	578	1 102	1 129
Variant 3 (Var. 3)	251	533	992	931

Table 21.5 Construction pattern of the proposed Asian Expressway Network (in km of four lanes)

	$t = 0$	$t = 1$	$t = 2$	$t = 3$	$t = 4$	*Total*
Variant 2 (Var. 2)	1 000	2 000	4 350	3 000	3 000	13 350
Variant 3 (Var. 3)	500	1 000	2 150	1 500	1 500	6 625

furthermore, borrow an amount equivalent to the public investment funds needed to complete the AEN (total length 13 350 km) on Chinese territory up to the end of the fifth period using: (a) an entirely four lane system or, (b) an entirely two lane system. This would be in addition to the amount of natural growth of the loan balance so far.

The procedure here was adopted as a temporary expedient; that is, the amount of investment funds for the total length of the AEN is used as a standard for the maximum permissible limit on the loan balance of borrowing from overseas. Though plausible, it is not based on a reasonable foundation. As mentioned above, Variant 2 does not necessarily guarantee that the Asian Expressway Network of 13 350 km will have been completed as an entirely four lane system by the end of the fifth period. For example, if there are more efficient investment targets than the proposed Asian Expressway Network, the surplus funds will be allocated to those targets. Alternatively, concentrated investment will be made for a link that shows relatively higher investment efficiency, which may bring about the creation of an expressway with more than four lanes.

If the products of industry and agriculture are quadrupled up to the year 2000 (GDP comes to be about US$1100 billion), the ratio of the loan balance of US$110 billion to GNP is relatively low compared to that of Brazil, Mexico, Korea, or Indonesia (20 per cent to 30 per cent respectively). However, it is obvious that the payment of interest equivalent to US$4.4–8.8 billion annually to overseas will be a considerable burden to the Chinese economy. (See Table 21.2.)

Table 21.6 Case setting

Case	*Borrowing interest rate %*	*Investment in the Expressway*	*Upper limit of the balance of borrowing from abroad*
1	4	With	Variant 2
2	6	With	Variant 2
3	8	With	Variant 2
4	6	Without	Variant 1

Case setting for analysis

The following four simulation cases differ in the amount of the borrowing interest rate and whether or not the AEN is invested in (shown in Table 21.6). It is taken into consideration that the weighted average interest rate was 6.65 per cent for the credit loan to China using the March 1979–November 1982 government base. This variation in interest rates is used to show the differences in the fund-raising environment during the construction of the AEN. For example, Case 1, with a rate of 4 per cent, shows that the supply of international investment capital is at a surplus, or that the managerial risk of project concerned is very low. Case 3, with an 8 per cent rate is the reverse of Case 1. (See Table 21.6.)

Optimum investment allocation by period to the link of expressway

The only one case with the Expressway is shown in Figure 21.1.

North China–South China route At the end of the fifth period ($t = 4$), the main route between North China–South China of Tianjin–Cheng-chou–Ch'ang-sha–Guangzhou (–Beihai) has already been opened to traffic, although the investment in the Tianjin–Cheng-chou link is small in amount. As for Case 2, in contrast, the amount of investment in the Guangzhou–Beihai link is zero.

As for Case 3, this main route has barely been opened to traffic through the Nan-ning route, although there is little investment in the links between Tianjin–Cheng-chou–Wu-han. The link between Heng-yang–Guanzhou has also been opened. In every case, the investment during the second period ($t = 1$) is made in the links of Wu-han–Ch'ang-sha–Heng-yang–Guangzhou, which includes the over-congested link of Heng-yang–Hsu-chia-tung, notorious for its excessive bottleneck.

Figure 21.1 Optimum transport investment allocation to the Asian Expressway Network by period (Case 1)

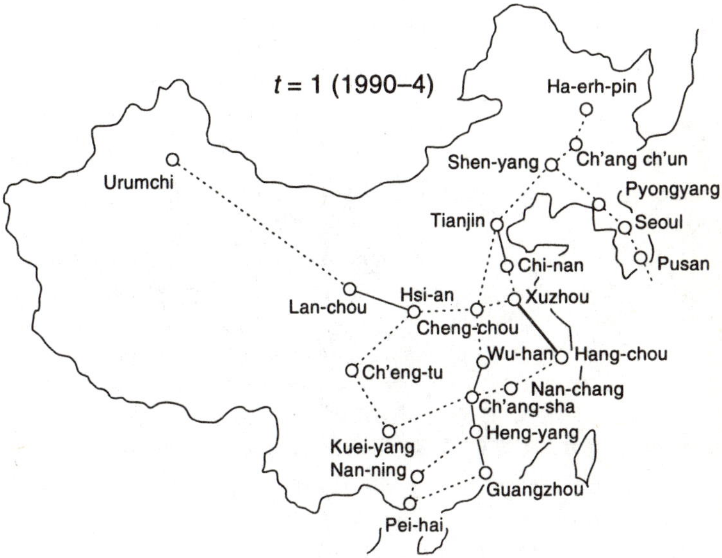

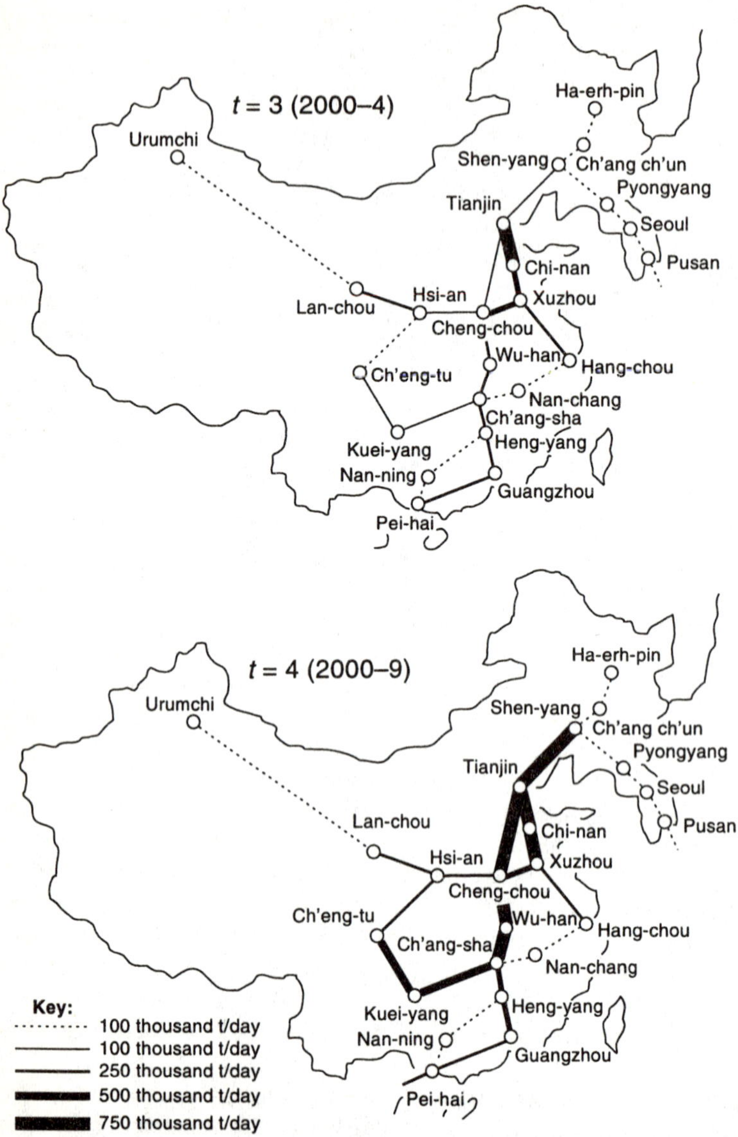

t = 3 (2000–4)
Ha-erh-pin
Urumchi
Shen-yang
Ch'ang ch'un
Pyongyang
Tianjin
Seoul
Pusan
Chi-nan
Lan-chou
Hsi-an
Xuzhou
Cheng-chou
Wu-han
Hang-chou
Ch'eng-tu
Nan-chang
Ch'ang-sha
Heng-yang
Kuei-yang
Nan-ning
Guangzhou
Pei-hai
t = 4 (2000–9)
Ha-erh-pin
Urumchi
Shen-yang
Ch'ang ch'un
Pyongyang
Tianjin
Seoul
Chi-nan
Pusan
Lan-chou
Hsi-an
Xuzhou
Cheng-chou
Wu-han
Hang-chou
Ch'eng-tu
Ch'ang-sha
Nan-chang
Heng-yang
Kuei-yang
Nan-ning
Guangzhou
Pei-hai
Key:
100 thousand t/day
100 thousand t/day
250 thousand t/day
500 thousand t/day
750 thousand t/day

As for the time until opening for the main route between Tianjin–Guangzhou, the fastest is for Case 1, where the opening occurs during the 3rd period. Its connection with the Japan–Korea Tunnel occurs in Cases 2 and 3 respectively. In the case where the borrowing interest rate is very high, on the other hand, a development pattern is chosen which puts the stress on the development of North-eastern China.

North China–East China route The Tianjin–Hang-chou (Shanghai) route which is the alternative North–South route, has opened to traffic. The opening time for the whole line is the soonest in Case 1 (in the 3rd period).

The western route The western route is open to traffic from Xuzhou to Lan-chou in Cases 1 and 2.

West China route The West China route of Hang-chou–Ch'ang-sha–Ch'eng-tu is open in Case 2.

Circular route The circular route of Tianjin–Xuzhou–Cheng-chou–Tianjin is open to through traffic for all the cases, though the amount of investment in Case 3 is limited. Though the investment is limited in amount for several links, the circular route of Xuzhou–Hang-chou–Ch'ang-sha–Cheng-chou–Xuzhou is opened to through traffic in Cases 2 and 3; however, the link between Hang-chou and Ch'ang-sha is not yet open in Case 1. The circular route of Cheng-chou–Ch'ang-sha–Kuei-yang–Ch'eng-tu–Hsi-an–Cheng-chou is open to traffic in Case 1 only, though the investment amount is small for several links.

In summary, Case 1 is to be the investment pattern if China pursues the completion of the expressway network; stress is placed on the development of the domestic inland. Case 3, in contrast, is the investment pattern which concentrates investment on any object; stress on the development of inland regions in North-eastern China, Northern China and Eastern China. Case 2, then, is an intermediate type of investment pattern.

With–without comparison of the value of the objective function

The various values of the objective function (= optimization of GNP) are shown in Table 21.7. This value is an index standing for the national welfare level over the entire planning horizon. In comparing these values, it is possible to identify which cases will produce a more affluent welfare level. These are the cases where the value of the GNP reverses itself

Table 21.7 Values of objective functions (US$100 millions)

Case	*FV*
Case 1	223085.7
Case 2	206493.6
Case 3	183123.9
Case 4	193920.5

$$FV = \sum_{t=1}^{5} (1 + 0.04)^{1-t}\ \mathrm{GNP}(t)$$

between cases at the intermediate period in the planning horizon.

When making a comparison between any two cases over the relatively short planning horizon of 25 years, it is understood that Case 3, with an 8 per cent per year borrowing interest rate, barely realizes a relatively lower value than that of Case 4, 'without expressway,' and the 8 per cent value proves to be a considerable burden which limits the catch-up effects of the Expressway.

This will be explained more explicitly by using Figure 21.2. The trajectory of Case 1 shows an example of economic growth which is under the planning type of economic administration with the premise of a large amount of foreign borrowing, with the AEN. The trajectory of Case 4 is without the AEN. Cases 2 and 3 are examples of economic growth under an economic administration in status quo as to the borrowing of foreign funds and other policies, with the AEN. The locational relation of these four cases is an example of the most typical ones. The growth trajectory of Case 4 is one in which the economic effects are revealed. Steady growth at the relatively high level is achieved earlier, as compared with Cases 1, 2 and 3, by efficiently investing the vast amount of funds in the existing transport network and its corresponding industries. Case 4 exhibits a satisfactorily realistic growth trajectory with due regard to the Chinese natural resources endowment, oversaturation of labourers and economic administration.

In comparison, it is clear that the trajectory of Case 1 has been stagnant in the early stage, far lower than the trajectory of Case 4, owing to the public investment policy. This policy intends to invest the large sum of funds not in an alternative expressway network which is optimal for the existing industrial location, but in the proposed AEN based on the premise that the industrial location, industrial structure and related factors will have been reorganized in order to receive greater indirect economic effects. However, as soon as the intended indirect

Figure 21.2 GNP derived from the model

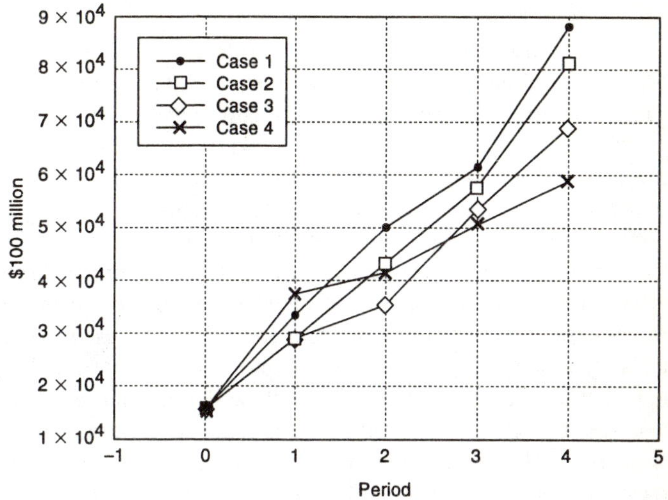

economic effects are revealed, the Chinese economy will start to grow rapidly until it catches up with the trajectory of Case 4, outruns it, and eventually reaches a far higher level of steady growth compared to the level of the Case 4, in the latter part of time horizon.

Case 1 (4 per cent) and Case 2 (6 per cent) produce differences of about 21.3 per cent and 12.3 per cent respectively compared with Case 4. The difference between Case 1 and Case 4, which is about a one and a half times difference in GNP for the fourth period, is quite large considering the relatively short planning horizon of twenty-five years; this difference may be significant.

ACCELERATION EFFECT ON THE CHINESE ECONOMY BROUGHT ABOUT BY THE ASIAN EXPRESSWAY NETWORK

There is a need to analyze the market directly relating to the goods and services which the project concerned will supply, regardless of how large it may be. It is very important to measure and evaluate the comprehensive and socioeconomic effects (which we intend to measure) using a measurement model of economic effects relating to the multi-markets in organic association with the direct market mentioned above.

The greater the economic effects of the project the more comprehensive a socioeconomic model will be needed. Moreover, this socioeconomic measurement model must be comprehensive in terms of both space and time in the sense that the bigger the project, the more the indirect economic effects may propagate and spread marketably, technologically, and spatially to more remote areas, and dynamically into the far distant future. The Asian Expressway Network is typical of the large projects and will embody all of the above characteristics. This is why our analysis is based upon a dynamic, multi-regional, multi-industry, multi-transport-modal programming model. The economic effects of large projects are of enormous value; however, the construction funds required are also immense. Regardless of whether these funds are raised by the Chinese economy alone or from foreign countries, it is certain that a vast amount of resources and labourers will be invested.

The economic effects of the AEN will be chiefly indirect and will only be realized after much time has passed. Therefore, had it not been for the AEN, it is reasonable to assume that a more efficient rate of investment and a higher growth rate trajectory would have been attained in an earlier stage by investing the funds earmarked for the AEN in other existing transport facilities or other industrial capital accumulation, associated with the existing facilities. However, with the passage of time, it is not long before the reorganization of industries and accumulation of capital associated with the AEN will ensue, allowing both producers and consumers to receive vast indirect economic benefits. In this way by the trajectory with the AEN we can catch up with and eventually surpass the alternative trajectory without the AEN.

It is expected that such a growth-accelerating effect on the Chinese economy will be typical of the early stages of large-scale projects such as the AEN. In short, nothing less than non-marketable and technological economic effects will result from making efficient use of function as an economic effect-generating apparatus. This is characteristic of large projects in the planning type of socioeconomic administration.

References

AMA (Administrative Management Agency) (1984) *1980 Industrial Input–Output Table of Japan – General Expository Manual*, pp. 1–330.

CNSB (People's Republic of China, National Statistics Bureau) (ed.) (1983) *Statistical Yearbook of China, 1983* (Chinese Statistics Publishing Corporation) pp. 1–330.

Dorfman, R., P. A. Samuelson and R. M. Sollow (DOSSO) (1958) 'Efficient Programs of Capital Accumulation' (ch. 12), *Linear Programming and Economic Analysis* (New York: McGraw-Hill), pp. 309–45.

Higano Y. and H. Kohno (1986) 'Optimal Reorganization of Greater Tokyo – An Industrial Complex of Agglomeration and Scale Economies', *Environment and Planning A*, vol. 20, nos. 8 & 9, August & September, pp. 1103–20 and 1145–64.

Kohno, H. (1969) 'Optimum Allocation of Public Investment Using Interregional Input–Output Programming Model', *Papers and Proceedings of the Pacific Regional Science Conference of the RSA*, vol. 1, pp. 53–93.

Kohno, H. (1987) 'Dynamic Optimization of Rural Development and Urban Re-growth', in P. Friedrich and I. Masser (eds), *International Perspectives on Regional Decentralization* (Baden-Baden: Momos Verlag) pp. 245–77.

Kohno, H., Y. Higano, Y. Matsumura and H. Mitomo (1992) 'Dynamic appraisal of the Asian Expressway Network Benefits on China', Paper read at the 39th North American Meetings of the RSAI, Chicago, Illinois, November 13–15, pp. 1–62 (obtainable from the authors).

Moses, L. N. (1960) 'A General Equilibrium Model of Production, Interregional Trade and Location of Industry', *Review of Economics and Statistics*, vol. 42, no. 4, pp. 373–99.

22 Identifying the Direct and Indirect Economic Effects of Electric Power Development Projects

Toshiyuki Hayashi and Sid Saltzman

INTRODUCTION

One of the primary methods for evaluating the economic effects of development projects in general, and electric power plants in particular, is cost–benefit analysis (CBA). This method typically compares the direct cost and benefit streams throughout a project's life (that is, its economic effects) which, in the case of electric power plants, includes both its construction and its operation phases. Typically, the direct economic costs of a project are evaluated using the notion of opportunity costs which, conceptually, reflect the economic scarcity of the resources that will be used by the project. For electric power projects, the direct economic benefits can be ascertained by estimating the economic price of electricity which, conceptually, also reflects its economic scarcity. Economic scarcity is reflected in the concept of consumers' surplus, which can be determined by estimating consumers' willingness to pay for electricity.[1]

The typical CBA described above is appropriate for evaluating not only the direct but also the indirect economic effects of most economic development projects including electric power plants. Although it is usually the case that the direct costs and benefits of many development projects represent their primary economic effects, that is not usually true with electric power plants and other very large projects. With such projects, the indirect economic effects of the project may be as large as, or larger than, the direct economic effects. In such cases, identifying and evaluating only the direct effects may well provide misleading results with respect to a project's economic viability.

Another problem in applying conventional CBA to evaluate the economic effects of an electric power plant is that there is no mechanism for incorporating a spatial component in the analysis. This is especially important in those situations where the region serviced by a power plant does not encompass the whole nation, which is the situation in most countries of the world. In such cases, it is deceptive to assume that the economic effects apply to the nation as a whole.

This chapter outlines an alternative approach to identifying the economic effects of electric power development projects that obviates the above shortcomings of the more conventional methods of evaluation. This alternative approach employs a regional, macroeconomic, semi-input–output (SIO) model which is based on the early work of Leontief (1951) as extended by Isard (1951), Tinbergen (1966), and others. Since its development, the SIO framework has been used for assessing comparative advantages of development projects in tradable sectors in a national economy (for examples, see Karunaratne, 1976, and Kuyvenhoven, 1978). However, the SIO framework has apparently not been used before for evaluating development projects in a non-tradable sector (such as electricity generation) rather than in a tradable sector, and in a regional rather than a national context.

The next section of this chapter provides an outline of the analytical framework upon which this approach is based. The following section summarizes how the direct and indirect costs and benefits of an electric power development project can be identified, and the chapter closes with concluding remarks.

ANALYTICAL FRAMEWORK

The regional semi-input–output model

The analytical framework for the proposed identification process has its beginnings in Leontief's input–output (IO) model, which can be written as follows:

$$AX + F = X \tag{22.1}$$

where A is a $(n \times n)$ technical coefficient matrix, X is a $(n \times 1)$ vector of total output, and F is a $(n \times 1)$ vector of final demand. Solving for the vector of total output (X) automatically accounts for both the direct final demand (F) and the indirect intermediate demand resulting from the structure of the relationships among the sectors (A) and the final demand (F). In this study, the model is closed with respect to households, because one of the major final consumers of electricity is the household sector which, in this case, is included as the nth sector in Equation (22.1).

The SIO model is developed from Equation (22.1) by grouping the sectors in that model into two different categories: tradable sectors and non-tradable sectors. In addition, one row vector representing capital coefficients, which specify each sector's need for capital per unit of input, is added to the model (Hewings, 1985). These two changes to Equation (22.1) will help make it possible to identify the direct, indirect and induced economic effects associated with electric power development projects (see the next section).

One further change to Equation (22.1) is necessary in order to modify the results of the analysis so that they are applicable primarily to the regional economy serviced by the electric power plant and not to the nation as a whole. This can be done by modifying the technical coefficients matrix, A, of equation (22.1) so that it is representative of a regional economy rather than the national economy. A relatively inexpensive way to accomplish this task is to use a non-survey method by which regional supply percentages are applied to the national technical coefficients, A, in order to estimate a regional direct input coefficient matrix, A^R, for region R (see Miller and Blair, 1985).

The dichotomy between tradable and non-tradable sectors of the regional matrix, A^R, produces a single-region, input coefficient matrix of a complete SIO model which can be written as:

$$\begin{matrix} \begin{bmatrix} A^R_{TT} & : & A^R_{TN} \\ \cdots & \cdots & \cdots \\ A^R_{NT} & : & A^R_{NN} \end{bmatrix} \\ [\,V_T \quad : \quad V_N\,] \\ [\,K_T \quad : \quad K_N\,] \end{matrix} \begin{bmatrix} X^R_T \\ \cdots \\ X^R_N \end{bmatrix} + \begin{bmatrix} F^R_T \\ \cdots \\ F^R_N \end{bmatrix} = \begin{bmatrix} X^T_T \\ \cdots \\ X^R_N \end{bmatrix} \tag{22.2}$$

where

A^R_{TT} = a regional input coefficient matrix within tradable sectors

A^R_{TN} = a regional input coefficient matrix from tradable sectors to non-tradable sectors

A^R_{NT} = a regional input coefficient matrix from non-tradable sectors to tradable sectors

A^R_{NN} = a regional input coefficient matrix within non-tradable sectors

V_T, V_N = row vectors of value added coefficients for tradable and non-tradable sectors
K_T, K_N = row vectors of capital coefficients for tradable and non-tradable sectors
X_T^R, X_N^R = column vectors of regional total output for tradable and non-tradable sectors
F_T^R, F_N^R = column vectors of regional final demand for tradable and non-tradable sectors

In this RSIO model, the value added and capital coefficients are the same as the national SIO model, because production technology in the region, in this case, is assumed to be the same as production technology in the nation as a whole.

Economic effects in a RSIO framework

Fundamental assumptions

The RSIO framework can be used to identify the direct, indirect and induced effects a project can bring to a regional economy. However, some fundamental assumptions were carried over from the original SIO framework in order to identify properly these economic effects in this application. The first assumption is that the production capacities of the non-tradable sectors are equal to the demand they are now fulfilling in the region, which implies that, in order to meet any increase in demand, new investment in non-tradable sectors will be needed. The second assumption is that increased demand for the goods and services of tradable sectors can be met by imports from other regions. Unlike the first assumption, the second assumption implies that new investment in the tradable sectors is not necessary in order to meet any additional demand. The third assumption is that any excess supply in the tradable sectors can be exported to other regions.

The direct effects

In Tinbergen's SIO framework, the direct costs of a project are obtained by multiplying the capital coefficient of the tradable sector of the project by the planned level of output of the project. Since the value of a capital coefficient represents the amount of new investment required to increase the total output of the sector by one unit, the direct costs the SIO framework identifies are essentially represented by the amount of the project investment.

Because a project in a tradable sector increases the total output of that sector, the amount of value added in the tradable sector also increases. The SIO framework identifies this increased amount of value added as the direct benefit of the project.

The indirect effects

In the SIO framework, indirect costs are identified, based on the first assumption in 'Fundamental assumptions', above, which states that the production capacities of non-tradable sectors are equal to the demand they are now fulfilling in the region. Once the project in the sector is completed, the project increases the total output of the sector. Suppose the project under study is of the *j*th tradable sector and is expected to increase total output of the *j*th sector by dx_j^R units. One result of this increase is the increase in the *j*th sector's inputs from other tradable sectors. According to the second assumption of the framework, the increased demand for the goods and services of other tradable sectors can be met by imports from other regions; consequently, new investment is not needed to meet the increased demand. Similarly, the *j*th sector also increases its inputs from non-tradable sectors. Unlike the tradable sectors, the increased demand for the goods and services of the non-tradable sectors cannot be met by imports. According to the first assumption, new investment in these sectors has to be made in order to meet increased demand. The SIO framework identifies this new investment as the indirect costs of the project.

Similarly, the SIO framework identifies the increased value added in non-tradable sectors as the indirect benefits. The increased value added will be realized by the increased total output in non-tradable sectors, which the increased total output of the *j*th tradable sector requires.

IDENTIFICATION OF THE ECONOMIC EFFECTS

The overall process

The regional SIO (RSIO) framework presented in the previous section is used as the basis for developing the specific models presented in this section for a project in a non-tradable sector. The overall approach taken to develop these models is first to estimate the increase in total regional output for both tradable and non-tradable sectors that will be generated by the proposed electric power plant. During the construction period, a standard closed IO model[2] is employed to estimate the increase in total output generated by the total investment in the project. During the operation period, a mixed type of closed IO model is used to estimate the increase in total output generated by the increased electricity supply. The RSIO framework is then applied to these increases in total output in order to derive the indirect costs and benefits.

Three additional considerations for the RSIO model

Given the increases in total regional output during the construction and operation phases of the project, it is possible to estimate the relevant costs and benefits associated with these increases. This section outlines the methods used to generate these estimates within a RSIO framework.[3] However, three issues should be considered before describing the models for estimating the costs and benefits that are of interest: first, modification of the capital coefficients; second, treatment of the household sector in a SIO framework; and third, excess production capacities in tradable sectors.

Modification of the capital coefficients

Capital coefficients, which reflect the requirements for capital per unt of input of an economy, are used to calculate the indirect costs needed to expand the regional production capacities in the non-tradable sectors other than those under study (that is, those other than the electric power sector). The indirect costs thus calculated represent the amount of investment that has to be made to establish new production facilities.

One difficulty in using capital coefficients in this model is that the new production facilities would continue for some years to produce goods and services in the respective sectors. However, the economic analysis of the facilities is on an annual basis and, for the sake of consistency, all the costs and benefits must be annualized. This can be done by calculating a capital recovery factor (see, for example, Kuyvenhoven (1978) p. 159) for each sector. A row vector of annual capital coefficients can then be calculated by

$$K_N^a = K_N \cdot H^\wedge \qquad (22.3)$$

where K_N^a is a row vector of annual capital coefficients and $H^\wedge$ is a diagonal matrix of a column vector of capital recovery factors.

Treatment of the household sector

As indicated earlier, the SIO framework used in this chapter is based on an IO model that is closed with respect to households (a non-tradable sector). However, because households are not considered to be one of the production sectors, they should not be treated in the same way as the other non-tradable sectors. For example, the capital coefficient for the household sector is assumed to be zero, whereas, for production sectors, capital is assumed to be a scarce resource (especially in developing countries) and it is considered a cost in the SIO framework (Karunaratne (1976) p. 282).

On the other hand, the value added coefficient for the household sector is assumed to be one. The outputs for the household sector (that is, wages and salaries) are remuneration for labour inputs to the production sectors and can be considered benefits in the SIO framework.[4]

Excess production capacities in the tradable sectors

An assumption that is made in this particular application of the SIO framework is that excess production capacities exist in tradable sectors because of insufficient electricity supply before the project under study is completed.[5] This assumption, which describes a typical condition in developing countries, results in increased indirect benefits in comparison with the indirect costs as derived from output expansion in the tradable sectors.

Identification of costs and benefits

Because an electric power development project entails significant resource use and creates one of the most important inputs to modern economic activities, implementation of a project causes extensive economic impact in a region. Generally, a project brings about an economic impact during two separate periods: the construction period and the operation period.

During the construction period

The length of the construction period varies depending on the type and the scale of the power station. Generally, the construction period of a hydroelectric power project may be from about five years to fifteen years. In the case of a thermal power project, the construction period is usually shorter, approximately three to five years.

During the construction period, the investment for a project is made in the form of annual disbursements to contractors.[6] In fact, these disbursements are the source of the economic impact of a project during the construction period, which can then be identified as direct and indirect costs and benefits.

(*a*) *Direct costs* Direct costs during the construction period are derived from the annual disbursements made to contractors. However, since the amount of the disbursements represents actual market value, the market value has to be evaluated by shadow prices in order to reflect the opportunity costs of the resources the project will absorb.

(*b*) *Direct benefits* During the construction period, no direct benefits are identified because the project does not produce any output until construction is completed and operation starts.

(*c*) *Indirect costs* Because the investment made in the form of annual disbursements adds to the final demand for goods and services of various sectors in the regional economy,[7] the investment generates an increase in total output of the economy. However, the increase in total output might not be realized without additional investments in the economy. These additional investments made to increase the total output of the regional economy represent the indirect costs of the project.

(*d*) *Indirect benefits* Like the indirect costs, the increase in total output generated by the project investment results in an increase in value added such as employee compensation, profits, and regional government taxes. These increases in value added are the indirect benefits of the project during the construction period.

During the operation period

Once construction is completed, the new electric power station starts to operate and begins supplying electricity to the regional economy. The additional electricity the regional economy receives becomes the source of the direct and indirect costs and benefits of the project.

Since insufficient electricity supply is often one of the factors behind lagging economies in developing countries, the indirect effects of the project are especially important. If insufficient electricity supply is mitigated, it is very likely that the increased electricity supply would stimulate a regional economy and generate a considerable amount of increase in total output in the economy. Thus, this increase in regional output is the source of the indirect costs and benefits of the project.

(a) *Direct costs* Operation and maintenance costs, including fuel costs in the case of a thermal power project, constitute the direct costs during the operation period. Like the annual disbursements during the construction period, these operation and maintenance costs are expressed in market prices. Therefore, they have to be evaluated by shadow prices so that the opportunity costs of these inputs can be accounted for as the direct costs of the project.
(b) *Direct benefits* After the power station starts to operate, it increases the total output of the electricity sector. Consequently, the value added to the sector increases. This increase in value added is identified as the direct benefits of the project.
(c) *Indirect costs* Increased electricity supply to the regional economy generates an increase in total output for various sectors in the economy. However, like the indirect costs during the construction period, the increase in total output for some sectors might not be realized without additional investment. Therefore this additional investment has to be identified as the indirect costs of the project.
(d) *Indirect benefits* Like the direct benefits, the increased total output of the regional economy brings about the increase in value added to the regional economy. This increase in value added is identified as the indirect benefits of the project.

The model of economic effects

The direct and indirect costs and benefits thus obtained can be summarized as follows:

(1) During the construction period:
  (a) *Direct costs*
  Project investment: D_c
  (b) *Direct benefits*
  No direct benefits
  (c) *Indirect effects derived from output expansions in the tradable sectors* (dX_T)
  Indirect costs: $(C_{NT}) : K_N^a \cdot (I - A_{NN})^{-1} \cdot A_{NT} \cdot dX_T^R$ (22.4)
  Indirect benefits: $(B_T) : V_T \cdot dX_T^R$,
  $(B_{NT}) : V_N \cdot (I - A_{NN})^{-1} \cdot A_{NT} \cdot dX_T^R$ (22.5)
  (d) *Indirect effects derived from output expansions in the non-tradable sectors*

Indirect costs: (C_N) : $K_N^a \cdot dX_N$ (22.6)
Indirect benefits: (B_N) : $V_N \cdot dX_N$ (22.7)

(2) During the operation period:

(a) *Direct costs*

Operation and maintenance costs including fuel costs in the case of a thermal power project: D_o

(b) *Direct benefits*

Increase in value added to the electricity sector: $B_D{}^*$

(c) *Indirect effects derived from output expansions in the tradable sectors*

Indirect costs: $(C_{NT}{}^*)$: $K_N^a \cdot (I - A_{NN})^{-1} \cdot A_{NT} \cdot dX_T^{R*}$ (22.8)
Indirect benefits: $(B_T{}^*)$: $V_T \cdot dX_T^{R*}$,
$(B_{NT}{}^*)$: $V_N \cdot (I - A_{NN})^{-1} \cdot A_{NT} \cdot dX_T^{R*}$ (22.9)

(d) *Indirect effects derived from output expansions in the non-tradable sectors*

Indirect costs $(C_N{}^*)$: $K_N^a \cdot dX_N{}^*$
Indirect benefits $(B_N{}^*)$: $V_N \cdot dX_N{}^*$

The variables are defined as:

D_c = Annual expenditure from the project investment (direct costs during the construction period);
K_N^a = Annual value of the capital coefficients for the non-tradable sectors including the household sector;
I = Identity matrix;
A_{NN} = Regional direct input coefficients within the non-tradable sectors of the closed input–output model;
A_{NT} = Regional direct input coefficients from the non-tradable sectors to the tradable sectors of the closed input–output model;
dX_T^R = The increase in regional production for the tradable sectors during the construction period;
V_T = Value added coefficients for the tradable sectors;
V_N = Value added coefficients for the non-tradable sectors including that of the household sector with the value of one;
dX_N = The increase in regional production for the non-tradable sectors during the construction period;
D_o = Operation and maintenance costs;
$B_D{}^*$ = Increase in value added in the electricity sector;
dX_T^{R*} = The increase in regional production for the tradable sectors during the operation period; and
$dX_N{}^*$ = The increase in production for the non-tradable sectors during the operation period.

CONCLUDING REMARKS

All the limitations inherent in using input–output models are carried over in this extension to a regional semi-input–output framework. These limitations are well known and need not be repeated here. Nevertheless, they do suggest directions for the future development of more comprehensive methods for the economic evaluation of large-scale development projects. One direction is in terms of the quantity, quality and type of data available. For example, a hydroelectric facility is expected to have an economic life of at least fifty years, but in this study it was assumed that various coefficients were fixed. Clearly, these coefficients will change over time as the use of electricity permeates the region. Estimates of these and other time-dependent changes could be readily incorporated into the model. More accurate and detailed data for the regional supply percentages and the capital coefficients, among other data, would be important contributions to more accurate results.

Another direction for future research concerns improvements in the structure of the models used in the analysis. For example, impacts of sectors with stronger forward linkages than backward linkages (such as electricity) can be better reflected by a supply-side model rather than a demand-side model. In this study, a demand-side model was used to estimate the increase in total output during the construction period. Therefore, using a supply-side model during the operation period would have introduced an inconsistency in the analysis. Other examples concern possible extensions to SAM models (Pyatt and Round, 1985) and general equilibrium models (Dervis *et al.*, 1982) in order to introduce the ability to analyze distributional impacts and to remove the limitations imposed by the assumption of linear relationships among the sectors.

Notes

1. A publication of the Asian Development Bank (Desai, 1985) describes practical methods for performing a CBA of the direct economic effects for electric power plants in developing countries.
2. Because private consumption expenditure is usually a significant portion of final demand, it is important to include household consumption as an endogenous variable in these models. For this reason, the IO-type models used here are closed with respect to households (for example, see Miller and Blair, 1985).

3. Since the costs and benefits are measured on an annual basis during the construction and operating phases of the project, the methods outlined here are also on an annual basis.
4. The 'true value added' of the household sector represents the households' tax payments to the government, and savings. Consequently, the value added coefficient can be considered to be less than one. However, because all the increase in total output for the household sector, which is the increase in wages and salaries, has to be accounted for as indirect benefits in the SIO framework and not just the increase in tax payments and savings, the value added coefficient of the household sector is assumed to be one.
5. This assumption is in addition to the three assumptions described under 'Fundamental assumptions' which were imbedded in the original SIO framework.
6. Practically, the disbursements to contractors are generally made monthly. Since cost–benefit analysis is usually made based on annual flows of costs and benefits, annual disbursements are assumed.
7. Annual disbursements that add to the final demand also have to be evaluated by shadow prices.

References

Dervis, K., J. de Melo and S. Robinson (1982) *General Equilibrium Models for Development Policy* (Washington, DC: World Bank).

Desai, N. (1985) *Economic Analysis of Power Projects*, Asian Development Bank Economic Staff Paper No. 24 (Manila: Asian Development Bank).

Hewings, G. J. D. (1985) *Regional Input–Output Analysis* (California, London and New Delhi: Sage).

Isard, W. (1951) 'Interregional and Regional Input–Output Analysis: A Model of a Space-Economy', *Review of Economics and Statistics*, vol. 33, pp. 318–28.

Karunaratne, N. D. (1976) 'Quantification of Sectoral Development Prospects in Papua New Guinea Using Tinbergen and Rasmussen Criteria', *Developing Economies*, vol. 14, p. 280.

Kuyvenhoven, A. (1978) *Planning with the Semi-Input–Output Method* (Leiden, Boston and London: Martinus Nijhof, Social Sciences Division).

Leontief, W. (1951) *The Structure of the American Economy, 1919–1939* (New York: Oxford University Press).

Miller, R. E. and P. D. Blair (1985) *Input–Output Analysis Foundations and Extensions* (Englewood Cliffs, NJ: Prentice-Hall).

Pyatt, G. and J. I. Round (eds) (1985) *Social Accounting Matrices: A Basis for Planning* (Washington, DC: World Bank).

Tinbergen, J. (1966) 'Some Refinements of the Semi-Input–Output Method', *Pakistan Development Review*, vol. 6, pp. 243–7.

23 A Multi-Regional Model for China Based on Price and Quantity Equilibrium

Asao Ando and Takanori Shibata

INTRODUCTION

To attain economic growth in developing economies, it is strategically important to provide them with appropriate infrastructure. As the installation of this could, at the same time, promote regional disparity within the country, the economic impact of such projects need to be studied carefully in advance. However, it is generally difficult to conduct such studies, particularly in the regional context, since sufficient regional statistics are difficult to obtain for developing countries.

The class of models known as the Applied General Equilibrium (AGE) or the Computable General Equilibrium (CGE) models (Dervis *et al.* (1982) and Scarf and Shoven (1984)) have been developed to describe the developing economies where economic statistics are poorly available. While their applications are naturally confined to the descriptions of national economies, the ultimate goal of our study is to develop a multi-regional model that can be used to evaluate the effectiveness of various projects designed to improve infrastructure without demanding detailed regional statistics. The model to be presented here cannot be called a multi-regional CGE model in the narrow sense, but it shares the motivation to build a model that can be operated with a limited set of data.

Our study area is China, which was subdivided into twenty-nine provinces in 1985. Because of its rapid economic growth in recent years, it is widely recognized that at least some provinces of China have reached the stage of full industrialization. Similarly, China is not a country where regional statistics are poor. However, it would still be necessary to adjust them to meet certain requirements relevant to comprehensive modelling, including estimation procedures to make the data consistent with the concept of SNA.

As the cost of collecting data is proportional to the data size, it is practically impossible to collect all the available data. Thus every model might be a compromise between the scrutiny of projections and their associated costs. Nevertheless, it is always desirable to construct the model from the least possible quantity of reliability data. Along these lines, this chapter is intended to present an acceptable *compromise* that can be employed to evaluate the impact of projects in developing countries in a multi-regional context. Meanwhile, we shall need some extra data above the quantity that is just enough to operate the model in order to check its validity. There are extra data available in China that are useful in this regard.

TRANSPORT PROJECTS AND PRICE EQUILIBRIUM

In developed economies, the direct benefits of a transport project tend to be marginal, and can mainly be evaluated by the reduction in travel time. When commodities, services, labour and capital are fully mobile, and a proper redistribution system through taxes and subsidies is established, it may suffice to evaluate the gross effect of a transport project in terms of increases in gross domestic product (GDP) and other macro indices.

But in economies with inadequate transport facilities, such a project could affect the structure of the commodity market with expanding trade possibilities. In this regard, the impact of the project could properly be evaluated by the *final approach*, where evaluations are made after the direct effects have been transformed through the market. Moreover, since such economies are likely to involve significant disparity among regions, it would be important to evaluate the impact by regions to make sure that the project will lead to a balanced development. This is why a comprehensive multi-regional model becomes relevant to the evaluation of the project.

A variety of such models have been developed so far (see Amano and Fujita (1970), for example). However not many models consider the commodity prices as being endogenous. As stated above, changes in prices and associated increases in inter-regional trade are among major impacts arising from transport improvement in developing economies. Accordingly, the models to be employed for assessing impacts should preferably be capable of describing a multi-regional Walrasian equilibrium concerning prices and quantities.

Remember that the direct effects of the project would appear as an increase in transport capacity rather than a reduction in travel time. Thus the model must consider capacity as a part of transaction costs when predicting inter-regional trade. Since transport costs work, in effect, as discriminating tariffs among regions, the reduction in transaction costs would certainly promote trade among regions depending on the comparative advantage. In this connection, the impacts corresponding to *trade gains* could be the most important ones in developing economies.

Our model is derived from the national input–output table based on producer prices, and we maintain these prices on average at the national level. Regional prices are determined endogenously so as to clear the inter-regional trade. Although prices under the planned economy would be determined by governmental initiatives, we calculate them here as a type of surrogate price. One way to justify this might be that it could be appropriate to evaluate the benefits in terms of fair market values rather than artificial prices when some foreign assistance is used to finance the project. Moreover, prices in the Chinese market have been liberalized increasingly since the early 1980s, and a free market now prevails in many sectors.

In the following, we consider railways to be the sole means of inter-regional transportation. Clearly, both water and road transportation carry an increasing share of domestic freight, but railways carried 44.9 per cent of the total traffic volume measured in ton-kilometres in the base year of our study (1985), followed by shipping at 41.9 per cent. When considering the fact that railways serve all the provinces apart from Tibet, and the share of trucks is still limited to somewhere around 10 per cent, railways could be the most important mode of long distance transportation.

NON-SURVEY ESTIMATION OF PROVINCIAL TABLES

The industrial sectors are classified into seven categories. These are agriculture, manufacturing, energy and resources, construction, transport and communication and commerce, plus services, which are referred to as Sectors 1 to 7, respectively. Figure 23.1 summarizes the notational composition of regional input–output tables. They are generated for each of the twenty-nine provinces from the national tables shown as the darkly-shaded panel at the back of the figure.

Figure 23.1 Composition of a national input–output table and its regional distribution

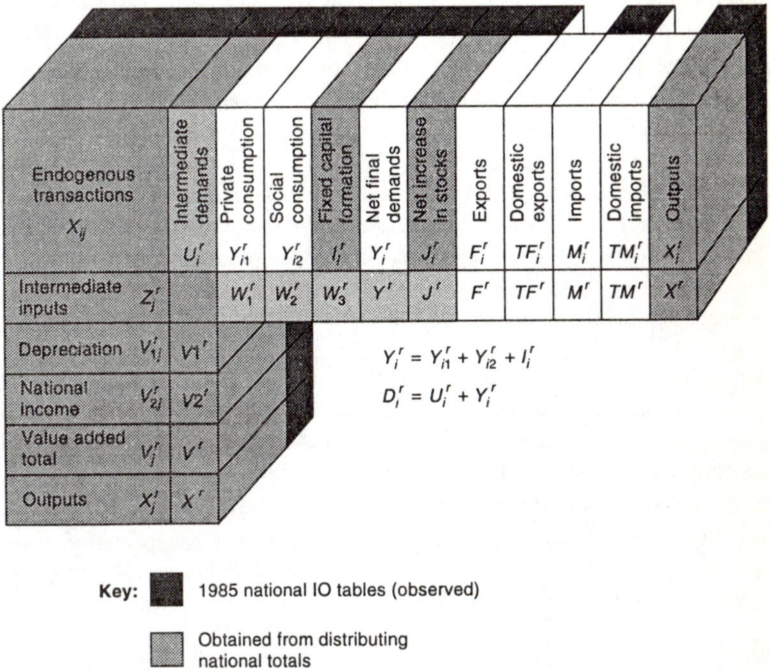

Regional exports and imports

Suppose that the regional output X_i^r (demand D_i^s) can be expressed by the potential based on the demands D_i^s (outputs X_i^r) in all the regions along with the relevant time distances d^{rs}, capacities CP^{rs} and relative prices p_i^s/p_i^r. Then we can assume the following relations when parameters α_{ik} are properly determined through an iterative process:

$$X_i^r = \alpha_{i0} \sum_s D_i^s (d^{rs})^{-\alpha_{i1}} (CP^{rs})^{\alpha_{i2}} (p_i^s/p_i^r)^{\alpha_{i3}} \tag{23.1}$$

$$D_i^s = \alpha_{i0} \sum_r X_i^r (d^{rs})^{-\alpha_{i1}} (CP^{rs})^{\alpha_{i2}} (p_i^s/p_i^r)^{\alpha_{i3}} \tag{23.2}$$

The inter-regional capacities are not as straightforward as the time distances, but it is possible to estimate them from the link capacities by applying a cut-flow algorithm to the network (Ando and Shibata, 1992). We shall return later to the procedure to calculate regional prices.

The quantities of provincial exports and imports are estimated from the national ones, F_i and M_i, given exogenously. Using the same parameters as above, distributions are made in accordance with a potential based on the freight handlings P^p at each of ten major ports p, along with the time distances and capacities to reach these:

$$F_i^r = \frac{\sum_p (X_i^r P^p)^{\beta_{Fi}} (d^{rp})^{-\alpha_{i1}} (CP^{rp})^{\alpha_{i2}}}{\sum_r \sum_p (X_i^r P^p)^{\beta_{Fi}} (d^{rp})^{-\alpha_{i1}} (CP^{rp})^{\alpha_{i2}}} F_i \tag{23.3}$$

$$M_i^r = \frac{\sum_p (D_i^r P^p)^{\beta_{Mi}} (d^{pr})^{-\alpha_{i1}} (CP^{pr})^{\alpha_{i2}}}{\sum_r \sum_p (D_i^r P^p)^{\beta_{Mi}} (d^{pr})^{-\alpha_{i1}} (CP^{pr})^{\alpha_{i2}}} M_i \tag{23.4}$$

where β_{Fi} and β_{Mi} are the parameters to be determined iteratively.

It must be noted that these expressions are applicable only to Sectors 1 to 3, since exports and imports in the transport and commercial sectors would be determined in accordance with those of *material products*. Trade, both domestic and international, in the construction sector is zero by definition.

Domestic exports and imports

As domestic trade will be cancelled out when summed up at the national level, the inter-regional trade T_i^{rs} cannot be obtained from distributing the national amounts. Instead, we employ a gravity-type model to estimate these, based on price differentials among regions reflecting generalized transport costs t_i^{rs}, to be determined later:

$$T_i^{rs} = (X_i^r - F_i^r) \frac{D_i^s \exp \gamma_{Fi}(p_i^s - t_i^{rs} - p_i^r)}{\sum_s D_i^s \exp \gamma_{Fi}(p_i^s - t_i^{rs} - p_i^r)} \tag{23.5}$$

where γ_{Fi} is an unknown parameter.

The domestic exports TF_i^r and imports TM_i^s are calculated by summing up the inter-regional trade around each province:

$$TF_i^r = \sum_{s \neq r} T_i^{rs} \quad \text{and} \quad TM_i^s = \sum_{r \neq s} T_i^{rs} \tag{23.6}$$

It must be noted that the values obtained above are not necessarily consistent with the regional input–output table. Therefore, they must be adjusted to satisfy the following relationship concerning the total regional imbalance:

$$TF^r - TM^r = V1^r + V2^r - Y^r - J^r - F^r + M^r \qquad (23.7)$$

The revised values of TF^r and TM^r are distributed proportionally over the commodities. Since this will alter the row and column sums of the inter-regional trade matrix for each commodity, T_i^{rs} is modified to meet these new sums, using Fratar's method.

Net final demand and value added

The net final demand, Y_i^r, is defined as the final demand to fulfil local needs. Three items, private and social consumption, and fixed capital formation, fall into this category. While the balancing items, including exports, imports and net increase in stocks are to be determined on a commodity basis, each net final demand item would have a stable composition of commodities. Thus the first approximation to the commodity composition of a regional net final demand item can be obtained as a product of its column sum, W_j^r, and the national final demand coefficients, c_{ij}:

$$Y_i^r = \sum_j c_{ij} W_j^r \qquad (23.8)$$

Once again, the value obtained above would violate the balance equation for the province:

$$Y_i^r = X_i^r - U_i^r - J_i^r - F_i^r + M_i^r - TF_i^r + TM_i^r \qquad (23.9)$$

So it becomes necessary to revise the final demand coefficient matrix for each region. This could be done through a three-dimensional extension of Fratar's method to determine Y_{ij}^r that satisfies the three constraining matrices comprising the left hand side of Equation (23.9), the regional final demand items, W_j^r, and the national final demands, Y_{ij}, by commodities and items. Once convergence is reached, the regional coefficients, c_{ij}^r, can easily be calculated.

A similar argument applies to the calculation of regional value added, V_{ij}^r, by items and sectors, where i represents either the capital depreciation or the provincial revenue. One of the constraining matrices in this case is defined by the regional values added by sectors, which are derived from the following relationship:

$$V_j^r = X_j^r - \sum_i a_{ij}^r X_j^r \qquad (23.10)$$

The rest of the constraints are provided by the regional value added items, $V1^r$ or $V2^r$, and the national value added, V_{ij}, by items and sectors.

Price indices and deflators

Suppose the initial values of regional price indices, p_i^r, by commodities and the deflators, w_j^r, for value added in respective sectors, are given. When we denote nominal values by asterisks, the price system in real terms can be written using nominal variables and price indices.

$$\frac{X_j^{r*}}{p_j^r} = \sum_i \frac{x_{ij}^{r*}}{p_i^r} + \frac{V_j^{r*}}{w_j^r} \qquad (23.11)$$

Considering that $x_{ij}^{r*} = <a_{ij}^{r*} X_j^{r*} = (p_i^r/p_j^r) a_{ij} X_j^{r*}$, this can be rewritten as follows:

$$\frac{1}{p_j^r}(X_j^{r*} - \sum_i a_{ij} X_j^{r*}) = \frac{V_j^{r*}}{w_j^r} \qquad (23.12)$$

We here assume that the technological coefficients in real terms hold constant throughout the country, although they may differ in nominal terms. Moreover, from the arithmetic conditions that the weighted average of regional price indices must be unity at the national level, we must have:

$$X_i = \sum_r \frac{X_i^{r*}}{p_i^r} \qquad (23.13)$$

The deflators, w_j^r, are obtained by dividing the nominal value added, V_j^{r*}, found in the statistics by the results from Equation (23.10). Accordingly, the initial values of price indices are to be chosen so as to satisfy Equations (23.12) and (23.13).

Network price equilibrium

The regional price indices would be linked closely with those in other regions through the transport network. For example, when p_i^r denotes the f.o.b. price of the ith commodity, its c.i.f. price in region s will be given by adding the generalized transport cost, t_i^{rs}, between the two regions, which is assumed to take the following form:

$$t_i^{rs} = \lambda_i (d^{rs})^{\alpha_{i1}} (CP^{rs})^{-\alpha_{i2}} \qquad (23.14)$$

where λ_i is a constant to be determined iteratively. Suppose that the local price of a commodity is determined as the weighted average of the c.i.f. prices of inflows of that commodity. Then we have the following relationship in the network price consistency:

$$p_i^r \sum_s T_i^{sr} = p_i^r T_i^{rr} + \sum_{s \neq r} (p_i^s + t_i^{sr}) T_i^{sr} \qquad (23.15)$$

Here, the inter-regional trade, T_i^{rs}, is determined by Equation (23.5), based on the price indices. In return, those indices must be modified in accordance with Equations (23.13) and (23.15) in the presence of inter-regional trade.

Note that we have total of 30 × 7 of these equations, while the number of unknowns is 29 × 7 price indices, p_i^r, along with seven constant terms, λ_i, in Equation (23.14). Thus the system is essentially solvable, but it can only be solved iteratively. It must be noted that the newly-obtained price indices, p_i^r, do not necessarily satisfy Equation (23.12) for the fixed technological coefficients, a_{ij}, in real terms. In other words, it is necessary to assume a different set of coefficients, a_{ij}^r, for each region for p_i^r to satisfy Equation (23.12).

$$\frac{1}{p_j^r} (X_j^{r*} - \sum_i a_{ij}^r X_j^{r*}) = \frac{V_j^{r*}}{w_j^r} \qquad (23.12')$$

While there are forty-nine coefficients to be modified, we only have seven Equation (23.12′) for each region. Thus we employ the RAS method, where only the column multipliers, s_i^r, are modified. The procedure is summarised in Figure 23.2, and will be repeated until the price indices, p_i^r, reach the convergence.

EMPIRICAL RESULTS

Model performance

The major outcome of our model includes provincial input–output tables as well as inter-regional trade. When we recall that the main

Figure 23.2 The procedure to estimate regional tables and inter-regional trade

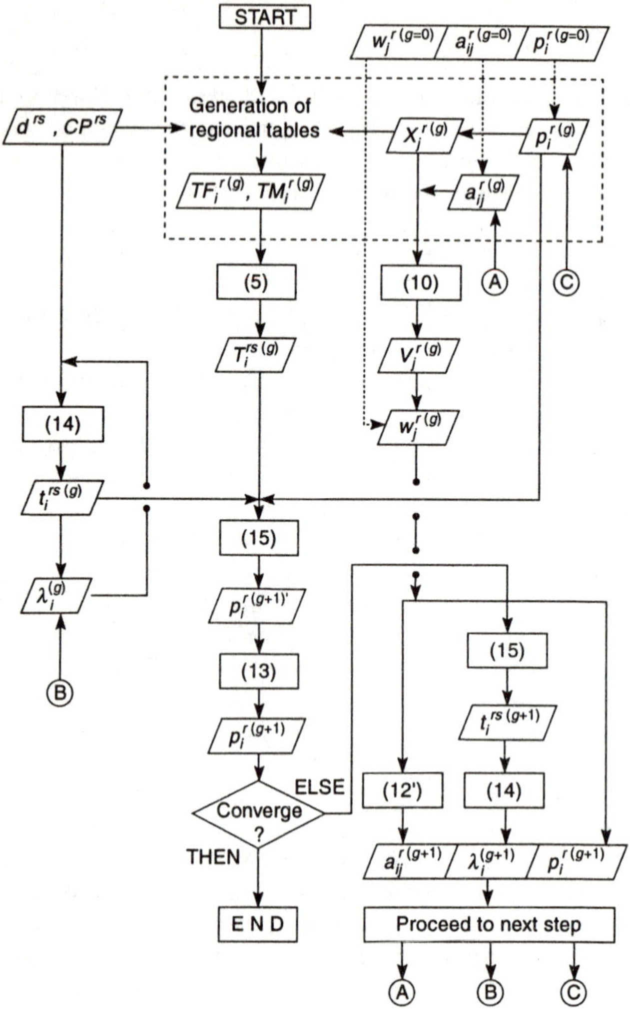

purpose of this chapter is to demonstrate a way of conducting multiregional analyses from a limited set of regional statistics, assessment of model performance would naturally be uneasy because of the difficulty of accessing certain extra data. For example, the only provincial input–output table available in early 1994 was the Beijing table for

Table 23.1 Correlation coefficients between Beijing tables estimated for 1985 and compiled for 1987

Intermediate demands *U*	*Private consumption* *Y1*	*Social consumption* *Y2*	*Fixed capital formation* *I*	*Net increase in stocks* *J*
0.9819	0.4748	0.9965	0.5502	0.9718

Exports *F*	*Domestic exports* *TF*	*Imports* *M*	*Domestic Imports* *TM*	*Outputs* *X*
0.9930	0.9958	0.9965	0.2170	0.9992

1987, despite the fact that the provincial tables for all the twenty-nine provinces are said to have been compiled for that year.

The observed Beijing table and the ones generated above differ in their base years, but at least the former may be utilized to examine the performance of our procedure. However, the difference in the base years would make a direct comparison of the two Beijing tables, the observed and generated ones, meaningless. Besides, they are conceptually different in the sense that the latter are compiled in *real* terms using national average prices, while the former is based on local prices. Thus we here compare the commodity composition of final demand items and output by means of correlation coefficients, and the results are summarized in Table 23.1.

The correlation coefficients for the items related to international and inter-regional trade are calculated for the six sectors, excluding construction, whose trade is definitionally zero. While the export, *F*, domestic export, *TF*, and the import, *M*, demonstrate satisfactory results, the correlation for the domestic import, *TM*, seems to command some refinement. However, it must be noted that these results are derived from using virtually no direct information on inter-regional trade. Thus our projections might possibly be improved when such information becomes available. Moreover, except for the problem associated with the projection of private consumption, *Y*1, correlations with other items are not particularly low when we consider the two-year difference in base years and the rapid changes the Chinese economy is experiencing.

Figure 23.3 Aggregated railway network and the virtual project examined

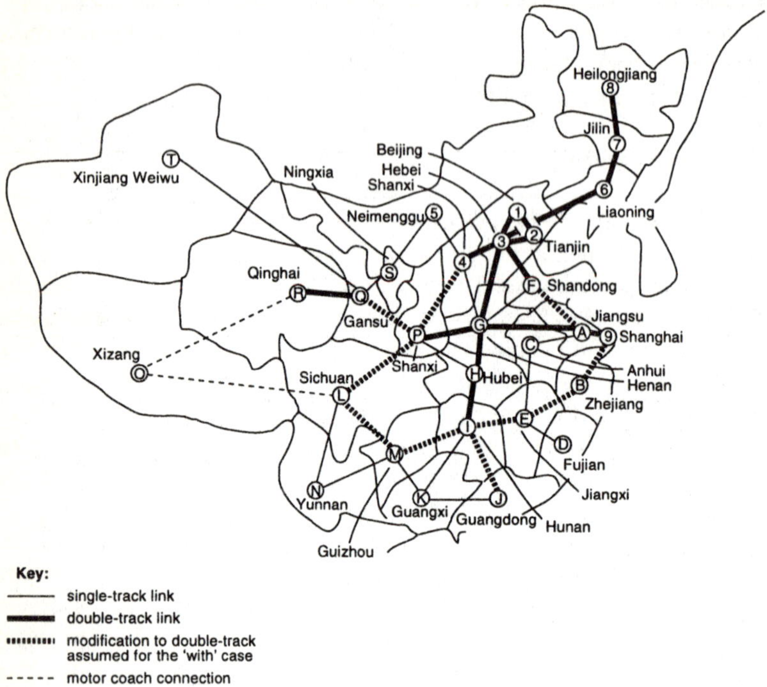

The railway network

Here railways are regarded as the sole mode of transportation for freight. The railway network originally considered in our study contains 132 nodes and 167 links. However, this original network is beyond our computational capacity when conducting the cut-flow calculations to assess inter-regional capacities. Thus we here aggregate the network by replacing the links across each provincial border by a virtual link with the combined capacity. This simplified network shown in Figure 23.3 has twenty-nine nodes corresponding to the provincial capitals, and forty-two links connecting them; the codes assigned to provinces are also shown for later reference.

In Figure 23.3, links are classified as double tracks if at least one of the original links, before aggregation, has double tracks. The effects of transport improvement on regional economies, including inter-regional trade flows and regional price indices, will be discussed later in this section. For that purpose, we establish a virtual project to modify some of the single-track links into double tracks. Links subject to modification in the project are shown by thick dotted lines in the figure. These links have been chosen by examining the ratios of the calculated link flows to the link capacities (see Shibata (1992) ch. 5.)

The basic results

Before proceeding to the evaluation of the transport improvement project, it may be worthwhile to summarize the basic results corresponding to the *without project* case. The prominent interregional flows are shown for the three material sectors on the left half of Figure 23.4. The major flows of agricultural products originate in the rice crop areas in the Central, South and Southwest areas (Huazhong, Huanan and Sichuan), and delivered to the densely-populated Shanghai metropolis as well as to the industrialized Liaoning Province. Other major cities, Beijing and Tianjin, also collect agricultural products from many parts of the country though these are not shown in the figure.

In return, manufactured products are mainly supplied from the Shanghai area, including Jiangsu Province. The shipments cover the nation widely, reaching as far as Xinjiang-Weiwu to the west and Heilongjiang to the north. The major flows of energy and resource products flow from Heilongjiang and Liaoning to several southern provinces, particularly Shanghai and its vicinity. Apparently the north-east is known to be rich in oil and coal, and this area includes a major industrial and consumer agglomeration.

Principal components are calculated from the price indices estimated for seven commodities. Figure 23.5 plots the provincial scores concerning the first two components. The weights attached to the figure indicate that the first axis may be interpreted as the overall price level. The second component will be large where energy is expensive, while construction and commercial services are relatively cheap. The far western provinces generally exhibit high price levels that may reflect the high transport costs, and similar results emerge in urbanized areas including the three metropolitan areas and Guangdong. The second component scores, which represent price discrepancies from the national average, are low in the energy-producing north-east and somewhat high in the southern provinces.

Finally Figure 23.6 shows the principal component scores based on a variety of economic indicators, including output, net final demand,

Figure 23.4 Inter-regional trade flows estimated for the cases without and with project

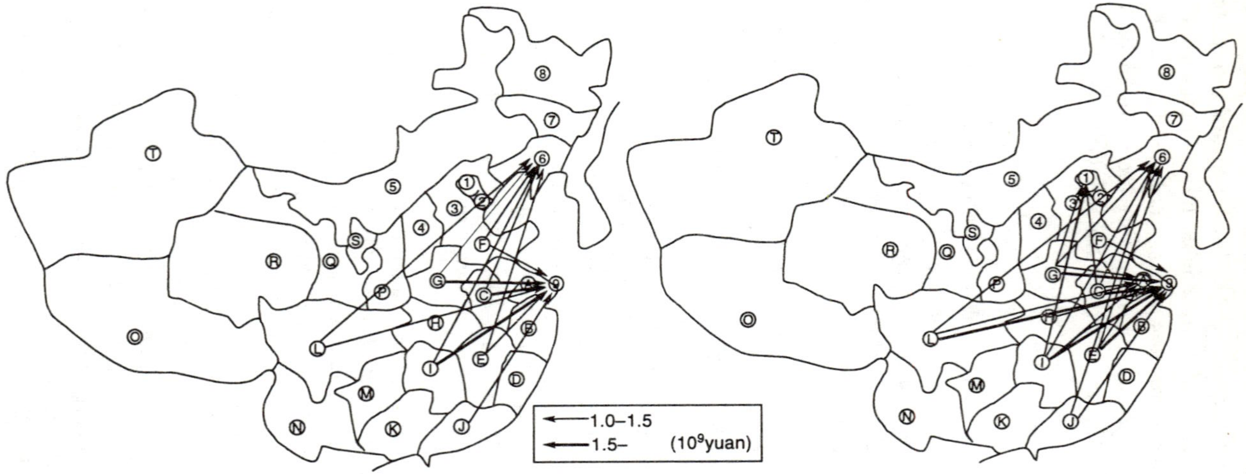

Without (a) Agriculture With

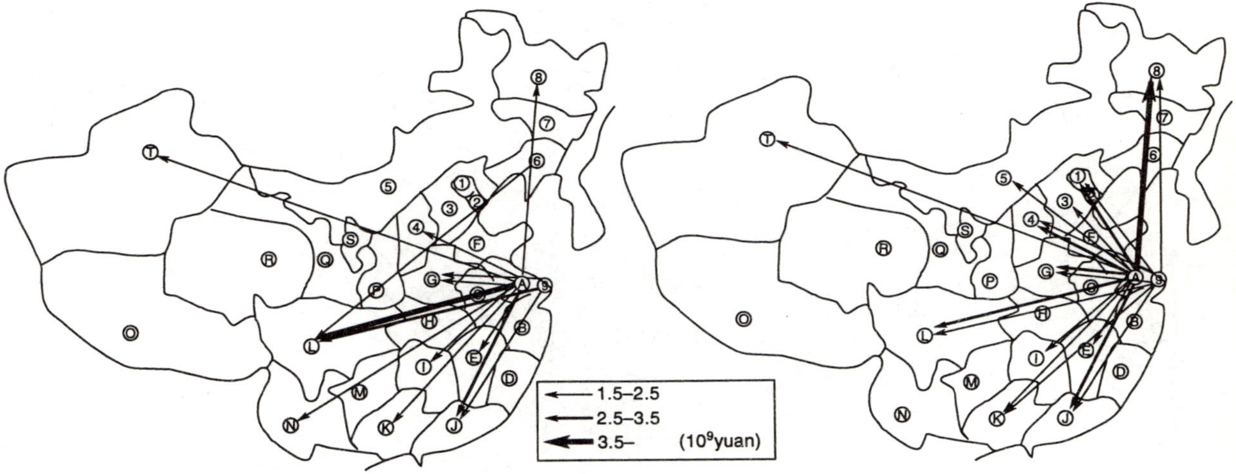

Without | With

(b) Manufacturing

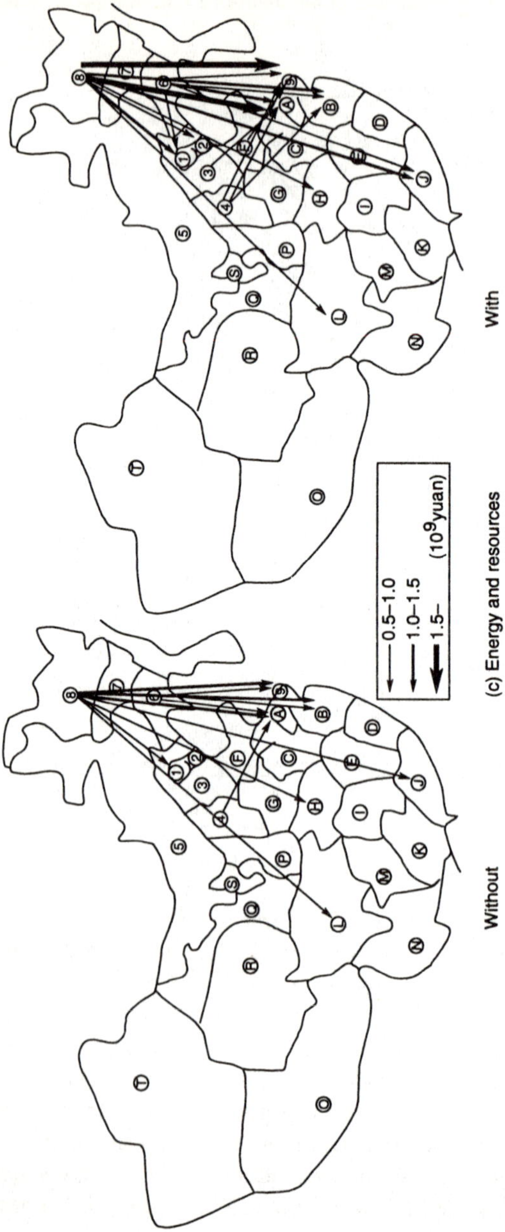

(c) Energy and resources

Figure 23.5 Principal components of regional price indices

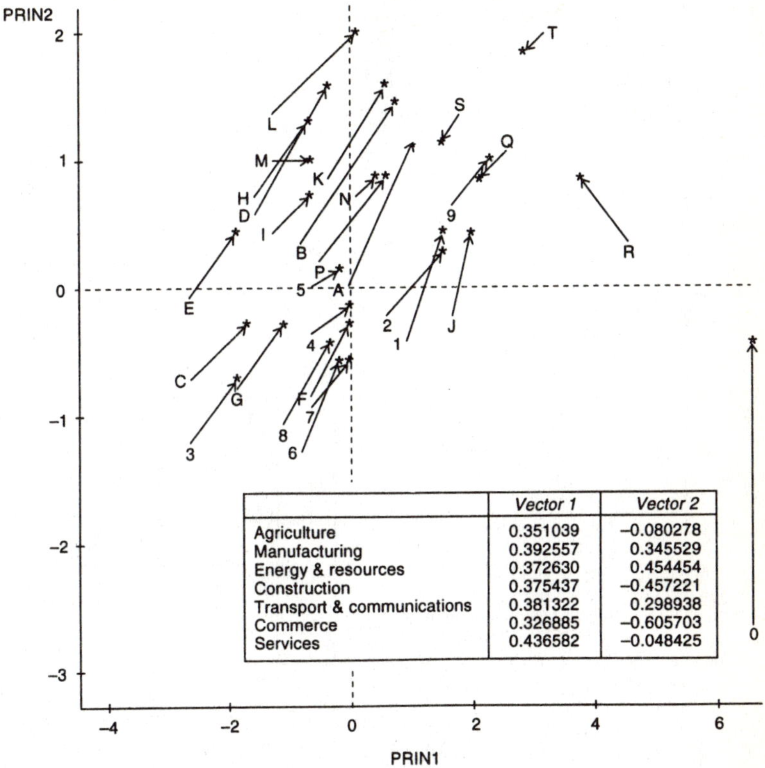

	Vector 1	Vector 2
Agriculture	0.351039	−0.080278
Manufacturing	0.392557	0.345529
Energy & resources	0.372630	0.454454
Construction	0.375437	−0.457221
Transport & communications	0.381322	0.298938
Commerce	0.326885	−0.605703
Services	0.436582	−0.048425

value added and population. The first axis indicates the general level of economic activities, and the second component will be large where external trade is active relative to the size of population. Accordingly, the coastal provinces and those along the Yangtze river are found to be more active in terms of their economies than the peripheral provinces. Meanwhile, the north-east as well as the cities of Beijing and Tianjin is found to be active in terms of external trade. When we recall that these results are based on the regional input-output tables derived through a non-survey procedure, we might safely say that they are fairly reasonable in view of our general notion of Chinese regional economies.

Figure 23.6 Principal components of economic indicators

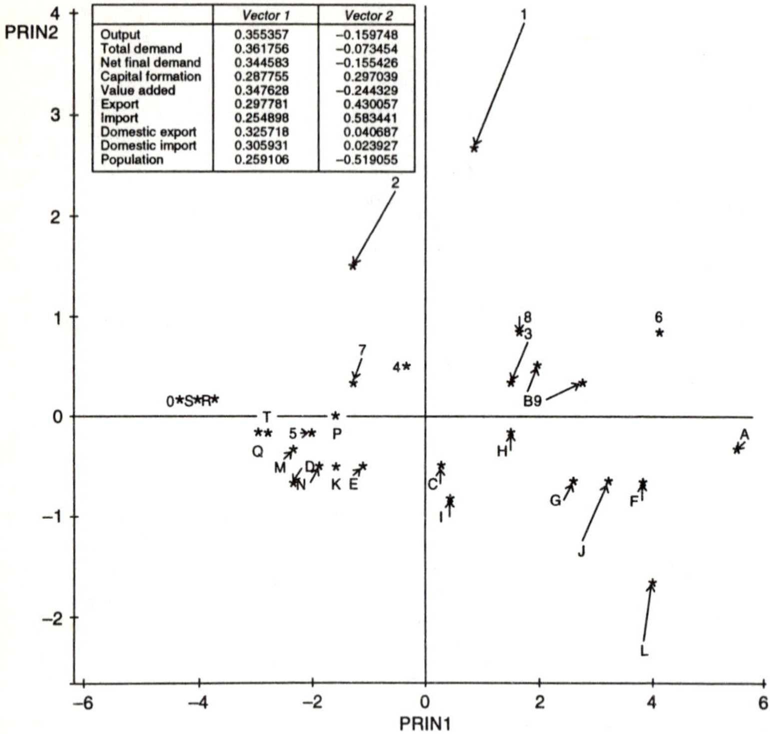

	Vector 1	Vector 2
Output	0.355357	−0.159748
Total demand	0.361756	−0.073454
Net final demand	0.344583	−0.155426
Capital formation	0.287755	0.297039
Value added	0.347628	−0.244329
Export	0.297781	0.430057
Import	0.254898	0.583441
Domestic export	0.325718	0.040687
Domestic import	0.305931	0.023927
Population	0.259106	−0.519055

The effects of transport improvement

Now we turn to the effects of the transport improvement project as described above, which is designed to enhance transportation along the circular corridor in eastern China. The prominent commodity flows corresponding to the *with-project* case are shown on the right half of Figure 23.4. They are essentially similar to the *without* case, but an increase in long-distance flows from the southern provinces to Beijing and Liaoning is observed concerning agricultural products. Jiangsu Province will benefit most from the project, as the major supplier of manufactured products, and the gross amount of flows will be increased in the case of energy and resource products with almost the same pattern of trade being maintained.

Figures 23.5 and 23.6 overlay the principal component scores calculated for the new indices or indicators corresponding to the with case on those of the without case while keeping the weights obtained from the latter. It must be noted that the transport improvement is expected to lead to an overall decrease in price discrepancies among regions, and Figure 23.5 suggests that such results are likely in the western provinces, particularly in Tibet. However, the provinces located in the left half of the figure, where prices are generally low, tend to move north-easterly even extending beyond both axes. This implies that the price increase caused by demand increase would wholly cancel out the reduction in transport costs, provided that the suppliers' conditions remain constant in the course of the project. This might be the case with energy products, and the expansion of market sizes would naturally cut down commercial margins.

As for economic activities, not much horizontal movement is expected from the project. While Shanghai and Guangdong seem to benefit most from the project to enhance their positions in the national economy, the remaining provinces are not affected much in this respect. On the other hand, the relative positions in terms of foreign trade will be enhanced in Zhejian, Guangdong and Sichuan along the circular corridor, and this in return lessens the positions enjoyed by Beijing, Tianjin and surrounding Hebei. The proposed project will extend the opportunity to engage in foreign trade from a few developed provinces to other parts of the country.

CONCLUDING REMARKS

In this chapter we have proposed a multi-regional model that can be used to evaluate the impact of transport projects on regional economies. The principal part of the model is devoted to the generation of regional input–output tables from the national table. The advantage of our model is that it can produce rich regional information while requiring only a limited set of regional statistics. With the model, we can estimate the inter-regional trade and the price indices corresponding to the network equilibrium.

The model was applied to China and its twenty-nine provinces for the year 1985. Although it is not generally possible to examine the accuracy of our model because of data limitations, a comparison with the Beijing table observed for 1987 might validate our procedure. A virtual project of improving railway facilities is introduced to examine the sensitivity of our model. The standard case without the project is compared against that with the project. The results are reasonable in the sense that transport improvement will promote both domestic and external trade, but price differentials among regions will not be reduced as expected.

This may be related to the profile of the present model that the size of the national economy is fixed despite the project, with relocation of industries and population being excluded. Thus the *with* case essentially affects only the regional distribution of economic activities within the country, and our results might underestimate the impacts of the projects. Although the goal of our study is to build a multi-regional CGE model on developing economies, the present model is confined to a sphere of producible commodities and services. Therefore it will be necessary to incorporate the factor market as well as a mechanism to explain the expansion of economies caused by projects.

Note

The authors would like to thank Mr Yasuhiro Nagao for his assistance in computational work.

References

Amano, K. and M. Fujita (1970) 'A long-run economic effect analysis of alternative transportation facility plan; regional and national', *Journal of Regional Science*, vol. 10, pp. 297–323.

Ando, A. and T. Shibata (1992) 'Estimating interregional trade in China for transport project evaluation on the regional I-O framework and railroad network capacities', *Selected Proceedings of 6th WCTR*, vol. 3, pp. 2311–22.

Dervis, K., J. de Melo and S. Robinson (1982) *General Equilibrium Models for Development Policy* (Washington, D.C.: World Bank).

Scarf, H. E. and J. B. Shoven (1984) *Applied General Equilibrium Analysis* (Cambridge University Press).

Shibata, T. (1992) *Development of a Project-evaluation System for Improving the Transport Infrastructures through Multi-regional Model Incorporating Price Differentials*, Ph.D. thesis, Kumamoto University, Japan.

24 Incorporating a Disaggregate Model for Trip Generation, Trip Distribution and Mode Choice

Ryosuke Ando, Shogo Kawakami and Naojiro Aoshima

INTRODUCTION

A major innovation in the analysis of transportation demand since the mid-1970s is the development of disaggregate travel demand models based on discrete choice analysis. In the modelling of travel demand, disaggregate models allow us to introduce an individual's attributes that influence travel behaviour, and to make more efficient use of the available individual data.

On the other hand, to guarantee the consistency in the choices of travel, conventional methods, which generally include four stages – trip generation, trip distribution, mode choice and trip assignment, have been partially replaced by combined models (for example, Evans (1976), Florian and Nguyen (1978), and Safwat and Magnanti (1988)). The combined model combines at least two of the four stages listed above. Among the combined models, most are based on the network equilibrium problem. On the other hand, a disaggregate model system (MTC model) was developed by Ruiter and Ben-Akiva (1978). However, the MTC model system cannot completely consider inter-relationships between trips. In general, a travel demand model is concerned with those households and individual decisions that result in trips being made. However, some other choices are so strongly interrelated with the trip-making behaviour that it is impossible to separate them.

To remove the interrelationship, Adler and Ben-Akiva (1979), Kondo and Kitamura (1987), and Kitamura (1988) proposed the treatment of

Figure 24.1 Typical tour patterns

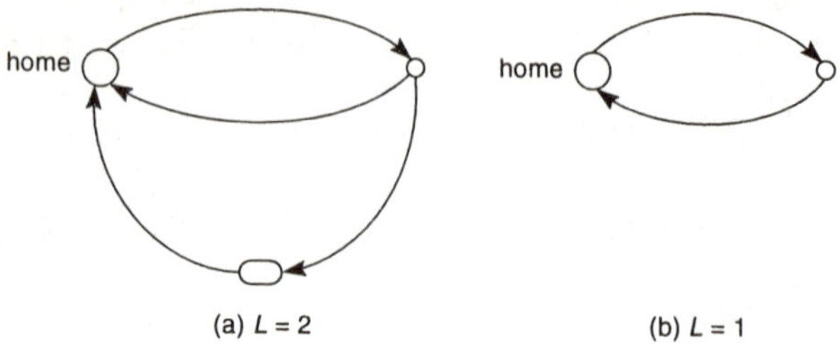

interdependent choices in a trip chain. Kawakami *et al.* (1989) first defined a tour as a chain of trips which starts from the traveller's home and end back at his/her home, and therefore proposed a disaggregate model that considered the inter-relations among trips in a tour. Figure 24.1 depicts the concept of the tour where $L + 1$ is the possible number of trips in a tour (L may also be thought of as the possible number of the non-base destinations in a tour). The model dealt with trip generation, trip distribution and mode choice for travel demand analysis. The model was further extended to workers' travel demand analysis (Kawakami and Su, 1991) by redefining a tour as a chain of $L + 1$ trips between two bases, where a base was redefined as the traveller's home or workplace.

In the previous studies (Kawakami *et al.* (1989) and Kawakami & Su (1991), people were divided into two groups of individuals: non-workers and workers. Further, the nested logit model (see Williams (1977) and Ben-Akiva and Lerman (1985) was used to express interdependencies among trip generation, trip distribution, mode choice and trip chain. The analysis of non-workers' travel presents much greater difficulties than does the analysis of workers' travel. Non-worker travellers typically can choose their trip frequencies, trip destinations and whether to combine trips into chains. Thus, in this study, the non-workers' model is taken as an example simply to introduce the discussion, so in the following discussion, 'the model' means the model for non-workers. In the model, a tour is defined as consisting of all trips of one cycle from home back to home. Then in terms of the maximum utility theory, the assumption was made that a traveler maximizes travel utility by each trip in a tour, conditional on the trips that have been made in the past and by considering a trip chain returning to his/her base, which consists of L trips (refer to Figure 24.1) at most. It is characteristic of the model system to incorporate all the trips during one day to measure tour utility maximization. Further, the traveller was considered not to change the mode in one tour.

In the study by Kawakami *et al.* (1989), it was stated that L may be set arbitrarily. However, it is debatable whether this hypothesis is correct, since the discussion was based only on 1981 data. Thus, in this study, a model is constructed by setting $L = 1$, that is, a tour is assumed to be a two-trips tour as shown in Figure 24.1(b). By investigating the temporal transferability of the estimated model, the effect of trip-chaining on the model development is shown, and finally a satisfactory model is given. In the model, the ideas from activity-based analysis are combined with the concept of a tour. Consequently, the combined model has an advantage that the previous studies did not have. That is, it not only reflects the effect of trips having been made, but it also incorporates the trips that the trip-maker will have in the tour. Further, it treats the effect of trip-chaining in the same model, combining the first three steps of the four-step process.

CALIBRATION OF THE MODEL BASED ON THE 1971 DATA

The data used to develop the model was taken from existing sources. The 1971 and 1981 person trip surveys which were carried out in Nagoya, Japan, are the most recent complete travel databases. The data on non-workers travelling by means of private car or public transportation system were extracted from these data sources.

Now let us set $L = 1$, since it was stated that L can be set as any integer (Kawakami *et al.*, 1989). In 1971 data, the non-workers were about four-tenths of the total samples. It was known that the number of non-worker trip-makers was 13 941, and 2741 non-workers took no trip. It was also understood that about 87.5 per cent of all trip-makers only performed 'piston trips (one destination trips starting from home to somewhere then directly returning home)'. If we consider all persons who did 'piston trips', the percentage will become 89.2 per cent.

Since it is too complicated to estimate a nested model with multi-stages simultaneously, the model system in this study is estimated sequentially. The interdependencies across choices are accounted for and the sequential approach is equivalent to the simultaneous approach. The advantage of the sequential approach is not only that it simplifies the problem but also allows us to check the model system at each stage by using statistical indexes.

In a nested model, if a lower-level choice is modelled by a random utility model, then an appropriate composite variable defined over these choice alternatives is the expected maximum utility for this choice process. If the outcome of this choice were known, then the composite variable would be taken as the utility of the chosen alternatives. For the logit model, this is equal to the natural logarithm of the denominator of the model. In addition, to satisfy the utility maximization theory, the coefficient of this explanatory variable (logsum) should be in the set (0, 1), that is, between 0 and 1.

Estimation of the nested model starts from the lowest level choice model. When the estimation was made by following the nested logit model with the order of trip generation choice, destination choice and travel mode choice, respective to the tour pattern shown in Figure 24.1(b), it was found that the logsum variable had a parameter that did not lie between 0 and 1. That implies the model system does not support the utility maximization theory based on the 1971 data.

Consequently the estimation was made by following the nested logit models illustrated in Figure 24.2, which exchanges the order of the trip destination choice and the travel modal choice. Thus, if denoting the levels in Figure 24.2 as g, m and d respectively; further let u_i^* be the maximum value of the composite utility of the node i, $\bar{u}_i$ be the common component of utility of the alternative i, and $P_i(\beta_i)$ is the probability of choosing i, which is with the parameters β_i. We can then write:

$$P_g(\beta_g) = \frac{\exp[\beta_g(\bar{u}_g + u_g^*)]}{\sum_g \exp[\beta_g(\bar{u}_g + u_g^*)]} \tag{24.1}$$

$$P_{m|g}(\beta_m) = \frac{\exp[\beta_m(\bar{u}_{gm} + u_{gm}^*)]}{\sum_m \exp[\beta_m(\bar{u}_{gm} + u_{gm}^*)]} \tag{24.2}$$

$$P_{d|gm}(\beta_d) = \frac{\exp[\beta_d(\bar{u}_{gmd})]}{\sum_d \exp[\beta_d(\bar{u}_{gmd})]} \tag{24.3}$$

where

$$u_{gm}^* = \frac{1}{\beta_d} \ln \sum_d \exp(\beta_d \bar{u}_{gmd}) \tag{24.4}$$

$$u_g^* = \frac{1}{\beta_m} \ln \sum_m \exp[\beta_m(\bar{u}_{gm} + u_{gm}^*)] \tag{24.5}$$

Figure 24.2 The nested logit model with L = 1

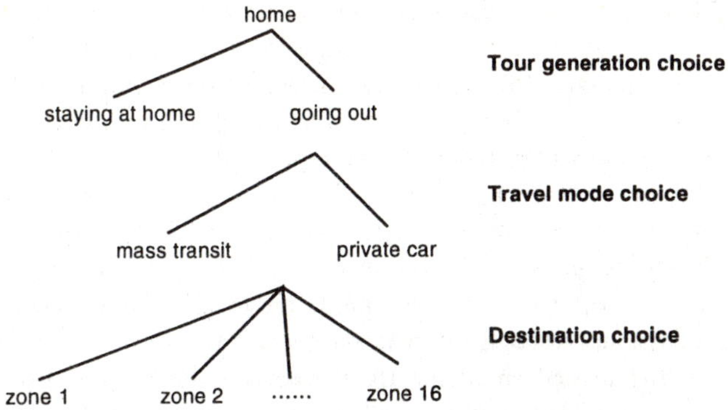

THE METHODOLOGY OF TRANSFERABILITY STUDIES

For a model system, the transferability can be defined at three levels:

(a) parameter level – transfer the model system without any change;
(b) variable level – transfer the model system with the re-estimation of all coefficients, based on the new data, for the old explanatory variables; and
(c) structure level – transfer the model system with the new estimation of all coefficients for the updated variable groups, without changing the structure of the travel decision-making tree.

Each of these criteria are discussed below (with reference to Koppelman and Wilmot (1982) and McCarthy (1982)).

Test of model parameter equality

The most common test used to determine equality is the *t*-test, with the null hypothesis that the parameters estimated in the old and new contexts are the same. Given an equation:

$$t_i = (\theta_{Ai} - \theta_{Bi})/\sqrt{var(\theta_{Ai}) + var(\theta_{Bi})} \tag{24.6}$$

where *A* and *B* denote the new and old context, respectively, θ_i means the *i*th parameter, and *var* denotes the variation of the parameter.

Disaggregate measures of transferability

By denoting:

$L_A(\theta_B)$ = the logarithm of the likelihood that the observed data in the application context A were generated by the transferred model estimated in context B

$L_A(MS_A)$ = the logarithm of the likelihood for a market share model, in which only alternative-specific constants are taken as the explanatory variable

$L_A(\theta_A)$ = the logarithm of the likelihood for a model estimated in the application context A

$L_A{}^*$ = the logarithm of the likelihood of a perfect model, which is equal to zero

the following measures can be defined:

(a) *Transferability Test Statistic (TTS)*

$$TTS_A(\theta_B) = -2[L_A(\theta_B) - L_A(\theta_A)] \tag{24.7}$$

This statistic is chi-square distributed with a degree of freedom equal to the number of model parameters, and it can be used to test the equality of the entire set model parameters or a subset of model parameters (Theil, 1971).

(b) *Transfer Index (TI)*

$$TI_A(\theta_B) = [L_A(\theta_B) - L_A(MS_A)]/[L_A(\theta_A) - L_A(MS_A)] \tag{24.8}$$

We use $TI_A(\theta_B)$ here to measure the predictive accuracy of the transferred model relative to a base or reference model (the market shares model). It will have an upper limit when the transferred model is as accurate as the base, but will have no lower limit. Negative values imply the transferred model is less than the base.

(c) *Transfer rho-square*

$$\begin{aligned}\rho_A^2(\theta_B) &= [L_A(\theta_B) - L_A(MS_A)]/[L_A{}^* - L_A(MS_A)] \\ &= 1 - L_A(\theta_B)/L_A(MS_A) \end{aligned} \tag{24.9}$$

This describes the degree to which the logarithm of likelihood of the transferred models exceeds that of the base model relative to the degree of improvement in logarithm of likelihood achieved with a perfect (predict all choice correctly) local model.

In summary, it can be said that $\rho_A^2(\theta_B)$ gives an absolute measure, that $TI_A(\theta_B)$ offers a relative measure; and that $TTS_A(\theta_B)$ provides a statistical test measure. Further, these measures can be also used for partial transfer (a model with some transferred parameters and some locally estimated parameters). In such a case, the logarithm of likelihood should always lie between $L_A(\theta_B)$ and $L_A(\theta_A)$.

Aggregate measures of transferability

As the planning process is primarily concerned with the prediction of aggregate rather than disaggregate travel flows, it is appropriate to consider transferability in terms of the accuracy of aggregate predictions. Especially for a model system without aggregate measures, it seems to be very difficult to make conclusions on the travel demand forecasting.

By denoting:

$$\text{REM}_{mg} = (\bar{N}_{mg} - N_{mg})/\bar{N}_{mg} \tag{24.10}$$

where

REM_{mg} = the relative error measure in prediction of alternative m from group g;

N_{mg} = the number of persons predicted to choose alternative m from group g; and

$\bar{N}_{mg}$ = the number of persons observed to choose alternative m from group other than g;

then the measures will be represented as follows:

(a)

$$\text{RMSE} = \Big(\sum_{m,g} \bar{N}_{mg}\text{REM}_{mg}^2 / \sum_{m,g} \bar{N}_{mg}\Big)^{1/2} \tag{24.11}$$

This weighted root mean square error measure is obtained by summarizing *REM* over alternatives and groups. Therefore it is an index of the average relative error in prediction weighted by the size of the prediction element and structured to place emphasis on large relative errors.

(b)

$$\text{RATE} = \text{RMSE}_A(\theta_B)/\text{RMSE}_A(\theta_A), \tag{24.12}$$

which is called the relative aggregate transfer error.

(c)

$$\text{APS} = \sum_{m,g} \bar{N}_{mg}\text{REM}^2_{mg} = \sum_{m,g} (\bar{N}_{mg} - N_{mg})^2/\bar{N}_{mg} \tag{24.13}$$

This, the aggregate prediction statistic, is defined to test the hypothesis that the observed frequencies of choice in each group are generated collectively by the prediction model. It is chi-square distributed under the assumption that the $\bar{N}_{mg}$ is predicted without sampling error, and the degree of freedom for full model transfer is (number of alternatives − 1)*(number of groups). However, it needs to be reduced to (number of alternatives − 1)*(number of groups − 1) when applied for local prediction or with locally adjusted alternative-specific constant.

As a summary, three measures are put forward from different perspectives: an absolute measure (RMSE), relative rate (RATE), and a statistical test value (APS).

As well as what has been described above, one additional criterion can be given. For a model system having been estimated, if the re-estimation by using the data of the application context cannot be achieved appropriately, the model system will be concluded, as not being transferable as a whole system.

ANALYSIS OF THE TEMPORAL TRANSFERABILITY

To test the temporal transferability, the non-workers' data about Nagoya from the person trip survey in 1981 was used to re-estimate the model system without recalibrating it. Among the trip-makers in 1981, the average number of trips during the day was 2.97, and the average number of tours was 1.35. Furthermore, the number of trips in a tour averaged 2.20. If the travel decisions were divided into two groups: home-based trips and non-home-based trips, then the mode choice for non-home-based trips can be assumed to be determined by the home-based trip mode choice, since the travellers, who accounted for 94.4 per cent of all tours, did not change their mode during a single tour.

Now the evaluating results for the temporal transferability are shown in Table 24.1, 24.2 and 24.3, which were obtained on the basis of the estimation and re-estimation results from 1971 and 1981 respectively.

Table 24.1 Evaluating results for the temporal transferability of the destination choice model

Variable	*Transit*			*Car*		
	$\theta_{71}-\theta_{81}$		*t-value*	$\theta_{71}-\theta_{81}$		*t-value*
Daytime population*	0.039		0.33	0.157		0.875
Travel time (min.)	–0.003		–0.7	0.015		1.8
$TTS_{81}(\theta_{71})$**		1.145			16.60	
$TI_{81}(\theta_{71})$		0.999			0.993	
$\rho_{81}^{2}(\theta_{71})$		0.147			0.366	
$RMSE_{81}(\theta_{71})$		0.197			0.234	
$RMSE_{81}(\theta_{71})$		0.203			0.213	
RATE		0.97			1.10	
$APS_{81}(\theta_{71})$***		61.8			62.0	

Notes: * = the logarithm of the actual number.
** = $\lambda^2_{0.50}(n = 2) = 1.386$, $\lambda^2_{0.001}(n = 2) = 13.815$.
*** = $\lambda^2_{0.001}(n = 15) = 37.697$.

First, let us examine the destination choice model (see Table 24.1). It can be seen that all *t*-values with respect to the differences of the two groups of parameters (taken from the 1971 data and the 1981 data respectively) have values that are less than 1.96. This indicates that there is no evidence of a real difference between the two parameters. With the values of TTS, an examination has to be made by separating the case of the public transportation system from the case of the private car. Since the value of 16.60 is obviously significant at the 0.1 per cent level, there seems to be considerable evidence of a substantial difference between the two values of the disaggregate measures obtained from the two different parameter groups in the case of the private car. The values of RATE (the relative error is 10 per cent) and APS ($62.0 > \chi^2_{0.001}(n = 15)$) also show that there is a real difference between the predicted number obtained by θ_{71} and that by θ_{81} in the case of the private car. Therefore it can be concluded that the model in the case of the private car is not transferable at the parameter level.

On the other hand, in the case of the public transportation system, the value of 1.145 is not significant even at the 50 per cent level, since it lies within the limit of 1.386. Hence, there is no evidence of a real difference between the observed and the predicted probabilities of choosing destinations. Although the value of APS (61.8) shows that there seems to be a real difference between the two predicted numbers (of persons) in the case of public transportation system, when we saw the value of RATE, it was found that RATE has the value of 0.97 in the case of public transport. It means that there is no real difference between the predicted number obtained by θ_{71} and that by θ_{81}, either. This conclusion differs from that drawn on the value of APS, suggesting that APS is sensitive to the sample size and that the sample was too large. Thus, it can be concluded that the model in the case of the public transportation system is transferable at the parameter level, while the model in the case of the private car is not transferable at the parameter level, but possibly at the variable level, since no explanatory variable is changed.

From Table 24.2, the *t*-values of the differences between the two groups of parameters, estimated from the 1971 data and the 1981 data respectively, apparently lie within the limit of 1.96. Hence it could be said that there is no evidence of a real difference between the two parameters for each pair of them. Since the values of TTS and APS are obviously significant at the 0.1 per cent level, there is considerable evidence of a real difference between the two values of the disaggregate measures and between the two predicted numbers of persons to choose a mode obtained from the two different parameter groups. Furthermore, RATE (= 67.0) shows that there is real difference between the predicted number of people to choose a mode obtained by θ_{71} and that obtained by θ_{81}, although TI (= 0.973) seems to indicate that there is almost no real difference between the predicted probability of choosing a mode by θ_{71} and that by θ_{81}. Thus, concerning this model in terms of the evaluating values, it can be concluded that the parameters cannot be transferred from 1971 to 1981 at the parameter level, but the model may be transferable at the variable level.

For the trip generation model, Table 24.3 shows that, excluding the pair of coefficients of logsum, the differences of any two parameters obtained from the 1971 data and the 1981 data respectively, have the *t*-values that are out of the set (−2.57, 2.57). That is, they are obviously significant at 0.1 per cent. Thus there is considerable evidence of a real difference between the 1971 and 1981 parameters. Moreover, since the value of TTS is obviously greater than 20.515, which is the limit of the confidence interval at the 0.1 per cent level, there is considerable evidence of a real difference between the two values of the disaggregate measures. Meanwhile, APS is also obviously greater than 10.827, the limit of the confidence interval at the 0.1 per cent level. There is considerable evidence of a real difference between the two predicted numbers of people choosing an alternative obtained from the two different parameter groups. Furthermore, the value of TI, 0.0806,

Table 24.2 Evaluating results for the temporal transferability of the mode choice model

Variable	$\theta_{71}-\theta_{81}$		*t-value*
logsum	−0.296		−1.47
car (*C*) constant dummy (*D*)	−5.18		−1.81
licence ownership *D* (specific to *C*)	0.233		1.31
$TTS_{81}(\theta_{71})$*		30.84	
$TI_{81}(\theta_{71})$		0.973	
$\rho_{81}{}^{2}(\theta_{71})$		0.297	
$RMSE_{81}(\theta_{71})$		0.067	
$RMSE_{81}(\theta_{71})$		0.001	
RATE		67.0	
$APS_{81}(\theta_{71})$**		12.3	

Notes: * $= \lambda^2_{0.001}(n = 3) = 16.266.$
** $= \lambda^2_{0.001}(n = 1) = 10.827.$

Table 24.3 Evaluating results for the temporal transferability of the trip generation model

Variable	$\theta_{71}-\theta_{81}$		*t-value*
logsum (specific to (S.T.) going out)	0.085		0.40
staying at home (*H*) constant	−4.78		−4.25
age 1 (≤ 34) dummy (*D*) (S.T.H.)	−1.25		−6.59
age 2 (35 ≤ age ≤ 49) D (S.T.H.)	−0.870		−4.07
housewife *D* (S.T.H.)	−0.621		−3.81
$TTS_{81}(\theta_{71})$*		385.7	
$TI_{81}(\theta_{71})$		0.0806	
$\rho_{81}{}^{2}(\theta_{71})$		0.007	
$RMSE_{81}(\theta_{71})$		0.096	
$RMSE_{81}(\theta_{71})$		0.0006	
RATE		160	
$APS_{81}(\theta_{71})$**		33.9	

Notes: * $= \lambda^2_{0.001}(n = 5) = 20.515.$
** $= \lambda^2_{0.001}(n = 1) = 10.827.$

and the value of RATE, 160, is so far from 1.0 that there is an almost conclusive difference between the predicted probability by θ_{71} and that by θ_{81}, and between the predicted number of people by θ_{71} and that by θ_{81}. In conclusion, this model is not transferable without re-estimating. This means that the model is not transferable at the parameter level, but it may be transferable at the variable level as the explanatory variables may not be changed at all.

In summary, the whole model system may be transferred from 1971 to 1981 at the variable level but it is not transferable at the parameter level.

EFFECT OF TRIP-CHAINING ON THE MODEL CALIBRATION

Why cannot the model be transferred at the parameter level? Is it because the L was set at a wrong value? To answer this question, statistics from the two years are summarized in Table 24.4.

As shown in Table 24.4, the situation in the case of mass transit was almost unchanged over the years. In the case of cars, the total number of tours became greater, while the percentages of tours consisting of less than 3 trips became fewer. However, the cumulative percentages changed very little. Thus, if we set L as 2 instead of 1, more than 92 per cent of tours for both modes will be covered in both 1971 and 1981 data.

Summarizing the above, to calibrate the model appropriately, L should be set as 2 based on the 1971 and 1981 data, and then the model becomes as shown in Figure 24.3 (refer to Figure 24.1(a)). Consequently, if we denote the levels by g, d, m, t and s from the highest to the lowest levels, and let u_i* be the maximum value of the composite utility of the node i, $\bar{u}_i$ be the common component of utility of the branch i, and $Pi(\beta i)$ is the probability of choosing i, which is with the parameters, βi. Then the formulations of the combined model are as the following:

$$P_g(\beta_g) = \frac{\exp[\beta_g(\bar{u}_g + u_g^*)]}{\sum_g \exp[\beta_g(\bar{u}_g + u_g^*)]} \tag{24.14}$$

$$P_{d|g}(\beta_d) = \frac{\exp[\beta_d(\bar{u}_{gd} + u_{gd}^*)]}{\sum_d \exp[\beta_d(\bar{u}_{gd} + u_{gd}^*)]} \tag{24.15}$$

$$P_{m|gd}(\beta_m) = \frac{\exp[\beta_m(\bar{u}_{gdm} + u_{gdm}^*)]}{\sum_m \exp[\beta_m(\bar{u}_{gdm} + u_{gdm}^*)]} \tag{24.16}$$

$$P_{t|gdm}(\beta_t) = \frac{\exp[\beta_t(\bar{u}_{gdmt} + u_{gdmt}^*)]}{\sum_t \exp[\beta_t(\bar{u}_{gdmt} + u_{gdmt}^*)]} \tag{24.17}$$

Table 24.4 Statistics on the number of tours for non-workers based on tour patterns in one day

		Mode: Cars			*Modes: Mass transit*		
No. of trips per tour	*Year*	*No. of tours*	*Percentage (%)*	*Accumulative percentage (%)*	*No. of tours*	*Percentage (%)*	*Accumulative percentage (%)*
2	1971	1358	92.8	92.8	605	85.8	85.8
	1981	1707	91.1	91.1	1418	79.1	79.1
3	1971	90	6.1	98.9	71	10.1	95.9
	1981	138	7.3	98.4	247	13.8	92.9
4	1971	14	1.0	99.9	15	2.1	98.0
	1981	28	1.5	99.9	92	5.1	98.0
≥5	1971	1	0.1	100.0	14	2.0	100.0
	1981	1	0.1	100.0	35	2.0	100.0

Figure 24.3 Depiction of the nested logit model for non-workers' travel demand modelling

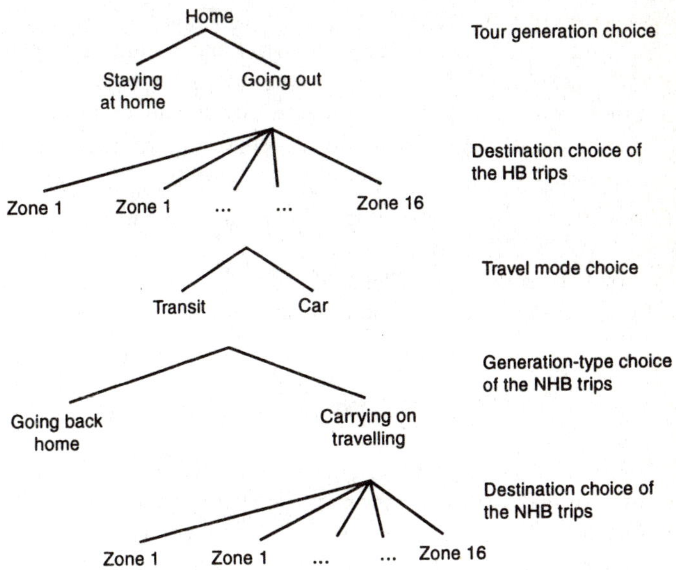

$$P_{s|gdmt}(\beta_s) = \frac{\exp[\beta_s(\bar{u}_{gdmts})]}{\sum_s \exp[\beta_s(\bar{u}_{gdmts})]} \tag{24.18}$$

where

$$u_{gdmt}^* = \frac{1}{\beta_s} \ln \sum_s \exp(\beta_s \bar{u}_{gdmts}) \tag{24.19}$$

$$u_{gdm}^* = \frac{1}{\beta_t} \ln \sum_t \exp[\beta_t(\bar{u}_{gdmt} + u_{gdmt}^*)] \tag{24.20}$$

$$u_{gd}^* = \frac{1}{\beta_m} \ln \sum_m \exp[\beta_m(\bar{u}_{gdm} + u_{gdm}^*)] \tag{24.21}$$

$$u_g^* = \frac{1}{\beta_d} \ln \sum_d \exp[\beta_d(\bar{u}_{gd} + u_{gd}^*)] \tag{24.22}$$

It is easy to understand that the effect of the proceeding trip to the current trip is represented in u_{gdmt}^*, which spreads its effect even to stage g, whereas the trips made in the past are taken account in the $\bar{u}_g$, which affects whether the workers go out or not.

Since there can be little change in the trip number in one tour during a short time period, the model seems to be capable of travel demand forecasting in a time period of 1 or 2 years. Furthermore, for a period of 3 to 5 years without exceptional change, the trip-makers may increase their trips in one tour. However, it is difficult to imagine there will be a big change of over 3 per cent with the tours consisting of less than 4 trips. Thus the model may also be applied to forecast travel demand for the time period of 3 to 5 years. However, for a long period of time, it is better to check whether the tour patterns changed much by using the latest data before the application context.

SUMMARY AND CONCLUSIONS

This chapter investigated the effects of trip-chaining on the disaggregate model of combined trip generation, trip distribution and mode choice. The temporal transferability of the nested logit model was also discussed. Unlike other studies, the transferability of the nested logit model was defined at three levels: (i) parameter level – transferring the model system without any change; (ii) variable level – transferring the model system with the re-estimation of all coefficients, based on the new data for the old explanatory variables; and (iii) structure level – transferring the model system with the new estimation of all coefficients for the updated variable groups, without changing the structure of the travel decision-making tree.

When the model was found not to be transferable at the parameter level, it was not simply transferred at the variable level as it could have been. We have improved the model by investigating the relationship with trip-chaining. Furthermore, the model was recalibrated since we knew it was inappropriate to estimate the model setting $L = 1$. Although it is expected to develop a model to predict the trip-chaining, it can be concluded that the improved model is capable of travel demand forecasting, especially for a short period where no change of trip-chaining can be assumed. Since the utility maximization was made in the unit of tour, the combined model has the advantages that previous studies had not. That is, it not only reflects the effect of trips made, but also incorporates the trips that the trip-maker will have in the tour. Further, it treats the effect of trip-chaining in the same model, combining the first three steps of the four-step process. The usefulness and the importance of the models can be understood from the fact that the combined models can be applied to take account of the possible effects of transportation policies, which is one of the most important subjects of transportation research.

References

Adler, T. J. and M. E. Ben-Akiva (1979) 'A Theoretical and Empirical Model of Trip Chaining Behavior', *Transportation Research*, vol. 13B, pp. 243–57.

Ben-Akiva, M. and S. R. Lerman (1985) *Discrete Choice Analysis: Theory and Application to Travel Demands* (Cambridge, Mass.: MIT Press).

Evans, S. P. (1976) 'Derivation and Analysis of Some Models for Combining Trip Distribution and Assignment', *Transportation Research*, vol. 10, p. 37–57.

Florian, M. and S. Nguyen (1978) 'A Combined Trip Distribution, Modal Split and Trip Assignment Model', *Transportation Research*, vol. 12, pp. 241–6.

Kawakami, S. and L. Su (1991) 'A Study on the Disaggregate Model for Workers' Travel Demand Forecasting', (in Japanese) *Proceedings of Infrastructure Planning*, vol. 14, pp. 39–44.

Kawakami, S., Y. Hirobata, Y. S. Bae and H. Nakajima (1989) 'A Model System for Non-Workers' Daily Travel Demand Based on Disaggregate Behavioral Model', *Selected Proceedings of the Fifth World Conference on Transport Research*, vol. 4 (Ventura, Calif.: Western Periodicals Co.) pp. 207–20.

Kitamura, R. (1988) 'An Evaluation of Activity-Based Travel Analysis', *Transportation*, vol. 15, pp. 9–34.

Kondo, K. and R. Kitamura (1987) 'Time–Space Constraints and the Formation of Trip Chains', *Regional Science and Urban Economics*, vol. 17, pp. 49–65.

Koppelman, F. S. and C. G. Wilmot (1982) 'Transferability Analysis of Disaggregate Choice Models', *Transportation Research Record*, vol. 895, pp. 18–23.

McCarthy, P. S. (1982) 'Further Evidence on the Temporal Stability of Disaggregate Travel Demand Models', *Transportation Research*, vol. 16B, pp. 263–78.

Ruiter, E. R. and M. E. Ben-Akiva (1978) 'Disaggregate Travel Demand Models for the San Francisco Bay Area', *Transportation Research Record*, vol. 673, pp. 121–8.

Safwat, K. N. A. and T. Magnanti (1988) 'A Combined Trip Generation, Trip Distribution, Mode Split and Trip Assignment Model', *Transportation Science*, vol. 22, pp. 14–30.

Theil, H. (1971) *Principles of Econometrics* (New York: John Wiley).

Williams, H. C. W. L. (1977) 'On the Formation of Travel Demand Models and Economic Evaluation Measures of User Benefit', *Environment and Planning A*, vol. 9, pp. 285–344.

25 Planning for National Development: An Agenda Guided by the Socioeconomic System's Social Philosophy

Stanley C. W. Salvary

INTRODUCTION

The idea of sovereignty, which involves self determination, is undermined with each suggestion for harmonization of socioeconomic systems and the globalization of trade, which is deemed to be inevitable. Being able to trade voluntarily with any country is highly desirable, but having to transform one's way of life – from one that is desirable to one that is not desirable – is a serious problem. In the interest of social harmony and social welfare, each country has to start out with its own social philosophy. Some countries wholeheartedly desire the free market to determine the goods and services that are to be produced, the number of unemployed workers, the investment in human capital, the rate of interest and so on. Other countries, however, are coerced in overt and covert ways to adopt the free market system although that system will not serve the needs of the citizenry of those countries. To say that the free market provides the answer for all socioeconomic systems is to ignore the fact that the free market is blind and indifferent to human needs. The unconditional requirement, that this system be adopted by developing countries, violates the rights of those sovereign nations to choose a mode of operation that would foster their desired development without infringing on the rights of other countries.

Indubitably, co-operation among members of the world community is highly desirable, since it would be a step in the right direction to alleviate some of the world's problems. However, the coercion of developing countries into becoming subjected to harsh, blind, confrontational competition, where ultimately those with the muscle to alter the rules of the game will prevail, is most unfair. For example, at the present time, one finds that the USA is asking Japan to observe certain targets for exports to the USA and imports from the USA into Japan. This clearly is managed trade – changing the rules of the game. The European Union (EU) objects to this approach; however, according to Leon Brittan, the EU will follow the approach of the USA so that the USA may not be the sole benefactor of favoured nation treatment [*Newsday* (1993) pp. 5, 95]. But some may, so who cares about what is fair! Nevertheless, to remove fairness from the agenda is indeed a denial of the rights of the citizens of those countries where the bedrock of the social philosophy is care, concern and compassion for other citizens. Unequivocally, some countries would prefer to control their own destiny (to the extent that it is possible) rather than have the invisible hand, which is blind, control it.

The basic assumptions in this chapter on planning for national development are: (i) each developing country is a sovereign nation with the right to shape its own destiny; (ii) the national government is the agent for planning; (iii) the objective function is social welfare maximization; (iv) the means to attain the objectives will be compatible with the objectives of an employment-based domestic economy; and (v) the economic system in each developing country will develop *pari passu* with evolving needs – continuous adjustments as circumstances reveal themselves.

SOCIAL PHILOSOPHY

The responsibility for the progress of developing countries and the direction that this development is to take belongs to the citizens and national governments of those countries. The governments of developing countries have to look inwards and not outwards for the means to undertake the necessary development – growth compatible with their social philosophies. The most available resource in developing countries is also the single most important resource of those countries – human beings/human capital. The challenge to developing countries is to harness the vast amount of that available resource and shape a bright future with and, simultaneously, for, those human beings.

First and foremost in any planning process is the recognition that human beings make up society. Society is an organization and not an organism; hence, there is no automatic adjustment process. To the extent that individual members of society feel they are part of the system, they can and will make a contribution to that system. With social welfare maximization as the objective function, individuals are to be made aware of the system's objectives: where the effort is for the betterment of the lot of human beings, the greater the willingness of individuals to contribute to that effort. The fact that a collective effort is being recommended in no manner implies a lack of incentives. It will not be a simple monetary question as to the level of participation of any individual. To permit maximum flexibility in the system, the emphasis is on educating the citizenry to the extent feasible, and then permit individual participation in the decision-making process at points in the operations where individuals feel comfortable. The interests of the many must have ascendancy over the interests of the individual.

The major concerns of any responsible society are the provision of sound health care, high quality education, adequate housing, uncontaminated food and meaningful retirement benefits. These are social imperatives which cannot be left to chance. It is doubtful that any developing country would willingly wish to become a warehouse for the larger industrial countries and be exporters of their own citizens (seeking jobs in those larger countries) to produce in those other countries goods that would be exported back to their own countries. There are many who contend that the profit motive and monetary incentives are sufficient to produce the best results. The evidence in today's world does not support such a contention. Today, privatization is seen as an end in itself, with shareholder wealth maximization as being the most pivotal consideration. Since the concerns of the many are not considered in this blind transition, the effect on the bulk of the citizenry in developing countries can be devastating.

In developed countries, the concern is made clear by Sherman (1991, pp. 391–2) that free market or market capitalist economies are incapable of dealing with the issue of full employment, among other things; only institutionalized macroeconomic planning can produce positive benefits to any and all societies. Henderson (1993, p. 204) maintains that it is the 'governed market theory' as expounded by Robert Wade which best explains the achievement of the South-East Asian countries. The roles of 'state leadership' and 'state followership', which are not captured by the 'invisible hand', are foremost (according to some observers) in this miraculous achievement. According to Weitzman (1993), the East European model based on contemporary neo-classical economic theory is failing. Yet, in spite of the fact that it is supposed to fail because it does not conform to the orthodox theory, the Chinese model has had remarkable success. The Township–Village Enterprise model, a communal organization having no well-defined ownership structure, is the Chinese model. It is an evolutionary approach which emphasizes collective organization and co-operation.

The measures employed by any developing country must take into consideration the type of society that exists. The measures employed by Western economies concern themselves with the amount of money spent on goods and services. However, in many developing countries possibly a significant portion of the output is not in the form of monetary expenditures (for example, self-supporting food growing; recreation – free access to beaches and a host of sporting activities; medical care; personal relationships and so on). Each developing country has to establish measures that would capture the essence of its philosophy of life. The measures employed by Western economies are incapable of measuring the essential qualities cherished by those social systems.

The needs of the developing countries can only be understood from within and the means necessary to attain those ends can only be provided from within. The challenge is there. It is up to these developing countries to accept the challenge and produce the necessary change.

NATIONAL PLANNING: ACCOUNTING INFORMATION AND MACROECONOMIC POLICY DECISIONS[1]

In any given country, the concern for macroeconomic policy can be appreciated in the light of incentives that are provided to stimulate the economy. For example, in the case of the US economy, in order to encourage investment in capital goods (primarily machinery and equipment), the investment tax credit was enacted in 1962 and repealed with the 1986 Tax Reform Act. Combating unemployment was the objective of the US government's fiscal policy. If the desired investments were to be made by business firms, then new jobs would be created. However, within a market economy, the effectiveness and efficiency in achieving the desired outcome is questionable, since such an incentive is generally made available to all firms. This condition obtains because it is the availability of money capital that determines the ability to invest in plant and equipment:

(i) Since money capital is not equally accessible to all firms in a market economy, the advantage of such a tax incentive can be enjoyed only by the 'money capital abundant' firms. The consequence of such a condition might very well be the construction of excess capacity.

(ii) For labour-intensive firms, the ability to secure the necessary money capital to invest in plant and equipment may come only at the expense of the labour force (substitution of machines for labour).

In Situation (i), if excess capacity ensues, then a misallocation of resources would be experienced. In Situation (ii), the condition to be ameliorated would be exacerbated.[2] Yet, such a tax incentive can be effective in a planned economy where resources are able to be directed to the areas that require development.

Economic stimulation and monitoring

For any national government, the means of stimulating the economy and how to monitor the effects of stimulants that are applied to the economy are of great concern. The remaining subsections of this section attempt to demonstrate a possible means of determining, through the medium of financial statements, whether optimal use is being made of the factors of production in a market or planned economy. This process/analysis constitutes the monitoring mechanism. In this analysis, the information content of financial statements is subject to marginal analysis; in essence, it is microeconomic analysis for the purpose of macroeconomic policy evaluation.

Technological frontier facing developed and developing economies

In developing countries, business firms are smaller than those in developed countries. They have limited funds, substitute labour for physical capital, use less modern technology, and have fewer skilled employees and a lower wage rate. In Figure 25.1, these conditions translate into dual zones of efficient production for developed and developing countries. The most efficient firms in developing economies would be operating at T_2 in M_2, while firms in the developed economies would be operating at T_1 in M_1. It is important to note that there is an efficient zone for both sets of firms; therefore, government planners in developing countries must guide their business firms to the efficient zone (T_2) in M_2, which is labour-employing rather than labour-substituting.

Figure 25.1 Technological frontier and substitution possibilities

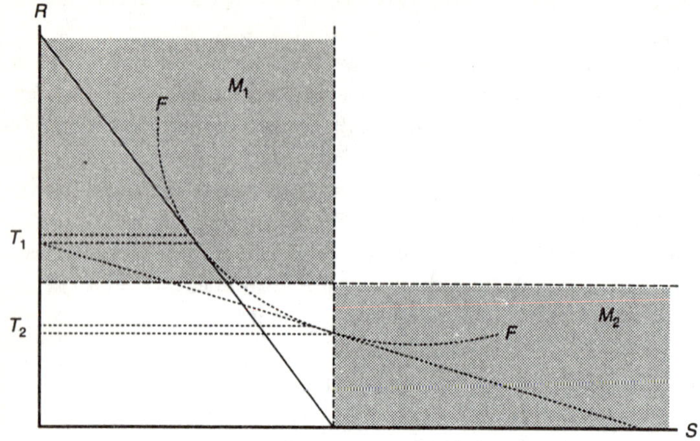

Notes: M_1 = Developed Economy M_2 = Developing Economy
T = Efficient Zone F = Technological Frontier
S = Degree of Labour Skill R = Range of Technology

Planners in developing countries should not try to upgrade their technology to the efficient zone (T_1) in M_1 because it is labour-substituting. In those economies, technology should be upgraded when the technology would increase labour productivity and/or increase employment opportunities.

Planning objective, problems and assumptions

The planning objective is to improve national economic policy decisions. The emphasis is on the usefulness of financial accounting information in contributing to more effective policy-making at the macro level. The model developed in this chapter permits observations of corporate factor utilization, enabling a better understanding at the micro level of the impact of some national economic policies on the economy's non-financial corporate sector. Hence a vehicle is provided for improving national economic policy decisions. The focus is on measuring at the micro level the productivity of the factors of production using factor costs[3] and not on the measurement of the impact of technology on the productivity of the factors of production.[4] The latter involves issues of technical changes that are not addressed in this chapter.[5]

Two serious problems to be confronted are: (1) the inefficient allocation of existing financial capital; and (ii) the arbitrary selection of accounting methods which affect the reliability of financial accounting data. One of the more crippling factors in economic growth is the inefficient allocation of existing financial capital. To ensure the availability of funds for expansion in desirable areas and industries, accounting information can be used to determine tax policy for redistributing financial capital. Assessment and monitoring is necessary to determine: (a) the impact of an industry on the economy; (b) individual firms' profitability, and (c) the effect of other factors on an industry as a whole. In assessing the allocational efficiency of financial capital, it is necessary to look at the individual firms[6] to determine: (i) the degree of variation in production performance (the level of efficiency attained), and (ii) the possible causes of such variation (the effects of factor substitution). The disaggregated approach avoids the problem of information concealment which occurs with the use of highly aggregated data.

In this discussion, the usefulness of financial accounting data is not assumed. The efficiency test to be applied to the firms should confirm the usefulness of financial accounting data. Indubitably, the use of financial accounting information requires an understanding of its structure, content and limitations (Salvary (1985) pp. 18–26). Care must be exercised to ensure the reliability of the financial accounting data used in the analysis.[7] It is necessary to group together firms with similar accounting methods within each industry; an individual firm's performance is to be compared to the aggregate group's performance. Because of the indivisibility of plant and equipment as a factor input, to overcome the problem of the arbitrary selection of a method of depreciation, gross plant and equipment are to be used in lieu of depreciation.

There are three basic assumptions underlying the planning model:

(i) A planned resource-optimizing decision confronts the firm. The various factor inputs of the firm are in great part determined in prior periods (plant and equipment from the preceding period and so on). In great part, the major constraint on the material factor input is the firm's existing technology and labour skills (for example, impracticality of substituting metal with plastic). Given this scenario, (a) the existing technology would constrain marginal investments (but not major investments) in plant and equipment and in labour; and (b) the impact that labour-displacing technology would have on the level of unemployment would constrain the level of labour-displacing technology that could be adopted.[8]

(ii) The firm is engaged in limited competition with foreign goods in the domestic market; thus its output is market-determined because factor costs are more or less market determined. The firm is faced with a closed, convex and negative monotonic production set, making profit the objective function to be maximized.[9] As income redistribution is an overriding concern, profits will be negative in some cases.

(iii) The firm is a price-taker. Production is based upon prices expected to prevail when output is sold and input is acquired. Because of uncertainty the expected prices would differ from the actual prices. The absence of information, on *ex ante* output selling prices and *ex ante* input factor costs, prevents two measures (output mix and input mix) of allocative inefficiency from being computed.[10] Except for large-scale investments in new plant and equipment, inefficiency (efficiency) in the firm's production is attributable to allocative inefficiency (efficiency) of scale versus technical inefficiency (efficiency).[11]

Evaluating resource allocation: macro vs. micro level

In most studies on factor productivity it is assumed 'that when entrepreneurs anticipate a relative increase in real wages, they will, in the short run, substitute capital for labor (provided that the elasticity of substitution is positive) and then concentrate on innovations which are labor saving' (Nadiri (1970) p. 1146). Such a business policy leads to more unemployment; thus the resource allocation process is not Pareto-optimal. Such a policy is highly undesirable for developing countries, where a major goal is 'full' employment or 'low' unemployment. Hence, business policies must be guided by effective national tax policies.

Highly aggregated information, though useful, does not enable an awareness of the variation in resource allocation among individual firms. Thus, factor utilization analysis at the firm level is a means of assessing the marginal efficiency of factor inputs for individual firms. Despite its crudity, the model offered in this chapter is useful for policy-making.

Data and methodology

The efficiency or inefficiency in the allocation of resources is to be determined using financial accounting information. The recommended financial accounting data is to be adjusted in certain areas for price-level changes. Since the analysis focuses on productivity analysis, the data to be employed consist of:

(i) *sales revenue* adjusted for price level changes using the specific industry's wholesale producers price index;
(ii) *the materials cost component of cost of sales*, adjusted in a similar fashion as (i);
(iii) *the overhead cost component of cost of sales* would be deflated by an appropriate price deflator;
(iv) *the labour cost component of cost of sales* would be deflated by the specific industry's wage index;
(v) *investment in plant and equipment* would be analyzed using current prices, on the assumption that new additions to plant and equipment embody new technology; and
(vi) *inventories* adjusted in a similar fashion to (i) above.[12]

Efficiency measures of factor utilization

To provide an indication of the efficiency of resource allocation at the firm (micro) level, three ratios have been developed: (i) Factor Utilization Optimality Ratio (F_r), (ii) Convergence to Optimality Ratio (O_r); and (iii) Labour Disproportionality Ratio (L_r). These three measures of efficiency relate to those of Fare *et al.* (1985, pp. 23, 49–53, 64, 79, 80, 93–6).[13]

(a) An 'overall input efficiency measure'
(b) An 'overall output efficiency measure'

The *input efficiency* measure determines whether a less expensive input vector exists to produce the given output vector. The *output efficiency* measure determines the output that should have been produced given the input vector. The validity of those measures hinges on the assumption that: (a) an output level is chosen by the firm that is consistent with market conditions and the firm's production capabilities; and (b) the firm selects the least expensive combination of factors consistent with its quality standards.

Because of uncertainty on the prices and conditions that will obtain, the firm will eventually reach optimal, suboptimal or superoptimal production results caused by differences between expectations and actual prices and conditions. The response to and impact of an unexpected upsurge in consumer demand, along with an increase in price, would differ for a firm operating at less than full capacity compared to a firm operating at full capacity.

The state of technology

In order to establish (i) the level of technology; and (ii) the full capacity level of production, two procedures have been devised.

1. *Level of technology* When new equipment is introduced, a period of adjustment ensues (that is, a learning period); therefore, for each firm, the year subsequent to the year in which the major investment in plant and equipment has taken place is considered as the benchmark – at this point, the firm's level of technology is deemed to have been established. The output/input factor relationship (O_t) is the standard output/input function at the micro level by which the actual output function (O_{tn}) in subsequent years would be judged. The calculation of the output/input ratios (OI) is as follows:

$$OI_{tn} = R_{tn}(C_{tn})^{-1} \qquad n = 1, 2, 3, \ldots \tag{25.1}$$

where OI = output to input ratio
R = revenue
C = cost of output sold
t = index.

$$OI_{t0} = R_{t0}(C_{t0})^{-1} \tag{25.1.1}$$

where t_0 = benchmark year

2. *Full capacity level of production* The year in which gross output (R) is at its highest level subsequent to the benchmark year (for determining the level of technology) is considered as an approximation of the full capacity level of production (FC_r) – the 'full capacity benchmark year' (t^*). The output/capital ratios (OC_r) are developed as follows:

$$OC_r = R_{tn}(K_{tn})^{-1} \tag{25.2}$$

In the 'full capacity benchmark year' (t^*), the output/capital ratio (OC_r) will be considered as the full capacity (FC_r). The output/capital ratio (OC_r) for every other individual year will be expressed as a percentage of the full capacity (FC_r) to arrive at the capacity utilization ratio (U_r). (In the presence of excess capacity, an increase in capacity usage can produce a change in output that would be an unexpected maximized situation.)

Production functions: ex ante and ex post

The development of the production function follows the approach suggested by Johansen (1972). Output {Revenue (R)} is a function of factor inputs (gross plant and equipment (K), labour (L), materials (M), and overhead (A) – without depreciation) reflected in the financial statements of individual firms: $R = f(K, L, M, A)$.

In each industry, by means of multiple regression analysis, estimates of the coefficients of factor inputs (CFI) will be calculated for each firm. Each estimate will represent a moving (forward-rolling) five-year period. That is, if the years 1983–93 constitute the period to be covered by the study, then seven estimates would be calculated for each firm. The *ex ante* production function would be the production function estimated for the period that contains the benchmark year as the last year of the five-year period. (If 1988 is deemed the technology benchmark year, then the *ex ante* production function would be the estimate calculated for the period 1984–8. The reason for this position is that it is expected that production after 1988 would be more efficient than production in the earlier periods.) Estimates calculated for the other periods will be considered as *ex post* production functions. The *ex ante* production function is estimated by Equation (25.3); whereas, the *ex post* production function is estimated by Equation (25.4).

$$R_x = (b_i K_{t0} + d_i L_{t0} + p_i M_{t0} + q_i A_{t0}) \qquad (25.3)$$

where x = *ex ante*, t_0 = benchmark year.
b_i, d_i, p_i and q_i = the coefficients of factor inputs (CFI) for the individual firm.

To arrive at the coefficients, the logarithmic form of the variables are to be used in order that the estimated partial regression coefficients can be interpreted as elasticities. The variables in Equation (25.3) are used to develop Equation (25.4):

$$R_y = (b_i K_{tn} + d_i L_{tn} + p_i M_{tn} + q_i A_{tn}) \qquad (25.4)$$

where y = *ex post*.

The 'overall input efficiency measure' (a vector {K^*, L^*, M^*, A^*}) and 'overall output efficiency measure' (R^*), for years after the benchmark year, are calculated using Equations (25.5) and (25.6).

$$R^a_n = (b_i K^*_{tn} + d_i L^*_{tn} + p_i M^*_{tn} + q_i A^*_{tn}) \tag{25.5}$$

where a = actual.

$$R^*_n = (b_i K_{tn} + d_i L_{tn} + p_i M_{tn} + q_i A_{tn}) \tag{25.6}$$

In Equation (25.7) changes in the magnitudes of the coefficients (Equations (25.3) and (25.4)) and direction of change in those magnitudes are captured in the aggregate by u:.

$$R^*_n = R^a_n + u \; (-k < u < k) \tag{25.7}$$

where u = random factor, $k < \infty$.

The standard output for a given capital input is the change in output (ΔR) in the year subsequent to the benchmark year. This standard enables the calculation of: (a) efficiency measures of marginal factor inputs; and (b) an efficiency measure of marginal output.

Optimality and convergence to optimality

Optimality in utilization of factors of production is determined via the 'factor utilization optimality ratio' (F_r). Changes in values of the variables in Equation (25.1) are the basis of this ratio, which is stated as follows:

$$F_r = (\Delta C_{tn})(\Delta R_{tn})^{-1} \tag{25.8}$$

where Δ = change.

Evidence on optimal use of the factors of production would be F_r = 1, or very close to 1 – that is, plus or minus some tolerance level/an adjustment factor (a): $F_r = 1 \pm a$. This adjustment (a) is for minor deviations which are caused by factors not related to optimum use (namely, idle time caused by mechanical problems; or transitory periods, including a learning period with the introduction of new machinery). Yet, in another way, the 'factor utilization optimality ratio' (F_r) can be derived and expressed (Equation (25.9)) as the relationship between the rate of change in the cost of output sold ($r\Delta C$) and rate of change in revenue (rDR):

$$\begin{aligned} Fr &= (r\Delta C)(r\Delta R)^{-1} \\ (r\Delta C) &= (C_{tn} - C_{tn-1})(C_{tn-1})^{-1} \\ (r\Delta R) &= (R_{tn} - R_{tn-1})(R_{tn-1})^{-1} \end{aligned} \tag{25.9}$$

W. E. G. Salter's (1966, pp. 30–1) equations for T' and T_r, and J. D. May and M. Denny's (1979, p. 760) equation for P_t (a measure of total factor productivity) are the counterparts of Equations 25.8 and 25.9, which are measures of technical advance (cost savings per unit of output).

According to W. H. Locke Anderson (1970, p. 153), 'when adjustment costs are important, firms will operate on the static production function only at seasonal or cyclical peaks. At other times, they will "hoard" labor in order to avoid adjustment expenses – referred to as "the presence of on-the-job underemployment" (You (1979) p. 97).' In this model, the existence of excess plant capacity or the hoarding of labour will be captured by the tolerance factor ($-a$).[14] There is the danger of a false lag in adjustment (Anderson (1970) p. 161). To eliminate (or at least to minimize) the false lag in adjustment that otherwise would appear, adjustments for changes in: (a) inventory levels; and (b) capacity utilization rates are to be undertaken. Since marginal analysis is employed in this model, inventory levels[15] have to be considered to avoid distortions in the measurement of F_r.

Convergence of optimality in utilization of the factors of production is discerned by means of the 'convergence to optimality ratio' (O_r). the firm's gross profit ratio (G) and its marginal gross profit ratio (Gm) are used in this ratio, which is the relationship between gross profit in period zero and marginal gross profit in subsequent periods:

$$O_r = (Gm_{tn})(G_{t0})^{-1} = \lim_{0 \to n} 1 \qquad n = 1, 2, 3, \ldots$$
$$(Gm = (\Delta R_{tn} - \Delta C_{tn})(\Delta R_{tn})^{-1};\ G = (R_{t0} - C_{t0})(R_{t0})^{-1}) \tag{25.10}$$

Convergence is intimated by Equation (25.10). The movement from period zero with a ratio of 100 (a grossly inefficient use of factors) and moving in each successive period closer to 1, or beginning in period zero with a ratio of 0.01 (an incredibly efficient use of factors) and each successive period moving closer to 1 is evidence on convergence to optimality.

Factor substitution – diminishing returns to factor input

Inefficiency, in this study, signifies continued substitution of one factor (for example, plant and equipment) for another (for example, labour). Factor substitution possibilities and the conditions necessary for factor substitution (for example, the decision to use a large factory with a single shift versus a small factory with double shifts, as indicated by Betancourt and Clague (1975) are factors that must be considered in order to obtain a better insight on the problem of capital availability.[16] Any firm experiencing diminishing returns on factor inputs can be indentified when the 'factor utilization optimality ratio' produces a result for any given year greater than $1 + a$. Diminishing returns on labour are discernible using the 'labour disproportionality ratio' (L_r), which is derived as follows:

$$L_r = (r\Delta L)(r\Delta R)^{-1}$$

where L = labour and related expenses.

$$r\Delta L = (L_{tn} - L_{tn-1})(L_{tn-1})^{-1} \qquad n = 1, 2, 3, \ldots \qquad (25.11)$$

Diminishing returns to labour are experienced whenever $L_r > 1 + a$. Factors that impinge on the measure of L_r are changes in employee mix and/or the quality of labour input (improved skills of previously unskilled workers). These factors should be isolated and accounted for (Chinloy, 1980). In this model, these factors are compensated for in two ways, on the assumption that: (i) wages reflect changes in employee mix where pay scales differentiate between skilled, semi-skilled, and unskilled workers; and (ii) wages are adjusted to reflect employees' upgrading of skills. If diminishing returns experienced by the firm are attributable to capital (a disproportionate use of that factor exists in relation to labour), then $F_r > 1 + a$, but $L_r \leq 1$. Similarly, Equation (25.12), which states that the relationship between the rate of change in investment in plant and equipment ($r\Delta K$) and the rate of change in revenue ($r\Delta R$), is used to determine the 'capital disproportionality ratio' (I_r):[17]

$$I_r = (r\Delta K)(r\Delta R)^{-1}$$

where K = investment in plant and equipment.

$$r\Delta K = (K_{tn} - K_{tn-1})(K_{tn-1})^{-1} \qquad n = 1, 2, 3, \ldots \qquad (25.12)$$

Given the complementarity of labour and physical capital, the use of a ratio which incorporates both factors is necessary. This approach addresses the problem that productivity measures related to a single input cannot measure the specific contribution of that factor. A number of interrelated influences (namely, technological change, substitution of factors, capacity utilization, change in skill levels and so on) are responsible for a change in output (Eisenberg (1974) p. 22). Indices, constructed from annual ratios, provide a basis for standardizing (offsetting the complementarity of) factor inputs. One form of standardizing is to use the ratio of L to K for each year to determine the coefficient of substitution. This ratio reflects the relationship between deflated labour dollars and investment in plant and equipment. Also, further refinement of the measurement of L_r and I_r would necessitate use of the level of plant capacity utilization (U_r) in the measurement process.

General comments

Regional economic conditions and their causes have to be considered carefully.[18] To produce the desired macroeconomic goals of income redistribution and full employment, economic incentives must be tailored to microeconomic level conditions. The preceding analysis focused on identifying change within and among firms and on measuring the direction of such change. The information generated in that analysis would reveal: (i) the existence of misallocations of resources within specific industries; (ii) the extent of such misallocations, and (iii) the peculiar geographic distributions of such misallocations. This knowledge enables policy prescription to be consistent with the existing economic situation.

ASSESSING REGIONAL ECONOMIC CONDITIONS[19]

Regions in developing countries, for the purpose of this presentation, are geographical areas with specific characteristics, be it land or natural resource features.

Regional economies within developing countries

Regional economies in developing countries are driven by agriculture, manufacturing or service activities. The agricultural regional economies tend to become more capital-intensive; this condition aggravates the labour excess problem. Hence, an introduction or expansion of the manufacturing sector in those regions would enable displaced labour from the agricultural sector to be absorbed back into the workforce. In some developing countries, small manufacturing regional economies are losing some of their industries to developed and other developing countries, entailing significant displacement of labour. These economies may then experience growth in the service sector (mainly tourism), which in turn may absorb the labour displaced from the manufacturing sector. Of necessity, planning in developing countries must begin with a sharp focus on identifying the strengths and weaknesses of regional economies within those countries.

Social welfare maximizing subject to a budget constraint is the basic assumption underlying this chapter; hence, public expenditures and tax decisions of national governments for regional development would be based upon a social welfare maximizing principle. In this analysis, the social welfare to be maximized in a region is the employment opportunities for its residents. A region's economic growth, the prime source of employment opportunities, can be influenced by a region's mix of public expenditure that paves the way for the region's employment portfolio of industries. Therefore, arriving at a proper allocation of tax revenues, among the various types of public expenditures to maximize the region's social welfare, is of the utmost concern to the national public administrator/regional planner. The model presented below demonstrates how national public administrators/regional planners can assess the economic conditions of the various regions in order to determine the fiscal policies compatible with the national current economic situation. Indubitably, the objective is to ensure that recognizable regional problems are ameliorated rather than accentuated.

Identification of economic conditions

This section is an exploration of dynamic analysis for regional policy-making which entails an identification/a determination of: (i) the distinct economic regions within the country; (ii) the economic needs of the country; (iii) the available resources (including the transportation network); (iv) the level of technology; (v) the skills of the labour force; and (vi) the compatibility of the various regions with certain economic activities. The planning perspective is on economic conditions identified with recognizable regions: (a) economic activities; (b) population growth; (c) unemployment rates; (d) regional output; and (e) public spending. The objective is to maximize regional employment opportunities in order to minimize relocation of citizens. The methodology for: (a) an assessment of the quality of a region's economic conditions; and (b) a measurement of the extent of the disparity in the quality of economic conditions among regions, follows.

Evaluative model

The quality of a region's economic condition (Q) is a function of the efficiency (E) with which the region absorbs its growing population into the labour force, and dependency (D) of the region on public spending – the degree of importance of public spending to the region's economy: $Q = f(E, D)$. The key variables are: the ratio of unemployment growth (or decline) rate to population growth (or decline) rate and the ratio of the rate of change of public spending to the rate of change of regional output. All regions cannot be expected to share the same quality level of economic conditions; however, through efficient management of the regional economies, a sharp contrast in the quality of economic conditions among the various regions can be avoided.

In general, the cause/effect relationship between a region's public and private expenditure would run from the former to the latter with a long time-lag. A national government can encourage economic activity in specified regions with appropriate expenditure of revenues. Planning for the long term would require public spending for the improvement of skills of the workforce and the infrastructure to produce a climate conducive to private investments. Public spending can be expected to grow in all regions. However, the pattern of public spending should differ because: (a) the economic climates of regions differ; and (b) the limits to public funds necessitate a trade-off among public expenditure to achieve short-term goals and those needed to produce long-term maximization of social welfare. Classification of regions by existing conditions enables a determination of the appropriate mix of regional public expenditure.

Regional classification

Regions in developed countries can be classified as congested, intermediate or lagging (Hansen, 1970). In a free-market system, it is assumed that when congested regions' agglomeration reach the point where the marginal social cost from external diseconomies for new and existing firms exceeds the marginal social benefit from the external economies, economic activities will flow from congested regions to intermediate regions. In many cases congested regions attract more investments, while investments opportunities in other regions go begging. Given market imperfections, developing countries cannot look to the market as a corrective device. Regional development has to be planned by directing investments to attain the desired results.

In developing countries, regions can be classified as either 'highly potential' (HP), 'moderately potential', (MP) or 'little potential' (LP). Each region cannot be developed in a similar fashion; each region has to be developed according to its potential. Redirection of economic activities can be achieved by investments in: (a) direct productive activities (DPA) – public investments; (b) social overhead capital (SOC) – investment in human beings (education, health, and so on); and (c) economic overhead capital (EOC) – basically work projects (roads, bridges and so on). In MP regions there should be public investments in EOC, while emphasizing SOC; LP regions should invest in SOC projects and DPA; SOC is to enable the mobility of displaced workers from LP regions.

Evidence on SOC projects indicates that there are more positive benefits than simply the mobility of the labour force. In the USA, New England's experience with SOC projects, particularly education, is indicative of the profound and positive consequence of such a policy – the attraction of specialized industries by the educated workforce (Business Week (1976) p. 98; *Wall Street Journal* (1985) p. 1; Rosengren (1990)). Unequivocally, each region's economic activities should be stabilized by directing spending related to the region's existing economic conditions. Empirical evidence does suggest that in a tight labour market, government spending may reduce the demand for labour in the private sectors (Crihfield (1989) p. 365). In most developing countries, a tight labour market does not exist; therefore government investments can be used to absorb displaced labour. Clearly, the government's role should be to: (i) create conditions conducive to the development of the private sector; and (ii) maximize the positive aspects of its own impact upon the economy.

Regional policy analysis: qualitative measures of regional economic conditions

To shape the region's development policy with its expenditure programs, policy analysis should be undertaken. Two ratios can furnish information on economic conditions of the regions: the efficiency ratio and the dependency ratio (Salvary, 1991).

Data and methodology

Data for analysis of regional economic conditions are: output, population, unemployment and public spending. Growth in regional output is a surrogate for regional economic growth. Exponential growth rates (regional output (V^g) and regional public spending (G^g) are to be calculated for each region. The growth rates can be calculated via 'exponential growth curve theory' (Glover (1930) pp. 470–83).[20] As fitted to the serial data in this analysis, it is based upon the mathematical formula: $y = ar^x$; where y = dependent variable; a = a constant; r = a rate of growth; and x = a time period.

The efficiency ratio (ER) – the relationship between exponential growth rates of levels of unemployment (u^g) and population (p^g): u^g/p^g – is a measure of a region's ability to absorb increases in its labour force and/or combat unemployment. ER = 1 implies that relatively no deterioration of the unemployment situation has occurred. A region with a ratio of ER < 1 is experiencing economic conditions which are qualitatively sound.

The dependency ratio (DR) measures the relationship between rate of change in total public spending (G^g) and rate of change in total regional output (V^g): $(G^g)(V^g)^{-1}$. This ratio measures the quality of a region's growth; the higher the ratio (DR > 1), the poorer is the quality of economic growth. DR = 1 is preferable to DR > 1; the ideal situation would be DR < 1. DR = 1 signifies no change in the quality of economic conditions; DR < 1 signifies that a healthy economic climate is developing. Low economic growth leads to a higher dependency on public spending. However, since public spending is a vehicle for ameliorating ailing regional economies, a long-term increasing dependence, while not desirable, is not bad. However, since the amount of financial capital needed is generally greater than the amount available for public spending in any region, there has to be a concern for the tax burden implicit in such spending.

CAPITAL AVAILABILITY

A primary capital market can be beneficial, but an unbridled capital market is a luxury, not a necessity. Banks are the facilitators of the flow of financial capital for the economic system, and interest rates are the means to ration financial capital for investment projects. While credit is a means to stimulate economic activity, if it is not controlled it becomes counter-productive. Banks, interest rates and consumer credit policy are items that have to be carefully managed. Banks in free market economies effectively transfer wealth from those who are the cogs of the economics system to those who are passive savers. The use of interest rates as a mechanism for controlling inflation has had serious consequences in terms of bankruptcies, unemployment, reduction of economic activities and exorbitant earnings for banks. Inadequate consumer credit policies can encourage unwise spending and lead to unnecessary business fluctuations.

The general belief among developing countries is that foreign capital is necessary to enable the development of the domestic economy. This is false. The initiative has to be taken by these countries to use the available natural and human resources and to finance the projects that are necessary and beneficial to their welfare with the savings generated in those economies. Both Germany and France have used the banking systems as partners with business. This is the ideal situation. Banks are the means for accommodating domestic thrift, which enables the internal financing of domestic projects. Unfortunately, banks in many developing countries invest available savings abroad to demonstrate their sophistication, while inadvertently sacrificing domestic growth opportunities.

CLOSING COMMENTS

In the planning process, it is imperative that national planners pay particular attention to local voices in the determination of needs and means to achieve those needs. Often, consultants whose recommendations achieve success are those who have obtained solutions from the local individuals. Accordingly, much time, effort and funds can be saved if national planners provide for the full participation of local individuals in the planning process.

Notes

1. Significant parts of the discussion in this section are drawn from Salvary (1990).
2. In the USA, the Economic Recovery Tax Act of 1981 permitted firms that were losing money to sell their tax benefits to other, profitable, firms. Since financial benefits are reaped by firms not contributing to new job creation, one can conclude that investment tax credit policy is inefficient.
3. On the use of factor costs to measure macro level productivity, see Kraus (1978) and Eisenberg (1974).
4. Problems encountered in the measurement of factor productivity are discussed by Nadiri (1970).

5. For an extensive presentation of measuring technical change, see Salter (1966, pp. 46–7).
6. For studies conducted on the US economy, see Alberts (1979); Clark (1984); Schmalensee (1985).
7. The issues discussed by Benston (1985), Schmalensee (1985), Salamon (1985), Jacobson (1987), and Scherer *et al.* (1987) must be considered by countries following the US model of accounting. Various methods exist in accounting to enable financial accounting measurement to capture the reality of the economic circumstances of the observed phenomena (Salvary (1989) pp. 15–16, 71–5). However, when accounting methods selected disregard the economic circumstances to be captured, measurement is not attempted and, hence, is not exacted (Salvary (1989) p. 69). The major accounting measurement problem is the *arbitrary use of inventory and depreciation methods*.
8. Studies conducted by Clark (1984) and Schmalensee (1985), have used micro data to focus not on national fiscal policy issues but on the impact of specific factors (for example, unionization, market and market share) on the profitability of individual firms in their sample.
9. This assumption on profit maximization is consistent with Varian (1984) p. 584.
10. Inefficient input mix: a better input mix could have been used given the output produced. Inefficient output mix: a better output could have been produced with the given inputs used.
11. Technical inefficiency: failure to maximize output that would maximize profit given an efficient allocation of inputs.
12. The use of various indices is to refine measurements and overcome issues raised by Fenoaltea (1976).
13. Also, these measures are suggested by Diewert (1980) pp. 263–4.
14. For evidence on the hoarding of labour, see Fay and Medoff (1985).
15. It is necessary to consider whether there are only a few firms in the industry. Efficient and inefficient firms alter their capacity utilization rates and inventory levels in concentrated industries over the cycle, while in competitive industries, price is adjusted rather than supply (Greer and Rhoades (1976) p. 1036).
16. Edmunds (1978, p. 30) used an approach similar to this approach, but conducted at the macro level.
17. Macro level measures to assess related policy issues are given by Coen and Hickman (1980, p. 218). In this study, the focus is on micro level measures for developing macroeconomic policies.
18. An 'ecologically-based theory' has been used in the development of models which can adequately quantitatively assess the quality of a region's economic conditions (Dendrinos (1984); Salvary (1991)).
19. Significant parts of the discussion in this section is drawn from Salvary (1991).
20. 'Exponential functions are closely related to logarithmic functions' (Chiang (1964) p. 281), and seemingly are superior to the logarithmic functions for serial data (Glover, 1930). The exponential growth curve is not free from all defects (Spurr and Bonini (1967) pp. 492–3).

References

Alberts, W. W. (1979) 'Do Oligopolists Earn "Noncompetitive" Rates of Return?', *Economic Journal*, September.

Anderson, W. H. Locke (1970) 'Production Scheduling, Intermediate Goods, and Labor Productivity', *American Economic Review*, March.

Benston, G. J. (1985) 'The Validity of Profits-Structure Studies with Particular Reference to the FTC's Line of Business Data', *American Economic Review*, March.

Betancourt, R. R. and C. K. Clague (1975) 'An Economic Analysis of Capital Utilization', *Southern Economic Journal*, July.

Business Week (1976) 'The Second War Between the States', 17 May.

Chiang, A. C. (1964) *Fundamental Methods of Mathematical Economics* (New York: McGraw-Hill).

Chinloy, P. (1980) 'Sources of Quality Change in Labor Input', *American Economic Review*, March.

Clark, K. B. (1984) 'Unionization and Firm Performance: The Impact on Profits, Growth and Productivity', *American Economic Review*, December.

Coen, R. M. and B. G. Hickman (1980) 'Investment and Growth in an Econometric Model of the United States', *Papers and Proceedings of the Ninety-Second Annual Meeting of the American Economic Association*, May.

Crihfield, J. B. (1989) 'A Structural Empirical Analysis of Metropolitan Labor Demand', *Journal of Regional Science*, August.

Dendrinos, D. (1984) 'Regions, Antiregions, and Their Dynamic Stability: The U.S. Case (1929–1979)', *Journal of Regional Science*, February.

Diewert, W. E. (1980) 'Capital and the Theory of Productivity Measurement', *Papers and Proceedings of the Ninety-Second Annual Meeting of the American Economic Association*, May.

Edmunds, S. W. (1978) 'Capital Productivity, Money Flows, and Inflation', *Business Economics*, May.

Eisenberg, W. M. (1974) 'Measuring the Productivity of Nonfinancial Corporations', *Monthly Labor Review*, November.

Fare, R., S. Grosskopf and C. A. Knox Lovell (1985) *The Measurement of Efficiency of Production* (Boston, Mass.: Kluwer-Nijhoff).

Fay, J. A. and J. L. Medoff (1985) 'Labor and Output Over the Business Cycle: Some Direct Evidence', *American Economic Review*, September.

Fenoaltea, S. (1976) 'Real Value Added and the Measurement of Industrial Production', *Annals of Economic and Social Measurement*, National Bureau of Economic Research, Winter.

Glover, J. W. (1930) *Tables of Applied Mathematics in Finance, Insurance Statistics* (Ann Arbor, Mich.: George Wahr).

Greer, D. F. and S. A. Rhoades (1976) 'Concentration and Productivity Changes in the Long and Short Run', *Southern Economic Journal*, October.

Hansen, N. M. (1970) 'Unbalanced Growth and Regional Development', in David L. McKee, Robert D. Dean and William L. Leahy (eds), *Regional Economics: Theory and Practice* (New York: The Free Press; London: Collier-Macmillan).

Henderson, J. (1993) 'Against the Economic Orthodoxy: On the Making of the East Asian Miracle', *Economy and Society*, May.

Jacobson, R. (1987) 'The Validity of ROI as a Measure of Business Performance', *American Economic Review*, June.

Kraus, J. (1978) 'Productivity and the U.S. National Income and Product Accounts', *Business Economics*, May.

Lovell, C., A. Knox and R. C. Sickles (1983) 'Testing Efficiency Hypotheses in Joint Production: A Parametric Approach', *Review of Economics and Statistics*, February.

May, J. D. and M. Denny (1979) 'Factor-Augmenting Technical Progress and Productivity in U.S. Manufacturing', *International Economic Review*, October.

Nadiri, N. (1970) 'Some Approaches to the Theory and Measurement of Total Factor Productivity: A Survey', *Journal of Economic Literature*, December.

Newsday (1993) 'G-7 Summit', 7 July.

Rosengren, E. S. (1990) 'How Diversified is New England?', *New England Economic Review*, November/December.

Salamon, G. L. (1985) 'Accounting Rates of Return', *American Economic Review*, June.

Salter, W. E. G. (1969) *Productivity and Technical Change* (2nd edn) (Cambridge University Press).

Salvary, S. C. W. (1991) 'Measuring the Quality of Regional Economic Conditions: Preliminary Evidence on Some US Regions', *Journal of Economic Democracy*, July–September.

Salvary, S. C. W. (1990) 'Financial Accounting Information and Microeconomic Analysis: A Basis for Macroeconomic Policy Decisions – A Research Agenda', *Journal of Economic Democracy*, January–March.

Salvary, S. C. W. (1989) *An Analytical Framework for Accounting Theory*, McQueen Accounting Monograph Series, vol. 5 (Fayetteville, Ark.: University of Arkansas).

Salvary, S. C. W. (1985) *Accounting: A Library of Quantifications*, McQueen Accounting Monograph Series, vol. 1 (Fayetteville, Ark.: University of Arkansas).

Scherer, F. M., W. F. Long, S. Martin, D. C. Mueller, G. Pascoe, D. J. Ravenscraft, J. T. Scott and L. W. Weiss (1987) 'The Validity of Studies with Line of Business Data: Comment', *American Economic Review*, March.

Schmalensee, R. (1985) 'Do Markets Differ Much?', *American Economic Review*, June.

Sherman, H. J. (1991) *The Business Cycle: Growth and Crisis Under Capitalism* (Princeton, NJ: Princeton University Press).

Spurr, W. A. and Bonini, C. P. (1967) *Statistical Analysis for Business Decisions* (Homewood, Ill.: Richard D. Irwin).

Varian, H. R. (1984) 'The Nonparametric Approach to Production Analysis', *Econometrica*, May.

Wall Street Journal (1985) 'The Road Back', 1 February.

Weitzman, M. L. (1993) 'Economic Transition: Can Theory Help?', *European Economic Review*, vol. 37.

You, Jong Keun (1979) 'Capital Utilization, Productivity, and Output Gap', *Review of Economics and Statistics*, February.

26 MegaProject Impact Assessment

Roger R. Stough and Kingsley E. Haynes

INTRODUCTION

The modern history of resource development began in the 1800s at the onset of the mass-production phase of the Industrial Revolution. During the transition from an agrarian to an industrial-based exchange economy, discrete jumps occurred in the number and scale of resource projects. However, during the past two centuries these 'phase jumps' have been associated increasingly with specific advances in technology (for example, the steam engine) and the amassing and targeting of major capital outlays (for example, for hydroelectric projects or construction of transcontinental railroads (see Anderson (1986), discussion on logistical revolutions). These 'jumps' have become increasingly larger steps (for example, the Erie Canal in the nineteenth century vs. Panama Canal in the twentieth century). As small, similar and near term resource development projects were completed, only larger, more difficult, more distant and unique projects remained for full development. Further, with the advance of technology, new projects became feasible that had not previously been possible. Hence, larger, more complex and higher-risk projects have become increasingly necessary to meet the rising demands of the world's population and the economic necessities of survival. This process does not seem to be abating, particularly in the developing world, where the need for more effective resource utilization is spurred by economic, political and population pressure, and where new technology is rapidly being adopted.

For large-scale development projects to occur, a financial assessment of the return on investment has gone hand-in-hand with project feasibility studies. However, with public-sector involvement in such investments, a broader demand for overall economic assessment, often described generically as economic analysis, has been used to complement purely internal financial evaluation of projects. The former is often operationalized as some form of social cost–benefit assessment.

The definition and tracing of benefits and costs has become increasingly complex as such items as social overhead benefits and environmental costs have entered into the equation for assessment of large, complex projects.

From this complexity has emerged a concern for appropriate assessment and evaluation of particularly large-scale irreversible projects that affect lives over generations across national boundaries and beyond the domain of the original decision actors. The term 'megaproject' refers to such large-scale, irreversible projects. For megaprojects, traditional economic cost–benefit cost analysis methodologies appear to be inadequate. The purpose of this chapter is to explore this conclusion.

THE NATURE OF MEGAPROJECTS

From the above discussion it might be assumed that megaprojects are primarily resource development endeavours and many of these projects are targeted directly towards natural resource exploitation objectives. However, many are not, and even those targeted to resource development objectives have major indirect effects. Some megaprojects are aimed at infrastructure expansion to facilitate more general economic development goals; for example, the interstate highway system in the USA or trans-continental railway development projects. Such projects are often rationalized with accessibility or market development goals. Other projects may be rationalized on technological development grounds, for example, the space exploration agency, NASA, or the construction of super-particle accelerators. In short, megaprojects take many different forms and are rationalized on different grounds.

There are three basic sets of forces that drive megaproject development: (i) engineering or *technological forces*; (ii) societal development or *social welfare forces*; and (iii) the complex of forces driven by multi-objective *national competitive development* goals. While these forces rarely, if ever, operate in a mutually exclusive fashion, most projects may be viewed as driven primarily by one or other of these basic forces. Examples appear in Table 26.1.

DEFINING MEGAPROJECTS

While the problems that are particularly germane to the measurement and evaluation of megaprojects stem largely from their size, it would

Table 26.1 Type of megaproject by motivating factor

Driven by technological forces
Aswan Dam
Itaipu Dam
James Bay (conversion to fresh water)
Lena and Ob Rivers, Snowy River (flow reversal)
Churchill Falls (hydroelectric)
North Africa Greenbelt
Brazilian to Belen Highway
Alcan Highway
Trans-Asian Expressway
The Channel Tunnel
A 2nd Panama Canal (proposed)
A new Siberian Baikal–Amur Railway (proposed)
Tokyo Bay Bridge (proposed)
Japan–Korean Tunnel (proposed)
Canadian Athabasca Sands Oil project
Russian–Siberian Natural Gas Project
Synfuels projects in US
Transcontinental railway in USA/Canada
NASA (USA)
ITS (USA, Europe, and Japan)
Driven by social welfare forces
Resettlement of population in Indonesia
National capital relocations (Brazil and Pakistan)
Development and settlement of modern Israel
Resettlement: Recife, Brazil
Resettlement: Orinoco and Coroni River confluence, Venezuela
Agricultural expansion in Khazakiztan, Russia
Eradication of hookworm, smallpox and malaria
Education/literary programmes – Libya and Mauritania
Driven by national development goals
Amur–Yakustsk mainline
Grand Canal, China
China and the Great Leap forward – unsuccessful economic development
Argentina – unsuccessful economic development

be an oversimplification to use size as an unqualified measure of impact. Work by Warrack (1987) and Romanoff and Levine (1989) identifies a number of megaproject characteristics. The first set of attributes includes distinguishing or definitional characteristics and incorporates size, divisibility, uniqueness, remoteness, duration, expenditure level, immobility, capital lumpiness, irreversibility, and monovalence (support or scuttle). Attributes of projects that generate large social, environmental, economic and market impacts are the second basic set of characteristics. These impacts, in addition to being large-scale and complex, are also unevenly distributed in time and space, unique to a region and may even change the structure of the regional economy and, more importantly, its social organization. The third set of attributes of these projects are related to their consequences. The potential scale impacts of megaprojects lead to a high level of government involvement, with a long construction period and potential time delays. The latter contributes to preference instability. Risk and uncertainty are high as a consequence of the potential large-scale impacts. This leads to difficulty in arranging financing and a need for risk spreading through multiple and joint sponsorship. Lastly, such projects have the possibility for what analysts of complexity refer to as increasing returns economics or synergistic growth interactions, which generate positive feedback on the economic growth or social transformation process (Arthur, 1990).

While considerable richness has been added to the concept of scale and to the idea of a megaproject from the above discussion, the question 'How big does a project have to be before it becomes a megaproject?' remains. Some investigators, for example, Blair and Carr (1981) and Beck and Dungan (1983), have used a financial magnitude of at least $100 million. However, Warrack (1987) observes that absolute size is likely to be misleading unless context is considered. A large metropolitan economy could incorporate and accommodate the cost of the construction of a $1 billion particle accelerator more easily than a town of 5000 could accommodate the impacts of a coal gasification plant. Resource- or technology-driven 'boom towns' would fall into the latter category. Similarly, the experience of project investors in a region with other megaprojects would tend to ameliorate some of the impacts of a large project. For these reasons, megaprojects should be defined in terms of relative rather than absolute scale.

Warrack (1987) has defined relative project scale as the ratio of absolute scale to context, for example, complexity, sophistication or size of the regional economy that will house the megaproject. Megaprojects may then be defined at or above some threshold. Schulman (1980) argues that such thresholds exist because of the indivisibility and size properties of most projects.

When context is held constant, projects may be defined in terms of three types of impact: (i) those with no spillovers beyond the immediate space/time context; (ii) those having spillovers beyond the immediate space/time context; and (iii) those having spillovers so large that transnational and/or trans-generational impacts are created. Most of the examples of megaprojects listed in Table 26.1 fall into the third category. It is the inability to bind projects into the geographic space of the community and into the time horizon of a single generation that makes them megaprojects. This defining characteristic of megaprojects requires a consideration of distributive justice issues in space and time.

Megaprojects may be viewed as being embedded in contexts that are complex and adaptive (see Waldrop, 1992). Such systems are seen to operate far from equilibrium, steady state or global optima, and as such they are subject to change by human agents and organizations that adapt their behaviour to changes in the surrounding context (Gifford, 1993). The social, economic, environmental and political conditions within which megaprojects unfold are continually in flux, and the institutions that guide megaprojects are continually adjusting and adapting to change. At the same time, unlike smaller activities with less of an impact, megaprojects are also major agents of change in their own right, and consequently change their surrounding contexts.

This complex and adaptive aspect of megaprojects has not been fully appreciated in earlier thinking on this topic. But, clearly, some megaprojects have had the goal of changing the national and regional context within which they have been implemented – in particular, projects that have been motivated by national development goals. The relevance of complexity thinking is that megaprojects will probably have major unforeseen and, in fact, unintended consequences caused by the non-equilibrating impact of projects on the context within which they are contracted.

The financial, managerial, logistic, and public policy inputs for large-scale, indivisible and unique projects are far more extensive and uncertain than for conventional projects. It is this underlying attribute which suggests that megaprojects may be defined as existing above some contextual impact threshold.

IMPACT ASSESSMENT METHODOLOGIES

Since the 1980s there has been increasingly wide experience with alternative analytic methods for linking projects to socioeconomic measures fundamental to evaluation. Aspects of impact studies that are critical include: (i) identification of essential spatial linkages; (ii) representation and integration of impacts across sectors; (iii) incorporation of households, final demand and demographic linkages to essential socioeconomic variables; and (iv) modelling of environment and consumption (including energy), with appropriate response and feedback systems. For these reasons it is important to examine large-scale models with blocks of environment, energy and socioeconomic/demographic variables as well as the traditional sectoral disaggregation. Some of these dimensions have been made explicit in an assessment of impact methods provided by Lonergan (1985). Concerns of temporal perspective, dependence on dynamic vs. static measures of adjustments, spatial scale (local to national) and inter-regional linkages, as well as the relevant policy levels, have been differentially addressed in large-scale energy models in the Canadian (Alberta Oil Sands Environmental Research Programme, AOSERP; and the Alberta Energy Resource Allocation Model, AERAM), and US contexts (Alaskan National Gas-Dynamic Simulation Model, called, after its maker, the Helliwell Model). A detailed assessment of these models appears in Stough and Haynes (1993). Here, we review the general conclusions of that assessment.

Impact studies have used numerous research methods (Richardson (1978), Pleeter (1980), Leistritz and Murdock (1981)). The most useful applications have been extensions of well-known methods such as economic base analysis (Richardson, 1978), shift-share analysis (Haynes and Machunda, 1989), input–output (IO) analysis (Isard, 1960) and related econometric methods together with cohort survival-migration analysis (Hua and Porell, 1970), and gravity/entropy models (Senior, 1979; Haynes and Fotheringham, 1985). Since the passage of the major US federal and state environmental legislation in the early 1970s, environmental impact analysis has expanded rapidly (Fitzsimmons (1980), Greenberg *et al.* (1978), Chapman (1981). This was followed by large-scale energy project assessment in the late 1970s, as noted above. Only in the 1980s had regional analysis begun to recognize fully the inter-relationships between large-scale technology-related projects (often environmental and energy-based) and their full economic, demographic and fiscal linkages (Fishkind *et al.* (1978), Lakshmanan and Johansson (1985)).

No regional impact analysis method has yet been demonstrated that can address this full problem adequately in an integrated, dynamic and comprehensive manner. Numerous efforts have been made at modelling the impacts of regional development projects within the context of an impact analysis model.

A widely used method applied to environmental impacts was input–output analysis in the late 1960s. During the ensuing years, numerous researchers developed national and regional IO models which attempted to account for many of the linkages between economic change and environmental impacts. Such regional IO models typically develop pollution or depollution coefficients for industrial activity. The pioneers in these efforts were Isard *et al.* (1968), although similar coefficients were developed earlier in air pollution engineering, and called the 'emission factor'. Other contributors to this field, which has seen numerous policy applications, include Cumberland (1966), Daly (1968), Isard (1969), Ayres and Kneese (1969), Leontief (1970), Isard and Cesario (1974), Johnson and Bennett (1979), Lakshmanan and Ratick (1980), Lesuis *et al.* (1980a, 1980b), and McConnell *et al.* (1982). Although these efforts are noteworthy, only a few abandoned the static IO model for a dynamic framework with an environmental focus (Miernyk and Sears (1974), Rose (1974)). Yet even the dynamic models were incomplete, since they relied upon change mechanisms in only a part of the IO system (for example, pollution control capital investment), and hence were not fully dynamic. For example, Rose (1976) has pointed out that both his own and W. Miernyk's dynamic environmental IO models incorrectly used an accelerator investment equation rather than a capital stock adjustment mechanism. No well-founded dynamic, environmental, regional IO model has been developed and applied in a completely satisfactory manner.

Problems with IO approaches constrain their application to large-scale problems, especially with long-run implications. Among these are the equilibrium assumption, the lack of intra-regional analysis capability, the huge commitment of time and money required to construct the data-intensive inter-industry transactions table, and the need to couple the IO model with other models to be truly integrative (Lesuis *et al.* (1980a and 1980b), Gordon and Ledent (1981), Ledent and Gordon (1981), McConnell *et al.* (1982)).

More pragmatic econometric methods which employ multiple regression and simultaneous equation models can also be used for regional impact studies (Fishkind *et al.*, 1978), and attempts at systems integration with demographic components under this framework have been under way (Comprehensive Planning Organization for the San Diego Region (1974)). Econometric models are often thought to be more useful than (IO) models for regional impact analysis, because of the former's flexibility in model design, spatial coverage, level of detail, modelling structure, functional form, estimation method and lower cost (about one-tenth that of IO models for comparably-sized regions; see Rubin (1981) p. 408). Although an IO model is also an econometric model, we follow convention and refer to the two separately (see Gerking,

1976). Econometric models can often be constructed primarily from secondary data; thus lowering the cost and increasing their accessibility to local government policy-makers. Only a handful of regional econometric models have included successfully large-scale environmental or energy impact sectors (Lakshmanan and Lo (1972), Lakshmanan and Krishnamurthi (1973), Fishkind *et al.* (1978), Fishkind and Milliman (1978), Milliman *et al.* (1978), Lakshmanan (1979), and Chatterji (1980) pp. 331–41). This scarcity of applications is undoubtedly due to historical data constraints, although the growing availability of time series data continues to render this approach increasingly amenable to dynamic impact modelling.

EVALUATION ISSUES

Project evaluation from a welfare economics perspective is concerned with economic efficiency and equity. The following discussion focuses first on the evaluation of megaprojects in terms of efficiency. The efficiency criterion is defined as the maximization of net social benefits (NSB), where NSB is defined as total social benefits minus total social costs.

Efficiency criteria

Measurement problems associated with benefit and cost estimation are central but generally manageable in conventional project evaluation through the use of techniques and concepts such as discounting, shadow pricing, option value, opportunity costs, and hedonic pricing. However, because of the scale, the uniqueness and the individuality of megaprojects, benefit and cost estimations become considerably more problematic. Further, these characteristics greatly increase project-related risk and uncertainty. The large scale coupled with uniqueness and indivisibility often make estimation of the financial risk to project sponsors difficult. Similar, if not greater, problems exist in estimating the probability of social and megaproject outcomes; these may be so high and monetizing measurement issues so great that it may be possible to estimate outcome probability and outcome effects only in a very general way. Further, long project time horizons mean that the nature of the environment within which these projects are completed may be very uncertain. As a consequence, megaprojects are usually best evaluated under assumptions of considerable uncertainty.

Decision theory offers several alternative rules for making decisions under conditions of uncertainty (Arrow and Lind (1970), Hirshleifer (1965). These all hinge on what the policy/decision-maker wants to maximize, and include: the Maximax criterion, where the option with the highest value is selected; the Maximin criterion, where the option with the least maximum cost is selected. The Index of Pessimism criterion, which weighs the best and worst outcome against the reciprocal probability can also be selected. The Laplace criterion is the decision rule of a risk-neutral agent, for example, government agencies as suggested by the Arrow-Lind theorem, while the Minimax Regret criterion is the rule of a cautious decision-maker but less so than the Maximin criterion.

There are variety of rules for making decisions under uncertainty, but the question of which to choose in the case of megaprojects is somewhat problematic. The selection of a rule depends upon what type of decision-maker – cautious, optimistic, pessimistic – is deciding. Thus, the rule 'selected is very much dependent upon the outlook of the decision maker . . . this outlook should take cognizance, as far as possible, of the views of society' (Pierce and Nash (1981) p. 83).

Equity Criteria

The second basic evaluation dimension is distributive justice or equity. From a Paretian perspective, if some members or groups in society are made better-off and no others are found to suffer a loss as a consequence of a decision or a project, then the project should be opted for. While this rule is clear conceptually, it is problematic in practice because it is difficult, if not impossible, to conceive of a decision or project where, if made, would not impose some hardship upon some member or members of society. The Pareto improvement criterion based on the Hicks–Kaldor compensation principle (Hicks (1939) and Kaldor (1939)) empowers the analyst and decision-maker to assume that all sorts of spillovers (inter-temporal, inter-sectoral, income and other class-based groups) are of no consequence if, in principle, compensation could occur. With the Pareto improvement approach, equity effects are often treated as pecuniary effects that 'erase' one another as they pass from submarket to submarket within an economic system. This, of course, begs the question of how equity considerations should be dealt with.

Sugden and Nash (1978) suggest an alternative called the 'decision-maker' approach, whereby benefits and costs are assessed in terms of the decision-maker's goals, which may well be redistributive in nature. With this approach, goals need to be accounted for explicitly in the estimation procedures.

Scale, uniqueness, indivisibility and space–time boundaries of megaprojects mean that there will be potentially large and significant distributive effects. Further, these spillover effects will be complex and multi-dimensional in nature, including inter-temporal, spatial, intersectoral, redistributive and exhibit inter-group equity considerations.

The indivisibility attribute of megaprojects means that it is difficult to think of the costs and benefits unfolding over time in an incremental fashion. Rather, the costs tend to be in advance, with the benefits unfolding over rather longer periods. Thus future generations may benefit or lose at the expense of the initial generation, depending upon a project's outcome. Moreau and Snyder (1987) offer some insight in the context of an examination of the distribution of the financial burdens and economic costs in urban water system capacity expansion decisions. They found that 'established residents pay less than the economic cost of facilities when facilities that can be efficiently expanded in an incremental manner are subject to demands that are growing at rates that are less than the real interest rate' (Moreau and Snyder (1987) p. 1139). To the extent that a megaproject can be built and expanded incrementally under rates of demand expansion that are less than the real interest rate, then future generations may be viewed as suffering an inequity. However, most megaprojects are indivisible and therefore probably do not satisfy these conditions. Moreau and Snyder also observe that lumpy investments with excess capacity to meet future needs, like most megaprojects, have an inequitable impact on existing residents which, they note, can be offset by small one-time charges to new residents, for example, impact fees. While this suggests a possible compensation approach for new generations of megaprojects benefactors, it may be that the initiating generation is no longer living. In short, the time horizons involved do not seem to warrant the use of such a compensation principle.

The review of the Moreau and Snyder findings serves to point out the very complex inter-generational equity problems that arise in megaprojects. Clearly, the long time horizons of these projects make it difficult to treat many of the associated equity problems from any perspective other than one of extensive uncertainty. This result reinforces our conclusion that megaprojects should be viewed as being characterized by high degrees of uncertainty, and evaluated accordingly. With respect to the inter-generational equity issue, Becker (1982) utilizes a Maximin criterion to estimate an inter-generationally equitable programme for the trade-off between environmental quality and capital accumulation. One problem with this interesting approach is that it assumes a constant utility path, difficult to achieve in reality, especially given the long time horizons of megaprojects. However, sensitivity analysis could be used to examine the limitations of this assumption.

Spatial equity issues of several general types arise with megaprojects, including intra- and inter-regional, national and international. Part of this issue stems from the difficulty that arises with respect to bounding the project impact area. If the project can be reasonably bounded at the regional level, (for example, the state or province) then associated spillovers can be compensated through fees and local tax mechanisms. Traditionally federal reallocation systems have been used to transfer benefits from one region, for example, the south of Sweden or non-maritime Canada, in the form of subsidized programmes in other regions, for example, the north of Sweden or the maritime provinces of Canada. Where spillovers are international, regional international compacts may arise via a treaty to provide amelioration.

Intra-sectoral equity issues occur both directly and indirectly (and induced) from megaproject construction. Measuring, and thereby tracing, these spillovers is critical if the differential impacts are to be compensated as discussed above. Compensation may occur through national and regional development planning via such mechanisms as regulatory and tax policy.

Redistributive (income groups) and other inter-group (minority vs. majority) equity impacts arise with the development of most megaprojects. Traditional progressive taxation policy or direct subsidies may be used to address redistributive equity impacts. Constitutional and statutory measures, such as affirmative action and native rights (for example, US Indians) and differential weighting of grant allocation formulas, for example, between urban and rural groups are more common cooperation measures for inter-group equity adjustment.

The potential for broad-ranging and complex equity impacts from megaprojects means that development and implementation are characterized by considerable conflict between advocates, protagonists and policy- and decision-makers. Consequently, the need for negotiation and bargaining is high to ensure the creation and adoption of acceptable compensation outcomes.

SUMMARY AND CONCLUSIONS

This chapter has examined a broad range of issues concerning the definition and evaluation of megaprojects and their impact. With regard to evaluation it is important to note that there are many approaches and dimensions. We have only touched on some of these, and in particular treated only the traditional cost–benefit approach in any real depth in an effort to consider the spatial and temporal (inter-generational) bounding problems associated with megaprojects. However, a second level of policy-making, and therefore evaluation of megaprojects, occurs in terms of institutional and political considerations. Here, only a short paragraph on conflict management and negotiation was provided. Megaprojects not only require considerable institutional inputs, but frequently have an institutional transforming impact. This type of impact assessment needs much more attention than has been possible here.

There is a third level at which the impact of megaprojects should be considered and this has only been treated very generally in this chapter. It is from the perspective of increasing returns of scale and complex adaptive systems that one must begin impact assessment from an alternative world view approach. Waldrop (1992, p. 333) begins with this formulation of alternative metaphors, that is, equilibrium and optimization vs. disequilibrium and chaos, and multiple optima. This would appear to be a highly fruitful area for future work.

References

Anderson, A. E. (1986) 'The Four Logistical Revolutions', *Papers of the Regional Science Association*, vol. 54, pp. 1–12.

Arthur, B. W. (1990) 'Positive Feedbacks in the Economy', *Scientific American*, February, pp. 92–9.

Arrow, K. and R. C. Lind (1970) 'Uncertainty and the Evaluation of Public Investment Decisions', *American Economic Review*, vol. 60.

Ayres, R. and A. Kneese (1969) 'Production, Consumption and Externalities', *American Economic Review*, vol. 59, pp. 282–97.

Beck, R. A. D. and P. Dungan (1983) *Major Canadian Investments 1983–1995* (Toronto: Canada West Foundation).

Becker, R. A. (1982) 'Intergenerational Equity: The Capital–Environment Trade-Off', *Journal of Environment Economics and Management*, vol. 9, pp. 165–85.

Blair, S. R. and S. G. E. Carr (1981) *Major Canadian Projects: Major Canadian Opportunities*, Report by the Consultative Task Force on Industrial and Regional Benefits from Major Canadian Projects, Ottawa, June.

Chapman, K. (1981) 'Issues in Environmental Impact Assessment'. *Progress in Human Geography*, vol. 5, pp. 190–210.
Chatterji, M. (1980) 'Energy Modeling with Particular Reference to Spatial Systems', *Regional Science and Urban Economics*, vol. 10, pp. 325–42.
Comprehensive Planning Organization of the San Diego Region (1974) *IPEF 73: Interaction Population–Employment Forecasting Model – Technical User's Manual* (San Diego: CPOSDR).
Cumberland, J. (1966) 'A Regional Interindustry Model for Analysis of Development Objectives', *Papers and Proceedings of the Regional Science Association*, vol. 17, pp. 65–94.
Daly, H. (1968) 'On Economics as Life Science'. *Journal of Political Economy*, vol. 76, pp. 27–31.
Fishkind, H. and J. Milliman (1978) *An Economic Assessment of Growth Management for Sarasota County* (Gainesville, Fla: Bureau of Economic and Business Research, University of Florida).
Fishkind, H., J. Milliman and R. Elson (1978) 'A Pragmatic Econometric Approach to Assessing Economic Impacts of Growth or Decline in Urban Areas', *Land Economics*, vol. 54, pp. 442–60.
Fitzsimmons, A. (1980) 'Environmental Quality as a Theme in Federal Legislation', *Geographical Review*, vol. 70, pp. 314–27.
Gerking, S. (1976) 'Input–Output as a Simple Econometric Model', *Review of Economics and Statistics*, vol. 58, pp. 274–82.
Gifford, J. (1993) 'Complexity, Adaptability and Flexibility in Infrastructure and Regional Development: Insights and Implications for Policy Analysis and Planning', Paper prepared for presentation at the International Workshop, Infrastructure, Economic Growth and Regional Development: The Case of the Industrialized High-Income Countries, Jönkoping, Sweden, 10–12 June.
Gordon, P. and J. Ledent (1981) 'Towards an Interregional Demoeconomic Model', *Journal of Regional Science*, vol. 21, pp. 79–87.
Greenberg, M., R. Anderson and G. Page (1978) *Environmental Impact Statements* (Washington: Association of American Geographers).
Haynes, K. E. and A. S. Fotheringham (1985) *Gravity and Spatial Interaction Models* (Beverly Hills, Calif.: Sage).
Haynes, K. E. and Z. B. Machunda (1988) 'Decomposition of Change in spatial Employment Concentration: An Information-Theoretic Extension of Shift Share Analysis', *Papers of the Regional Science Association*, vol. 65, pp. 101–14.
Hicks, J. R. (1939) 'The Foundations of Welfare Economics', *Economic Journal*, vol. 49.
Hirshliefer, J. (1965) 'Investment Decisions Under Uncertainty: A Choice-Theoretic Approach', *Quarterly Journal of Economics*, vol. 74, no. 4.
Hua, C. and F. Porell (1978) 'A Critical Review of the Development of the Gravity Model', *International Regional Science Review*, vol. 4, pp. 97–126.
Isard, W. (1960) *Methods of Regional Analysis: An Introduction to Regional Sciences* (Cambridge, Mass.: The MIT Press).
Isard, W. (1969) 'Some Notes on the Linkage of the Ecologic and Economic Systems', *Papers and Proceedings of the Regional Science Association*, vol. 22, pp. 85–96.
Isard, W. and F. Cesario (eds) (1974) *Working Papers on the Use of Regional*

Science Techniques in Environmental Management (Ithaca, NY: Center for Urban Development Research, Cornell University).

Isard, W., K. Bassett, C. Choguill, J. Furtado, R. Izumita, J. Kissin, E. Romanoff, R. Seyfarth and R. Tatlock (1968) 'On the Linkage of Socio-Economic and Ecologic Systems', *Papers and Proceedings of the Regional Science Association*, vol. 21, pp. 79–99.

Johnson, M. and J. Bennett (1979) 'An Input–Output Model of Regional Environmental and Economic Impacts of Nuclear Power Plants', *Land Economics*, vol. 55, pp. 236–52.

Kaldor, N. (1939) 'Welfare Comparisons of Economics and Interpersonal Comparisons of Utility', *Economic Journal*, vol. 49.

Lakshmanan, T. (1979) 'A Multiregional Policy Model of the Economy, Environment and Energy', *NSF Working Paper*, no. 79–1 (Boston, Mass.: Center for Energy and Environmental Studies, Boston University).

Lakshmanan, T. and B. Johannson (eds) (1985) *Large Scale Energy Projects: Assessment of Regional Consequences* (Amsterdam: Elsevier).

Laksmanan, T. and S. Krishnamurthi (1973) *The SEAS Test Model: Design and Implementation* (Washington, DC: US Environmental Protection Agency).

Lakshmanan, T. and F. Lo (1972) 'A Regional Economic Model for the Assessment of Effects of Air Pollution Abatement', *Environment and Planning*, vol. 4, pp. 73–97.

Lakshmanan, T. and S. Ratick (1980) 'Integrated Models for Economic-Energy-Environmental Impact Analysis', in T. Lakshmanan and P. Nijkamp (eds) *Economic–Environmental–Energy Interactions* (Boston, Mass.: Martinus Nijhoff).

Ledent, J. and P. Gordon (1981) 'A Framework for Modeling Interregional Population Distribution and Economic Growth', *International Regional Science Review*, vol. 6, pp. 40–56.

Leistritz, F. and S. Murdock (1981) *Socioeconomic Impact of Resource Development: Methods for Assessment* (Boulder, Col.: Westview Press).

Leontief, W. (1970) 'Environmental Repercussions and the Economic Structure: An Input–Output Approach', *Review of Economics and Statistics*, vol. 52, pp. 262–71.

Lesuis, P., F. Muller and P. Nijkamp (1980a) 'An Interregional Policy Model for Energy-Economic-Environmental Interactions', *Regional Science and Urban Economics*, vol. 10, pp. 343–70.

Lesuis, P., F. Muller and P. Nijkamp (1980b) 'Operational Methods for Strategic Environmental and Energy Policies', in T. Lakshmanan and P. Nijkamp (eds), *Economic–Environmental–Energy Interactions* (Boston, Mass.: Martinus Nijhoff).

Longergan, S. C. (1985) 'Resource Extraction in Canada: Modeling the Regional Impacts', in T. R. Lakshmanan and B. Johansson (eds) *Large Scale Energy Projects: Assessment of Regional Consequences* (Amsterdam: Elsevier).

McConnell, V., C. Harris and J. Cumberland (1982) 'Forecasting Economic and Environmental Impacts of Energy Policy', Paper presented at the Annual Meeting of the Southern Regional Science Association, Knoxville, Tennessee.

Miernyk, W. and J. Sears (1974) *Air Pollution Abatement and Regional Economic Development* (Lexington, Mass.: Lexington Books).

Milliman, J., H. Fishkind and J. Gonzalez (1978) *A Methodology for Assessing the Physical, Economic and Social Trade-Offs Between Increased Economic Development and Enhanced Environmental Quality* (Gainesville, Fla: Bureau of Economic and Business Research, University of Florida).

Moreau, D. H. and T. P. Snyder (1987) 'Financial Burdens and Economic Costs in Expanding Urban Water Systems', *Water Resources Research*, vol. 23, no. 7, pp. 1139–44.

Pierce, D. W. and C. Nash (1981) *The Social Appraisal of Projects* (New York: Hastead Press, John Wiley).

Pleeter, S. (ed.) (1980) *Econometric Impact Analysis: Methodology and Applications* (Boston, Mass.: Martinus Nijhoff).

Richardson, H. (1978) *Regional Economics* (Urbana, Ill.: University of Illinois Press).

Romanoff, E. and S. H. Levine (1989) 'Combined Regional Impact Dynamics of Several Construction Megaprojects', Paper presented at the 18th Annual Meeting of the Northeast Regional Science Meetings, Northeastern University, Boston, Mass., May.

Rose, A. (1974) 'A Dynamic Interindustry Model for the Economic Analysis of Pollution Abatement', *Environment and Planning A*, vol. 6, pp. 321–38.

Rose, A. (1976) 'A Note on the Investment Equations in Some Recent Environmental Management Models', *Environment and Planning A*, vol. 8, pp. 477–8.

Rubin, B. (1981) 'Econometric Models for Metropolitan Planning', *Journal of the American Planning Association*, vol. 47, pp. 408–20.

Schulman, P. R. (1980) *Large-Scale Policy Making* (New York: Elsevier Holland).

Senior, M. (1979) 'From Gravity Modeling to Entropy Maximizing: A Pedagogic Guide', *Progress in Human Geography*, vol. 3, pp. 179–210.

Stough, R. R. and K. E. Haynes (1993) 'Megaproject Impact Assessment', Paper presented at the International Conference on Regional Science in Developing Countries, Beijing, People's Republic of China, 11–14 October.

Sugden, R. and A. Nash (1978) *The Principals of Practical Cost–Benefit Analysis* (Oxford University Press).

Waldrop, M. M. (1992) *Complexity* (New York: Simon & Schuster).

Warrack, A. A. (1987) 'Ten Characteristics of Megaprojects', Paper presented at the Annual Meeting of the Western Regional Science Meeting, Kona Beach, Hawaii, February.

27 Regional Science and Nation State Development

Takashi Takayama and John Williams

INTRODUCTION

China is about to embark on an unprecedented transformation of its economy and society. Its economy is steadily opening up and establishing links with the rest of the world. This will have the effect of changing the form of the Chinese economy. As a result of its interaction with more market-orientated economies, the Chinese economy will also become more market-orientated.

In this chapter we present a comprehensive model of nation state development using differential game theory. We examine the dynamics of the development of states with multiple tiers of government within a framework which highlights the need for the co-ordination and synchronization of national and regional development plans. We argue that, in countries such as China, leadership at both national and regional levels is essential to the creation of a prosperous future for the nation.

DEVELOPMENT OF A NATION STATE

As W. W. Rostow has observed, the economic development of a nation state is a process in which a traditional society conditions itself for 'take-off' and, if the conditioning is successful, sustains a vigorously growing economy which subsequently matures and becomes a society of high mass consumption.[1]

What are the necessary conditions for this take-off into sustained economic growth? There are a number of disparate views on this question, but the following three conditions appear to be essential:

1. Among the people there must be a spirit or willingness conducive to development.
2. Capital must be available.

3. The society must be stable; in particular, law and order must prevail.

The importance of these three requirements was recognized at an early stage in the development of the Japanese economy. A Vice-Minister in the Finance Ministry during the Meiji Period (1868–80) argued:

> Which requirements should be considered as most important in the present efforts of the government in building Japanese industries: It can be neither capital or laws and regulations, because both are dead things in themselves and totally ineffective. The *Spirit/Willingness* set both capital and regulations in motion. . . . If we assign weights to these three factors with respect to their effectiveness, spirit/willingness should be assigned five parts, laws and regulations four, and capital no more than one part.
>
> Capital provides nourishment and the legal system shows how to maintain a state of health. Whether or not these measures can help the patient recover depends on his *willingness* to recover.[2]

The World Bank and other international organizations have, in the past, placed heavy emphasis on capital in the implementation of development programmes. But without leadership from the government and individuals within the developing country – leadership which identifies development priorities and directs the development effort, capital injected may well be wasted and the development effort fail.

Acceptance of this leadership role by government and others is a manifestation of spirit or willingness conducive to national development. It also points to the fact that 'development' is not just 'economic development'. National development is the development of the entire society and economy of a nation state. Development is a process of change in the technological, institutional and religious–cultural environments of the developing country. It is a process of change in which these three spheres of environment within the developing country interact with each other, and interact with the technological, institutional and religious–cultural environments of other countries. These interactions are shown in Figure 27.1: e_t, e_i and e_{rc}, and E_T, E_I and E_{RC} are the technological, institutional and religious–cultural environments of the developing country and the rest of the world respectively.

If the national government is to lead the process of development it must identify clearly the initial state of each environment. For instance, it must survey production technology in each of the country's indus-

Figure 27.1 Three elements of environment and their interaction

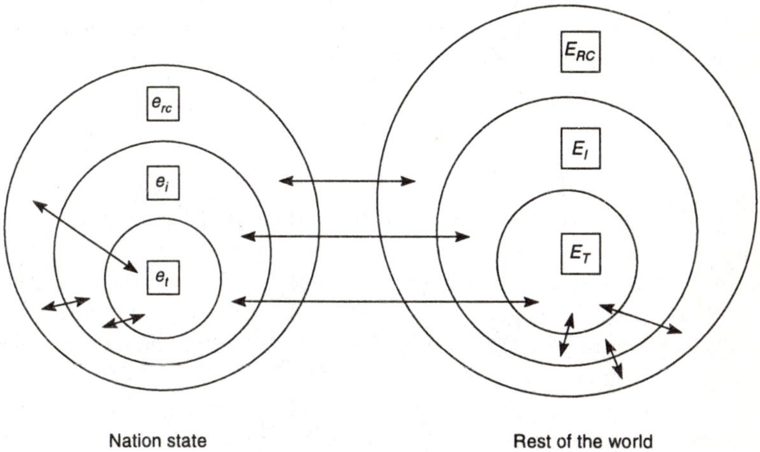

tries and compare it with technology available in the rest of the world. If superior foreign technology can be transplanted, the implications of technology transfer must be carefully explored, the rate at which new technology is to be introduced decided upon, and appropriate policy implemented.

Comparative assessment of the institutional environment may also lead to government-initiated changes to meet the challenge of national development. Furthermore, the national government might initiate changes in the religious–cultural environment, but there is likely to be a long delay before such changes affect the society materially.

The interactions between the technological, institutional and religious–cultural environments can be formalized in a system dynamics framework.

SYSTEM DYNAMICS IN NATIONAL AND REGIONAL DEVELOPMENT

Let $x(t)$, $y(t)$ and $z(t)$ be, respectively, vectors of technologies, attributes of institutions, and religious–cultural factors. Each is defined over the period of a development plan, and each is a state vector. If the nation comprises a 'centre', the jurisdiction of the national government, and n regions, the national state vectors are functions of the state vectors for the centre and for each of the n regions. The aim of a national development programme is to effect a desired change in each of the components of the national state vectors.

The dynamics of national and regional development are described by the system of differential equations:

$$\begin{aligned} \dot{x}(t) &= f(x(t), y(t), z(t), u(t), v(t), t) \\ \dot{y}(t) &= g(x(t), y(t), z(t), u(t), v(t), t) \\ \dot{z}(t) &= h(x(t), y(t), z(t), u(t), v(t), t) \end{aligned} \tag{27.1}$$

where

$$\begin{aligned} x(t) &= (x_1(t), \ldots, x_{n+1}(t))' \\ y(t) &= (y_1(t), \ldots, y_{n+1}(t))' \\ z(t) &= (z_1)t), \ldots, z_{n+1}(t))' \\ u(t) &= (u_1(t), \ldots, u_{n+1}(t))' \\ v(t) &= (v_1(t), \ldots, v_{n+1}(t))' \end{aligned}$$

The dynamics of the centre and of each region can then be written:

$$\begin{aligned} \dot{x}_i(t) &= f_i(x(t), y(t), z(t), u_i(t), v_i(t), \mathrm{t}) \\ \dot{y}_i(t) &= g_i(x(t), y(t), z(t), u_i(t), v_i(t), t) \qquad i = 1, 2, \ldots, n+1 \\ & \qquad \text{(the centre and } n \text{ regions)} \\ \dot{z}_i(t) &= h_i(x(t), y(t), z(t), u_i(t), v_i(t), \mathrm{t}) \end{aligned} \tag{27.2}$$

$u(t)$ and $v(t)$ are, respectively, the policy variable (control) vectors of the national and regional governments and of business leaders (the private sector) making national and regional investment and employment decisions.

A national development plan integrates central and regional government plans with the plans of the private sector so as to achieve national objectives set by government and also by the private sector. The government and private sector objective functionals are, respectively:

$$\Phi(x, y, z, \dot{x}, \dot{y}, \dot{z}, u, v, t) \qquad \Psi(x, y, z, \dot{x}, \dot{y}, \dot{z}, u, v, t)$$

Given these components, we can represent the system dynamics of the development of a nation state as shown in Figure 27.2:

Figure 27.2 Nation state and rest of the world interaction differential game scheme

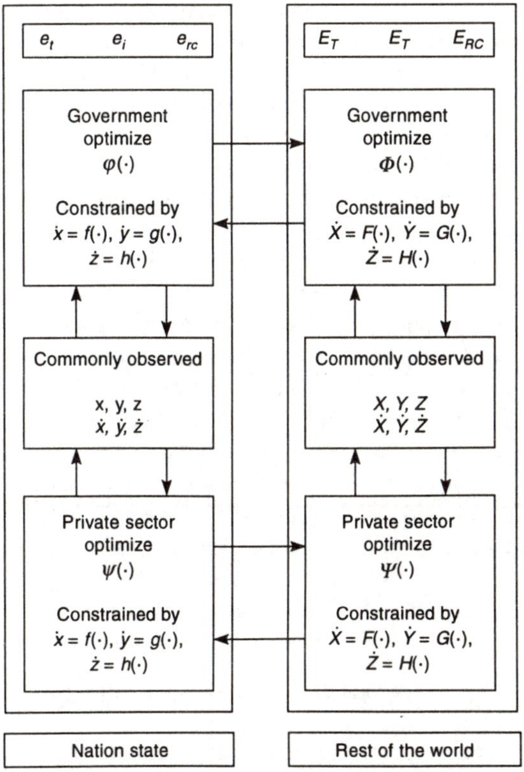

The central and regional governments carefully observe the regional dynamics of technology, institutions, and religion and culture, and then select from among the available policy options. In the early stages of national development, only a limited number of observations will be available for each of the three spheres of environment, and governments can take a leading role in creating the required database (as the United Nations, the World Bank and other international organizations have done in some cases). This database is a set of records of the past; it is a 'dead thing' on its own. Only the spirit/willingness of national and regional leaders to pursue development can put life into it. They identify the dynamics of the three environments, $\dot{x} = f(\cdot)$, $\dot{y} = g(\cdot)$ and $\dot{z} = h(\cdot)$, influence the process of change through their policy directives, and make information (including objectives and policy directives) available to the private sector and to the people.

With a clear understanding of the objectives and policies of national and regional governments, and after carefully observing the system dynamics, the private sector seeks to attain its objectives.[3]

The dynamics of the national development process cannot be closed to the rest of the world. Institutional innovations, like new technology, diffuse across national borders, but perhaps less rapidly. Developments in communications technology have accelerated change in national religious–cultural environments by means of exposing people to other ways of living and organizing their societies.

The development of new technology and its transfer across borders is taking place almost continuously throughout the world. National economic development requires the intensive efforts of national and regional governments and the private sector jointly to determine an optimal set of technologies to achieve development priorities currently and in the intermediate term. (The World Bank has played a key role in assisting a number of developing countries in this respect.) If, in the early stages of development, superior foreign technologies are available, their introduction will require the assistance of foreign engineers and other specialists. Government to foreign government, government to foreign private sector and private sector to foreign private sector interactions take place and usually in this order.

NATIONAL DEVELOPMENT AND REGIONAL SCIENCE

National development is a process for which system dynamics in its time varying form provides a most suitable framework for analysis. The framework presented in the previous section highlights the interaction of national and regional planning in the development process. The tools of regional science may, in specific circumstances, prove useful in exploring this interaction.

Regional science draws on a number of fields or disciplines, including economics, finance, management science, geography, urban and regional planning, mining (petroleum) engineering, civil (transport) engineering, sociology, and political science. Therefore, it is almost impossible to review all its techniques and methods. In this section we review only some of the tools of regional science developed by economists that may prove useful for developing countries.

Location of regional production centres

J. H. von Thünen's original insight into the location of production has now been fully exploited with the use of linear and non-linear programming methods to determine the optimal locations for different types of economic activities. If regional demand and supply quantities are known and fixed, the Koopmans–Hitchcock transportation cost minimization problem can be set up and solved for optimal product flows between regions. The shadow prices generated provide a basis for determination of absolute market prices by a planning authority.[4]

This type of modelling has been used widely by international organizations such as OPEC, the World Bank, and FAO, and by government agencies including the US Department of Energy and the Environmental Protection Agency. Even though the modelling structures were simple (LP or similar models) the dimensions of these models were large. The OPEC LP models each had more than 10 000 equality and inequality constraints and variables. Models with such large dimensions take a very long time to solve, even on modern computers. We believe that, given our current modelling capabilities, planning authorities should refrain from investing heavily in very large-scale modelling exercises, even though the temptation to do so may be extremely high.

Determination of efficient production, consumption and inter-regional trade

As a nation starts to develop its trade with the rest of the world, the volume of its exports is small, and limited by both its capacity to produce export goods and by domestic consumption (which will be intentionally discouraged in order to improve the balance of payments). Once the volume of exports rises to a level at which the country in question can influence prices in world markets, 'market-oriented' modelling can be used to determine efficient levels of production, consumption and inter-regional trade.[5]

There is always a nagging problem in modelling of this type that the planning horizon is not clear because the models are static. One way of overcoming this problem is to create a multi-time period model, with each period being clearly defined as, say, one year.[6] In practical application, model dimensionality is increased significantly and rapidly becomes too large for solution even in LP format. In quadratic (non-linear) programming or linear complementary programming format, the model dimensionality is severely limited (to say 500 × 500 or 1000 × 1000) on average mainframe computers. This curse of dimensionality may be overcome with advances in computer technology. Anna Nagurney has recently reported that a super-computer could solve a ten commodity–ten region–ten time period model within ten or twenty minutes.[7] Provided a modelling group has free access to high-powered computing facilities, market-orientated regional modelling can be used effectively to assist economic decision-makers in the market place, or policy makers within government.

NATION STATE DEVELOPMENT AND THE MARKET ECONOMY

During the 1950s, economists and policy advisers thought that freer trade would contribute to the equalization (relatively and absolutely) of factor prices among trading nations. The equalization of factor prices would, in turn, facilitate structural change and accelerate the process of development. It was therefore desirable that developing nations have freer trading arrangements with the market economies of Japan, North America and Western Europe.

This view was widely held. P. Samuelson himself argued: 'when many were despairing of Europe's future, I was led by my factor–price model to make the different suggestion that moving goods by trade might be able to do nearly as much for living standards as moving Europeans to Australia or elsewhere.'[8] It may, however, have been a statement about politics rather than a statement founded in an understanding of development economics. Trade liberalization may have trickled its effects through the international economy following the Second World War; however, it did so accompanied by major changes in labour mobility as new nation states emerged and as new national borders were declared – and disputed.

Reflecting on the war and its aftermath, Ludwig von Mises argued:

> None of these conflicts could have emerged in an unhampered market economy. Imagine a world in which everybody were free to live and work as entrepreneur or as employee where he wanted and how he chose, and ask which of these conflicts could still exist. Imagine a world in which the principle of private ownership of the means of production is fully realised, in which there are no institutions hindering the mobility of capital, labor, and commodities, in which the

> laws, the courts, and the administrative officers do not discriminate against any individual or group of individuals, whether native or alien. Imagine a state of affairs in which governments are devoted exclusively to the task of protecting the individual's life, health, and property against violent and fraudulent aggression. In such a world the frontiers are drawn on the maps, but they do not hinder anybody from the pursuit of what he thinks will make him more prosperous. No individual is interested in the expansion of the size of his nation's territory, as he cannot derive any gain from such an aggrandizement. Conquest does not pay and war becomes obsolete.[9]

A world like that which von Mises asks us to imagine has never existed. The fundamental prerequisites for his conclusions have, at no time in history, been fulfilled.

In von Mises' view, as long as nations exist, the organization of economic activity within national borders as a market economy, and liberal individualism as the dominant social and political philosophy, are fundamental to vigorous development:

> In the market economy the individual is free to act within the orbit of private property and the market. His choices are final. For his fellow men his actions are data which they must take into account in their own acting. The coordination of the autonomous actions of all individuals is accomplished by the operation of the market. Society does not tell a man what to do and what not to do. There is no need to enforce cooperation by special orders or prohibitions. Non cooperation penalises itself. Adjustment to the requirements of society's productive effort and the pursuit of the individual's own concerns are not in conflict. Consequently no agency is required to settle such conflicts. The system can work and accomplish its tasks without the interference of an authority issuing special orders and prohibitions and punishing those who do not comply.[10]
>
> The only reason why the market economy can operate without government orders telling everybody precisely what he should do and how he should do it is that it does not ask anybody to deviate from those lines of conduct which best serve his own interests. What integrates the individual's actions into the whole of the social system of production is the pursuit of his own purposes. In indulging in his 'acquisitiveness' each actor contributes his share to the best possible arrangement of production activities. Thus, within the sphere of private property and the laws protecting it against encroachments

> on the part of violent or fraudulent action, there is no antagonism between the interests of the individual and those of society.[11]

In these circumstances, government has a very limited role. Its purpose is to ensure peaceful social co-operation by the 'violent prevention and suppression of antisocial action on the part of refractory individuals and groups of individuals'.[12]

What would be the ultimate state of a society if this extreme individualism were exercised in every sphere of activity? We do not know the answer to this question; no nation state in history has organized itself in this way.

In East Asia, each of the sovereign states carries within itself over a thousand years of history, religion and culture which constrain the actions of individuals. The exercise of individual freedom has been bounded by the individual's recognition of his or her social responsibilities. Nevertheless, the economic growth of these states has become an object of envy for the rest of the world.

The further national development progresses, the weaker historical and cultural influences become and the more pronounced capitalism and liberal individualism. In system dynamics terminology, System x influences the institutional System y, and eventually influences the religious–cultural System z. The latter effect may be gradual, or it may be sudden, as is the case when there is a change in ideology.

Von Mises postulated that a system of national states would merge into a borderless society only if 'everybody were free to live and work as entrepreneur or as employee where he wanted and how he chose'. Until, if ever, these conditions are realized, governments will have a much greater role to play in the process of national development than von Mises advocated.[13]

China's development policy cannot be *laissez faire* in its purest form. The national government should play a leading role. Exposure to more open market economies than Japan was exposed to in the nineteenth century will exert a pressure for industrialization at a much greater rate than was experienced in Japan. At the same time, the national government must maintain law and order in a population exceeding 1 billion and distributed over 10 square kilometres. This is a challenge that no nation state in history has had to accept. The government of the People's Republic of China must use its own cumulative experience and wisdom to control the speed of adjustment in technology, in institutional structures, and in religion and culture if national development is to succeed.

Regional governments within China must play a similar role. At both national and regional levels, the government must sponsor infrastructure development, in particular of highways, railways and the internal air transport system. Without improvements in transport, development may well remain confined to centres along the country's eastern seaboard. More generally, national and regional governments must demonstrate leadership and assist the private sector in creating a prosperous future for the nation.

CONCLUDING REMARKS

The development scheme of a nation state may be conceptualized as a dynamic system closely connected with the dynamics of the rest of the world. There is a great concern that, within this global dynamic system, nation state development may become a secondary priority if governments relinquish control of economies and allow the fullest operation of 'the market'. A short review of von Mises' ideas on 'liberal individualism' and 'the market economy' leads us to conclude that, as long as completely free movement of labour is not realized, the nation state must continue to play a major role in the process of development.

National and regional governments must then demonstrate leadership and assist the private sector positively in creating a prosperous future for the nation. In this process 'regional science' will play an important role in the formulation of policy for regional development and nation building.

Notes

1. W. W. Rostow (1960) *The Process of Economic Growth* (2nd edn) (Oxford: Clarendon Press).
2. From *Kogyo Iken* (A Proposal for Economic Development), vol. 18. The economy of Meiji Japan at the time was in a state of chaos, with high inflation and a large number of government-run enterprises failing.
3. This dynamic scheme is referred to as a 'differential game' in T. Takayama (1988) 'The Japanese Economy: Past, Present and Future', *International Journal of Development Planning Literature*, vol. 3, pp. 178–220.
4. The details are presented in T. Takayama and G. G. Judge (eds), (1971) *Spatial and Temporal Price Allocation Models* (Amsterdam: North-Holland). Various applications are discussed in G. G. Judge and T. Takayama

(eds) (1973) *Studies in Economic Planning over Space and Time* (Amsterdam: North-Holland). See also T. Takayama (1979) 'An Application of Spatial and Temporal Price Equilibrium Model to World Energy Modelling', *Papers of the Regional Science Association*, vol. 41, pp. 43–58.

5. Market-orientated modelling strategies are comprehensively documented in parts III, IV and V of Takayama and Judge (1971) (see Note 4 above). Later applications are partially documented in T. Takayama and W. Labys (1986) 'Spatial Equilibrium Analysis', in Peter Nijkamp (ed.), *Handbook of Regional and Urban Economics Vol. I* (Amsterdam: North-Holland). See also W. Labys, T. Takayama and N. Uri, (1989) *Quantitative Methods for Market-Oriented Analysis over Space and Time* (Aldershot: Avebury), and O. Guvenen *et al.* (eds), (1991) *International Commodity Market Models; Advances in Methodology and Application* (London: Chapman & Hall).
6. This strategy was developed in part IV of Takayama and Judge (1971), and in T. Takayama (1976) 'Market-Oriented World Petroleum Modelling', Department of Economics, University of Illinois, Venezuela Project Report no. 9.
7. A. Nagurney (1993) *Network Economics: A Variational Inequality Approach* (Boston, Mass.: Kluwer).
8. P. Samuelson (1964) 'Theory and Realism: A Reply', *American Economic Review*, vol. LIV, pp. 736–9.
9. L. von Mises (1949) *Human Action* (New Haven, Conn.: Yale University Press) pp. 680–1.
10. Ibid. p. 720.
11. Ibid. pp. 720–1.
12. Ibid. pp. 715–99.

Index

acceleration 311–12
accounting
  energy 160–1
  enterprise 32–7
  financial *see* financial accounting
  information and national planning 364–75
  linked system 38–40
  managerial 27, 28–9
  social *see* social accounting
  see also national input–output accounts
acidification 183
actors: innovative environments 97–9
adjusted NRP 110, 121
adjustment mechanisms *see* market share adjustment mechanisms
administration 265–7
administrative–territorial units 261
agglomeration
  comparative analysis of intercity agglomeration 4, 219–31
  urban and product variety 8–11
aggregate prediction statistic (APS) 352, 353–5
aggregates, social accounting 121–2
agriculture
  economic geography 209, 214
  multi-regional model project 337, 338
  NAFTA 237, 244
  simulating regional systems 158
Aguilar, L. 235
air pollution 119–21
Albegov, M. 252
'aliens' 254
Alps 200–1
amenities
  economic geography 210, 213–15
  environmental 93, 94
Anchor Glass Container Corporation 236
annual growth ratio 224, 225
Anshan Iron and Steel Corporation (AISC) 36–7, 38–9
apparel and textiles 235–6
applied general equilibrium (AGE) models 326
applied spatial informatics 166–80
appraisal, project *see* project appraisal/evaluation
appreciation of QOL 81–2, 83–4
ASEAN 3
Asia
  East 7, 408
  governed market 363
  see also China; Japan
Asian Express Network (AEN) 5, 296–313
  acceleration effect on Chinese economy 311–12
  dynamic optimal appraisal model 299–302
  dynamic optimal planning model 302–3; simulation result 304–11
  economic effects-measuring model 297–8
  investment allocation by period 306–9
aspiration level 75, 76–9
assets, net increase in 110, 113, 122
attrition pattern 135–6
AUTOPLAN 176, 177
AUTOROUT 176
awareness effect 46, 47, 51, 52

balance sheet 27–32
banks 379–80
barriers to foreign investment 285
Bartelmus, B. 203, 204
basic needs 93, 94
Bassand, M. 95–6
behaviour
  and climate change 189, 193; environmental perception and climate change information 197–206
  and structure in system dynamics 147–8, 162
Beijing tables 334–5
benefit-cost analysis *see* cost-benefit analysis
benefit denial principle 67
big push models 21–2
bilateral seminars 253
biodiversity, loss of 183
biogeochemical cycles 182–3
Border Environmental Co-operation Commission 242
border region, NAFTA and 237–42

borrowing, foreign 304–5
bottom-up development 90
bounding: project impact area 394
Bracero Program 240
Britain: Economic and Social Research Council (ESRC) 184–5
Brundtland Report 181, 195
Brussels Agreement of Association 1991 273
Bulgaria 286, 287
business *see* firms; industry

Caldwell, L. K. 197
California 237, 245
  and Mexican immigration 242–4, 245
Canada 232, 233, 238
capital
  allocation of financial 367
  availability 379–80, 399–400
  formation 302
  human 114–15, 362–4
  industrial 300, 302
  social overhead capital 378
capital coefficients 316, 317, 319
capital disproportionality ratio 374–5
capital projects *see* infrastructure projects
capital recovery factors 319
capital structure 279, 281
cash-flow statement 27–32
Central and Eastern Europe
  foreign investment 5, 276–87
  integration processes 272–6
  regional pollution 294
  socioeconomic transformations 4–5, 263–71
central planning, local 256
centralization 219–20, 250
Chapin, S. 129
chemical pollution 241–2
China 363–4
  AEN 297; acceleration effect on economy 311–12; dynamic optimal appraisal model 299–302; dynamic optimal planning model 302–11
  input–output accounts: enterprises 32–7; linked system 38–40
  multi-regional model 5, 326–44
  nation state development 399, 408–9
chlorofluorocarbons (CFCs) 290, 291
cities
  comparative analysis of intercity agglomeration 4, 219–31
  and environment 294–5
  size and congestion 121
  transitional economies 265–6
  urban systems and regional development 3, 7–25
Ciudad Juárez 242
civilian society 97, 98
classification, regional 377–8
climate changes 4, 290
  human practices and climate change information 202–3
  impact of humans and society 187–8
  marketable commodity 193–4
  measuring responses to 199–201
  perception 188–90, 198–9
  policy 184–6, 190–1
  regional planning implications 197–206
  response strategies and attitude change 190–1
  and social sciences 181–96; research agenda 183–4; research methodology 192; role of social sciences 186–92
  technology assessment 189–90
climate impact analysis (CIA) 192
climate sensitivity 197–206
coalitions, economic 254
coercion 361–2
cognitive psychology 198–9
collaboration
  inter-organizational in innovative environments 94–5
  scientific 3, 70–9, 268
collective reflection 99–100
  strategic reflection tables 101–2
comfort 81–2, 83–4
command and control (CAC) 119
Commission for the Study of Natural Productive Forces (KEPS) 249
committed costs 132–3
  and expenditures 130–1
  postponing 133–4
  trajectories 134, 135
  uncertainty analysis 134–40
Commonwealth of Independent States (CIS) 254
  see also Russia
communal councils 265
communes 267
  obligatory association of 266
community 97, 98
Companies with Foreign Capital Act 1991 (Poland) 277–8
competence statutes 267
competition
  environment and 5, 289–95

price patterns in spatial oligopolistic markets 43, 45, 61, 63, 66, 67
competitiveness, international 245
computable general equilibrium (CGE) models 326
computer training programmes: natural disaster planning 4, 166–80
concave adjustment mechanism 49–51, 62–6, 68
concentration
of pollutants 119
spatial agglomeration 219–20, 222, 226–8
concurrent engineering 133
confirmation effect 46, 47–8, 49–50, 52
conflict 267, 394
congested regions 377
congestion 121
construction period 320–1, 322–3
consumer credit policy 379–80
consumer responses, lagged 43–69
consumption
economic geography 210–12
income and consumption matrix 122–4
natural development planning and efficient 405–6
consumption goods 8–10
continental expressway *see* Asian Express Network
contingency studies 190
convergence to optimality ratio 369, 373
Cooper, R. 27
co-operation, international 264, 291–3
see also scientific collaboration
Corning 236
corporation input–output accounts 32–7
linked system 38–40
cost approach to human capital 114–15
cost-benefit analysis (CBA) 384–5
electric power development projects 314–15, 320–2, 322–3
infrastructure planning 4, 127, 131–2
cost commitments *see* committed costs
cost-effectiveness analysis 185
costs: direct and indirect 317–18, 321–3 *passim*
Council for the Study of Productive Forces (SOPS) 249
CPPOLDER 176, 178
creative destruction 274–5
credit 379–80
cultural–religious environment 400–4
culture, organizational 95–6
cyclone disaster 170
Czech Republic 274, 286, 287

data base, territorial 100–1
decentralization 219–20, 250
decision-makers
approach to equity in evaluation 392–3
innovative environments 97–9
decision-making
infrastructure projects 130–40
in scientific collaboration 70–9
decision rules 68, 392
deconcentration 219–20, 222, 226–8
demand clusters 155–7
demand and supply 299–302
dependency ratio 378–9
depletable resources 115–16
destination choice 348–9, 353–4, 357
determined costs 140
developing countries 2–3
regional classification 377–8
regional economies 375–6
regional sustainable development 194–5
technological frontier 365–6
development
bottom–up 90
disaster planning 174–6
economic *see* economic development
industrial 158
nation state development *see* nation state development
planning for national development *see* national development planning
regional *see* regional development
sustainable *see* sustainable development
development funding 269–70
development programmes, strategic 269
development projects *see* infrastructure projects; megaprojects
dimensionality, model 405–6
direct benefits 321–3 *passim*
direct costs 317–18, 321–3 *passim*
directed divergence 138–9
disaster planning 4, 166–80
discriminant analysis 139–40
distributive justice 392–4
divergence, directed 138–9
division of labour 4, 207–18
DOSSO model 297, 298
duocentric spatial configurations 15, 17, 18, 21
dynamic adjustment 20–2

dynamic environmental IO models 390
dynamic optimal appraisal model 297–302
dynamic optimal planning model 302–11

Eastern and Central Europe *see* Central and Eastern Europe
ECCO (enhancement of carrying capacity options) 159–61
eco-commodities 293
ecological reform tasks 258
econometric models 390–1
economic coalitions 254
economic development
  asymmetrical 270
  levels and the environment 5, 289–95
  social accounting and 122–5
  see also development
economic geography 4, 207–18
  amenities 213–15
  equilibria 212
  model 207–12; agricultural sector 209; consumer behaviour 210–12; industrial sector 209–10
economic growth: acceleration in China 311–12
economic indicators/activities 337–41, 342, 343
economic integration 257, 258–61
economic reforms: Russia 253–5, 257
  see also transitional economies
economic regulation 89
economic restructuring programmes 269
economic stimulation 365
Economic Union 254
education 93, 94
effect analysis 192
efficiency
  evaluation of megaprojects 391–2
  measures of factor utilization 369–75
  in production, consumption and inter-regional trade 405–6
efficiency ratio 378–9
El Paso 242
electric power development projects 5, 314–25
  indentification of economic effects 318–23
  semi-input–output model 315–18
emergency announcements 176, 178
emission charges 119
employment
  Central and Eastern Europe 264
  NAFTA's impact 236–7, 238–9, 242, 245
  simulating regional systems 153, 154
endowment
  net increase in 110, 122
  regional 110, 112, 114–17
energy accounting 160–1
energy consumption 291–2
energy costs 337, 340
enhancement of carrying capacity options (ECCO) 159–61
enterprise input–output accounts 32–7
  linked account system 38–40
entrepreneurship 93, 94
entropy 135–6
environment
  climate changes *see* climate changes
  disaster mitigation 174–6
  global change *see* global environmental change
  'hidden foot' problem 181–2
  levels of economic development and 5, 289–95
  pollution *see* pollution
  social accounting 117–21
environmental amenities 93, 94
environmental committees 293
environmental perception 188–90, 197–206
environments, innovative *see* innovative environments
equations: system dynamics models 149–50
equilibria/equilibrium
  economic geography 212
  Nash 43, 59, 62–6, 68
  path equilibria 68
  spatial configuration 14–19; structural instability of multiple equilibria 20–2
equipment/machinery 93, 94, 235
equity 392–4
Europe 2–3
European Union 293, 362
  and Central and Eastern Europe 269–70; integration 272–6
evacuation routing 176, 178
evaluation function 81–2, 83–4
evaluation of projects *see* project appraisal/evaluation
expenditures, commitments and 130–1, 132
experimental studies 192
expressway, continental *see* Asian Express Network

factor substitution 365, 365–6, 373–5
factor utilization 366–75
  efficiency measures 369–75
factor utilization optimality ratio 369, 372–3
federalism, financial 259–61
feedback 145
  importance in system dynamics 148–9
  loops 147–8
Fiat 281–2
final approach 327
financial accounting
  input–output accounting 27–32
  planning for national development 364–75
financial capital 367
financial federalism 259–61
financing 93, 94
firms
  multi-locational 22–3
  pricing behaviour in spatial oligopolistic markets 54–66
  small and medium-sized 91
  social accounts 109–11
  see also enterprise input–output accounts
flexibility 189
flooding disasters 173–4, 176, 178
flow diagrams 149
flow-of-funds statement 27–32
food production 290
forecasting models 2
foreign borrowing 304–5
foreign investment 5, 272–88
  distribution by country of origin 283–4
  incentives and barriers 285
  locational preferences 286, 287
  Polish legal regulations 277–8
  role and characteristics 276–7
  sectoral distribution 282–3
  structure and spatial distribution 278–84
  value of commitments 286–7
forests, degradation of 290
Forrester, J. W. 144, 147
forum, territorial 99–100
France 289, 292, 380
Friedman, J. W. 66–7
Friedmann, J. 97, 99
fused regional accounts *see* social accounting

game theory
  nation state development 399–410
  pricing in spatial oligopolistic markets 43–69
geographic information systems (GIS) 188
Germany 293, 380
  investment in Poland 284
  shock therapy 274–5
glass 236–7
global environmental change 182–4
  climate changes *see* climate changes
  economic responses 289–93
  key factors 187
  policy 184–6, 190–1
  see also pollution
global infrastructure fund (GIF) 296
global seawater level rising 171–2
global warming *see* climate changes
go/no go decisions 130, 131–2, 137–8, 139
governed market 363
governments
  industrial development role 158
  leadership role in nation state development 400–1, 408–9
  social accounting 110, 111; programmes and investments matrix 124–5
  see also state
grain production 290
greenhouse gases 183, 290, 291
Greenpeace 292
gross national product (GNP) 309–11
growth pole models 21–2

hazard functions 49
hazards, responses to 199–201
'hidden foot' problem 181–2, 188
hierarchical city systems 8, 10, 17–19
households
  SIO model for electric power development projects 316, 320
  social accounting 110, 111
housing 158, 265
human activities
  climate change information and 202–3
  impact on global change 187–8
human behaviour *see* behaviour
human capital 114–15, 362–4
Hungary 274, 286, 287

identification, territorial 95–6, 97–9
immigration 242–4, 245

Immigration Reform and Control Act (IRCA) 1986 (USA) 243–4
impact studies 108
incentives
  economic stimulation 364–5
  foreign investment 285
income
  approach to human capital 115
  income and consumption matrix 122–4
  personal 110, 111
  simulating regional systems 153, 154
income accounts 108
income statement 27–32
indirect benefits 321–3 *passim*
indirect costs 318, 321–3 *passim*
individualism 406–8
Indonesia 223–8
industrial belt 15
industrial capital 300, 302
industrial development 158
industrial pollution 120–1, 241–2, 292
industry
  competition and the environment 292–3
  economic geography 209–10
  see also firms
informatics, applied spatial 166–80
information
  climate change and human practices 202–3
  innovative environments and access 93, 94
  territorial data base 100–1
  value of in project evaluation 132–4, 140–1
information costs 45–6, 67–8
information management systems 179
information systems 192
infrastructure 259
  China's need for development of 409
  innovative environments 93, 94
infrastructure projects 4, 127–43
  continental expressway 5, 296–313
  electric power development 5, 314–25
  evaluation 129–32
  evolution 128–9
  multi-regional model for transport 5, 326–44
  uncertainty analysis 134–40
innovative environments 3, 88–107
  actors 97–9
  collective reflection 99–100
  definition 92
  emergence of new theory 88–92
  octagonal model 93–5
  research of tactical execution 103–4
  role definition 100
  strategies for 101–2
  structuring actions 102–3
  territorial data base 100–1
  territorial identification 95–6
input efficiency 369
input–output accounting 3, 26–42
  enterprise 32–7
  financial 27–32
  linked system 3, 33, 38–40
  managerial 27, 28–9
input–output analysis 389–90
  see also semi-input–output model
institutions
  building and disaster planning 178–9
  human behaviour and climate change 190
  innovative environments 94–5, 97–9
  nation state development 400–4
integration
  Central and Eastern Europe with EU 272–6
  economic 257, 258–61
  regional 2–3
intercity agglomeration 4, 219–31
interdisciplinarity 193
interest rates
  AEN borrowing 305, 306
  capital availability 379–80
  pricing and 61
inter-ethnic relations 258
intergenerational equity problems 393–4
intergenerational transfers 108–26
inter-group equity adjustment 394
intermediate goods 10–11
intermediate state administration 266–7
international climate change policy 184–6, 190–1
international competitiveness 245
international co-operation 264, 291–3
  see also scientific collaboration
International Geographic Union 253
international input–output accounts 38–40
International Institute for Applied Systems Analysis (IIASA) 252
international regional science 251–3
inter-regional trade
  multi-regional model project 329–30, 333–4, 337, 338–40
  nation state development and efficient 405–6
inter-republican interactions 255

investment
AEN 304–5, 312; allocation by period 306–9
electric power development projects 317–18
foreign *see* foreign investment
planning for national development 364–5, 377–8
social accounting 110, 112–13; governments' programmes and investments 124–5
Isayev, B. 252
isolated state 15

Japan
foreign investment 283, 284
spatial-cycle stages 223–8
trade with USA 362
Jiangsu Province 342
Johnson, H. T. 27
justice, distributive 392–4

Kaplan, R. S. 27
knowledge networks 70–9

labour
economic geography 4, 207–18
substitution 365, 365–6
labour disproportionality ratio 369, 374–5
labour markets, local 91–2
lagged quantity adjustments 3, 43–69
land 117
land rent 212, 213–15
land-use zoning 176, 177
Laplace criterion 392
Latino immigrants 243–4, 245
leadership 400, 409
Leontief, W. 252
level variables 148–9
Li Bingquan 33
liberal individualism 406–8
life cycle, project 130–1
linear adjustment mechanism 52
linked input–output accounts 3, 33, 38–40
living populations 116–17
loan balance 304–5
local administration 265–6
local central planning 256
local externalities 194
local/global policy compatibility 191
local labour markets 91–2
location equilibrium condition 14
location of production 405
logistic adjustment mechanism 47–9, 62–6

Maastricht Treaty 272
machinery/equipment 93, 94, 235
macroeconomic policy 364–75
managerial accounting 27, 28–9
manufacturing 337, 339
East–West Europe co-operation 264–5
maquiladora programme 240–1
market
free 361
governed 363
mechanisms 266
solutions for global change policy 191
spatial oligopolistic markets 3, 43–69
market economy
nation state development and 406–9
see also transitional economies
market potential function 14
market share adjustment mechanisms 46–54
and pricing behaviour 54–66, 67–8
Marketable Emission Permits 119
Marshall, A. 89
Maximax criterion 392
Maximin criterion 392, 393–4
megaprojects 384–98
defining 385–8
evaluation issues 391–4
impact assessment 388–91
motivating factors 385, 386
nature of 385
Menshikov, S. 252
meso-analytical perspective 90
Mexico
migration to California 242–4, 245
and NAFTA 232–47
migration 242–4, 245
mill pricing (MP) 43, 52–4
Minimax Regret criterion 392
Mises, L. von 406–8
mitigation programmes 179
mode choice, travel 5, 345–60
model dimensionality 405–6
model validation 150–1, 160, 163–4
monitoring, economic 365
monocentric spatial configuration 15–17, 21
monopoly prices 59–61, 63, 66, 67
Montreal Protocol 291
Moreau, D. H. 393
motor vehicles 235
mountainous areas 200–1, 203
MTC model 345
multi-criteria matrix 83–4

multi-locational firms 22–3
multiple equilibria 14–19
  structural instability 20–2
multipliers 125
multi-regional model project 5, 326–44
  basic results 337–41
  effects of transport improvement 342–3
  model performance 333–6
  non-survey estimation of provincial tables 328–33; domestic trade 330–1; net final demand and value added 331–2; network price equilibrium 332–3; price indices and deflators 332; regional trade 329–30
  railway network 336–7
multi-time period models 405–6

Nash equilibria 43, 59, 62–6, 68
nation state development 5–6, 399–410
  and market economy 406–9
  and regional science 404–6
  system dynamics 401–4
national development goals, megaprojects and 385, 386
national development planning 5, 361–83
  accounting information and macroeconomic policy 364–75
  capital availability 379–80
  regional economic conditions 375–9
National Disaster Management Plans 179
national input–output accounts
  linked systems of accounts 38–40
  multi-regional model project 328, 328–9
natural disaster planning 4, 166–80
natural resources 115–17
needs, basic 93, 94
nested logit models 346, 347–9
  transferability 349–59
net final demand 331–2
net increase in assets 110, 113, 122
net increase in endowment 110, 122
net increase in wealth 110, 122
net regional/national product (NRP) 110, 111
net social benefits 391–2
Nijkamp, P. 252
'no regret' strategies 185, 189
non-linearities 146
non-renewable resources 115–16
North American Free Trade Agreement (NAFTA) 3, 4, 232–47
  California and Mexican immigration 242–4, 245
  Texas and the border 237–42
  and US regions 233–7
North Carolina 236
Nuevo Laredo, Tamaulipas 241, 242

objective functions 309–11
obligatory association of communes 266
oligopolistic markets 3, 43–69
operation period 321–2, 323
optimality: and convergence to optimality 372–3
optimization input–output table 35
organizational culture 95–6
output 317–18
output efficiency 369
ownership structure 278–9
ozone depletion 183

Pacific Rim 3
parameter-level transferability 349, 352–9
Pareto improvement criterion 392
Pareto superior strategies 62–6
path equilibria 68
payoff matrix 185–6
perception, environmental 188–90, 197–206
personal income 110, 111
personal trips 304
pessimism, index of 392
phase jumps 384
physical input–output table 34, 36
physical-value input–output table 35, 36
Piore, M. 89
piston trips 347
planning
  dynamic optimal planning model 302–11
  linking enterprise to state 36–7
  local central planning 256
  for national development 5, 361–83; planning objective 366–8
  natural disaster planning 4, 166–80
  regional and climate changes 197–206
  stages of process 204
  transitional economies 269
  urban 228–9

Poland 272–88
foreign investment 5, 276–87; incentives and barriers 285; regulation 277–8; structure and spatial distribution 278–84
integration process 272–6
polder flooding 176, 178
pollution 118–21
air 119–21
congestion 121
industrial 120–1, 241–2, 292
levels of economic development and 289–95
US border with Mexico 241–2
water 118–19
see also environment
Polonia enterprises 276
pools of labour 91–2
population
comparative analysis of intercity agglomeration 4, 219–31
simulating regional systems 152–3, 157–61
ports 259
postponing cost commitments 133–4
potential function, market 14
Power, T. M. 80–1, 85
prices
dynamic price patterns in spatial oligopolistic markets 3, 43–69; firm behaviour 54–66; mill pricing 52–4; uniform delivered pricing 46–52
multi-regional model project 343; indices and deflators 332; network equilibrium 332–3; price equilibrium and transport projects 327–8; regional indices 337, 341
private investment 112
private sector 264
innovative environments 97, 98
Poland 278–9, 280
probability law 135–6
product accounts 108
product variety 8–11
production
nation state development: determination of efficient 405–6; location of regional production centres 405
transitional economies 263–5
production capacities 317, 318
excess 320
full 370
production functions 371–2
productivity
factor 366–75
scientific collaboration 70–2
total factor productivity 114
profit maximization 54–66
project appraisal/evaluation 129–32
AEN 297–302
megaprojects 388–94
multi-regional model 5, 326–44
uncertainty analysis 134–40
value of information 132–4, 140–1
project life cycle 130–1
protection of home producers 275
prototyping 133
provincial input–output tables *see* regional input–output accounts
public expenditure 377, 378, 379
public investment 112–13
public sector 278–9
public transportation system 353–4

QUALIFLEX 83–5
quality of life (QOL), regional 3, 80–7
quantity adjustments, lagged 3, 43–69

railways 259, 328, 336–7
rate variables 148–9
reflection, collective *see* collective reflection
regional accounts 2
fused *see* social accounting
regional administration 266–7
regional associations of economic interaction 260
regional classification 377–8
regional development
system dynamics 401–4
urban systems and 7–25; regional development strategies 20–2
regional economic conditions 375–9
identification 376
qualitative measures 378–9
regional endowment 110, 112, 114–17
regional governments 409
regional input–output accounts
linked system of accounts 38–40
multi-regional model project 328–33, 333–5
regional planning: climate changes and 197–206
regional policy
analysis and national development planning 378–9

regional policy *continued*
  Central and Eastern Europe 267–8
  Russia in transition period 255–61
regional pollution 294
regional production centres 405
regional quality of life 3, 80–7
Regional Science Association (RSA) International 252, 253
regional semi-input–output (RSIO) model *see* semi-input–output model
regional sustainable development 194–5, 245–6
regional systems 144–65
  characteristics 145–6
  ECCO 159–61
  RUSIM 155–9
  Susquehanna River Basin model 152–5
  system dynamics 146–51; utility and validity 161–4
regional utility simulation model (RUSIM) 155–9
  description 155–8
  use of model 158–9
regionalization of economic reforms 257
regulation
  economic 89
  environmental 190
  legal and foreign investment 277–8
relative aggregate transfer error (RATE) 352, 353–5
religious–cultural environment 400–4
renewable resources 115, 116–17
rents 265
  land rent 212, 213–15
resource allocation 367–75
resources
  multi-regional model project 337, 340
  natural 115–17
  use in transitional economies 265
rest of the world
  nation state interaction with 403–4
  social accounting 110, 111
retail sales 239–40, 244–5
return on investment (ROI) 4, 127, 131–2, 137–8, 139–40
Rhône, River 292
Rio Grande 241–2
risk 188–9
  see also uncertainty
Romania 286, 287
root mean square error measure (RMSE) 351, 352, 353–5
routing, evacuation 176, 178
ROXY Index 220–3, 223–7, 230
rubbish tips 267
rural attractiveness 214–15
Russia 4, 248–62
  Comprehensive Program 249
  Constitution 1993 260–1
  General Scheme of Development 249
  General Scheme of Settlement 249
  international and Soviet regional science 251–3
  regional policy in transition period 255–61
  regional studies 248–51
  transformation of former USSR 253–5

Sabel, C. 89
sales, retail 239–40, 244–5
Saline Water Conversion Corporation (SWCC) 155
satellite cities 17, 21
Saudi Arabia: RUSIM 155–9
savings 110, 112, 113
scientific collaboration 3, 70–9, 268
scientification 130
seawater level rising, global 171–2
sectoral flows matrix 122, 123
self-government 263, 265–6, 266–7, 271
semi-input–output (SIO) model 315–25
  direct economic effects 317–18
  excess production capacities 320
  household sector 320
  identification of costs and benefits 320–2
  indirect economic effects 318
  model of economic effects 322–3
  modification of capital coefficients 319
semi-isolated states 17
sequential engineering 133
settlement clusters 155–7
shipment balance 300
shock therapy 274–5
Simulation of Traffic Assignment on the Network (STAN) 298
Slovak Republic 274, 286, 287
small and medium-sized enterprises 91
Snyder, T. P. 393
social accounting 3, 108–26
  aggregates 121–2
  detailed accounts 122–5
  environment 117–21
  investments 110, 112–13, 124–5

regional endowment 110, 112, 114–17
static accounts 109–11
social accounting matrices (SAMs) 108, 109
social actions 93, 94
social conflict 267, 394
social dilemma 186–7, 189, 193
social impact analysis 187–8
social overhead capital 378
social philosophy 361, 362–4
social reform tasks 257
social sciences: and climate change 181–96
social systems 162
social welfare *see* welfare
society: impact on global change 187–8
software programs: disaster training 167–78
sovereignty 361–2
spatial configurations, equilibrium 14–19
structural instability 20–2
spatial-cycle hypothesis 4, 219–31
spatial-cycle path 228–9; and ROXY Index value 220–3
spatial-cycle stages of four countries 223–8
spatial economy: formal model 11–14
spatial informatics, applied 166–80
spatial oligopolistic markets 3, 43–69
spatial plan design 176, 177
spillovers 394
spirit 399–400
stability
society 400
structural of multiple equilibria 20–2
state
innovative environments 97, 98
transformation of Russia and 4, 258, 268; administration 266–7
see also governments
state planning 36–7
static accounts 109–11
Stolp, C. 238–9
strategic reflection tables 101–2
structure: and behaviour 147–8, 162
structure-level transferability 349, 351–2, 352–9
Struder project 269
subsidies 394
subsoil resources 115–16
substitution
factor 365, 365–6, 373–5
regional quality of life 82–3, 84–5
successful innovative environments 91, 94–5
supply and demand 299–302
Susquehanna River Basin model 152–5
description 152–4
use of model 154–5
sustainable development 182
regional 194–5, 245–6
simulating regional systems 159–61
Sweden 223–8
system dynamics 144–65
applications to regional systems 151–61; ECCO 159–61; RUSIM 155–9; Susquehanna River Basin 152–5; utility and validity of models 161–4
characteristics of approach 146–7
importance of feedback 148–9
model formulation 149–50
model validation 150–1, 160, 163–4
national and regional development 401–4
structure and behaviour 147–8, 162
systematic perspective 90

take-off 399–400
taxation 260, 292, 394
technical coefficients matrices 315–16
technical progress 114
technological frontier 365–6
technology
assessment and global change 189–90
competition and the environment 292–3
motivation of megaprojects 385, 386
nation state development 400–4
planning for national development 370
territorial data base 100–1
territorial forum 99–100
territorial identification 95–6, 97–9
territorial self-government 263, 265–6, 266–7, 271
Texas 237, 237–42, 244–5
textiles and apparel 235–6
time 145–6
total factor productivity 114
tourism 202–3
tours 345–6, 356–8
see also travel demand model
township-village enterprise model 364
trade
inter-regional *see* inter-regional trade
liberalization 406

trade *continued*
multi-regional model project 328, 343; domestic 330–1; regional 329–30
NAFTA *see* North American Free Trade Agreement
traffic routing 176, 178
transfer index (TI) 350, 351, 353–5
transfer rho-square 350–1, 353–5
transferability 349–56
temporal 352–6
transferability test statistic (TTS) 350, 351, 353–5
Transferable Emission Permits (TEPs) 119
transitional economies 2
foreign investment *see* foreign investment
integration processes 272–6
socioeconomic transformations 4–5, 263–71
see also Central and Eastern Europe; Poland; Russia
transport infrastructure facilities (TIF) 301–2, 302, 304
see also Asian Express Network
transport network, Russia 259
transport projects 4, 326–44
effects of improvement 342–3
and price equilibrium 327–8
travel demand model 5, 345–60
analysis of temporal transferability 352–6
transferability studies methodology 349–52
trip-chaining and model calibration 356–8
tricentric spatial configurations 15, 17, 19, 21
trip chaining 345–7, 356–8
trip distribution 5, 345–60
trip generation 5, 345–60
twin plant programme 240–1

uncertainty 4, 127
analysis in project development 134–40
climate changes 188–9
megaproject evaluation 391–2, 393
UNDECAD umbrella approach 168
United Nations Conference on the Environment and Development, Brazil 291
United Nations Conference on the Human Environment, Stockholm 194
uniform delivered pricing (UDP) 46–52
United States of America (USA) 283, 364, 378
coercion 362
National Academy of Sciences 183–4
policy analysis 129
regions and NAFTA 232–47; California and Mexican immigration 242–4, 245; Texas and the border 237–42
spatial–cycle stages 223–8
urban changes 219–20
see also intercity agglomeration
urban congestion 121
urban planning 228–9
urban systems
characteristics 145–6
and regional development 7–25; equilibrium spatial configuration 14–19; formal model of spatial economy 11–14; product variety and urban agglomeration 8–11; structural instability 20–2
urbanization 7

validation, model 150–1, 160, 163–4
value added 317, 318
provincial tables 331–2
value-input–output table 34–5
variable-level transferability 349, 350–1, 352–9
variety, product 8–11
Vernadskky, V. I. 249
volcanic eruption disaster 175

wages 212, 213–15
Warsaw Voivodeship 280, 281
water resources 118–19
simulating regional systems 153, 154, 154–5, 158
wealth, changes in 110
net increase 110, 122
Weill, H. B. 151
Weintraub, S. 238–9
welfare, social
AEN planning model 309–11
maximization 362–4, 376
motivation for megaprojects 385, 386
West Virginia 236
White, G. 199
willingness 399–400
World Bank 404